JUST ASKING

Restoring the Soul of Prayer

Stuart McAlpine

WestBow Press books may be ordered through booksellers or by contacting:

WestBow Press
A Division of Thomas Nelson & Zondervan
1663 Liberty Drive
Bloomington, IN 47403
www.westbowpress.com
1 (866) 928-1240

ISBN: 978-1-9736-3530-7 (sc)
ISBN: 978-1-9736-3531-4 (hc)
ISBN: 978-1-9736-3529-1 (e)

Library of Congress Control Number: 2018908910

Print information available on the last page.

WestBow Press rev. date: 08/16/2018

"Ask of Me" - Psalm 2:8

To Terry, Tammy and Alden
who were God's answer to our asking

To all the members of the Ask Network who are gathering
all generations to pray for all nations, asking God to do what
only He can do, and doing whatever He asks of them.

Honoring the centenary of the publication of
'The Soul of Prayer' by P.T.Forsyth

"There is nothing that will so preserve a life of prayer – its vigor,
sweetness, obligations, seriousness and value – so much as a deep
conviction that prayer is an approach to
God, a pleading with God, an asking of God."
- E.M.Bounds

Contents

"There is no secret. It is only ask and receive." – Evan Roberts upon being asked about the secret for revival

"Let him ask now that never asked before,
And him that asked before but ask the more."
– author unknown

"In a broad sense, asking is the essence of praying. Whatever else we do in religion builds around the activity of asking as its center." – J. Packer and C. Nystrom

"Whether we like it or not, asking is the rule of the kingdom. 'Ask and you shall receive.' It is a rule that never will be altered in anyone's case … If the royal and divine Son of God cannot be exempted from the rule of asking that He may have, you and I cannot expect the rule to be relaxed in our favor. Why should it be? ... If you may have everything by asking, and nothing without asking … I beseech you to abound in it." - C.H.Spurgeon

Introduction
Asking about Asking

Why Asking?

You are right if you thought that this was going to be a book about prayer. It is, but for our purposes, the word 'prayer' is often unhelpful, given that so many make a subject out of it, as if there is something out there by that name that it is our job to acquire by any and all means. The French theologian and sociologist Jacques Ellul wrote: "One cannot speak of prayer, but only of what the person does who prays." [1] What do they do? They ask and their asking assumes a hearer who will respond. There are so many words and terms that describe the act of praying: *calling on, crying out, beseeching, pleading, entreating, appealing, inquiring, communing, travailing, seeking, knocking, interceding, listening, petitioning, supplicating, prevailing,* to name a few. You could add other biblical phrases and expressions to the list. However, though different terms, they have a common meaning and purpose: asking.

Prayer is asking, but sadly, the word *prayer* becomes generalized in many people's minds and practice. All sorts of expressions pass for prayer that maybe are not prayer but more like recitations, observations, incantations, reflections, or spiritual-sounding conversations with oneself. Fundamental to a biblical understanding of prayer is *asking.* All of Jesus's teaching about prayer is all about asking. *"ASK!"* is His one-word compendium on prayer. It is when our confidence in asking erodes that prayer dissipates into general and tentative conversation. We back off the specific asking. Why? That is a good question to ask. There are many reasons that we will look at, but make no mistake about it, by talking about asking we are dealing with the heart of prayer. "If prayer is the heart of religion, then petition is the heart of prayer ... Petition is, and must ever remain, the heart and center of prayer." [2]

When you begin to ask about asking, it is not surprising that a number of questions present themselves. Why ask at all? What is the point and purpose of it? Is uncertainty about this the reason why we do not ask that much, for much? If God is going to do what He is going to do, is our asking just a therapeutic exercise to help us to talk about what we think that we need? Does our asking actually secure help or is it more an exercise of self-help? Is asking a condition of God's answering? What does my asking assume about God? What does my asking imply about me? Before I ask anything of God, are there things that God asks of me? Am I the only one doing the asking in this relationship? Are there things that God actually asks me to ask about and for? Are there things that God says we should not ask for, and we are wasting our time if we do? Are there kinds of asking that are welcomed but still may not be answered? What provokes our asking? Why do we stop asking? Is asking presumptuous? How and why does God respond to our asking? If He does respond to what I ask for, do I assume that He does so for the same reasons that I asked for it? Are there conditions to our asking or does anything go? Can we really ask whatever, whenever, wherever for whoever, or is it not quite as unconditional as that suggests? Are there things that encourage and help our asking? Are there things that hinder or subvert asking? When asking does not seem to be answered, what are we meant to conclude about it? There is plenty to ask about asking.

Psychological research is fascinated by the nature of asking. One leading child psychologist writes, "We all take for granted the fact that human beings ask." [3] According to another, a child asks about forty thousand times between the ages of two and five. [4] It would seem that our asking is an admission that there is so much that we need. Developmental research acknowledges that this innate drive to ask is intrinsic to our understanding of how humans are wired. As Christians, we know that. We were created to ask, because as creatures, we are dependent on our Creator.

So Why Are You Asking about Asking?

A few years ago, my wife Celia and I became part of an international prayer network called **THE ASK NETWORK** whose mission statement is: "Gathering all generations to pray for all nations, asking God to do what only He can do, and doing whatever He asks of us." [5] Although I had been exposed to intercession all my life, through praying parents, and through personal involvement in prayer ministries and movements, it was the simplicity and specificity of that word *ask* that caught my attention and imagination afresh, and provoked me to ask myself how much I really knew and understood about asking? I committed myself to renewed biblical study on the subject, which led me to a conclusion that inspired this book. Despite all my commitment to the necessity and practice of prayer, I was overwhelmed by how much more I could ask of God. Or to put it a little more pointedly: how little did I ask of God when all was said and done.

George Mueller, of Bristol in England, was renowned for his care for over ten thousand orphans and for his faith in God's ability to provide for them. In his journal he wrote:

> It struck me that I had never asked the Lord for anything concerning it (the Orphan House) ... and then I fell on my knees and opened my mouth wide, *asking him for much* ... I prayed that He would give me a house. [6]

And God did. Likewise, a fresh focus on the nature and necessity of *"asking Him for much"* serves to unclog the channel of anyone's silted communication, and release a fresh and forceful flow of abandoned but specific asking of God. In a book on spiritual formation, the author included a chapter on asking and then asks: "Does it appear too self-serving to devote an entire chapter to prayer as request?" So how self-serving is an entire book going to appear? I agree with the author's answer: "Not according to Jesus." [7]

In pursuing this matter, I began to notice how little was actually written or taught about asking, certainly recently. After surveying a large number of well-known and high-circulation books on prayer, most of them already on my shelves, I was surprised to find very little that was specifically about asking. It was always just assumed. One notable exception was Andrew Murray's gorgeous volume, *With Christ in the School of Prayer.* [8] There are other voices like his that need to be heard again, and I want to introduce you to some of them. In one of the rare books that devoted an entire chapter to asking, Jim Packer and Carolyn Nystrom observed that:

> for adults to practice the petitionary mode of prayer in a way that honors God and leads to the joy of seeing answers, *more is needed.* [9]

That shared conviction was an encouragement to my task.

So What Are You Asking For?

This book's purpose is to convince us that prayer is about specific asking, and to the extent that we do not specifically ask, we are not praying. I am asking God that before you finish reading this, you will be asking more and for more. Indeed, *more is needed.* I am asking boldly for exactly the same thing that P.T.Forsyth asked for one hundred years ago, in *The Soul of Prayer*: "What we ask for chiefly is the power *to ask more and to ask better.*" [10] It was Spurgeon who said that we should study the Bible until our very blood becomes "bibline"[11]. Our inquiry about asking will require that kind of study, and hopefully we will conclude with George Herbert that asking is equally "the soul's blood". [12] We need a *theology of asking* that transfuses life like a spiritual blood bank.

However, this subject of asking raises some challenging questions for personal life and circumstance that require wisdom and tenderness in their resolutions. For some there may be the jumbled, confusing and disappointing emotions that cling like spores to the things that have been asked for, but have not yet been answered or delivered. We have to acknowledge these realities. There may be emotions of discouragement and helplessness given the current health of our praying. But there are other emotions that if not experienced yet, can be anticipated. Was it not Jesus Himself who said, "Ask ... and your *joy* will be complete" (John 16:24)? Did not Paul express the joy he experienced as he asked for others? "In all my prayers for you I always pray with *joy*" (Philippians 1:4). So I am asking that this conversation will be pastoral, opening new horizons of possibilities in our understanding of praying, in our practice of praying, and in our expectation of praying.

There is much teaching about prayer that is not the scope or concern of this book. There are no chapters on different kinds of prayer (e.g. contemplative, sacramental, conversational) or on the many other kinds of designated prayers. There are no chapters just dedicated to exposition of the Psalmists' prayers, of the Lord's Prayers or Paul's prayers, though they are frequently referred to and commented upon. There are no extended chapters on everything you should ask about: family and friends, neighbors and nations, governments and governed, causes and crises, prospects and provisions, healings and deliverances, revivals and transformations. That is quite another kind of book. My concern is simply to invite you to think about asking and then to do it, and let whatever is needed get into its stream. It is amazing how asking even gets squeezed out of organized prayer meetings. I leave many of these gatherings asking myself what we specifically asked for, when all was said and done? Sometimes we do need to state the obvious – prayer is about asking. Deny that, dilute that, diminish that, and we will find that the bones of our prayer life will start to suffer from spiritual osteoporosis. Prayerlessness is a failure to ask and keep on asking.

Though C.S.Lewis was a man of prayer, he was diffident about his understanding of it. How would he have responded to many of the books written about the subject? "However badly needed a good book on prayer is, I shall never try to write it." This is humorously ironic as Lewis wrote this in *Letters to Malcolm* that was published posthumously and happens to be a brilliant book on prayer because he did not try to write it as such. He said, "For me to offer the world instruction about prayer would be impudence." [13] I feel the same way. However, I am going to take comfort that the aspect of prayer that we are going to address and be encouraged to grow in, is probably the very kind of praying that Lewis would have selected too, given what dominates most of his writing on the subject, particularly in his essays *The Efficacy of Prayer* and *Petitionary Prayer: A problem without an answer.* It is this business of *asking* that consumes his interest and inquiry. In his typically humble way, he was quick to admit the challenges that asking presents to all of us, with which we can all identify. But surely, we all know what asking is and how to ask?

So If We May Ask ...

So where do we go from here? Origen, the spiritually influential, third-century biblical scholar and teacher, wrote in the introduction to his treatise *On Prayer*:

> I pray as a man – for I by no means attribute to myself any capacity for prayer – that I may obtain the spirit of prayer before I discourse upon it, and entreat that a discourse full and spiritual may be granted to *us.* [14]

Together, we can ask for no less, so let *us* begin this investigation by asking of the Father, whom Jesus promised would "give the Holy Spirit to those who ask Him" (Luke 11:13).

"Dearest Father, We are so thankful that we can ask you for what we need. Right now, we need the help of your Holy Spirit, to use this book as an encouragement to just ask. We ask you to consecrate the time that will be spent in reading it, and may there be an accompanying sense of your presence. We ask you to incite wonder at the intimacy of relationship that you desire with us through this asking and answering relationship. We ask you to direct us to your Word and to give us an increased understanding about how to ask according to your will. We ask that we will be asking more and for more before the reading is completed. Please help us to know when to stop reading and to start asking. We are so thankful that you have invited us to ask of you, and that your Son Jesus taught us that this was a way to bring glory to you. We are asking, therefore, not primarily for our answers, but for the sake of your awesome glory. We ask this in the name of Jesus. Amen.

Towards a Theology of Asking

"Beginners at prayer – children, new converts – find it easy. God speaks to us … and we answer. In a word, we pray. It's that simple. But prayer doesn't stay simple. We spend years slogging through a wilderness of testing and begin to question the child-like simplicities with which we started out … It happens to all of us. Everyone who prays ends up in some difficulty or other. We need help."
– Eugene Petersen

"Petition is not a lower form of prayer. It is our staple diet."
– Richard Foster

"God's children are taught that they are to get things by asking."
– John Rice

"Prayer, or praying, is simply asking." – Karl Barth

1

Asking is for Beginners ... or is it?

Asking Is For Beginners

To ask or not to ask? That is the question. Asking often gets treated as if it is *Prayer 101* and has been described by some as "simple prayer" because it is equated with the communication of little children to their father. Although acknowledged as the most common form of prayer in scripture, which surely suggests that it is the most important and the most necessary to be understood, asking has been described as *"beginning* prayer ... the prayer of *children* yet we will return to it again and again." [1]

Asking is not altogether marginalized, but it ends up getting compared to more "mature" forms of prayer. Inevitably, it is then assumed to be more immature, like the requests of immature children. This is not the view of the Bible, nor of this book. It is not that asking is "simple prayer" but that all prayer is simply "asking".[2] It is crucial to discern between what is simple and what is simplicity. When explicit asking ceases, spiritual simplicity goes out the window and fleshly complexity comes through the door of our "mature" prayer rooms.

Or Is It?

It is important to distinguish the *childish* from the *childlike.* Though the former is a description of immaturity, the latter is the necessary qualification to both receive and enter the kingdom of God according to Jesus (Mark

10:13–16). When the disciples ask what constitutes greatness in the kingdom of God, which implies self-assumed maturity, Jesus affirms that such a disposition is predicated on the humility of a child (Matthew 18:1–4). "Unless you change and become like *little children*, you will never enter the kingdom of God."

Presumably, such a "change" to "little children" is one in a maturing direction, though it would seem to be going backward, given the chronology of the image. Asking, therefore, is clearly a response of humility that is not about reverting to immature childishness but advancing to mature childlikeness. What is most significant and strategic is that Luke places an incident with little ones following two parables about asking. The text says that "babies" (Luke 18:15) were brought to Jesus. What does this mean for asking? B.B.Warfield, the eminent Princeton Reformed theologian, argued that though humility (as inferred in Matthew 19:13–15), simplicity, or trustfulness are legitimate characteristics of being childlike, the focus on the babies can only mean that the qualifying characteristic is absolute dependence. As Warfield argued, babies have "no disposition of mind" as the other qualities imply.[3] So asking is the evidence of dependence and is its necessary expression.

Like babies we cannot secure our own spiritual births and sustain our own lives. Given this dependence, why would asking not be organic to our daily maturing existence? If the kingdom of heaven belongs to "such" (not "them") then the dependent asking of the helpless becomes the nonnegotiable expression of that kingdom and its essential DNA. Professor Farmer's conclusion about asking is this:

> The reason why it appears early in the religious life ... is not that it is childish and must be discarded like milk-teeth, but that it is basic and must abide all through, like the skeleton on which the body at all stages of its development is built; that to eliminate it from prayer, therefore, so far from helping man to the proper maturity of his personal life in relation to God, is definitely to hinder and prevent it.[4]

Seldom noted is the fact that in all three synoptic gospels [5] the very next incident after the comments on childlikeness is Jesus's encounter with the Rich Young Ruler who was bound by his possessions. What is the contextual connection with "asking"? Jesus identified this man's independence and self-sufficiency. He neither wanted Jesus to ask about it, nor did he want to be in a position where he would have to ask for provision. The only way to recover the dependence that would ask of Jesus was to forsake his independent means. It is the publican in the parable preceding Luke's account of the babies who knows that he has no ability or capacity to bring anything to the table but his need. He has nothing to commend himself to God except his helplessness and absolute dependence. That is precisely why he becomes Jesus's illustration of why and how we need to ask. As Augustine said, "The best disposition for praying is that of being desolate, forsaken, stripped of everything." [6]

We have already referenced how developmental psychological research is discovering how the capacity to ask is a unique strength of children, but it is puzzling that this seems to weaken in expression in adult life. Research is revealing how brilliant and strategic the asking of children is when in pursuit of answers. When it comes to asking, Alison Gopnik observes in her study 'The Philosophical Baby': "Human children are equipped with extremely powerful learning mechanisms and a strong intrinsic drive." [7] That sounds like a capacity for the importunity that Jesus said was necessary in asking.

Simply because children may be regarded by an adult as immature chronologically, it is assumed that they are undeveloped in all other ways. Cognitive psychologists are now discovering the immeasurable capacities of a child's brain but also how many of these seem to be lost with presumed chronological maturity through what is called "synaptic pruning." So it would seem that the analogous relationship between asking and a child has everything to do with strength and not weakness, capacity and not limitation.

Richard Wurman, creator of the TED talks, notes: "In school, we are rewarded for having the answer, not for asking a good question." This may explain why the trustful asking that is so instinctive in a young child gradually wanes with educational progress and with our know-it-all independence. Regardless of culture, it is estimated that preschool children ask about one hundred questions a day but almost none by middle school. It is argued that this is responsible for two things: the decline of creativity and the loss of relational engagement. [8] How interesting is it then that scripture relates childlike asking to creativity ("more than we can imagine"; Ephesians 3:20) and to intimate relationship ("if you remain in me"; John 15:7).

Knock ... Seek ... Ask

It has been said that anyone can ask. This is true. However, often the implication is that not anyone can seek or knock. This is just not true. What has not helped, as a consequence of the simple view of asking, is the habit of many to make hierarchical distinctions between asking and other descriptive words like *interceding* or *prevailing* and to also make evaluative differences between what are considered big and worthy requests and small and less worthy ones. After all, the sequence is to ask, then seek, and then knock (Luke 11:9). Does this not move from the lesser to the greater, representing an increasingly mature expression of prayer? This presents asking as the bottom rung of a ladder, a good starting place, but not our stopping place.

This approach is presented by the ablest of saints. In his otherwise excellent book, *The Life of Prayer,* A.B.Simpson, the founder of the Christian Missionary Alliance, writes:

> In its *simplest form* prayer is represented as asking. 'Ask and it shall be given unto you.' This expresses *the most elementary* form of prayer – the presenting of our petitions to God in the *simplest* terms and manner ... There is a *higher form* of prayer, 'Seek and you shall find'. This denotes the prayer that waits upon God until it receives an answer, and that follows up that answer in obedience ... 'Knock and it shall be opened unto you.' This is *more than* seeking. This is the prayer that surmounts the great obstacles of life." [9]

Of course, seeking and knocking seem more vigorous and engaging than asking. Is not an increase of intensity and urgency implied? Is that not how we are encouraged to perceive them? But you could look at this in a different way. It all depends where you start. If you begin with *knocking*, this is coming from the outside. *Seeking* suggests an entry, a strengthening of the pursuit, pressing in and getting closer, but *asking* suggests something on the inside, the personal face-to-face. Thus it could be argued that asking is the most mature and most intimate expression of communication. My point is not to argue for either view but simply to say that there is no ground to reduce asking in a manner that treats it as an immature and undeveloped form of communication with God. It is not helpful to understand seeking and knocking as different and more mature expressions of prayer.

Leveling The Levels

In so many books about prayer, the word *levels* appears, as if asking, seeking and knocking were hierarchical. Here is an example:

> In order to prevail, the intercessor must often increase the intensity of his or her praying from one level to another. *I suggest seven such levels.* The first three are listed by Jesus in His Sermon on the Mount. To these I add four more levels from scripture. [10]

With all due respect, why did Jesus short-change us when He knew there were other levels to aspire to, and is it any wonder that so many have missed all seven carriages of this prayer train and feel confused about how to catch up? Two bad results come from this. First, we may become proud about our mastery of the levels and in our status as intercessory black-belts. Any talk about levels makes unbiblical distinctions, and though well-meaning in the attempt to bring a sense of organization to so many biblical teachings about prayer, it ends up imposing an order on prayer itself whereby we advance through a prescribed sequence to effectiveness. The second bad outcome is that in the face of all these levels, like unclimbable steps to the throne, many resign themselves to a self-perception of immaturity or inability that they are stuck with. The more levels and steps are added, the further away the throne seems to get. This is unhelpful, misleading, and frankly unscriptural. It is not altogether surprising that more levels are added by those exponents of the need for more and better prayer. The zeal is to be appreciated but Jesus used all these different words to describe not distinctive and easily distinguishable levels but different dimensions of asking that included undeterred pursuit (seeking) and unstoppable persistence (knocking), both of which are definitely expressed by asking children should you still wish to equate asking with childish and immature prayer.

As well-meaning as this presentation of levels may be, it can be damaging and at worst very deceiving. We end up stratifying prayer and those who pray, determining the efficacy of various forms of prayer on our own terms. Well-intentioned people end up believing unbiblical things about what they are doing or achieving at the place of prayer. An erroneous theology will usually lead to an erroneous methodology. The enemy of our souls will be happy to sponsor the competitiveness between different schools of prayer, and of spiritual warfare, simply because we are tempted to take pride in our own insights on prayer and our own assumed effectiveness in doing battle. It ends up being more about style than spirituality; more about rhetoric than revelation; more about tradition than truth; more about deception than discernment; more about presumption than prayer.

We know how deceiving this can be from the teaching of Jesus Himself. The Pharisee and the Publican (Luke 18:9–14) went up to the temple *to pray.* The difference between them was that one asked for something with untutored desperation and one asked for nothing with religious technique. If we cease to ask rightly then other kinds of communication will predominate. In this case, the Pharisee's prayer was all about himself. He was making pronouncements, not asking. He was presenting himself and his insights. It was a soliloquy. Pride and independence simply do not ask, though they masquerade as doing so. They have no need to do so. This might suggest that our asking is a fairly good barometer of our humility and of our dependence on the Lord. The paucity of our asking will reveal what we have decided we have no need to ask the Lord about. The potential pride in our perception of our level that has us praying "not like other men" will not be the kind of asking that leaves us "justified before God."

Does Anyone Want Anything?

If we can only enter the kingdom as a child, then communication with the King will be child-like. Asking is then indeed *"the prayer of children"* that needs to be understood, not as a passing phase of immature communication, but as the non-negotiable description of all mature prayer. A proud grandfather described how his grandson, upon leaving the room to go and say his evening prayers, asked the assembled adults, "Hey everybody, I'm going to pray. Does anyone want anything?" [11] Learning to ask again as a child makes eminent sense when you ask the question, "How does a child ask?" Several answers come to mind: incessantly, helplessly, indiscriminately, repetitively, insistently, trustingly, noisily, honestly, unselfconsciously, dependently, desperately, needily, audaciously, inarticulately, verbally and non-verbally, frankly, directly, appealingly, emotionally. Add your own adverbs. Does that describe our asking of God? I would add "ungrammatically". Children do not always know the rules of language, nor the social manners of asking, but that neither discourages nor invalidates their asking. Nor should our thoughts about our immaturity discourage our asking of God.

Theological and grammatical rectitude is not always the best expression of personal spiritual reality. We are no more heard by God because of our articulate and immaculate asking, than a parent only hears the asking of the child by virtue of their command of the language. An adult will often ask, *"What was it they said?"* when listening to an asking child. Of course intelligibility helps but the lack of it is not an obstacle. What makes the child's asking recognizable as an understandable request is not the way the child asked it, but the way the parent heard it. It is the hearing of God that transforms our emotionally guttural and spiritually ungrammatical asking into something that a mature intercessor might recognize as a prayer, but only after God has sorted it out, or as one observer puts it, "fixed it up." [12] The famous Boston preacher, Phillip Brooks, was once described as having prayed the most eloquent prayer "ever offered to a Boston audience." It may have been a paragon of prayer but it was offered to the wrong audience. It is better to be a child whose asking of the Father has to be translated and interpreted by the Holy Spirit because no one else quite gets it, than to be the model of invocatory eloquence. In the same way that a parent is ready to respond to the cry of the child, even so our Father is disposed to our asking: "The Lord waits to be gracious to you; He rises to show you compassion" (Isaiah 30:18). Like a loving parent, He is already up and moving towards the child who is asking before they have even finished their request. And if David the psalmist is right and the Lord knows what we are asking before the word is even on our tongue (Psalm 139:4), then regardless of how jumbled and mangled, how upside-down and back-to-front, how immature-sounding is the asking, and no matter how it tumbles out, God can fill in the blanks, supply the missing words of need, and read the hidden heart. The grammar of grace can parse every word and sentence of the son or the daughter that asks of the Father.

Isn't It Rude To Ask?

When associated with the communication of a child, asking attracts other objections. When a child says "open it", they can present both inquiry and insistence, since both a question-mark and exclamation-mark accompany their intonation, as they manage to ask and demand at the same time. Importunity is always lurking in their request. To some ears it may indeed sound a little rude, but the child will learn to say "please" and "thank-you". Hopefully, that will not be at the expense of their asking being squashed or suspended until they learn how to ask properly. Asking is instinctive to a child and its inquisitiveness, but also the dominant form of communication given their inabilities to be self-sufficient. Sadly for many adults, the maturation process is marked by becoming acquisitive (having more and therefore asking less for resources) and ceasing to be inquisitive (knowing more and therefore asking less for revelation). Such maturity could not be more 'anti-asking'.

Is there any parent who has not been pressed to the limit, whose emotional and intellectual resources have not been completely exhausted by the random, spontaneous and annoying asking of a child, oblivious to the degree of difficulty of what they ask for or about? Legitimate inquiring is heard as precocious asking. It is easy to regard their endlessly bold asking as rude and insensitive to social manners or the patience of others. Children do ask about anything and everything, things that Jesus understood asking to be about. Inevitably, justifiable lessons in social graces (dressed up as spiritual manners) train them not to be so bold. In fact, they learn that it can be considered impertinent and rude to ask. Charles Hodge, another respected Princeton theologian, was reported by his son as saying: "In my childhood, I came nearer to 'praying without ceasing' than in any other period of my life. I had the habit of thanking God for everything I received and asking for everything I wanted." [13] Or as Walter Wangerin expressed it: "Children prevail where their elders fail." [14] As children, somewhere along the way, it seems that our innate gift of asking, rather than being developed and nurtured, was suffocated and knocked out of us. Spiritually, we ended up being seen but not heard. With adult maturity came independence, control, self-sufficiency, cynicism, doubt, distrust, self-awareness, and the pride that does not ask. What the asking child will not let us forget is that they are powerless and cannot manage their limited resources or manipulate the world to get what they need. The power and efficacy of asking is not in the child who asks, but in the father they are talking to. Thus the principle is established that our asking is only effective because of the one we ask. And He does not consider our asking to be rudeness.

Isn't It Selfish To Ask?

Those who describe asking as "simple" are usually those who also describe it as "selfish", as "self-serving" prayer, as "egotistical". [15] Perhaps this is a hangover from assumptions about the 'child' image. B.B.Warfield was not the first to acknowledge that: "There is no period of life so purely, sharply, unrelievedly egotistic as infancy." [16] The argument given is that we have to move through this kind of self-centered prayer (notice that asking is assumed to be self-serving) in order to get beyond it to "other-centered prayer." Presumably, the idea is that if you are consumed with your own navel, then you will never ask for nations. The truth is that if you do not know how to ask rightly for yourself it is unlikely you ever will ask for anyone or anything else. It is interesting that one of the largest selling books ever written about prayer, and one of the few books to have ever sold more than 10,000,000 copies, is *The Prayer of Jabez* which many would classify as a totally selfish prayer if ever there was one. "O that you would bless **me** and enlarge **my** territory. Let your hand be with **me**, and keep **me** from harm so that **I** will be free from pain" (1 Chronicles 4:9-10). While we are tut-tutting, and saying under our breath, "It's not all about YOU!" the very next words read: "And God granted his request." So there! How can we be surprised that Wilkinson entitles his second chapter, *'So why not ask?'* The rest of the book rests on these appealing questions:

> Is it possible that God wants you to be 'selfish' in your prayers? To ask for more and more – and more again – from your Lord? I've met so many Christians who take it as a sign of immaturity to think such thoughts." [17]

There again is that link between asking and immaturity.

Of course, the demanding concerns of self may well end up wrongly occupying our asking. It has been suggested that it is because devout writers so feared the self-centered aspects of asking that they shunned any possible focus on asking for the self that would lead to selfishness and narcissism. Andrew Murray is a rare voice in his understanding of asking. To those who say that direct petitions are "but a subordinate part of prayer" and that for those who are mature in prayer they "occupy but an inconsiderable place", Murray writes:

> If we carefully study all that our Lord spoke of prayer, we shall see that *this is not His teaching* ... everywhere our Lord urges and encourages us to offer definite petitions, and to expect definite answers.

He then acknowledges that asking has been given "a subordinate place" precisely because "it has been thought needful to free it from the appearance of selfishness." [18] If indeed our asking is selfish, then it will be ineffective for the reason that James gives: wrong motives (James 4:3). But there is a dependent, humble, submissive and needy asking for ourselves that has to be expressed, that is neither selfish nor immature and that asks for that which Jesus asked for us, and gave His life to secure for us. That puts a high value on that kind of asking for self which is not to get our "pleasures" (James 4:3) but to give God pleasure in our conformity to do His will and our maturity in the character of His Son.

The correct response to wrong selfishness is not to cease to ask, but to disallow our asking to be dominated by selfish need. If our passion is for God to be glorified through us, then we will ask much for ourselves, not for our selfish sake, but for God's sake. If there is any justification in what we are asking for self then we are rehearsing what needs to be asked for others. For this reason, so much that first appears as private and personal asking, reappears as public intercession for others. The asking that might appear particular to me, and therefore selfish, becomes the asking for the common good. Jonathan Graf, the founder of "PRAY" magazine, testifies to the bad consequences that came from this fear of selfishness:

> For some reason I, like many believers, began to pray less and less for myself. I'm not sure why. Maybe we think praying for ourselves is a sign of selfishness or immaturity. [19]

That is exactly what we are talking about. It is the fear that asking is likely to be simple, and therefore rude and selfish, perhaps precocious and presumptuous. I so appreciate that Graf went on to assert that it was Jesus Himself who instructed us to ask for ourselves.

Ask Nicely

Sadly, spiritual manners and the liturgical propriety of form and phrase begin to suppress the child-like asking of desperate need, deep desire, passionate affection, and compassionate intercession. There is a temptation to become dependent on the asking of others, because they know how to ask properly, or because they seem more mature and confident. Scripture exhorts us to ask for one another, but is not encouraging us always to get someone else to ask *for* us, in a way that they end up asking *instead* of us. The priests and military leaders who came to Jeremiah (21:2; 42:2) and asked him to do the praying on their behalf represent a multitude that makes a similar request of others. Of course, it is necessary that we humble ourselves and seek the ministration of others for things that are needed in our lives, about which they have experience, wisdom, discernment, authority, faith and spiritual giftedness. Jesus assumed this mutuality of asking when two or three are gathered together. But asking others to ask for us should not displace the primacy of asking of God for ourselves.

Many only feel confident to ask if using the words of others, which over time may diminish their own personal asking. The place and role of 'set prayers' has been discussed through the ages, particularly among the Puritans. Thomas Fuller remarked that formal prayers were "lawful for any and needful for some" [20] and suggested that if you begin with them, you will learn to ask better without them – a bit like trainer wheels on a bicycle. How different this is to the idea that liturgical prayer is somehow a mature form of prayer for adults. But Fuller was a realist and given the strange things that he heard people ask about, suggested that "set form was better than nonsense"! Others, like John Owen, saw the unquestioned dominance of set prayers as "occasion of quenching the Spirit in hindering all progress or growth in gifts and graces." [21] Never one to mince words, John Bunyan observed:

> For as he that feels the pain needs not to be taught to cry O! even so he that has his understanding opened by the Spirit needs not to be so taught of other men's prayers, as that he cannot pray without them. [22]

When it comes to our asking about *what* most matters to us, and *why*, set prayers cannot fully help us. They capture the general feelings, and clearly point us in the right direction, but do not deal with the particularities of what is 'me and mine'. If asking is a means of intimacy with God, then we are not going to get another to ask for us most of the time and be our go-between. There are just not enough Hallmark-card style prayers to cover our personal needs. The love poems of literature, the songs and the sonnets, are generally helpful in increasing the vocabulary and imagination of romance, but they do not hold a candle to the personal covenantal love-letter or poem that a husband could write for his wife, in his own words. As C.S.Lewis put it: "A ready-made form can't serve for my intercourse with God anymore than it could serve for my intercourse with you." [23] He did not completely exclude the "ready-made" for he was equally concerned about an over-familiarity in prayer that resulted in becoming "too cosily at ease in Zion." He acknowledged that the liturgical, historic prayers are helpful in reminding us of things that we ought to ask for when tempted to be distracted by our immediate needs and crises. Understandably, when our greatest need is the need to ask about our needs, we can feel isolated and alone in bearing them. The proven, scripture-based words of others may be especially helpful in providing a sense of connection with other askers, who we feel are asking with us and for us. However, this should be a support to our asking and not its substitute. If not, it may result in a false trust in the formulation rather than in the God who we are asking. It can come to be treated as a magical incantation. We may mistake what we describe as spontaneous asking as somehow less worthy, less efficacious and less mature than that which is liturgical. The familiarity that Lewis feared in the free is no less a concern than the impersonality that can result from the formulaic. If asking ceases when we are not using the words or liturgies of others on our behalf, then the problem is a lack of intimate personal asking of our Lord. The loss of ritual exposes a lack of relationship.

Truly, children do learn to speak by listening to the words of others and by repeating them, so they are tutored by the language of others. This is good and necessary. However, if all future conversation and relationship required another's words, we would recognize that as evidence of immaturity at best and serious incapacity at worst. The liturgical and devotional formulations that are a crucial and non-negotiable part of our Christian worship and intercession are not being questioned here. Liturgical prayer is helpful in recovering a corporate and united asking. The New Testament contains liturgy. As we will see later, asking is never just free-style and free-wheeling, if at the end of the day it is scripted, explicitly or implicitly, by the will of God and the Word of God. The point is that while acknowledging the place and purpose of our use of the words of others in our asking, it will not do if it becomes the major form of our asking. Donald Bloesch, who was one of the great pastoral theologians of our time, put it like this:

> The growing liturgical worship in the mainline churches more often than not signifies a formalizing of the prayer life that spells the death of a realistic communion with a living God.[24]

It need not be an either/or; it must be a both/and.

Simple But Not Easy

Child-like asking preserves simplicity in prayer, but it comes with challenges that should be recognized. Few have written as persuasively about prayer as E.M.Bounds:

> The simplicity of prayer, its child-like elements, form a great obstacle to true praying. Intellect gets in the way of the heart. The child spirit only is the spirit of prayer ... *It is no easy work* to have this child-like spirit of prayer. [25]

He is challenging the idea that what is simple is thereby both less challenging and less mature, and consequently somehow easier to accomplish. On the contrary, he suggests that child-like asking is in fact very hard work. Asking is not an easy act for beginners, but in the words of Bishop Ryle, the godly nineteenth century pastor and theologian, "it is the simplest act." [26]

The notion that asking might be avoided precisely because of its many tough challenges was not lost on one "mere Christian". C.S.Lewis acknowledged the good reasons why there would be more emphasis on other expressions of faith, like adoration, than on asking. He conceded that these may be "nobler forms of prayer" but he admitted the challenges of asking when he added, "they are also a good deal easier to write about!" [27] Those who consider asking-prayer as the simple prayer of children would not find Lewis in agreement.

> Whatever the theoretical difficulties are, we must keep making requests of God. And on this point *we can get no help from those who keep on reminding us that this is the lowest and least essential kind of prayer.* [28]

For Lewis, far from 'asking' being an immature or elementary expression, it was the communication of those who were maturely advanced in the faith.

> My own idea is that it occurs only when the one who prays does so as God's fellow-worker, demanding what is needed for the joint work. It is the prophet's, the apostle's, the missionary's, the healer's prayer that is made with this confidence justified by the event. [29]

In other words, these people are so in tune with God, as sons and daughters (children) of their Father, and so know His will, that their specific asking is reflective of a mature faith in the evidence of things not seen (Hebrews 11:1ff).

Asking Is For Beginners ... Or Is It?

Psychologists say that if they could ascertain what the mechanisms are by which children can ask so well, then they would learn something crucial about human nature. For Christians this is no mystery, because we have learned that we are created to be in a dependent and intimate relationship with the Creator of the universe who loves our asking of Him to be the sign of our trust and the means for Him to show His answering love. The process of maturity is not about moving *out* of asking into some more mature means of communication that appears less 'childish', but it is about progressing *in* our continual asking in a manner that increasingly matures in 'child-likeness'.

"Christian prayer is our word answering God's ... Our prayer is the answer to God's. Herein is prayer, not that we prayed Him, but that He first prayed us, in giving His Son to be a propitiation for us ... So God inspires all prayer which finds and moves Him." – P.T.Forsyth

"In the biblical history, prayer is not introduced as a separate spiritual discipline: it rises as man's answer to God's address."
– Edmund Clowney

"Only the prayer which comes from God can go to God. The dove will only bear a letter to the cote from which it came, and so will prayer go back to Heaven if it came from Heaven. We must shoot the Lord's arrows back to Him. That desire which He writes upon our heart will move His heart." – C.H.Spurgeon

"Prayer is the attention we give to the one who attends to us."
– Eugene Petersen

"The essence of prayer does not consist in asking God for something but in opening our hearts to God ... it does not mean asking God for all kinds of things we want; it is rather the desire for God Himself."
– Sadhu Sundar Singh

"Our petition is a response to the initiative of God." – Donald Bloesch

"The hearing really precedes the asking. It is the basis of it. It makes it real asking, the asking of Christian prayer." – Karl Barth

2

Asking as Answering

My Initiation Or His Invitation?

It usually feels to us that we are the ones initiating the asking and the conversation with God. That is understandable, especially on those occasions when our asking is coming from a place of pressure or desperation and we assume that we are trying to get God's attention. In our theology of asking we are saying that before we even ask, God's initiative precedes ours. You can understand why Eugene Petersen rightly describes asking as "answering prayer" [1] or why long before him, P.T.Forsyth wrote:

> If our prayers reach or move Him it is because He first reached and moved us to pray ... Before prayer can receive an answer it must be itself an answer ... The Answerer provides the very prayer. [2]

This is why all of our asking is a response to His prior asking of us. It is His invitation before it is our initiation or invocation. Forsyth observes: "He beseeches us which makes us beseech Him." [3] Our asking is always an answering, if our asking is according to the Word of God which He has already spoken, and in response to what He has first presented as His will, as what He has prescribed, and what He has promised. This is why the Puritan pastor William Gurnall described prayer as "the promise reversed." In our asking, we direct back to God the divine purposes and promises that were first initiated by Him, and consequently revealed and delivered to us.

All arguments against asking are a denial of the possibility of relationship with God: a relationship which has been initiated by a loving God who made the first move, in which asking and answering constitute the very core of intimate communication. The fact that God not only invites us, but then commands us to ask, seems to settle it. Why would initiating love not command what is best for the beloved in order for the relationship to be lovingly maintained and sustained, deepened and directed? Did not Jesus say that we "ought" always to ask, and then tell the parable of the insistent, persistent widow who would not stop asking (Luke 18:1-8)? God's moral imperative, His encouragement of our intentional and intense asking, solicits our response to just ask. God has desired, chosen and commanded our asking as a way for Him to give of Himself to us, and for us in turn to receive of His love.

Just Give The Answer

Why ask for that which God desires to give us anyway? Why does He not initiate by just giving us our answers and cutting out the middle-man of our asking? As we will affirm again and again, it is because He wants to relate to us, and like any one who desires relationship, He needs to hear us express our heart, not merely for what we need, but for who He is as the answerer. In any love relationship is it not the intimate interplay of asking and answering that unveils who we are? In our answers to being asked, we entrust ourselves to the one who inquires of us? Why asking? Because if there was no need for loving solicitation and His answers were without our asking, then there would be no need for humble dependence and we would be the first to believe that either we deserved the answers, or God was somehow obliged to provide them at our beck and call, according to our will. The greatest potential deception would be that we would end up assuming that what was given by His hand had been gained by ours. God would somehow be obliged to us, and we would cease to be debtors to His grace. Furthermore, we would end up treating what was precious and purchased at a price as if it was of no account. As Spurgeon put it:

> If we had the blessings without asking for them, we should think them common things, but prayer makes the common

> pebbles of God's temporal bounties more precious than diamonds.[4]

If asking the Father was the response of Jesus Himself to what the Father's initiating love asked of Him, and if in that asking was His dependent identity as a Son, then how much more so for us. Our asking, that answers the same Father's initiative, is the evidence of our dependent relationship as sons and daughters of our Father.

The self-consciousness of our need is suddenly transformed into a much-more needed God-consciousness and in that moment, despite the incontrovertible reality of neediness, our cares are truly all cast on Him, simply because He initiated the invitation to do so. Thus comes the revelation that despite having felt uncared for, despite beginning to feel like we could not care any more, despite being overburdened with cares, or that we could not care less – we know in that instant of asking that He cares for us, and always did. His care preceded our cares, as His asking of us, and His answering of us, preceded our asking.

Divine Kick-Starts To Our Asking

So given God's eagerness that we ask of Him, what happens when gracious initiations and commanding invitations are ignored or neglected? Of course, we are quick to ask when we are in need or in crisis; when we want something that we do not have or have something that we do not want. Not all asking is good or acceptable. Scripture gives examples of asking for wrong things, asking of wrong sources, asking in wrong ways or with wrong motivations and desires. But if we cease asking altogether, then because God loves us and needs our asking as our loving and intimate relational response to Him, we should not be surprised that He does things to kick-start our asking so that the calls of His heart are answered.

Sadly, we give little thought or preparation to what our asking should be, simply because we are not asking at all. Day after day passes with little expression of our need or our dependence on Him. Our lack of asking is an evidence of our self-satisfaction, of the fact that we think we can manage without Him, and in fact are doing so. But because God wants to relate with us and relate us to His work in the world, and because this relationship is fueled and fed by our asking and His answering, God has ways of interrupting and invading our prayer-less state with His own ways and means for getting us to respond to His neglected initiative. How?

By Asking Us Questions

The first communication of God after the Fall was a question. What had precipitated the Fall was some satanic asking, "Has God said?" (Genesis 3:1). This sought, in a single blow, to subvert God's goodness, His justice and His Word. We have only been reading the Bible about five minutes when we see how the devil wants to corrupt our trustful asking of God and turn it into unbelieving questioning of God. There is asking and asking. We can ask of God in a way that is impertinent and imperious, cynical and supercilious, doubting and distrusting. We need to know the difference between right and wrong ways to ask. The initiating asking of God started early. In Genesis 3:9 we hear Him ask: "Where are you?" It is the evidence of God's initiating grace that He would come into our helpless and hopeless situation with asking of His own in order to lovingly provoke responsiveness; to raise an awareness of His availability and ability on our behalf; to draw us to Him from places of distance and unbelief, sin and seduction, brokenness and neediness; to get us to ask Him for help.

There are few of us who have not known this kind of divine asking of us and for us that enquires about where and how we are, because like Israel of old, we have forgotten Him "days without number" (Jeremiah 2:32). Jeremiah's opening prophecy to these people is a torrent of divine asking that is seeking to kick-start their asking of God. Their spiritual failure was a failure to ask. "The priests did not ask, 'Where is the Lord?'" (Jeremiah 2:8) Even when they did appear to ask ("My Father, my friend from my youth, will you always be angry?" 3:4) it was not sincere asking and therefore was not heard because God said that they continued to do "all the evil you can." In Genesis 18:9 we have another example of the way God asks: "Where is Sarah?" This is His way of getting a response from a pained and mocking heart. Through the prophet Isaiah, God says: "When I asked, no one could answer a word" (Isaiah 41:28). God knew what it felt like to continue to be ignored despite continuing to initiate. In the gospels, we often find Jesus kick-starting the necessary asking that the needy one should be expressing, by first asking of them: "What do you want me to do for you?" (Mark 10:36) What is implied here? "Ask Me!" Although the disciples should have been asking for provision, it is Jesus who asks, "How many loaves do you have?" (Mark 6:38) Rather than being silenced by their need and their limitations, He wanted them to ask Him to use what they had. Will we respond to what God asks of us and understand that this is God's loving move to get us to ask of Him? He wants us to answer Him by 'just asking.'

By Telling Us What We Should Be Asking For

Through Jeremiah, God pleaded with the people to just ask so He could answer. Everything is about to collapse and no one had any idea about what the future held. God wanted them to bring their ignorance to Him because they needed to be asking about both their present predicament as well as their future prospects: "Call to me and I will tell you great and unsearchable things you do not know" (Jeremiah 33:3). God takes the initiative to get them to ask Him for what they need, which is exactly what He longs to give them: "health and healing ... abundant prosperity and peace." Asking is a recovery of a posture of openness to listen, to respond and to receive.

One of the best examples is in Luke 11:1 when the disciples actually do not know how to ask, or what to ask for. They need Jesus's initiative to tell them. Asking for help to ask is where all humble asking needs to begin. And there is an answer. The answer is the asking that Jesus then models for them that we know so familiarly as the *Lord's Prayer.* It is simply a divine aid that is telling us what to ask for: a revelation and knowledge of holiness, manifestations of kingdom life, daily provision, forgiveness, protection and deliverance. Through this example of what Jesus asked for, we are told what we should be asking for.

Another gospel record of what Jesus asked of the Father serves as a key resource. By listening to the specific things He is asking for us, we are being taught what we can and should ask for ourselves. Study John 17 in detail and make your own ask-list from your meditations. It might go like this: "Lord, I ask: that I will accept and obey your Word (6,8); that I will be assured about who you are (8); that I will know the Father (6,7); that I will be assured of His specific and special care of me (9); that I will choose to live under His protection (11,12); that I will experience His joy in my life (13); that I will practice and pursue unity and reconciliation in all my relationships (21); that I will be holy and set apart for Him (17); that I will bring others to Him through my witness (20); that I will be filled with His love (23,26); that I will abide and live in His presence (24); that I will receive increasing revelation of His glory (24)." Have we been told enough here about what to ask for? If this is what Jesus Himself is asking for us, would this not be a safe and assured place to begin our asking? Is there not sufficient in these two asking prayers of Jesus (Luke 11 and John 17) not merely to turn the ignition of our asking, but keep it fueled for the rest of our lives? God tells us what to ask for so that we will 'just ask.'

By Being Explicit About What He Asks Of Us

By initiating the conversation God wants us to realize that we are incapable of doing what He asks of us without His help, and that consequently, we will have to ask Him for the resources that we need in order to give Him what He both requests and requires. "What does the Lord your God require of you, but to fear the Lord your God, to walk in His ways, to love Him and to serve Him with all your heart and with all your soul, and to observe the Lord's commands and decrees" (Deuteronomy 10:12). We cannot do this unaided, therefore we must ask for enablement. In Micah 6 the Lord Himself is feeding the people the questions they should be asking of Him. "With what shall I come before the Lord and bow down before the exalted God?" Obviously, God's heart is pained because they are not asking of Him, but if He can get them just to ask, then hopefully they will start asking about their lostness and loss, and God will answer them in order to restore them. God gives them no less than three questions to ask, one after another. "Shall I come before Him? ... Will the Lord be pleased? ... Shall I offer?" God is prompting the asking by telling them explicitly what He is asking of them so that they in turn will have to ask Him for mercy and for help: "And what does the Lord require of you? To act justly and to love mercy and to walk humbly with your God" (Micah 6:6-8).

Jesus said, "From the one who has been entrusted with much, much more will be asked" (Luke 12:48). That sounds explicit about what is being asked of us. Does this not spur our asking of God for all we need so that we can give a good account of our stewardship, and continue to ask about the "master's will" that the servant is expected to do? Paul is more than aware of this: "Now it is required that those who have been given a trust must prove faithful" (1 Corinthians 4:2). Paul was clear about what God had explicitly asked of him, so it is no wonder that he asked incessantly so much of God, and humbly asked others to ask on his behalf: "Pray also for me" (Ephesians 6:19). God is explicit about what we should be asking about because He wants us to 'just ask.'

By Using Adversity To Get Us To Ask Why Things Are So Bad

Like frogs boiling to death in the pot that is being slowly heated, we continue to live in cultural contexts that never raise the alarm to ask about what is happening, or where things are heading. Scripture tells us that God will sometimes use adversity to kick-start our asking. "Many disasters and difficulties will come upon them, and on that day they will ask, 'Have not these disasters come upon us because God is not with us?'" (Deuteronomy 31:17) God was orchestrating external events and agencies to get people to ask about their lives and through their asking, to come to the conclusion that "God is not with us". This awful realization would hopefully convince them to come back to God and ask Him for some things: like forgiveness, like a gift of repentance, like revival and restoration. In Jeremiah 13:22 God is warning His people of the consequences of their back-sliding: "And if you ask, 'Why has this happened to me?' – it is because of your many sins." When they ask, God gives answers that can deliver them. Again, God is using external circumstances ("Those who are coming from the north" *v20*) to incite them to ask for forgiveness when they realize what has caused their problems: "you have forgotten me and trusted in false gods" (v25). The threat of judgment and the onset of adversity were allowed by God in order to urge the kind of asking that God desired. In the next chapter there are two petitions that though spoken through Jeremiah, are in fact the voice of God giving them the words for what they should be asking for. So eager is He for them to ask that in the context of adversity He gives them the script and begins to prompt them on how to ask: "Although our sins testify against us, O Lord, do something for the sake of your name ... do not forsake us ... for the sake of your name do not despise us ... remember your covenant with us" (Jeremiah 14: 7, 9, 21). God uses adversity to get us to 'just ask.'

By Telling Us To Ask Of Someone Or Something Else

If God is not going to be asked Himself, when questions need to be asked in order to get His answers, then He suggests other shocking sources, like idols and pagan nations, as a way to provoke our eventual asking of Him. Through Isaiah, it is God who tells the people to go and ask of the idols "so that we may know you are gods" (Isaiah 41:22-24). God is confronting them with the fact that they are asking of all the wrong sources. God tells them to ask their gods about: "what is going to happen", "what were the former things", what does "the future hold", what is the "final outcome." God is the only one who can answer what we ask about the past, the present and the future. By asking of gods that could not answer their pleas to be saved (Isaiah 45:20) it would hopefully dawn on them that they should be asking of God, and would then choose to do so again. When others suggest that we ask of counterfeit sources (epidemic in our culture of alternative spirituality) it should stir us to ask God: "When men tell you to consult mediums and spiritists, who whisper and mutter, should not a people ask of their God?" (Isaiah 8:19) The emptiness, ignorance and silence of these sources is a confrontation that should bring people to their senses, in the same way that the questioning of his situation by the prodigal son of a life-style that was providing no answers, goaded him to return to the Father and ask the Father to receive him back. There are even rhetorical suggestions in scripture to ask beasts, whose knowledge of the ways of the Lord was meant to shame people into their lack of knowledge and their need to ask of God. At least the ox and the donkey, images of stupidity, were models of instruction, by simply fully being who they were created to be, and knowing their master. They obviously knew something that the people of God should be asking about for themselves (Isaiah 1:3). God seems to commit us to the logic of asking of the idolatries we serve in order to realize the futility of their falsehood and their lack of answers, in order to kick-start the recovery of turning to Him and 'just asking'.

By Commanding Us To Ask

When God says *"Ask"* it is His grace that initiates and invites our asking to answer Him. However, He is not just giving us a permission to ask but a prescription. The invitation is a command that emphasizes both the need of God to hear our asking, and our need to ask. Asking ceases to be optional. It is essential. It is how we relate to God. The command to inquire of the Lord comes through the psalmists and the prophets. "Ask of me and I will give you the nations ... Ask of me of things to come ... Ask the Lord for ... Ask the Lord of the harvest ... Ask and you will receive" (Psalm 2:8; Isaiah 45:11; Zechariah 10:1; Matthew 9:38; John 16:24). Asking is not just a matter of faith; it is a matter of obedience. Our responsive asking is not only requested but also required by God. He goes to great lengths to initiate and invite it, to provoke and promote it. As we have seen, He even takes extreme measures when necessary to command and demand it. The failure to ask is not presented as a lapse or as a sad refusal to take advantage of an amazing opportunity, or even as immature discipleship. It is disobedience to a commanded response. This is why it is the recovery of the repentant asking for forgiveness for our disobedience that is the recovery of all other asking.

It's All About Relationship

Why does God pull out these stops to get us to answer Him by our asking? Because He wants relationship with us, and that interplay of asking and answering is the heart of all intimate conversation. Asking relates us to God and God's answers relate us to God. Every which way, He uses our asking to draw us to Himself. Then, in His humility, He says things to Moses like, "I have forgiven as you asked" (Numbers 14:20), or to Solomon like, "I will do what you have asked" (1 Kings 3:12). Our asking invites God's acting and He acknowledges that personally. "The Lord did the very thing that Moses asked" (Exodus 8:31). God had said He would do it, but He seems to describe it as much in terms of Moses' asking as His acting. "I will do the very thing you asked, because I am pleased with you" (Exodus 33:17). Our asking is a way for God to show how He loves us, how irresistible we are to Him, and through it He affirms our relationship that we are covenant partners with Him and that He treats us as co-workers, as collaborators in His actions. That gives motivation and encouragement, delight and joy to our asking when we are tempted sometimes to think it is just a hard slog to be asking for things for people that they are not even asking for themselves. We forget that God's answers have everything to do with the relationship He treasures with those who are doing the asking, as well as the relationship He desires with those who are being asked for.

Lion's Den to Upper Room

Anybody who was somebody in scripture did it. Abraham remained asking before the Lord, Moses asked, Gideon asked, David inquired of the Lord. The greatest of all, Jesus, asked. Scripture tells us what people asked for, and why they wanted to ask, but time and time again, we see that their asking is in response to something God had already asked or said. Their asking is answering. Daniel's asking affected nations and generations, future dynasties and events. His job was to be able to answer whatever was asked of him. No wonder he was a man who knew how to ask of God. (Read the wonderful sequence in Daniel 2: 11-23.) By the way, it is often overlooked as to why Daniel was thrown to lions: "Have you not signed a decree that every man that shall ASK a petition of any god or man within 30 days, except of you O king, shall be cast into the den of lions?" (6:12) Asking was his offense and it was punishable. Daniel pleaded guilty as charged. Would we be judged guilty by our present asking? This shows you how desperately Satan opposes the asking church, and the asking saint. In his miraculous rescue, it was Daniel's asking that was vindicated. One of the momentous records of asking in scripture is Daniel's prayer in Daniel 9. He was not being original but yet again, his asking was an answering response to what God had already said: "I Daniel understood from the scriptures, *according to the word of the Lord given* Jeremiah the prophet that ... so I turned to the Lord God and pleaded with Him in prayer and petition" (vs.2-3). The revelation of God's revealed will through Jeremiah triggered the asking of Daniel. When we ask according to Scripture and the revealed will of God, our asking is always answering what God has already said. When we do not hear God speak, or when we hear but do not listen, then we do not answer and therefore we do not ask.

Closer to home, the church as we know it was not born out of an original prayer on their part. Before the day of Pentecost, the 120 disciples were *asking*: "These all continued in one accord in prayer and supplications" (Acts 1:14). Jesus told them what to expect as an answer to their asking: the gift of the Holy Spirit. He initiated all this and they responded to His invitation. The Upper Room was asking as answering. The whole of the Godhead gets involved, thus mid-wiving the birth of the church in this spiritual maternity ward of asking. Jesus had first said that He would ask the Father to send the Comforter, the Holy Spirit. He also said that if they asked, how much more would Father God give them the Holy Spirit (John 14:16). So Father, Son and Holy Spirit, in an exchange of asking and answering, combined to include 120 asking people in the experience of Trinity presence, unity and power. The prior asking of the Godhead and the present asking of the disciples combined in an incredible prayer meeting. Consequently, it is the loss of the will to ask of the Godhead in the church that is one of the causes for the great loss of presence, unity and power. Think about that next time you pass up an invitation to be in an asking-room in the privacy of your home or in a gathering of your church community, or in a meeting with friends. The church was born, maintained and sustained through asking that answered the initiating invitation of the Godhead.

Getting My Head Around The Godhead

We need to understand how central asking is to our understanding of the Godhead's relationships with each other and of our relationship with every one of their three persons, before we even see the relationship of our asking to our lives and to this world with all its needs. If our asking is just rooted in a response to human need then it will not be consistent. Sometimes we are just not engaged by that need so we do not ask. But if it is rooted like all truth in the very nature of God, in the very heart of our relationship with God, and if it is normative behavior for the Godhead, then we have a much surer basis for the consistency and confidence to ask and keep on asking.

If our asking has something to do with us responding to something God has already initiated, then this is so much bigger and better than our own fickleness that asks only when we are moved to do so. It is not just about what we want to ask about, but what the Godhead is already asking about, in a conversation that I am invited to join.

To say that the two sufficient grounds for us to ask are that we have a need and God has the supply is actually insufficient grounds for a theology of prayer. If we are interested in a theology of asking, then like all truth it must first be established on who God is, even though at first it would seem to us that asking begins with us and with our need. So where does that leave us, or lead us? Before we ask God about anything, or for anything, what is it about God, about who and how He is, that validates our asking? What is it about God that assures us about our asking? In what way is our asking of God premised on the attributes of God, or the initiative of God? If we do ask, why should we expect the possibility of an answer to our questions and our petitions? If our understanding of God's character is amiss, will not our asking be amiss? As P.T.Forsyth asked: "Is the subsidence of petition not due to a wrong idea of God?" [5] Daniel's aforementioned powerful, intercessory prayer is such a good example of what we now need to address. Daniel gives us a clue:

> O Lord, the great and awesome God, who keeps His covenant of love ... Lord you are righteous ... The Lord our God is merciful and forgiving ... hear the petitions of your servant ... For your sake O Lord ... Give ear O God and hear ... We do not make requests of you because we are righteous but because of your great mercy ... O Lord listen! O Lord forgive! O Lord hear and act! For your sake O my God do not delay! (Daniel 9: 4-19).

Before we talk about *our need* that instigates our asking, we have to first talk about *God's nature* that initiates it and invites it.

Asking is answering. In the words of Spurgeon, on the frontispiece of this chapter, our asking is like the dove returning to the cote. More than two centuries earlier George Herbert captured this same idea in one of his most famous sonnets about prayer. He described asking as: "God's breath in man *returning to his birth*" and as nothing less than *"reversed thunder"*.[6] Thunder normally booms down from heaven to earth, but in our asking, God has given us His own authority to reverse it and boom back: to thunder back at Heaven in response to His thundering initiative. Let that ring in our ears. Our asking is answering, whether it is gentle like a returned dove, or forceful like reversed thunder. Asking is answering.

"I urge then, first of all, that requests ... be made for everyone."
– 1 Timothy 2:1

"Devote yourselves to prayer, being ... thankful."
– Colossians 4:2

"After adoration, therefore, prayer is thanksgiving and petition."
– P.T.Forsyth

"Prayer and thanks are like the double motion of the lungs; the air that is sucked in by prayer is breathed forth again by thanks."
– Thomas Goodwin

"Thanksgiving is inseparable from true prayer; it is almost essentially connected with it. One who always prays is ever giving praise, whether in ease or pain, both for prosperity and for the greatest adversity. He blesses God for all things, looks on them as coming from Him, and receives them for His sake - not choosing nor refusing, liking or disliking anything, but only as it is agreeable or disagreeable to His perfect will." – John Wesley

"Prayer and praises go in pairs,
They have praises who have prayers."
– Unknown

3

Ask, Ask, Thanking at Heaven's Door

So Many Ways To Ask About So Many Things

There are so many passages in the Bible to which we could go to learn about the need for asking, and the variety of ways to ask. Paul captures this when he referred to "all kinds of prayers and requests" that are made "on all occasions" (Ephesians 6:18). Furthermore, there are many different words and phrases, like *desiring,* or *longing for* or *seeking after* that are used to suggest the wide range of emotions and intensities with which our asking is presented. Different words like *intercede* or *request* are sometimes used to distinguish different kinds of asking. As we have already noted, one helpful way to understand all this is to see these terms less as qualitatively different kinds of prayer, or different levels of prayer, but as descriptions of our asking at different speeds, under different pressures, with different intensities, and in some cases, indicating different subjects that are being asked for. But at the root of them all is specific *asking* and lots of it.

The Private and Public Priority Of Asking

Paul's words to Timothy (2:1-8) are a great example of his enthusiasm for unceasing, subject-specific asking. He is addressing practical matters of public, corporate, community worship, particularly prayer, and he is emphatic about its importance. Worship is composed of three non-negotiable constituents: praising, preaching and praying. Sadly, prayer is the element that is most commonly reduced or excised in our public church gatherings. Praying is arguably the least evidenced and the least missed. Do we go to church ready and willing to pray – expecting to ask of God? Paul knew that the limits of our asking represented the limits of our vision and our outreach. Reaching out to God precedes reaching out to people. We access people less when we ask God less. When we cease to ask God we cease to answer people and thus witness declines. No wonder that Paul, the apostle and evangelist, was concerned that the church grasped the urgency and the priority of asking. It is of note that early church records up until the 2nd and 3rd centuries show that intense, prolonged and urgent asking-prayers were an integral part of all public meetings. These were not by-rote liturgical prayers. Much of what is presented as prayer in our services can end up as nothing more than cultural comfort or religious observance, but not asking.

Asking Served Four Ways

What Paul does is to list what is "urged": requests, prayers, intercessions, and thanksgivings. His priority is that Timothy is enabled and empowered (literally 'in-strengthened') to ask. Referring to the different words used for prayer here, at least Calvin was honest: "I do not understand completely the differences."[1] There is no need for too much confusion. All these expressions are just variations on the theme of asking. In four different ways Paul is saying, "ASK! ASK! ASK! ASK!" Like a good chef, he is serving asking four ways on the same dish. This emphasizes the variety of things to ask for and the many ways they can be asked for.

- **Requests**: *(deesis)* The idea here is that specific things are being asked for which are need-sensitive. There is a suggestion of an asking that involves compassion and a deep emotional concern in relation to what is being asked for. It is the word used to describe Jesus's entreaties in Gethsemane (Hebrews 5:7) or Zechariah's request for a son (Luke 1:13).
- **Prayers**: *(proseuche)* The word used here is the more general word for prayer, and is about things that can only be asked of God. This emphasizes the need to ask less of others and more of God; to talk less to everyone else about things and more to God. He is the audience we need. A sense of reverence is implied in this asking,

so this cannot just be a functional, selfish shopping list, given the awareness of God's presence. It is the word used in Luke19:46 to describe the temple being a "house of prayer", the temple that was the dwelling place of His awesome presence. It is often used in Acts to describe the community prayer that was so aware of the consuming presence and character of God when they asked for something (1:14; 2:42). This reinforces the conviction that our asking seeks answers that we know that God alone can give. The loss of His presence is always manifested in a lack of asking. It is this sense of His presence that takes the raw material of our desires and starts to transform them into the kind of asking that is desired by the God who is present.

- **Intercession**: *(enteuxis)* The idea here is that this is the kind of asking that we can make because God can be approached and we can be free to ask "whatever" of Him. Used in other contexts it emphasizes the kind of asking that is for others, not for self. It is asking on behalf of another, which again implies an asking that identifies with compassion and affection for the object of asking. There is also a nuance here that this kind of drawing near assumes both intimacy and confidence. This suggests an asking that can use familiar language with someone known intimately.
- **Thanksgivings**: *(eucharistia)* "Ah!" you might say. This has nothing to do with asking. This is praise not petition. On the contrary. It is an echo of what Paul wrote to Lydia's church: "In everything by prayer and *petition with thanksgiving,* present what you *ask* to God" (Philippians 4:6). Please note that the thanksgiving is not on hold until we have the answer we want. It is part and parcel of the asking itself. Thomas Goodwin wrote: "As asking abounds so will thanksgiving." [2] This indivisibility of asking and thanksgiving is evident in David's practice: "I will sacrifice a thank offering to you and call on the name of the Lord" (Psalm 116:17). It is evident in Paul's practice: "I cease not to give thanks for you, making mention of you in my asking ... I thank my God in every remembrance of you, always in every prayer of mine, asking for you with all joy" (Ephesians 1:16; Philippians 1:3,4,8,9). In our asking we inhale as it were, and then, having asked, we exhale thanksgiving. Like Paul,

when we find ourselves thanking God for someone or something, how quickly does that thanksgiving become asking. Asking and thanksgiving are equal components of the breath that is our communion with God. P.T.Forsyth raises the same issue: "Has petition a true place in the highest and purest prayer?" But then he asks: "Does adoration move as inevitably to petition as petition rises to adoration?" He concluded that "what kills petition kills praise." [3] Do you see how the praise is contingent on the petition? "Upon offering the sacrifice of praise, the heart is further enlarged to pray for fresh blessings. We are never fitter to pray than after praise." [4] Gratitude then expresses itself in more adoring, and the more we adore and worship God and become more convinced of who He is, the more our confidence in His abilities on our behalf is strengthened, and the more our confidence to ask is emboldened, and therefore the more our asking.

Please ... Thank You

Jesus said, "Ask whatever you wish, and it will be given to you. This is to my Father's glory" (John 15:8). The very act of our asking is by definition God-glorifying. Earlier, Jesus told his disciples: "I will do whatever you ask in my Name, so that the Son may bring glory to the Father" (John 14:13). Is this not overwhelming? How can asking be treated as immature if it is the chosen means by which Jesus Himself is able to give glory to His Father? Our asking is part and parcel of our worship, and Jesus's worship, because by definition, if we are asking from a place of abiding in Jesus, we are tacitly acknowledging everything that is dependable, powerful, compassionate and miraculous about His nature. This means relationship with Jesus, not human need, is the starting place of our asking. It informs it, provokes it, enables it and emboldens it – and on top of all that, Father God loves it, and cannot get enough of it, for in the very act of our asking He is glorified. Do you really want to be a thankful person? Then ask of Him! Do you really want to glorify God? Then ask of Him! Your asking implies: your inability but His ability (Hallelujah!); your ignorance but His knowledge (Glory!); your need but His provision (Thank you, Lord!); your lack but His supply (Jehovah Jireh!); your want but His wealth (Majesty!); your weakness but

His power (Mighty God!); your fear but His strength (Praise the Lord!) Did you hear any thanksgiving or worship in that asking? It is our way of saying, "I'm not praising you out of a place of fullness in my life right now, but my asking, that cries for help, is letting you know God, that you are God! In the act of asking, I'm honoring and worshiping you as the only hope for this matter. Though my asking may even sound tentative, please hear in it, 'Yeah God!' I am so thankful that I have you to turn to in my need; that I can ask of you." Can we ever forget what Mark records before Jesus went to Gethsemane (the oil press) for the most pained and impassioned asking of all? "When they had **sung a hymn**, they went out to the Mount of Olives" (Mark 14:26). The praising was not contradictory to the 'pressing' but necessarily complementary. Out of the assurance of His thanksgiving came His asking about His suffering.

Antibiotic, Antidote and Preservative

The point is that asking and thanking are inseparable, and whichever you begin with, the other follows. How often does thanksgiving serve to sift and purify our asking, as our experience of God's presence serves to shape our desires, and as our engagement with Him helps us to have a better understanding of what to ask for? Thanksgiving and the interplay between asking and adoring is forever settled. And if for any reason our asking is born out of sorrow, then thanksgiving seals it with the balm of joy, the "pure joy" that James speaks of when trials are faced and faith is tested. Thanksgiving, as so many have acknowledged [5], purifies asking by not allowing it to be focused only on our requests, which can lead to putting faith in the asking rather than in the One we ask. Paul was right in presenting asking as an antidote to anxiety. The difficult circumstances that we ask about solicit many other possible emotions, like discouragement or bitterness, resentment or hopelessness. The thanksgiving that is integral to our asking, like a good antibiotic, opposes the viral effects of these contrary emotions and helps us to remember that God is good, that we can ask for what is good and that He does work all things together for good (Romans 8:28).

Thanksgiving is the necessary antidote to ingratitude. Surely you have experienced it! The sheer relief that we can ask of God at all, results in a spontaneous overflow of gratitude and thanksgiving and we have not even asked for anything specific yet. We are overcome by the surfeit of grace and goodness in the One we are asking, and not by the concern or struggle that got us to think of asking in the first place. Do you get it? The fact is that if our asking outruns our thanksgiving we can become impatient, untrusting, unexpectant, complaining, ungrateful, and even demanding with a sense of personal rights. Having thanksgiving as a constituent element of our asking preserves the necessary humility and dependence that is fundamental to the act of holy asking. They team-up to disallow our egotism or selfishness to strut in the presence of God. It is normal when you ask to say please and thank you. You can now see how the lack of asking actually affects our worship. The less asking (please?) there is, the less thanksgiving (Thank you!). It is when God is diminished in our eyes, and perceived as limited, that we cease to ask. The lack of praiseful and grateful conviction about the greatness and goodness of God subverts our trust and faith in the love and power of God to respond to us, and thus subverts our asking.

It is our thanksgiving, in relation to our asking, that is the way that we express our desire for, and submission to the will of God in all things asked about. Thanksgiving is the way we agree with the rightness and praiseworthiness of anything and everything that God does for His reasons and purposes.

Asking For 'All' and 'Every'

In case we think this asking is a part-time business every now and again and requires only an occasional visit to heaven's door, Paul (1 Timothy 2: 1-8) takes the words "every" and "all" and repeatedly presents them back to us: this asking is for "everyone" (v1), "everywhere" (v8), for "all" those in authority (v2), for "all" men to be saved (v4) because Jesus was a ransom for "all" men (v6). This reason for asking provides an understanding that is basic to a theology of asking – our asking is possible because of Jesus's death on the cross. Furthermore, we ask for everything that Jesus's salvific work on the cross has made possible. Our asking is because of His atoning. Atoning first opened up the way for us to have access and to ask. Furthermore, if Jesus died for all, then God must desire the salvation of all, which means our asking for others is in tune with the heart and passions of God when we ask for the knowledge and acceptance of that atonement by everyone. Paul then references the "Gentiles" (v7) which means our asking is about all nations. Is anyone still in need of an ask-list? This is an important passage in a theology of asking, particularly as it also describes the need to ask for three specific nonnegotiables: our peace (2:2), God's pleasure (2:3) and the proclamation and propagation of the gospel (2:6-7). This is our ask-list.

Because of this inclusivity, this "all men" and "all nations", asking is one of God's ways and means by which we continue to identify and break the demonic bondages of pride and prejudice (racism, nationalism, classism, materialism – whatever opposes God's creational, redemptive and reconciling purposes for everyone). These are revealed and unmasked as we ask about them. Asking of God for all men and for all nations becomes such a place of revelation and instruction as we learn on location what God's will in heaven is for what is going on in the earth. This kind of asking often results in *conviction* about our own prejudices and irreconciliations, and in a *confession* that is necessary to free us to ask for all without accusation or condemnation, without hypocrisy and insincerity.

This passage is but one example of how much there is to exegete and learn about asking, out of any single biblical context dealing with prayer. For Paul, and for us, specific asking is intrinsic to all of the different terms used for prayer, and the nature of asking is revealed when we examine the terms used and their context. We ask, ask, ask at heaven's door, which means we are also thanking, thanking, thanking the One who meets and greets us His side of that door. Asking with thanksgiving ... try it.

"Prayer, which began simply enough by paying attention to God, can only recover that simplicity by re-attending to God."
– Eugene Petersen

"True theology is warm and it steams upward into prayer."
– P.T.Forsyth

"Ask nothing of God save God Himself." – Augustine

"So many of us pray because we are driven by need rather than kindled by grace ... Prayer's power answers to the omnipotence of grace." – P.T.Forsyth

"My God, thy creature answers Thee!" – Alfred de Musset

"The theological discussion of prayer is justified, not only by the importance of the subject, but by its difficulty." – Wayne Spear

4

Towards a Theology of Asking

Asking and Theology

Our asking must be theological, and our theology must inspire our asking. However, we do not have to wait for a theology of asking in order to ask. We just ask! Yet given the challenges that asking raises for many of us, ranging from our ability to ask, to our perceptions of God's ability to answer, some theological validation is needful and helpful to support the principles and practice of asking. Prayer is not some minor topic in a compendious systematic theology. Theology itself is the outcome of prayer, and can only be pursued as a spiritual exercise if it is maintained by the submissive humility of asking. If theology ceases to be conducted in this context and spirit, it will not remain a prayerful biblical theology but will degenerate into a philosophical unbiblical theology. To reinforce this point, one theologian used to urge his students to do their theologizing with a window in the room left open to the heavens in order to remind them that:

> The first and basic act of theological work is prayer . . . But theological work does not merely begin with prayer and is not merely accompanied by it; in its totality it is peculiar and characteristic of theology that it can be performed only in the act of prayer. [1]

Only in asking of God, assured that He hears what we ask, "is theological work at any time a successful and useful work." So a theology of asking is necessary for the very foundations and premise of *all* theological inquiry, not just inquiry about prayer. "All its questions, inquiries, reflections, and declarations can only be forms of this petition."[2] John Piper, a prolific author of pastoral theology, recalled hearing one of his seminary professors as saying that "one of the best tests of a person's theology was the effect it has on one's prayers." [3] An unprayerful theology, like untheological prayer, is a contradiction in terms. Don Carson writes: "Something is amiss in our theology if our theology becomes a disincentive to pray." [4] All that said, we need to agree a biblical, theological basis for our asking, to serve as a validation of it, given that we have noted the questioning of asking itself that arises in the minds of many. These difficulties come from three broadly different groups.

Categorical Unbelief

There are those who have no belief at all, in either the existence of a knowable, personal God or in the authenticity and veracity of scripture. Warfield argued:

> The scriptures themselves tell us that to come to God implies that we believe that He is ... We must really believe in the existence of God and in His care for the works of His hands, *or we cannot pray to Him*. Not only then cannot the atheist, or the agnostic, or the pantheist, pray; nor yet the deist or the fatalist. [5]

Obviously, if there is no God to respond to our asking, such petition is vain and self-deceived. It is totally ineffective, because it cannot effect anything. In a world of ruling scientism and determining natural laws of causality, where cause and effect are inviolable, what grounds are there for any interruptive or creative initiative by a divine being, even if there was such a one? There are no grounds for asking. Friedrich Heiler, the twentieth century German theologian and historian of religion, feared that: "Rational philosophical thought means the disintegration and dissolution of prayer." [6] However, it is duly noted that so great is God's grace and His forbearance, that should such a one yet ask of Him, He will answer, and in some extraordinary ways too.

Camouflaged Unbelief

The second group are those who may present themselves as theologians, or religious, or adherents of a version of spirituality "which baptizes itself with the Christian name" [7], but who are essentially secular philosophers. Their talk of a "Being" and of personally "becoming" amounts to nothing more than a conversation with themselves, since again, there is no personal God to converse with, and consequently, no grounds for asking. There are no prayer meetings in their Theology Faculties. They have contempt for any personal language that describes relationship with God, which in the words of one of my theology professors at Cambridge University, "needs to be radically discounted." [8]

Paul Tillich rejected a traditional view of the Trinity precisely because of the problems he thought it posed for asking: is asking one person of the Trinity different to asking another? Frankly, what this betrays is a lack of personal relationship with the Trinity. Without that intimacy there is no way that Tillich could understand the notion of asking of God. It would seem, tragically, that the search for intimacy in his life was misdirected, given his inclinations to pornography and his many affairs. Though these theologians talk of prayer, sometimes in ways that are hardly intelligible, they are really describing a process of self-communing. Their use of 'God' is about philosophical terminology not biblical theology. They seem to be as confused and confusing as those who talk about finding "within" the God who is not there! Once "the God who is there" [9] is denied, you are left with the tortuous task of keeping all the juggling balls of contradiction in the air, all the time. Juggling is the art of clowns, the fools of Psalm 14:1. It is interesting that in the next verse God says that no one is asking of Him. "The Lord looks down from heaven on the sons of men to see if there are any ... who seek God" (Psalm 14:2). This juggling is a thankless task. The balls of unbelief fall on the head at some point and further wound both head and heart. Liberal, anti-scriptural theology, if it wants to maintain its agnosticism and still talk about prayer, has to present prayer as engaging a "presence" or a "feeling" or a "consciousness" or whatever. Declaring that God is dead or absent, they talk as if there is some ethereal and eternal fragrance that can be smelled in the room. It is psychobabble dressed in religious-sounding terms. They are cheats, denying a Person but still talking about Presence. They practice what Francis Schaeffer described as "semantic mysticism". [10] Having denied the message (scripture) and the messenger (Jesus Christ), they still pretend there is meaning and thereby offer an illusory hope, a mirage that has no substance. No wonder the demons oblige to occupy such a vacuum, and draw people into the world of nirvana and mantras, of spirit-guides and gurus. There is usually no place for asking, for petitionary prayer, in any church that has embraced theological liberalism. Where faith fails, asking ceases. Where grace is denied, asking ceases. Where hopelessness gets entrenched, asking ceases. Charlotte Bronte responded to the first work of avowed atheism and materialism that she had ever read: "We are called on to rejoice over this hopeless blank, to receive this bitter bereavement as great gain – to welcome this unutterable desolation as a state of pleasant freedom?" [11] The "pleasant" state of satisfaction and peace that is claimed by those who commune with themselves, and call it prayer, is indeed an "unutterable desolation."

Confessed Belief

The third group, though they say they believe the scriptures, are not absolutely questioning the possible effectiveness of asking God, yet they struggle to be sure about why such asking is actually needed. On a bad day, they may even scoff politely at the need to ask at all, if God by His nature is indeed omniscient and omnipotent. You know how it goes: why ask about anything if God already knows everything, and if "Father knows" then does He not know what we need before we ask him? "Does God not know ... so that it may seem in a sense superfluous that he should be stirred up by our prayers?" [12] If God's purposes are indeed changeless, then our asking cannot cause anything to happen. So why bother? Furthermore, if He is able to do "more than all we ask or imagine" then why waste our time given our limited, uncertain, uninformed and unimaginative asking? How does sovereignty relate to supplication? Why ask for what is already determined? What possible relation can there be between God's sovereign will and my free will? If my asking cannot compel God to comply, what is the point of it all?

One of the reasons we need a revived attention to the theology of prayer is precisely because the simple act of asking has taken such a hammering, and has been so opposed and belittled by rationalism, liberalism and secularism, and possibly by some "Calvinian" (thought influenced by John Calvin) articulations about prayer. Clearly, it also poses problems for philosophic theologians grappling with the relationship between apparently irreconcilable matters like human free will and divine immutability, with divine foreknowledge and the inquiry of petition. Thus there is a need to champion and defend prayer's normalcy and necessity, its purpose and its outcomes, its pains and joys, without denying the patent and blatant realities of life and circumstance, of rational thought and spiritual powers, of human ignorance and divine knowledge, of theology and practicality, that would first seek to subvert us and then silence us.

Grace-Asking

The challenge was not lost on P.T.Forsyth:

> To common sense, the fact that God knows all we need, and wills us all good, the fact of His infinite Fatherhood, is a reason for not praying. Why tell Him what he knows? Why ask what He is more than willing to give? [13]

But is not an omniscient father exactly the best person to ask? And anyway, when you know something, is it not a joy to be asked? You want to be asked. The argument continues that if God is omnipotent, He is going to do what He is going to do, when He is going to do it, so what is the point of asking about it. There is no need to ask because it is up to Him. This is why many who pride themselves on being the defenders of divine sovereignty have little passion for asking. (These may find themselves more in the third group above than they dare to admit.) Getting life all sorted out by propositions, albeit good doctrinal-sounding ones, does not leave much that needs to be sorted out by prayer. It should be somewhat puzzling that those who present themselves as the defenders of doctrinal rigor are less responsive when it comes to adoring with abandon and desperate asking. As Jim Packer argues [14] it is precisely those of a Calvinistic persuasion who should be rabid in witness and vigorous in intercession in their co-operation with procuring election's outcomes.

The lack of impassioned asking becomes less mysterious when you understand the way that prayer has been treated within some theological traditions. It is not our purpose to engage those who argue the nuances of different Confessions and Catechisms when it comes to understanding whether or not our asking is a means of grace. In a monograph by Wayne Spear, Professor of Systematic Theology and Homiletics at Reformed Presbyterian Theological Seminary we read:

> Calvin treated prayer as the *expression of faith*, not as a *means of grace.* Continental theologians followed his example in the enumeration of the means of grace, with the result that prayer was all but eliminated as a topic within the system of theology ... Modern Reformed theologians, such as Bavinck, Berkhof, Berkouwer and Hoeksma, true to the continental Reformed tradition, fail to accord any separate discussion to prayer. [15]

In my library, I have systematic theologies and writings of all the men named above, and have often consulted them, and learned from them with gratitude. The scriptural position is that asking is not either/or but both/and. Calvin rightly defended prayer as God's means for us to express, exercise and expand faith. We have already agreed that asking is perhaps one of the most symptomatic expressions of faith, but it is only by God's grace that we have access to present our "asking by faith", and that same asking is clearly a means of grace if it facilitates the kind of spiritual outcomes and benefits that Calvin himself noted were the fruit of answered asking. These included: a stirring and strengthening of love for God, an increased knowledge of His will, a deeper faith in God, a truer gratitude to God, an assured conviction about His goodness, greater joy in God, and bolder confidence in God. [16]

John Piper asserts that prayer is a means of grace. "I don't know of a better way of describing how God's decisive work relates to our dependent work. Or, to be specific in this case: how God's sovereign governing of all things relates to human prayer." [17] He acknowledges that when Jude exhorts his "dear friends", who are under persecution and pressure, to "build themselves up" in their "most holy faith", and to "keep themselves in the love of God", the connector that services these necessities (building and keeping, growth and guardianship) is "pray in the Holy Spirit" (Jude v20-21). We cannot by our own efforts and smarts either build ourselves "up" or keep ourselves "in". Asking is thus nothing less than the means of grace by which we find our place of safety, maturity, and integrity and keep ourselves in the love of God. The grace of asking becomes one of the vital means by which God sustains and maintains the spiritual life that He gave us. Our asking invites the reception of grace, and we appeal to the God of grace, at the throne of grace, in order to obtain grace. Precisely because it is an expression of conscious, reciprocal intimacy, it is a means by which God communes with us, and therefore a means of grace. As B.B.Warfield put it: "What is prayer but the very adjustment of the heart for the influx of grace." [18] The lack of asking may well be an explanation for so much graceless experience.

It is interesting to read what Hebrews (10:1) teaches about the law as a "shadow". Whenever legalism and the requirements of men begin to take control, the result will be a return to shadow-lands and the liberty of access into this grace will be reduced, as will the confidence to enter. The law is not a friend of asking. Regulation always obscures, limits and quenches revelation. The law impedes confidence by giving another ground of confidence other than the outrageously generous and welcoming grace of God. The law introduces frisk tests for spirituality that oppose and frustrate the grace of God. The law convinces us of our unworthiness to ask, and if we do perchance get as far as asking, it will begin with an apology, not with boldness. If the great goal of asking is to bring us closer to the God of whom we ask, how is this not a nonnegotiable means of grace?

Of course, prayer does lend itself to become a work. But our faith is not in our asking. There are many who excuse themselves from asking because they do not feel they have enough faith to ask, as if faith was measureable by the pound, and it took certain weights of faith in order to secure certain answers or to move particularly heavy mountains. If the command to ask is an invitation to intimate relationship with God, then it is a means of grace for me to relate to God, not a method of religious law by which I relate my need to Him. It is the sufficiency of grace, especially in our need and weakness, that encourages and empowers us to ask for the supply and the strength that we need. It is worth remembering that Paul's revelation of the sufficiency of grace came as a result of intense asking about something, his thrice unanswered asking for the removal of his thorn in the flesh. It could be said that his asking was answered, not with removal but with revelation, including the understanding that the tormenting "messenger of Satan" was God's answer "to keep me from becoming conceited because of these surpassingly great revelations" (2 Corinthians 12:7-9). Paul's asking became the very means by which grace was revealed to him. It was also the means by which he received that grace for the perfecting of power in his weaknesses. When Paul said God would make "all grace abound ... unto all good works", among those spiritual works was 'asking' which then became a means of grace.

There is a deliverance from failures in prayer, from the "wretchedness" that Paul refers to (Romans 7:24), and as he explains a few verses later (Romans 8:1-17) the Spirit of life sets free, and by that Spirit, the wretchedness is put to death, and the slave to the law who once feared to ask, is now the son who is free to ask of the Father with abandon and assurance. As much as any who have ever written about prayer, Andrew Murray understood the consequences for asking, when "grace abounding" was understood only as it relates to pardon and a free justification, and not as it relates to "grace abounding" in our sanctification, our reigning through righteousness.

> Beloved child of God! What think you? Is it not possible that this has been the want in your life, the cause of your failure in prayer? You knew not how grace would enable you to pray, if once the whole life were under its power. You sought by earnest effort to conquer your reluctance or deadness in prayer, but failed ... What you see no possibility of doing, grace will do ... pray the prayer of faith, 'Heal me and I shall be healed.' [19]

That kind of grace-asking opens the heavens for just more of the same.

The Amazing Grace of Asking

John Newton's universally known hymn 'Amazing Grace' is not the only one he wrote about grace. One that is little known does not present the working of grace in quite the same benevolent way as its better known relative, so it is not surprising that it is not used much in worship settings. He wrote it at a challenging time in his life when a friend who was helping him assemble a hymnal for worship went insane. What is interesting is that it is essentially a hymn about asking and its relation to grace.

> I *asked* the Lord that I might grow
> In faith and love and every *grace*;
> Might more of His salvation know,
> And seek more earnestly his face.

So far, so good! Would we not all ask along with him for more asking and for more growth in grace? He continues:

> 'Twas He who taught me thus to pray,
> And He, I trust, has *answered* prayer; (I am still singing)
> *But* it has been in such a way
> As almost drove me to despair. (Singing stutters.)

Everything is fine as we agree that Jesus is the one who invited us to ask and taught us to do so, and we are singing heartily until that word *"BUT"*. The hymn goes on to tell how the request he had hoped to be answered "at once" remained pending. However, it was not that nothing happened. "Instead of this" Newton describes a series of things that occurred: he was made to feel "the hidden evils" of his heart; God "crossed all the fair designs" he had schemed, "blasted my gourds and laid me low". His woes were actually aggravated not assuaged. Not surprisingly, this invites some more asking:

> "'Lord why is this?' I trembling cried,
> 'Wilt thou pursue thy worm to death?'

"'Tis in this way,' the Lord replied,
'I answer prayer for *grace and faith*.'"

The final verse reveals that both the work of grace through the asking, and the work of grace that was the needed answer to the asking (after all he did ask for "every grace") were the indispensable means for God's will to be done:

"These inward trials I employ,
From self and pride to set thee free,
And break thy schemes of earthly joy,
That thou mayest seek thy all in Me!" [20]

Before our asking is ever about our faith, it is about God's grace; before it is ever about our faithful concern to ask, it is about His gracious desire to answer. In keeping with principles already presented, God's initiating words and actions to us come before our asking, so our grasping and gasping effort is preceded by his gracious empowerment. He calls before we answer and answers before we call (Isaiah 65:24). By grace we ask through faith – it is not of ourselves but of Him who asks through us. In the same way that it is about presence-asking before it is problem-asking, so it is grace-asking before it is ever about faith-asking. But it is never an either/or as Newton attested. God answers our grace-asking for both "grace and faith."

Because thanksgiving is an organic part of our asking, as we have already discussed, it is therefore grace-asking. Why? "Devote yourselves to prayer, being ... thankful" (Colossians 4:2); "by petition with thanksgiving" (Philippians 4:6). The same word, 'eucharistia', is used for thankfulness in these two passages. The heart of this word is 'charis', grace. One of the great reasons for thanksgiving being inseparable from asking, is that it is the constant reminder that it is by grace that we ask, for grace that we ask, and with grace that we ask, utterly conscious that our asking has no other grounds of appeal, other than that grace in which we stand. Indeed, it is grace-asking, so what encouragement this is to us to 'just ask.'

Thou art coming to a King,
Large petitions with thee bring;

For His grace and power are such,
None can ever ask too much. [21]

Asking In a Round-about Way

C.S.Lewis rightly argued that objections to asking could not be "that absolute wisdom cannot need to be informed of our desires, or that absolute goodness cannot need to be prompted to beneficence." [22] Like all of us, Lewis was fascinated by asking but puzzled about why God took the "long way round" by inviting our petitions. Despite what he saw as divinity's "roundaboutness" he chose to marvel that the Omniscient still invites us to ask. There is no way round that. This explains Lewis' love for Pascal's dictum: "God instituted prayer in order to lend His creatures the dignity of causality." [23] Augustine had an interesting take on this: "God does not ask us to tell Him our needs that He may learn about them, but in order that we may be capable of receiving what He is preparing to give." [24] What if, as Professor Farmer argues, the idea that an all-knowing God renders asking redundant, does not take into account the possibility "that the divine purpose may be such that petitionary prayer is indispensable to its realization." [25] In other words, it is true and right that we should ask, because the omniscient and omnipotent God ordains it so, and commands it so. Whether it is divinity asking for our asking through the prophetic voice of the Old Testament ("I will yet for this be enquired of by the house of Israel to do it for them" Ezekiel 36:37) or through the pastoral voice of the New Testament ("In everything by prayer and petition … present your requests to God" Philippians 4:6), our asking is presented as a real factor in the shaping of the world's destiny, and our understanding of what it means to be a "co-worker" with God. Not only does the Omniscient choose to invite us to ask, the Omnipotent chooses to work in and through us "to will and to act according to His good purpose" in effecting His answers. "Creation seems to be delegation through and through", concludes Lewis. [26] In another context when he is grappling with asking, he reaffirms that God "seems to do nothing of Himself which He can possibly delegate to His creatures." [27] So our asking is not just a gracious invitation but a delegated responsibility. So what?

Asking As Show-and-Tell

That we are known by God and known to God is not in question. But what is *our* role in this relationship? As we continue to observe, our understanding of asking is all about our understanding of this relationship, because all communication is conditioned by relationship. Lewis grasped this in a wonderful way. He knew that we were known to God, that we were objects of divine knowledge "like earthworms, cabbages and nebulae." [28] He argued that when we become aware of that fact, and assent with our will to be so known "then we treat ourselves, in relation to God, not as things but persons ... Instead of merely being known, we *show,* we *tell,* we offer ourselves to view." [29] Our asking is essentially a "show and tell" experience with the living God. We are taking off the coverings of our lives and showing who we are to God. We are breaking our silence, because we know God is not implacably silent, and we are voluntarily and trustingly telling Him things about ourselves in what we ask for. Our asking is nothing less than two important things. It is an awareness and acknowledgement that *God is a Person*; He is personal, knows me and can be known by me. But it is also a manifestation of *our personhood* that brings all that we are, all that is on our mind, all that we need, openly to God. Whenever we ask, we come in full view into the fullness of God's revelation of Himself.

Being Asked to Ask

Our asking affirms this most incredible truth about God and about us – we can know each other personally, and communicate personally. Asking affirms this personal relationship. In the face of every demonic lie about the nature of God, every philosophic denial of God, every dehumanizing lie about myself, every mechanistic, materialistic explanation of who I am, my single act of asking of God incontrovertibly establishes who He is and who I am. Why would we take asking for granted or treat it as an immature thing? How soon in this relationship does my asking of Him become indistinguishable from my adoring Him. Petition is transformed into adoration. Do you see how vital this understanding is for our asking? Our asking of God becomes the answer to His asking of us. While we are thinking, in our need, that our asking is a means to the result we want, God is using our asking as a means to draw us into the relationship He desires with us.

Loving to Ask Because We Are Loved

The deciding factor is the truth that God is Love. "Love loves to be told what it knows already. Every lover knows that. It wants to be asked for what it longs to give." [30] P.T.Forsyth is pointing to the fundamental justification and persuasion for asking: we are inquiring of a *love* that is all-knowing and all-powerful. It is a love that invites us to intimate asking. Thus our asking is never just a matter of needing to know something, of informing God or being informed by God. It is more about needing to be known by Someone, and being formed and transformed by the asking and answering of intimate communication. What we most deeply desire, and what we in fact receive, is not merely what we need, but who we need; not merely the result but the relationship; not merely the answer but the Answerer. All asking is answered with the gift of Himself in the very act of asking. There is no wait-time for that. Even if our asking does not seem to be answered in our immediate terms, yet our spirits are immediately satisfied.

Knocking at Heaven's Door

Of course, some may still argue against this kind of asking because it seems to be impertinent at best and an illusory exercise at worst. Again, this is where a theology of asking is so important. The matter can only be decided based on how God Himself validates it. What is the answer to our fears of presumption? What right have we to ask anything of God? When Lewis admits that it could be regarded as somewhat arrogant to ask of God and thus put ourselves on a personal footing with Him by virtue of the exchange, he responds by arguing that it is God Himself who "gives us that footing. For it is by the Holy Spirit that we cry 'Father'. By unveiling and confessing our sins and 'making known' our requests, we assume the high rank of persons before Him ... and He reveals Himself as a Person." He adds: "The door in God that opens is the door He knocks at." [31] This is biblically brilliant. Note yet again where the initiative lies. Our asking is knocking on a door that God has already knocked on from His side of it, wanting to get our attention, seeking to get entry into our lives and circumstances. Indeed, He stands at the door and knocks, before we ever got to our ask-seek kind of knocking.

Speaking of Knocking

"Behold I stand at the door and knock" (Revelation 3:20). Most often, when this verse is discussed, more attention is given to what it is that Christ is coming to: a table where He is going to sup with us. There always seems to be insufficient provision for a one-course meal for one, let alone a two-course meal for self and a visiting guest. The need of the house that Christ seeks to enter is apparent. Indeed, there is so much to ask for. All that is true, but three verses later John writes: "There before me was a door standing open in heaven" (4:1). The Victorian paintings, like Holman Hunt's 'Light of the World', depict Christ standing against a bleak background, knocking at an ivy- overgrown door, with a wan and forlorn look on His face as if He has been traveling for days in search of a bed. This could not be further from the truth. The issue has less to do with the need that we are asking about that Christ sees on our side of the door, than it is about what we see behind Him, through that now open door, over His shoulder, on His side of the door. "There before me was a throne in heaven with someone sitting on it!" First you see the open door, then you see the throne. How much of our asking assumes a closed door? Does not scripture present our asking as access to the throne? Our need, all that is on our side of the door, and all our asking about it, is suddenly connected with the one who initiated the knocking and invited us thereby to come through the door to His side of things, to see things from His perspective and vantage point, to see revelation and resources that will leave us every bit as overwhelmed as John. Our asking is a response to an initiative towards us that God has already taken, supremely in Jesus Christ, and this revelation not only validates our asking, but verifies that the vision of heaven that comes with it can sufficiently supply the fulfillment of His will on the entire earth, and His will for me behind my closed door of need. So yet again, our asking is less about asking God something than it is answering something He has already said or asked of us. And even if that door had only a peep-hole, would we not see and sense enough of the grandeur of God, of the largesse of His heart, of His purpose for our lives, that we would realize that even peep-hole size revelation invites us to heaven-size asking? But no,

He wants us to open the door to Him, to get undone by the vision of the throne of grace, and realize that life here, before we get there, is just too short to ask all that can be asked for that kingdom to come to this earth, to my side of the door, as it is in heaven.

Moving Closer Towards a Theology of Asking

It is not only the nature of God but the nature of man that insists that we should ask. Simply put, man's nature is creaturely in relation to God's nature as Creator. Therefore, by definition, there is a creational dependency of man upon God, which means asking is a basic human action and an essential response to the human condition. Recent research is expressing interest in the fact that man seems to always have been a praying creature. According to anthropologists, prayer is "a human phenomenon" [32] and they say that it is one of the earliest recorded human behaviors. We were created to ask, so this creational dependency is specially and specifically communicated in our need to ask. This speaks of our creaturely limitations and needs, but more so of God's greatness and provision as Creator. Because we are not God, and are finite and limited, ignorant and powerless, our nature requires that we ask. However, though it confirms it, the nature and need of man is not our starting place for a theology of asking. The nature of God is where we begin, and it is God alone who can validate our asking. Our starting point must be the doctrine of God, not the doctrine of man.

It is interesting that in the New Testament the only prayer which is treated with disdain and not responded to is the prayer of the Pharisee in the parable of the Publican and Pharisee (Luke 18:10). From Jesus Himself we are getting nothing less than God's take on things. The prayer is treated as an aberration of humanity for one reason – he asked God for nothing. This reinforces asking as an expression of our dependence on God, our necessary humility, and our trusting submission to His will. Pharisaical independence just does not ask. The lack of our asking presumably means we are doing fine and have need of nothing. We get so used to self-management that we do not inquire of the Lord. God's nature invites us to ask. Our nature insists that we do. Not to ask is to defy God's nature and to deny ours.

Drawn Into the 'Three-Personal' Life

Having established that God has invited us to ask, we are going to look at three aspects of God's nature that irrefutably establish:

1. the possibility of our asking (*He hears*)
2. the desirability of our asking (*He responds*)
3. the achievevability of our asking (*He is our Father*)

All three persons of the Trinity are presented in scripture as asking and answering each other, thus establishing that asking is a fundamental constituent of spiritual relationship, and that all three persons are vitally linked in the transmission process that is activated whenever we ask for whatever.

- *God the Father* is the one we ask.
- *Jesus the Son* is the one who invites our asking, is the mediator of our asking and gets in on the asking of the Father on our behalf.
- *The Holy Spirit* motivates and guides our asking, not only teaching us what to ask for, but making our requests His own so that He is in fact asking for us, not just through us.

In his sublimely simple manner, C.S. Lewis has captured this necessary understanding of how a Christian is drawn into the "three-personal life" when in his or her ordinariness, the promptings of God are experienced, to ask of Him.

> God is the thing to which he is praying – the goal he is trying to reach. God is also the thing inside him which is pushing him on – the motive power. God is also the road or bridge along which he is being pushed to that goal. So that the whole three-fold life of the three-personal Being is actually going on in that ordinary little bedroom where an ordinary Christian is saying his prayers. [33]

Our 'ordinary' asking is always 'extraordinary' given its engagement with Father, Son and Holy Spirit.

Asking of Them and With Them

Far from asking being some immature form of prayer, asking is the very means by which we are drawn near to God, and invited into the counsel of the Trinity. This is why Andrew Murray understood that our asking becomes "a real factor in God's rule of this earth" and how God "rules the world by the prayers of His saints." [34] In other words, our asking engages the outworking of divine strategies and kingdom actions.

It would be an error to give the idea that our asking is the be-all and end-all of *everything* God does. Yes, God invites us to ask of Him, and He receives because He hears, and He responds because He is loving, and He gives because He is our Father, but our asking does not determine everything God does or does not do. Philosophically speaking, it is a necessary not a sufficient condition. That is why it is important to be aware of the curve balls that God throws us. "I will give you *what you have not asked for*" (1 Kings 3:12); "I revealed myself to those *who did not ask for me*" (Isaiah 65:1); "Your father knows what you need *before you ask Him*" (Matthew 6:8). That does not mean we do not have to ask (we do) but it does mean that we cannot make our asking the necessary pre-condition of all that God does, in a way that it can become a source of pride or control.

If this engagement with the Trinity is just too good to handle, there is more. "*Ask of me* and I will make the nations your inheritance" (Psalm 2:8). Who is addressing who here? The previous verse tells us: "You are my Son, today I have become your Father" (v.7). The Father is addressing the Son. This is a huge Godhead moment, in what can be argued to be an extraordinary Trinitarian psalm when it comes to asking. Asking is a constituent element in the communication of the Godhead and gives meaning and fulfillment to the relationships. Think of it. Christ's asking had a place in God's eternal plan for the universe. His intercessional asking is an intrinsic part of the eternal Father-Son relationship. Therefore our asking of the Son accesses the Deity as it were, and becomes part of the exchanges of heaven, especially as Jesus is presented as the one who "ever lives" (Hebrews 7:25) to ask for us at the right hand of God. Now jump forward a few hundred years. The apostles have been banned from preaching. What do they do? They quote this very psalm and imitating the example of the Son, they ask the Father for a manifestation of healings and wonders. By asking they break through all the limitations and confinements imposed on them by men and go straight into the Operations Room of the Trinity. What could be more persuasive for asking, more supportive of our theology of asking. Andrew Murray writes this about Psalm 2:

> The Son's asking wasn't just for show. It was one of those life-movements in which the love of the Father and the Son met and completed each other. The Father had determined that he would not be alone in His counsels: their fulfillment would depend on the Son's asking and receiving. Thus *asking* was in the very life and being of God. Prayer on earth was to be the reflection and outflow of this. [35]

What more permission, freedom and confidence do we need to ask of God the Father, Son and Holy Spirit?

Trinitarian Asking

To ask is to experience the Trinity. The indwelling of the Holy Spirit, the intercession of the Son and the intentionality of the Father's will combine to work in and through us in the asking we express. The opening of the twenty-first century has seen what some theologians have described as "a Trinitarian renaissance". This is to be welcomed given the lack of Trinitarian awareness in much contemporary Christian worship. Despite this resurgence of attention and the renewed acknowledgement of the Spirit and the Word, it is an emphasis on the Word in the *context of proclamation* that gives the understanding of our participation in the Godhead's life for most people, way more than the *context of prayer*. In a similar way, participation in mission, especially in some theological traditions, seems to be more by proclamation than prayer. The reported recovery of Trinitarian prayers is encouraging, like the 'Prayers for Illumination' in the Reformed tradition, or like the 'epicletic' prayers (from the Greek *epikaleo* meaning 'to call upon') that consciously invoke the presence and help of the Holy Spirit. [36] But this cannot just be about prayers that acknowledge the Trinity by name, or pay liturgical lip-service to their role. It has to be about the need to both acknowledge and understand the participation of the Trinity in our personal asking, not just our public assembling.

> Christian theologians have a remarkable opportunity to serve God's people with a renewed vision for the triune beauty of God's own life and the Trinitarian dimensions of divine activity ... but also to engage the church in practices that elicit and sustain Trinitarian faith. [37]

Asking is one of these non-negotiable "practices", and the hope is that our continuing pursuit of asking will be a theological and pastoral contribution to that recovery of Trinitarian faith and worship. In the words of John Newton's hymn, let us first ask together for a Trinitarian blessing.

> May the grace of Christ our Savior
> And the Father's boundless love
> With the Holy Spirit's favor
> Rest upon us from above. [38]

Asking and God

"The goal of prayer is the ear of God." - C.H.Spurgeon

"The arm of the Lord is not too short to save or
His ear too dull to hear." - Isaiah 59:1

"The power of prayer rests in the faith that God hears it ... Faith in a prayer-hearing God will make a prayer-loving Christian ... One great reason of lack of prayer is the want of the living, joyous assurance: 'My God will hear me!'" - Andrew Murray

"The power of prayer is not in us, that we speak. It is in God, that he listens! It is His hearing that causes a true connection between us."
- Walter Wangerin

"Before they call I will answer; while they are still speaking
I will hear." - Isaiah 65:24

"True prayer is prayer which is sure of a hearing." - Karl Barth

"Inspirer and hearer of prayer,
Thou Shepherd and Guider of Thine,
My all to thy covenant care,
I, sleeping or waking, resign."
- Augustus Toplady

5

He Hears

By His Nature God Hears When We Ask

When it comes to asking, there are three profoundly simple truths about God that must be believed: God hears, God responds and God fathers. These truths are so important to know, not just to have a theology of asking, but to be someone who is confident in their asking of this kind of God.

In any relationship it is helpful that the other person speaks. However, at some point you are going to want to speak yourself. Though comforted that they speak, you will only be satisfied if they can also listen, in order that what they then speak actually relates to what they have just heard you say. Not surprisingly, one of the sections of scripture that is most populated by asking is the collection we know as the Psalms, the Prayer Book of scripture. It is there that we discover one of the great descriptions of God: "O you who *hears* prayer, to you all men will come" (Psalm 65:2). God, by virtue of His nature, exists to hear what we ask, whether we ask as a friend like Abraham, or like the outcast maid, Hagar (Genesis 16:5-11). Three verses later the psalmist declares, "You answer us", and then reels off a whole series of examples of God's answers to asking, affirming that God hears. Our asking is in vain if God does not hear, so the psalmist's description of God's nature is essential truth: God hears. In Psalm 85, the writer begins by asking for several big things one after another: for national restoration, for the assuaging of God's anger against their sin, for revival and for a demonstration of God's unfailing love and His power to save. Then he writes: "I will listen to what God the Lord will say" (v8). If there is a reason to listen, because God is going to speak, then it is assumed that He has heard exactly what has been asked for.

The very next psalm begins as many do: "*Hear* O Lord and answer me!" (86:1)

Living In the Answer-Gap

It is because of this assurance that God hears that we can live in what sometimes feels like a credibility gap between the expression of our asking and the experience of God's answer. The seventeenth century divine, Samuel Rutherford, assured his congregants that Christ "heareth when He doth not answer – His not answering is His answer." [1] It is because Micah can affirm, "My God will hear me" that he can also say, "I will look to the Lord, I will wait" (7:7-9). Living in the answer-gap would be impossible without the prior assurance that God had heard him. It was the common experience of the prophets to ask of God and then wait to see what happened. Desperately, Habakkuk (1:1-4) asked God about the lawless conditions of his day ("the law is paralyzed"), about the life-threatening dangers ("destruction and violence are before me"), about the collapse of justice ("justice never prevails"), about the state of the nations and the menacing arousal of Babylon. However, what was at the heart of Habakkuk's asking was his complaint and frustration about not being sure if God was hearing. "How long O Lord must I call for help but you do not listen?" He was not denying altogether that God could hear, but he was not sure that He actually listened. When you desperately need to be heard by someone it is equally demoralizing if you fear their inability to hear or their refusal to listen. Deafness and disinterest are equally bad.

For Habakkuk, asking questions of God had now degenerated into the questioning of God's character, capacities and capabilities, not by way of seeking answers but of making accusations. But God proves to the prophet that He hears by answering his complaint, and encouraged by this Habakkuk asks again and goes to his watch-tower and says "I will look to see what He will say to me" (2:1). The assurance that God hears strengthened him to wait in the answer-gap. The prophecy ends with his famous assertion that despite no provision and no immediate answer, he will "rejoice in the Lord", and "will wait patiently for the day of calamity" to come on the invading nation (3:16-18). Micah put it like this: "I will bear the indignation of the Lord till he plead my cause" (7:9). Both prophets shared the conviction that their asking was not in vain, not because everything suddenly made sense, or that everything was sorted out; or that God was evidently present in power to do what was asked. It was simply because God was present to hear. The apostle John experienced it no differently as he declared that his confidence, when he asked was: "we know that He hears us" (1 John 5:15).

Asking Post-Its

But John goes a step further. The certainty that God hears is also the assurance that "we have what we asked of Him." What "we have" may not necessarily be the immediate acquisition of the answer, but it is immediate attention and attentiveness. To believe anything less is to impugn both God's name and His nature. It is interesting to note how Solomon ends his historic asking of God at the dedication of the temple. Everything he had asked for was accompanied by the appeal, "*Hear* from heaven!" (1 Kings 8: 30, 32, 34, 36, 39, 43, 45, 49, 52). All his asking assumed the hearing of God. The text says that he finished his asking, and concluded with blessing and praise. Nothing has been answered yet so wherein lay his confidence and his gratitude? On what sure grounds did his theology of asking rest? "May these words of mine, which I have prayed before the Lord, *be near* to the Lord our God day and night, that He may uphold the cause of His servant and the cause of His people Israel according to each day's need" (1 Kings 8:59). Thomas Goodwin, a seventeenth-century pastor, took this to mean that our asking was always "before Him, and He sets them in His view, as we do letters of friends which we stick in our windows, that we may remember to answer them; or lay them not out of our bosoms ... so the petitions of His people pass not out of His sight, till He sends an answer." [2] What God hears is presented not just verbally but visually. He sees what we ask. The things that we ask for, that are not yet, are given shape and form. They are like post-its on God's window.

We will not ask confidently if we are uncertain about God's hearing. It has been argued that the criterion for the genuineness of prayer "is that it will be made in certainty that it will be heard." [3] If there is skepticism about this, the one who asks will have no idea what he is actually doing "when he entreats the Father in the name of the Son and the Holy Spirit." C.S.Lewis observed that we do not talk about the "results" (impersonal effects) of asking but of "answers" (personal responses). That we are heard is therefore assumed. "We can bear to be refused but not to be ignored." [4] We are not ignored, because we are heard. But the fact that God hears is both good news and bad news for our asking.

First the Good News

All spiritual life is premised on the fact that God has ears to hear. You bank on it. There is no salvation, no prayer, if God does not hear. Scripture affirms that God hears. "Does He who implanted the ear not hear?" (Psalm 94:9). "His ear is not dull to hear" (Isaiah 59:1). The deliverance of a future great nation was couched in the words, "God heard the boy crying" (Genesis 16:11). The whole story of the Exodus-deliverance was determined by one thing: "God heard their groaning, and remembered His covenant" (Exodus 2:24). There are other kinds of cries that God hears: " the cries of the workers reached God's ears" (James 5:4). The conviction and relief that God hears is presented in so many ways as people talk about the "ears of the Lord" (1 Samuel 8:21), or testify with relief that "my cry came into His ears" (Psalm 18:6). Consider the ways this is presented: "Give ear O Lord" (2 Kings 19:16); "You hear O Lord" (Psalm 10:17); "May your ear be attentive" (2 Chronicles 6:40); "Incline your ear to me" (Psalm 17:6); "Listen to my cry" (Psalm 5:2); "Bow down your ear" (Psalm 31:2); "His ears are open" (Psalm 34:15); "Give ear to my words ... to my prayer ... to my voice" (Psalm 5:1, 17:1, 141:1); "Hear me when I call" (Psalm 4:1); "Hear me in the day of trouble ... hear me speedily" (Psalm 20:1, 143:7).

Assurance is given, not only *that* God hears, but *what* God hears, like the "desire of the afflicted" (Psalm 10:17) or "the prayer of the righteous" (Proverbs 15:29). One of the most quoted chapters on intercession in scripture contains the most quoted verse: "If my people who are called by my name will humble themselves and pray, and seek my face then *I will hear* from heaven and will forgive their sin and will heal their land" (2 Chronicles 7:14). There is no healing if there is no hearing. If God's hearing is impaired, we remain impaired. God's opening words to Solomon in this communication are, "I have heard your prayer" (7:12). This is the clear response to what was asked earlier: "Hear the asking of your servants ... when they pray toward this place" (6:21). Any lack of assurance about this, any doubt about His loving attentiveness to us, will undermine our confidence and our will to ask. God's hearing invites our asking. Our asking is heard. Without that confidence we will not ask. And even if we do, and go through the motions, it will not be with any faith at all.

Nowhere is the assurance of God's hearing more emphatic than in the repeated testimony of Jesus Himself at Lazarus' tomb: "Father, I thank you that you have heard me. I knew you always hear me" (John 11:42). Do we catch the confidence, joy, relief, gratitude and love in this statement? The grounds of Jesus's confidence are the same grounds as ours: God hears when we ask.

And Now the Bad News

The assuring fact that God hears, also has a less comfortable outcome. He hears what we speak that we would maybe prefer that He not hear: "God heard their murmurings" (Exodus 16:8); "The Lord heard what you said and was angry" (Deuteronomy 1:34). He hears the blasphemies of nations (Ezekiel 35:12); He heard Sarah's mocking cynicism and unbelief behind the tent flaps (Genesis 18:13-15). What does He hear us saying beneath our cold sheets, under our breath, in the dark, into the wind, through our tears, behind our hands?

Having established that God hears, scripture presents not just what God *chooses* to hear, but also what He *refuses* to hear. This has huge implications for our assumptions about prayer, and our expectations of our asking. It is salutary to go through the scriptures and discover how many times God explicitly says He will not listen to what is asked of Him, or He will choose not to hear. Sometimes His choice not to hear is a response to our choice not to listen or heed His word and commands. Just as Jesus said that our refusal to forgive runs interference with our own reception of forgiveness, so God makes clear that there is a divinely reciprocated response in His hearing, to our refusal to hear. After all, is it not true that we cease to speak to someone who has ceased to listen to what we are saying, and cease to listen to someone who repeatedly fails to respond to what we have said? Surely, before we ask, it is worth checking if there are any reasons which might contribute to our asking being in vain, simply because God will choose not to hear. It will feel to us that He has not heard or cannot hear. No, God hears. What he does is refuse to hear for specified reasons; He chooses not to listen.

The following scriptural examples are important because they affirm that God is a Person and not some cosmic impersonal slot machine where certain input gets certain output; as if we ask and out pops the answer, custom wrapped for our fleshly consumption. We are not heard simply by virtue of our asking. We have already noted that there are many reasons for unanswered asking: asking for wrong things, asking of wrong sources, asking in wrong ways, asking when in the wrong. What follows will be a helpful list to check two things: our possible presumption in asking, and the continuance of those things in our lives that are not consistent with those whose asking is an expression of their intimate trust of God. Some requests may have a reasonable and laudable face value when verbalized, and may even pass theological muster, but the Lord not only hears our words, He sees our heart. While I am asking for and about those things that affect my relationship with my world, God is concerned about what affects my relationship with Him. Here are some of the biblical reasons given for God's refusal to hear what is asked:

Choosing other lordship: "Give us a king to lead us ... you will cry out for relief from the king you have chosen, and *the Lord will not answer* you in that day" (1 Samuel 8:18). Divine lordship has been abandoned in favor of human leadership. Trusting men has been preferred to trusting God. Human security and protection is more desired than the presence of God. If we serve other lordship God will not hear.

Willful disobedience: "The Lord was angry with me and *would not listen* to me" (Deuteronomy 3:26). Why? Moses was disobedient. Basically, God is saying: "There is no point in asking me again. Do not ask for something that I cannot and will not do." If there is willful disobedience God will not hear.

Meaningless religion: "When you spread out your hands in prayer I will hide my eyes from you – even many prayers *I will not listen*" (Isaiah 1:15). This is preceded by: "Stop bringing meaningless offerings!" (v.13) God has heard and seen enough and is taking no pleasure in their asking. He "cannot bear" what they are doing, and His "soul hates" their liturgical rituals which have "become a burden" to Him. When living faith is reduced to dead religion and what is spiritually real becomes fleshly ritual then God will not hear.

Living a double life: "Do not plead with me for *I will not listen* to you" (Jeremiah 7:16). This is God's response to His people's private worship of the Queen of Heaven, while paying public lip-service to the temple. They were asking while they were "two-timing" God. "Will you steal and commit adultery and follow other gods and then come and stand before me in my house?" (vs. 9-11) You can ask for blessing and immunity all you want but God will not bless what you are asking for, because of the conditions of the asking heart. "Has this house, which bears my name, become a den of robbers to you?" This is a chilling passage because it is the same one that Jesus quotes when He casts the money-changers out of the temple and re-establishes it as a house of "asking" (Matthew 21:12-13). It is clear at the end of the chapter that God is responding in kind because He says to Jeremiah, "When you tell them all this, they will not listen to you; when you call to them they will not answer." They do not answer God about what He is asking of them through the prophet, yet they expect Him to answer what they are asking of Him. When there is the deception and duplicity of a double-life God will not hear.

Refusal to be compassionate to others: "Administer true justice; show mercy and compassion to one another ... But they refused to pay attention ... When I called they did not listen; when they called *I would not listen*" (Zechariah 7:13). The chapter begins with God answering something they had asked about ("should I mourn and fast?" v3) with asking of His own ("Was it really for me that you fasted?" v5). The problem is that their asking is utterly self-consumed and self-enhancing. It was all about "feasting for themselves" (v6). Despite what God was asking of them, it says "they refused to pay attention ... they stopped their ears" (v11). This refusal to heed God's justice provoked the divine response to "not listen." When a compassionate response is asked for oneself while withholding compassion for others, God will not hear.

Disregard for injustice and denial of justice: "If a man shuts his ears to the cry of the poor, he too will cry out and *not be answered*" (Proverbs 21:13); "On the day of your fasting you exploit all your workers ... you cannot fast as you do today and *expect your voice to be heard* on high" (Isaiah 58:4); "Should you not know justice? They will cry out to the Lord but He *will not answer him*" (Micah 4:2-4). The deliberate avoidance of the afflictions of those who are the victims of injustice, results in a divine refusal to hear what they ask for. A lack of generosity is also implied here as there is a contradiction between asking more for oneself while denying what another needs. When Paul tells the Philippians that God will supply their needs when they ask, it is clearly because they have already been generous in supplying the needs of others. Effective askers are usually those with generous spirits. We have received freely in response to our asking, therefore we give freely. If God's justice is willfully disregarded He will not hear.

Appearance without reality: "They seek me out; they seem eager to know my ways as if they were a nation that does what is right ... They ask me for just decisions and seem eager for God to come near them" (Isaiah 58:2). They appear to be concerned and desirous but there is a divine "YET!" (v.3) What they "seem" is not what they are and it negates their asking. God explains that the answers to their asking are conditional on their choice of what He has chosen, not their self-oriented choices. He clearly spells out what that will require of them (vs.6-7). "THEN ... you will call and the Lord will answer, you will cry for help and the Lord will say 'Here I am'". Where there is appearance without reality, God will not hear.

Unconfessed and unrepented sin: "If I had cherished iniquity in my heart *the Lord would not have listened*" (Psalm 66:18). The problem here is the expectation that God will be responsive to anything we ask while we persist in ignoring the things that interfere with relationship, and that are an offence to God. "Your sins have hidden His face from you so He *will not hear*" (Isaiah 59:2). This is referring to a habitual life-style of sin that results in God not listening to what is asked, so there will be no answers. Where the eyes of God are covered, the ears of God are covered too. If iniquity is harbored, God will not hear.

Failure to acknowledge and accept God's wisdom: "Wisdom calls aloud ... since you rejected me when I called ... since you ignored all my advice ... and would not accept my rebuke ... they will call to me but *I will not answer*" (Proverbs 1: 20-28). You have to listen in order to be listened to. Fools will not be given a wise answer. "Answer a fool according to his folly" (Proverbs 26:5). The answer to the fool's asking is silence. Those addressed did not choose the fear of the Lord, and they would not accept the advice of wisdom. In the New Testament, the book of James is like a commentary on Proverbs and it makes clear (James 1:5) that if we are humble and admit our need of God's wisdom, then an amazing invitation is extended: "let him *ask* of God who gives generously." Submission to the wisdom of God attracts a generous and a gracious response to our asking. Where there is a failure to submit to God's wisdom, God will not hear.

Deliberate rejection of God's law: "If anyone turns a deaf ear to the law even *his prayers are detestable*" (Proverbs 28:9). Again, here is an example of God's refusal to respond to what is asked for by someone who insists on shutting their ears to the holiness and justice of God, rejecting truth and disdaining God's laws. In such a case, God will not hear.

Pride: "If my people ... will humble themselves and ask ... then will I hear from heaven" (2 Chronicles 7:14). Humility is loud in the ears of God. Pride therefore closes them to our asking. "I will break down your stubborn pride and make *the sky above you like iron*" (Leviticus 26:19). There is no responsiveness from heaven to the prideful, because God will not hear.

Idolatry: "These men have set up idols in their hearts and put wicked stumbling blocks before their faces. *Should I let them ask of me* at all?" (Ezekiel 14:3). "You continue to defile yourselves with all your idols ... Am I to let you inquire of me? ... *I will not let you inquire* of me!" (Ezekiel 20:31) The only answer the Lord says He will give is to separate Himself from anyone who separates themselves from Him by their indulgence in idolatrous thinking and living. That separation is a break-down of communication which means no possibility for asking, so God will not hear.

Ritualistic repetition: "Do not keep on babbling like the pagans, for they *think they will be heard* because of their many words" (Matthew 6:7). Vain, fleshly, superstitious verbosity and volubility is not the way to ask if you want to be heard. God will not hear it.

Unforgiveness: "If you do not forgive men their sins, your Father will not forgive your sins" (Matthew 6:15). Our asking for forgiveness will go unheeded if we bear unforgiveness in our hearts. There may be many things that are maintaining the unforgiveness, like bitterness, unhealed pain, continuing strife, the vindictive desire for punishment, or the ongoing wishing of ill upon the offender. If we willfully retain unforgiveness in our hearts, God will not hear.

Disunity: "If two of you agree about anything you ask for it will be done" (Matthew 18:19). If unity is a condition for asking effectively, then lack of agreement and dissension will invalidate our asking. Disunity, irreconciliation and disagreement render our asking null and void. God will not hear.

Enmity: Jesus addresses the consequences of anger and enmity in His teaching, and points out that the posture of worship, whether we are giving or asking, is rendered ineffective, unless we first "go and be reconciled" to our brother (Matthew 5:23-24). Wesley taught that if asking was "to have its full weight with God" then it was imperative that we be living "in charity with all men" [5] or God will not hear.

Hypocrisy: "They love to pray ... to be seen by men ... I thank you I'm not like other men ... God have mercy on me ... this man rather than the other went home justified before God" (Luke 18: 9-14). The Pharisee in Jesus's parable did not leave justified like the asking Publican, but left just the same. The Pharisee was not heard. Insincerity was not heeded. Where there is hypocrisy, God will not hear.

Double-mindedness: "When he asks he must believe and not doubt ... That man should not think he will receive anything from the Lord" (James 1:6-7). Where there is double-mindedness and doubt there will be no authority in asking. Equally, there will be no capacity to receive, even if answered. Jesus was so clear that the one who asked for a mountain to be moved should have "no doubt in his heart." Although some of the things we ask for are staggering, we are exhorted to heed Abraham's example who "staggered not at the promise of God through unbelief, but was strong in faith giving glory to God" (Romans 4:20). Where doubt persists, asking eventually ceases. As Calvin remarked, "If you doubt you do not pray." Where there is double-mindedness there will be no authority in asking and God will not hear.

Broken marital relationships: "Husbands ... be considerate as you live with your wives ... treat them with respect ... so that nothing will hinder your prayers" (1 Peter 3:7). Inappropriate, un-Christ-like behavior and sins against spouses run interference with our asking. Trading presumptuously on a sense of intimacy with God, when marital intimacy is not being cherished or protected, is inviting a hindrance to our asking. If we are sinning against our spouse God will not hear.

Condemnation: "If our hearts do not condemn us, we have confidence before God and receive from Him anything we ask" (1 John 3:21). Where there is condemnation there is a block both on the freedom to ask with assurance, and on the reception of what we ask for. If our hearts condemn us, God will not hear.

Not asking according to His will: "If we ask anything according to His will He hears us" (1 John 5:14). God cannot be asked to act against His own character or purpose. If we do not ask according to His will, God will not hear.

Asking with wrong motives: "You do not receive because you ask with wrong motives, that you may spend it on your pleasures" (James 4:3). When asking is fueled by wrong motives rooted in the lust and covetousness, fighting and warring that James refers to, there will be no answers. It is clear that the motive for asking is utterly self-serving and good things can be requested for bad reasons. Simon Magus asked for the Holy Spirit, a good thing, but with godless motives (Acts 8:18-19). If the motivation for the request is not to delight oneself in the Lord, then the asked-for desire is unlikely to be given (Psalm 37:4). The Lord searches the heart and discerns the motivation behind our asking. The litmus test for our motives in asking is simple but direct: is what we ask for to gratify ourselves or to glorify God? If wrong motives are present, God will not hear.

Asking wrong sources: "My people ask counsel of their stocks, and are answered by a stick of wood" (Hosea 4:12). Asking of wrong sources, from God's perspective, is "a spirit of prostitution". When they do have a need to ask, "they will not find Him" (Hosea 5:6). The divine pain is explicit whenever Israel appointed prophets, priests and kings of their own making, and ceased to inquire of the Lord. "They have not asked at *my* mouth" (Isaiah 30:2). "They didn't ask, 'Where is the Lord?'" (Jeremiah 2:6) They carried out their own plans, asking counsel of unholy consultants and forming alliances other than relationship with God. When Saul chose to ask of the witch of Endor instead of the Lord, he lost his kingdom (1 Samuel 28:7). When Ahaziah sent messengers to consult Baal-Zebub, the god of Ekron, God told Elijah to ask these emissaries, "Is it because there is no God in Israel? ...You will surely die!" (2 Kings 1:3). When wrong sources offer themselves, the need to ask of God is imperative. "When men tell you to consult mediums and spiritists, who whisper and mutter, should not a people inquire of the Lord?" (Isaiah 8:19) Getting direction from others displaces asking of God. The consequences are dangerous and disastrous. God will not hear.

Asking for wrong things: "They put God to the test by demanding the things they craved" (Psalm 78:18). This is rooted in the same lust that James speaks about. When Solomon asked for wisdom, the difference between asking for right and wrong things is made clear. "The Lord was pleased that Solomon had asked for this ... and not for long life or wealth for yourself ... I will do what you have asked" (1 Kings 3:10-11). If we ask for wrong things God will not hear.

Asking that is really accusing: The prophet Isaiah foresaw Jesus as a lamb that was dumb before its shearers: "so He did not open His mouth" (Isaiah 53:7). There was plenty of asking going on, and in any other context they would have been good questions to ask. "Are you the one who was to come?" (Luke 7:20) when asked of Jesus by John the Baptist, is very different to: "Are you the Christ?" (Mark 14:61) when asked by Caiaphas. As with all these points, it is not that God is deaf. He chooses not to hear. The silence of Jesus, as if he did not hear, is the divine response to that which is asked in anger and contempt, in mockery and accusation. It is not genuinely interrogative but deliberately derogatory. How much asking is addressed to God from the place of bitter cynicism, or challenging defiance, or personal enmity? Asking that is accusing will not be heard.

Failure to ask: "You have not because you ask not" (James 4:2-3). It is important to state the obvious. God cannot and will not hear what is not spoken. God presents Himself, time and time again in scripture, as the God who wants to be addressed, wants to be asked. "Ask of me!" (Psalm 2:8) Go to God and "take words with you" pleads Hosea (14:2). If we will not ask, God will not hear because He has nothing to hear! It has been said that the greatest tragedy of life is not unanswered prayer but unoffered prayer. God cannot hear what is not asked.

We Know That He Hears Us

It would be easy to be disheartened by all this and limit our asking to the question: what hope? But that would be to completely miss the point. God is not trying to make Himself less approachable but more so. If we are going to ask rightly and effectively, it makes sense that we know as much as possible about wrong kinds of asking. God has a vested interest that nothing hinders our asking, because He wants to relate to us. Thus the practice of asking is such an invitation of grace to live in a manner that is worthy of our confession of Christ. Not to ask of God is actually not to ask some crucial questions of ourselves. The neglect of asking turns out to be a neglect of personal spiritual health, and a weakening of discipleship.

The bottom line is that we should be awe-struck that God hears: "There is a divine hearing - on the basis of the incomprehensible grace of God an incomprehensible hearing - even of the creature which is sinful." [6] This is amazing grace indeed. "The Lord has heard me and I will call on Him as long as I live" (Psalm 116:1-2). The psalmist has committed himself to a lifetime of asking just because of the wonder that God hears him - and there is not an answer in sight. God's responsiveness is joyfully affirmed because He hears, not because He has answered at this time. No one expresses this joy better than John: "And this is the *confidence* that we have in Him, that if we ask anything according to His will, *He hears us*. And *if we know that He hears us*, whatsoever we ask, we know that we have the petitions that we desired of Him" (1 John 5:14). The most fundamental of these petitions to God, exampled by Jesus, is "Your will be done." We should be disheartened about anything that would interfere with His hearing of our asking. This encourages asking that is righteous and just. Two chapters earlier (1 John 3:22) John makes clear that our confidence in asking is related to the keeping of His commandments and doing "those things that are pleasing in His sight."

What we have said so far, in our theology of asking, is that fundamental to God's nature is that He hears and that this is both good news and bad news. Let us first ask for a renewed conviction in our relationship with God that can express itself in those words of Micah way back at the beginning of this chapter: "My God will hear me!" Let us ask for the removal of every reason for why God would not hear our asking. Let us ask for forgiveness for what God has heard from our lips, from the speech of our spirits, that has unrighteously and unjustly questioned His loving care and provision for us and that has doubted His faithfulness in the responses we think we have received to our asking. Let us respond immediately to any conviction from the Holy Spirit about anything mentioned above. The recovery of asking begins with the repentant asking for forgiveness, healing and deliverance from those patterns of life and thought that have resulted in the breakdown of our intimate asking-answering communications with God.

This leads us to the second essential truth about God that we need to know when it comes to our theology of asking: He responds.

"The prayer that gets what it asks is the prayer that is unto God."
- R.A.Torrey

"We never dare enough in petitioning God, in putting Him to the test of what He can do." - Jacques Ellul

"What we receive in our prayer is not simply a boon but communion – or if a boon, it is the boon which Christians call the Holy Spirit, and which means, above all else, communion with God." - P.T.Forsyth

"He is not deaf, He listens; more than that He acts. He does not act in the same way whether we pray or not. Prayer exerts an influence upon God's action." - Karl Barth

"Our asking is not a cause that makes God's response inevitable, it is the reason for His response: God does what He does because He is asked." - Vincent Brummer

"God's response to our payers is not a charade. He does not pretend to answer our prayers when He was only going to do what He was going to do anyway. Our requests really do make a difference to what God does or does not do." - Dallas Willard

6

He Responds

By His Nature God Responds to Those Who Ask

A theology of asking is essentially an affirmation of what it is about God that validates our asking of Him. We ask and keep on asking, less because of our awareness of our need, but more because of our assurance of His nature. "Anyone who comes to Him must believe that He exists and that He rewards those who earnestly seek Him" (Hebrews 11:6). It is not only about believing that God exists, but that He exists to both hear and respond to those who ask of Him. It is important that the person to whom we are presenting a request is able to hear what we ask (not just listen passively) and actively respond. God will not allow these things to be separated: that He lives and that He listens; that He receives our requests, and that He responds to them. This is precisely what separates the true God from false gods. "Their idols cannot speak" (Jeremiah 10:5). "Their idols ... have ears but cannot hear" (Psalm 115:4-6). "Ignorant are those who carry about idols of wood, who *pray to gods that cannot save*" (Isaiah 45:20). False gods are dead, deaf and dumb idols and cannot answer when asked. Yahweh is a living, listening and answering God.

The monumental confrontation between Elijah and the prophets of Baal was all about this matter of asking and answering. Regardless of how the Baalites "shouted" we read that "there was no response; no one answered" (1 Kings 18:16-39). Elijah got right to the point: "The God who *responds* ... He is God." The difference between true and false religion is this: the true God hears our asking and responds to it. Our asking demonstrates that our God is the true God of heaven and earth. Elijah asked, "Answer me, O Lord. Answer me, so that these people will know that you, O Lord, are God." When the fire fell and licked up all the water, it was more than impressively convincing. But the point of it all was not just about what the people's eyes saw. It was about what God's ears heard. When they cried, "The Lord, He is God!" they had just recovered a theology of asking. God receives our requests and is responsive to what is heard. He is not impassive and implacable. From this truth alone, that God exists to hear what is asked of Him, we can infer the other divine attributes, especially His love, His mercy and His grace. This speaks both of His desire to respond, and His need to be asked so that He has reason to respond. Scripture presents us with a God who invites people to ask of Him, in order that He might be responsive. As theologian Vincent Brummer puts it, our asking "creates the conditions necessary for God to be able to give us as persons that which we need or desire." [1] He responds because we ask.

Response As Ventriloquy

However, there are many who struggle with the idea that God can be responsive to their asking. Are such responses real or are they mirages, imaginative delusions, coping mechanisms? Kenneth Woodward, a Newsweek journalist, wondered if asking was just "an exercise in narcissism and dishonesty." [2] Is it just about self-responsiveness, an internalized conversation with oneself, a self-administered therapy? Nothing can really change, but apparently, according to some Job's comforters, we are changed in the process, hopefully in a positive sort of way. (Surely not getting what you asked for may have very negative results.) Does this not sound like a specious attempt to salvage some benefit from something that cannot in fact procure the beneficial outcomes that we most desire and need? It has been wryly observed that it is not that there are no benefits to asking but it is just that a response to what we ask for is not one of them. Are the responses less about prayer and more about pragmatism, with our faith in the fact creating the fact, thus convincing us of a response? Does that not sound like self-deception? As others have argued, you do not even need God for any of these benefits, if they are essentially self-induced and self-authenticating.

Is It Inappropriate to Expect a Response?

So what is the relationship between providence and prayer? A paragraph will be insufficient to cover what others like Terrance Tiessen have done well in 400 pages [3] and I urge you to consult their excellent work. Is our asking "presumptuous ... insulting ... impudent ... impertinent ... impious" as some have claimed and therefore unworthy of response because unworthy of God? After all, if God's mind is unchangeable, if everything He does is inevitable, then according to Aquinas "it is not fitting that we should pray to God." [4] Is this suggesting it is morally inappropriate to do so, and that it is an offence to God? Has asking that seeks God's blessing now become a blasphemy, in that it questions His control or runs the risk of implying lack of trust in His disposal of things? The expectation of a response is then considered unspiritual and out of order. Similarly, Ambrose remarked to Origen that if "none of the things He wills can be changed, prayer is vain." [5] Jonathan Edwards, because he saw God as being self-moved, remarked that it was "not as if He were moved or persuaded" by prayer.[6] These are all prodigious and prolific theologians, but just based on these insights, although you may want them to teach a seminary class and do a 'revival week' they may not be the guys you want as your prayer-partners. So what do we do? Is God powerless to change His own mind, and tethered to His own inevitable will? It would seem that either asking or immutability has to be jettisoned if the ship of prayer bearing the cargo of our need is not going to sink. But we already know that asking is spiritually in order, and in fact we could say, ordered by God in every sense of that word. And if God chooses to change His mind it cannot contradict any aspect of His holy character, so any such 'change', whether perceived as such by us, or described as such by God, will still be immutably perfect.

Admittedly, there are some things that we cannot ask God to do with any expectation of a response, like contradictory requests that are either contrary to His character and nature, His goodness and His will, ("ought presupposes can") or contrary to sense, to what is logically possible. However, that said, asking still remains a "besetting problem" if someone holds a theological position, notably one that is "Calvinian" [7], that seems to present the personhood and purposes of God as immutable "fixities" and thus impenetrable and impervious to what we want to ask about. Does that not scotch the idea that "prayer changes things"? That bumper-sticker would need to be bumped. We can cede that God is benevolent and will always have His best foreordained intentions for us in mind, but the fact is that in terms of a live, here-and-now, relationally interactive response to what I am asking for – forget it. God is going to do what He is going to do in accord with His predetermined will and there is nothing that our asking can do about it. To those who presented God as an unresponsive benefactor, a mischievous theologian had an iconoclastic reminder: "He is not alone in His trinitarian being." [8] Most Calvinian discussions on asking convey no sense of the fertile intercommunication of asking and answering and personal responsiveness within the Trinity, to which we have already alluded. When we ask of God, we are conference-calling with this amazingly interactive Godhead. How different is this intimate conversation from an intellectual construct. If God cannot be freely responsive to what I am freely asking, then asking has no meaning at all. The inevitable determinability of what is going to be, renders asking null and void and reduces it to a God-doubting, self-deceiving exercise in futility. My asking is ineffective because it can have no effect on God and therefore elicit any response. If nothing can be obtained by prayer that is already ordained by providence then why ask about anything that is present or prospective?

The attempts by most 'Calvinians' to make asking viable, purposeful and desirable are usually tortuous, and in some cases, philosophically obtuse and theologically selective. It would be hard to use their essays as hand-outs if you were trying to encourage more passionate asking of God in your church. Though they may try to secure asking as a necessary spiritual duty (which is good) I have yet to read a defense of a Calvinian theology of prayer that generated much delight. Despite all the talk about being satisfied that God's will is going to be done and He is going to be glorified (which is all good and true and most pre-eminently desirable), why is one not overjoyed at the prospect of prayer? I am not making a god out of personal feeling, or saying that all asking is delightful, but I am saying that in any relationship, asking and answering is affective, not just cognitive. Relationship assumes lovingly mutual responsiveness. The wife whose husband's answer to every question is, "I've taken care of that already," is going to be discouraged and distanced, regardless of how well he means. He may think he has relieved her of a burden but for her there is no relief if she is unable to interact in a way that conveys a sense of the significance and meaning of her specific needs for specific reasons.

One begins to wonder if these argumentations are more philosophical than theological, or less theological and more temperamental, determined less by 'providence' than by perhaps a more melancholic, or even morose disposition that finds emotional and intimate relationships challenging anyway, and whose insecurities require a self-authenticating fool-proof system of thought to give them assurance that they are right and therefore righteous. The common defense against the pointlessness of asking if everything is pre-ordained is the notion that our asking itself is ordained for the ordained answers that God will give. It should be pointed out that asking here is not a preface to anything, not a holy engagement with what God is about to do. It is more like an ordained after-thought, a consequent necessity because the response that is asked for is already ordained. In this view, there is nothing causal about asking. It is always consequential. True, our asking is never causal in the sense that it gives God an idea that He never had or creates a reality that never existed. Perhaps a better word to use would be 'instrumental'. Scripture seems to be clear on the instrumentality of our asking, since God personally invites it, and specifically says what His responsive outcomes will be if we do so. He answers us because we ask. A young company-founder attended a marketing event sponsored by a well-known designer who often appeared on the TV show *Good Morning America.* After giving her stage-presentation pitching her company, the young entrepreneur boldly asked the TV host to put her product on his national program. The designer agreed and later sought out the intrepid asker and said, "Do you want to know why I said yes to you? Because you asked." [9]

It is sad when a theological system becomes unwittingly God-proof and the voice of God cannot be heard when He calls us to engage in asking for, say, His intended acts of judgment to be averted. There is nothing that quite quenches the outpouring of a heart, whether desolate or delirious, than the dutifully 'ordained' pause, to register that the utterance about to be spilled is also ordained in its entirety. So at the end of the joyless time of asking, one is told to be content with the fact that asking effects nothing out there but may affect the one asking in some beneficial ways. Oliver Crisp, one of a new generation of Calvinian theologians, concedes that asking is a useful exercise to remind one of the need for God's help, and that any benefits that derive from it "proceed from His hand." [10] He trusts that something moderately encouraging will be learned in this "exercise of patient submission to His will and in the hope of salvation, come what may." [11] While appreciating these best wishes, why does that bring no consolation? Even though it is named as 'grace', why does it feel more like 'grit and grind'?

Calvin argued that God instructed us to pray "for he ordained it not so much for His own sake as for ours." [12] Of course there is truth in that because any means of grace is going to have gracious effects. But is this entirely consistent with the biblical record? Asking is reduced to a training exercise in faith that gets us to align our will with God's will and have faith in the exercise of that will, however and whenever that is ordained for whoever, wherever. As Aquinas put it: "We do not pray in order to change the decree of divine providence, rather we pray to acquire by petitionary prayer what God has determined would be obtained by those prayers." [13] Thanks for nothing, Thomas. Why am I not encouraged to learn that our pointless asking is purposefully ordained? Trying to salvage some benefit for the asker, Aquinas writes: "We must pray, not in order to inform God of our needs and desires, but in order to remind ourselves that in these matters we need divine assistance." [14] So we acknowledge our need of help but we cannot be specific about the help we need? Not helpful at all! Frankly, there is only a fine line between these theologisms and the view held by atheists who would accept that 'prayer' can only be a conversation with self, since there is no divine response possible. Again, if God cannot be responsive then asking has no meaning at all. If God has no need to respond because He has determined everything then asking is ineffective. We cannot argue convincingly that prayer is necessary or essential, either for our sake or for God's. What is fascinating is that biblically, petition and praise are indivisible, so those traditions that suppress asking are often equally suppressed when it comes to the affective freedoms of worship. The two are inextricably linked.

And another thing, talking of worship. When asking has no meaning, there is less sense of what is received as a gift. Yes, there is no question about God's glorification, but God is not threatened by our legitimate gratification that expresses itself in grateful thanksgiving. Of course, we should be worshipful that God is always God, and true to Himself, but we also need the sense that He is our God, and true to us, as we desire to be true to Him. Is that not the nature of faithfulness in a relationship? The loss of any sense of personal causality in our asking reduces the experience of intimacy because what is being received is more ordained by God than asked by us, and the assurance about being personally known and personally cared for, suffers. Assurance in the doctrine has to make up for the lack of assurance in the relationship.

Asking of Sovereignty As a Son

It does not need to be this complicated and excruciating. Surely we are not negotiating trade-offs, though it feels that a little more of this means a little less of that: a little more of answered asking means a little less of sovereignty; a little more of unanswered asking means a little less of omnipotence; a little more of asking for things to change, or for God to relent, means a little less of immutability. It is important to understand this discussion about 'response' in the context of the following chapter's theme of God's fatherhood. If we only deal with asking in relationship to His unchangeable sovereignty we will only have half the truth. He is the sovereign God who is also our loving Father. He is comprehensively sovereign and intimately personal. We are free moral agents, accountable and responsible for our choices, not programed pawns in a fatalistic universe. We can be obedient or disobedient sons and daughters.

Suffice it to say that we have to hold several things together that are all true, all complementary, and not contradictory. God has chosen not to act alone and has given us the dignity of being His agents in His work, as His partners and fellow-participants – co-heirs, co-workers, co-laborers. He has chosen our asking as a means by which He chooses to act and furthermore, include us in His responsive answers and actions. Given this, our asking is far from pointless, but rather influential, purposeful, significantly proactive in what is accomplished by God. His amazing grace then shares the rewards of the divine outcomes as if we had input. I am reminded of the story of the mouse walking over the bridge with the elephant. The bridge shuddered and swayed, rocked and reeled. When they got to the other side, the mouse looked up at the elephant and said, "We really shook it this time!" Graciously, the elephant did not argue.

As our Father, there is no contradiction between God's paternal love and His providential order; between his omniscient foreknowledge and our freedom as sons and daughters; between the sovereign fulfillment of His will and His fatherly responsiveness to our needs and desires; between His cosmic rule and our Father-Son personal relationship; between our asking as dependent sons and daughters, and His acting as a kingly father. It is so important to note the words of Jesus himself when He was asking the Father, just before the cross: "Holy Father" (John 17:11). This is the only occurrence of this phrase in scripture and its timing is hugely significant. In the Old Testament, holiness was God's calling card. Jim Packer observed: "The whole spirit of Old Testament religion was determined by the thought of God's *holiness* ... Everything that makes the New Testament new ... everything that is distinctively Christian as opposed to merely Jewish, is summed up in the knowledge of the *Fatherhood* of God." [15] In the New Testament His Fatherhood is His calling card. It is not either/or but both/and, but it was not until Jesus's atoning death and resurrection that we could know God intimately as both, or ask Him as such. Jesus, having asked "Holy Father", was now going to open the door that would give access to all who believed on Him to ask in the same way with the same intimate confidence, fearless assurance, and joyful expectation. When we ask, it is no longer just "His holiness" or "His sovereignty" that we address in our asking. 'Abba' is now our primary address not Jehovah. He is no less Jehovah but He is now Jehovah-Abba. How did Jesus ask? That should settle it. He asked "Holy Father" and there was no contradiction.

If asking is an intrinsic, irreplaceable, God-required part of the divine process by which His divine intentions and providential actions are done, then asking becomes an awesome invitation and responsibility, a high privilege and honor, a human need and godly necessity, for the accomplishment of that which is divinely purposed by God, through the means of willing askers who are totally desirous of God's will to be done, and who are personally submitted to that same will. The commitment to ask is the expression of that submission and of that co-operation in covenant partnership with a God who needs to be responded to, and who responds.

By His Nature God Asks Us to Ask So That He Can Respond

There is a remarkable incident when the Lord gives an extraordinary invitation to King Ahaz: "Ask the Lord your God for a sign" (Isaiah 7:11). There were no conditions and no limitations. There were no divine requests for the sign to "be within reason". What would our response have been if we had received that invitation? Normally we assume that requests for a sign are an evidence of little faith, of doubt, and therefore illegitimate. If you remember the Gideon incident in Judges 6, he asked for a sign but this is not presented as something wrong or faithless. He really wanted to be sure: it was the expression of someone who was trying to believe and be faithful to what the Lord was saying. And of course, Gideon was granted it. We know it is legitimate here too, because it is God Himself who is asking Ahaz to ask. God is eager for an excuse to demonstrate His responsiveness to Ahaz who is clearly being addressed as a believer here: "the Lord *your* God" (v10). The king is in a desperate situation and should not have needed to be persuaded and prodded to ask. He had every urgent reason to be asking God, and God wanted him to ask, as He wants us to do so, because He wants our crises and cries for help to be the exercise room for the strengthening of our faith and trust in Him. He wants the place of the disorientation of our pain to become the venue for the demonstration of His power. This shows us that so often God is more desirous to be asked, than we are willing to ask. He wants to respond to us but are we responding to Him?

So what was Ahaz's response? "I will not ask: I will not put God to the test" (v.12). Most people would say, "How wonderful! How spiritual! How trusting! How faithful!" But the fact is that it is nothing of the sort here. Of course, there is a real sin of testing God that is an expression of rank unbelief. The Israelites did it all the time. The Pharisees did it in asking Jesus for a miracle: it was a 'test' rooted in their unbelief not their faith. By not asking, Ahaz is hiding his unbelief and trust in an incense cloud of fake spirituality.

His failure to ask was an evidence of faithlessness not faith. He actually denies the Lord's request to be trusted. He resists the responsiveness that God wants to show to his asking. Look what God offered: "Whether in the deepest depths or the highest heights!" (v10) He could have asked for the moon! The failure to ask of God here, the God who hears and responds to those who ask Him, is a terrible manifestation of unbelief. Do you know what is incredible here? It seems that sometimes God is so desirous to be asked, so longing to give a sign, that if He is not asked, He will do it for Himself for His own sake and satisfaction. What would that sign be that would be beyond any dimension that Ahaz, or anyone else for that matter, could possibly imagine? What could be a sign worthy of the "deepest depths" of desire and the "highest heights" of hope? God answers our question. "A virgin will be with child and will give birth to a son and will call Him Immanuel!" (v14) Jesus no less! Could Ahaz not at least have asked for God's presence to be active in his situation? He did not. God breaks through the localized needs of Ahaz and promises a Presence, "God with us", that will give a new motivation and access for our asking of God. So desirous was God to be asked that He reveals a sign that will, when fulfilled, secure forever His availability to be asked, and our access to Him to ask: "We have a great high priest ... Let us then approach the throne of grace with confidence so that we may receive ... Let us draw near to God ... in full assurance of faith" (Hebrews 4:14-16; 10:22). That is response is it not?

Asking When the Desired Response Seems Impossible

The response that God said He would give anyway, after Ahaz had failed to ask for anything, became a fulfilled reality in the birth of Jesus. The answer to Mary's asking about the sheer impossibility of what was required for this to be, becomes the foundation for all future asking. "For nothing is impossible with God" (Luke 1:37). Sometimes we are tempted to question the possibility of a response to what seems to us to be the impossibility of our request. Our perspective is so often limited by both the unchangeable facts of the situation as well as by the lack of personal faith. Jesus Himself acknowledged such circumstances: "With man this is impossible, but not with God. All things are possible with God" (Matthew 19:26). Our estimations about the viability or possibility of divine responsiveness should not in themselves deter our asking, or expectation of a response. It is because He responds that we know that our impossibility has just become a precedent for other possibilities. But what about the impossibility of a situation that we deem to be so, not because it only seems impossible for man to do anything about, but because, for whatever reasons, we believe that it is something that God Himself will do nothing about?

As challenging as it is to our theological algorithms, scripture presents us with situations in which God's response to man's asking would suggest that He had been persuaded to act in a way that He had already decided against. No event captures the idea of a Fall for the Jewish people like the idolatry of the golden calf. The text clearly says that God intended to "destroy" them (Exodus 32:10), so much so, that He wanted to be left alone to do it without any interference or dissuasion. It seems that Moses did not register what God had said about making him into a great nation, so undone was he by the impending disaster. The impossibility of this situation is conveyed through God's language. He had called the Israelites "My people" but now he tells Moses they are "your people" (v7) and "these people" (v9). It sounds sarcastic because it is rooted in the deep pain of being rejected so quickly (v8), resulting in God distancing Himself, disowning them and determining to end the relationship. "Now leave me alone." What if Moses had done that? Calvin of all people, commenting on this scripture, said that it was because God was not left alone that He was not able to freely execute His vengeance. Is there an implied invitation here to Moses not to leave Him alone, but to argue the case, and ask for another outcome?

This is one of the most poignant and holy exchanges between an asking man and an angry God. It is a furnace of emotion. God the lover of the people who has spared nothing for their deliverance and welfare is abandoned in an act of adulterous idolatry. Moses was the loving intimate of God but also deeply torn by his love for the Israelites. The asking that follows is born out of a relational intimacy that bears and shares the burdens of the heart with boldness and safety, oblivious of impossibilities, limitations and arguments against, and is as pure a text on asking as one will find in the Bible. "Moses sought the favor of the Lord" (v11). The premise of his asking was a conviction that he could appeal to the grace of God at this late hour, though running the risk of appearing irreverent, insolent and even defiant. When everything is wrong in a situation we can still be right about God, and was Moses ever! Would not God reveal Himself a few days hence on Sinai, as "the compassionate and gracious God, slow to anger" (34:6)? There are plenty of other things that Moses could have sought in his asking: his own security at a time of crisis, his own future life and ministry with a new nation to boot, his own ticket out of there. As important as Abraham's intercession for Sodom was for our understanding of how and when and why to ask of God, Moses' asking here is perhaps on an even deeper plane. He is not asking with a persuasive appeal for the "righteous" but for sinners who have absolutely nothing to recommend themselves to God's mercy. Abraham's asking pleads for less and less people, as he seems to be heading towards zero righteous. Moses goes below ground zero in his asking and offers his own life and eternal security: "Perhaps I can make atonement for your sin ... Blot me out of the book you have written" (32: 30,32). Here is a tacit acknowledgement of the price that is exacted for our asking and God's answering. There is never a facile response. The Atonement of Christ, no less, is the cost paid for our access to ask of God's grace, and for that grace to respond.

The depths of this passage should be plumbed, since there is so much to discover here about how to ask for a divine response, despite how far gone the situation has plummeted into the dark domain of executable judgment. At least note these observations in Moses pursuit of God's response.

- His asking which began with an appeal to God's changeless character continues with an appeal to a precedent, to a mighty action of God already done: "whom you brought out of Egypt" (v11). Like Moses, our response-seeking asking brings the precedents into the presence. We plead for a response on the basis of prior responses. Respond!
- His asking is a repeated "why?" God wants to be left alone and he is getting in God's face, with driving and argumentative questions. No wonder he knew God face to face. Here is the advocacy of asking that seeks the desired decision from what seems to be an implacable judge. Respond!

- "Why should the Egyptians say ...?" (v12) What will the neighbors think? His asking is zealous for God's name that he does not want to be smeared and shamed by the Egyptians when this rescue fails in a God-forsaken terrain. How can you choose to be so misinterpreted? The whole world is looking on. How can you impugn your name by pulling out now? You will have no street credibility. Respond!
- "Turn ... relent" (v12). His asking appeals to mercy and outrageously, yet reasonably, asks God to change His mind. Respond! Relent!
- "Please forgive their sin" (v31). He asks primarily for forgiveness. Respond!
- "Remember your servants Abraham and Isaac and Israel, to whom you swore by your own self ... I will give your descendants all this land I promised them" (v13). Having begun by arguing the precedents, he ends by pleading the promises. Respond!
- "Then the Lord relented" (v14). There is no need to get our theology wrapped around the axle here. This is an awesome, heart-stopping, voice-hushing, knee-bending, head-bowing anthropomorphic moment. There are 36 times when 'relenting' is described in scripture and on 30 of those occasions the subject is God, and 24 of those 30 times it speaks of God changing His mind. In the majority of those incidents (19 out of 24) He changes His mind away from judgment. The lavish outpouring of the gracious and merciful heart of God has a way of flooding the chambers of our philosophical theologies. We have to listen beyond the limitations of the language to hear what is being said, and the primary thing we need to hear is not that God changes His mind, but that God responds because He desires to save and will go to the uttermost to do so. The irony is that being true to His infinite self, to His character and His promises, His 'relenting' appears to be untrue to His unchangeable self as perceived by our finite minds. The common reason for God to relent, to respond beyond the pale, is because of a repentance that asks first for forgiveness. "If at any time I announce that a nation or kingdom is to be uprooted, torn down and destroyed, and if that nation I warned *repents* of its evil, then I will *relent* and not inflict on it the disaster I had planned" (Jeremiah 18:7-8). The response of relenting is to the asking of repenting. Through the prophet

Joel, God invites the people to ask with fasting in order to change His mind about sending an already intended calamity. "Rend your heart ... Return to the Lord your God for He is gracious and compassionate, slow to anger and abounding in love and He relents from sending calamity" (Joel 2:12-13). So hundreds of years after Moses' asking at Sinai, Joel affirms the same grounds for asking for a response from God, for the inevitability of judgment to be averted. Because indeed God changes not, we can depend on His responsiveness and plead those same grounds in our asking today.

Neither Vending Machine Nor Butler

That we do not receive a response to our asking on our terms (the what, the when, the how) does not mean that God does not respond. Any response to God's apparent non-response – complaints and even accusations about God's apparent inaction, deafness, silence, absence, indifference, non-engagement, distance – is wrong. Thereby, we imply His culpability and then impugn His character. If the response is not good for us, then God's goodness ends up being questioned. God hears and He responds to what He hears: "God is not a man that He should lie" (Numbers 23:19). That God may have other responses other than the ones we would prefer, comes as a challenge to those who would treat Him as if He is obliged to vend only according to the buttons they push, and provide only the benefits they seek to procure. They stare in dismay at the empty compartment of their need-space and wonder at the silence of the machine. Is anyone at home in there? They cannot believe that God, like a waiter who serves our table, could not bring from His kitchen anything that is asked for from the tasting-menu of their need. The subject of "unanswered asking" will be discussed in a later chapter, but for now, suffice it to affirm that we have seen that there are many reasons why God chooses not to hear. That is a response, but of course, not one we want. Such responses are utterly consistent with the righteousness of God's character, and with His love for us that will not dispense what is contrary to His will and His word, His plan and His purpose for our lives. We may feel the worst when He knows what is best, but as surely as we know that God hears what we ask for, so surely can we know that He will always respond to the matter, in a manner, in a moment, by a means that will ultimately bless us and glorify Him.

First Responder

"First-response" is a common phrase in our troubled world that we usually employ in a context of emergency and crisis. The concern of "first response teams" is that the time lapse between the asking and the responding is a minimum. In their emergencies, the psalmists wanted God to "come quickly" (Psalm 102:2; Psalm 141:1) and we do too. The temptation is to conclude that if God does not respond with what I have decided I need, when I have determined that I need it, then He has not responded.

Long before any response to our asking, God has been responding. He has always been the "first responder" on the scene of our spiritual wreckage. No sooner had our first parents slipped into their fig-wear, than God initiated a conversation by asking: "Where are you?" (Genesis 3:9). It was His asking response to our fallen parents that was seeking to solicit their response to Him. Redemption's rescue was fully engaged. Long before Abraham asked anything of God, the Lord responded to his situation in Haran and spoke to him, and the rescue of the nations was fully engaged (Genesis 12:1). The enslaved Israelites' groans were heard by God and He responded to them, and the rescue of His people from bondage was fully engaged (Exodus 1:24). The silence of four hundred years was broken by God as He responded to those living in darkness and in Zechariah's words, the rescue from the hand of enemies was fully engaged (Luke 1:74). While we were still sinners, Christ responded to us and died for us to rescue us from the present evil age. Before we ever asked for anything, God had already responded to our need and the plan for our salvation was fully engaged. This is why we have already argued that our asking does not initiate anything, so much as serve as an answer to what God has already said and already done throughout redemption history, but superbly and supremely in these last days through what He has said to us by His Son Jesus. All our asking is in fact our response to His first-response to us.

The point is that *God is a responder to those who ask* and as we have noted, He takes the initiative to get us to invite His response, to receive His gifts and rewards. And then of course, He responds over the top, in His "more than we asked" style. Luther commented on the number of times we ask for silver and He gives us gold. He wants to respond – it is His nature, therefore He asks us to ask Him so He can have an excuse to keep giving and blessing. The Psalmist speaks of the divine response as the "reward of the righteous" (58:11) but the greatest reward of all is the same for us as it was for Abraham. It was not the promised land nor even the generations that he would ask God for, in his nomadic and childless state. God said, "*I am your very great reward*" (Genesis 15:1). It is this experience of intimacy with God, this responsiveness of love, this relationship with the Giver, that is always the greatest response and reward to our asking. As Oswald Chambers commented: "Have you been asking God what He is going to do? He will never tell you. God does not tell you what He is going to do; He reveals to you who He is." [16] Like children who have asked for something, we judge the response by what is in the hand of the one asked, not what is in the heart. God responds and comes to us in His presence, even if the 'present' we want does not come. In any loving relationship, we always want the person more than the present, the giver more than the gift, the answerer more than the answer. Requesting is but the bedroom door to relating. His first response to what we ask for is always His presence: "The Lord is near to those who call on Him ... You will call ... and He will say, 'Here I am'" (Psalm 145:18; Isaiah 58:9).

Your Call ... My Response

It is so important that we are sure about God's heart for us, and about how His ear, His hand, and His eye all bend towards response. Any who doubt God's responsiveness will minimize the need to ask anything of God. This is a denial of the possibility of a personal relationship with God, in which responsive asking and answering is the very core of intimate communication. If you have experienced any intimacy in any relationship, you will know the freedom there is, the safety and assurance that you can ask about anything, assured of a response. Asking ceases to be just about being functional: we are not just asking to get information or knowledge, or just to do something, or satisfy self-interest. Our asking in this intimate context is an expression of faithfulness, more than functionality. It matters to us what the other thinks. It is a way of getting inside them as it were. It is a way of pleasing them and blessing them, that we would include their counsel as necessary in our decision-making; that we would value their insight or input; that we would humbly acknowledge our need of their answer and response; that we would want them to be involved in the direction and outcomes of our life; that we would simply ask and ask because we just wanted to know everything about them in and through their responses.

It is important to reiterate that whether or not we receive what we asked for, when we asked for it, God responds. This is what Forsyth called "response even when we get no compliance." [17] He goes on to remark that when we ask in faith, although that does not necessarily mean that we are absolutely sure that we will receive what we ask, we are sure that our "prayer is heard and stored." The 'storing' was the divine response. The "prayers of the saints", answered or not, were responded to by heaven (Revelation 5:8).

God has chosen our asking as a way for Him to respond to us. When God calls through Isaiah, "Ask of me" or says through Jeremiah, "Call on me" or through the psalmist, "Ask me", the assurance of His desire to respond is premised in the invitation. Not surprisingly, in case we did not get that, often God follows up by explicitly saying, "and I will ... answer ... give ... send ... show you ... save ... deliver ... turn back the enemies ... keep ... forgive ... heal ... restore to full well-being ... relieve your distress ... uphold their cause ... send a word." Do your own study. God's response is never just about getting things done, even good kingdom things. Fundamentally it has to do with the deepening of the responsiveness of intimate relationship with Him. Listen to John 15:7 again: "If you remain in me and my words remain in you, ask whatever you wish and it will be given you." The response is assured ("it will be given") but note that the invitation here to ask is not unconditional. It is not about Him responding to anything we want, any way we want it, any time that works for us. It is conditionally premised: "if you remain in me." Asking is the response of abiding, to which God responds. In other words, our asking and His responding is the outcome of our union with Christ. We should be amazed at ourselves that even when in desperate straits, the obvious times to ask of God, the consequence of our lack of intimacy is still to huff and puff and sweat and fret, and shout and pout and curse and worse, as if God is not willing and ready to respond. We need to stop reacting to circumstance and start relating to Him. When it comes to asking – God responds.

"Father, if it is possible... Yet not as I will, but as you will." - Jesus

"Because you are sons, God sent the Spirit of his Son into our hearts, the Spirit who calls out, 'Abba, Father!'" – Apostle Paul

"We doubt not to take ourselves to Him in a familiar manner, as to a Father." - John Calvin, Genevan catechism Q250

"He petitions God ... as if he was in the divine presence, and yet with as firm a hope and confidence as we would address a father and friend." – someone describing Martin Luther praying

"There is no father who would be satisfied that his son should take everything and ask for nothing ... Petition is not mere receptivity, nor is it mere pressure; it is filial reciprocity ... If God is really the Father that Christ revealed, then the principle is – take everything to Him that exercises you." - P.T.Forsyth

"O how great a task it is, for a poor soul that becomes sensible of sin and the wrath of God, to say in faith but this one word: 'Father!' ... Here is the life of prayer ... when he comes, I say, in the strength of the Spirit and cries Father." - John Bunyan

"Prayer is ... the acknowledgement of God's fatherhood." - Alfred de Quervain

"We shall not have the reserve of a slave but the loving reverence of a child." - C.H.Spurgeon

7

He Fathers

By His Nature God Is Our Father

God is the one who hears our asking and the one who responds. We have seen that both of these attributes give "confidence" (1 John 5:14) to our asking. But there is a third truth that is the foundational one that Jesus most emphasized in His teaching and exampled in His practice. To those who love God and are His sons and daughters by spiritual adoption, *He is the Father*. It is this familial and filial relationship and trust that grounds our confidence in asking. As Forsyth described it, Jesus "made the all-knowing Fatherhood the ground of true prayer. We do not ask as beggars but as children." [1] We have already seen that our asking is answering and that we are invited to ask in a child-like way of the Father. Dietrich Bonhoeffer understood the relationship between these two truths. "The child learns to speak because the father speaks to him. He learns the speech of his father. So we learn to speak to God because God has spoken to us and speaks to us." He understood that the reason we can ask in the first place, is because we have the speech of the Father, and when we ask, we are simply repeating the Father's "own words after Him." [2] It is the most natural thing in the world for children to ask the father. If earthly fathers will give their sons what they ask, "How much more will your Father in heaven give the Holy Spirit to those who ask Him?" (Luke11:13) And how does the prayer that Jesus taught as a model for all our asking begin? "Our Father." How did Jesus always ask? "Father, Lord of heaven and earth" (Matthew 11:25); "My Father if it is possible, may this cup be taken from me" (Matthew 26:39). Following the raising of Lazarus, Jesus makes clear the ground of His assurance for His own asking: "Father I thank you that you have heard me" (John 11: 41). If last words give any indication to what is of utmost importance, then it should be noted that in the Last Supper discourse, Jesus references the Father 44 times and 6 times in His 'high priestly' prayer. "I will ask the Father" (John 14:16); "Father, the time has come" (John 17:1); "Do you think I cannot ask my Father for twelve legions of angels" (Matthew 26:53). Our asking does not begin in *our* relationship with Father, Son and Holy Spirit, but in *their* relationship with each other.

Do you see what all this means for our asking? It is not just some expression of our need initiated by us. The asking Godhead invites us to boldly ask. Our asking has been elevated, honored, and blessed. The Father invited the Son to ask Him. The Son did. The Son now asks us to ask the Father. We do. They invite us to insert our asking into their communications with each other. They all get in on it, and they respond to it, and thereby we discover this relationship between asking and accessing. To ask is to access the Trinity no less. How can we minimize asking or treat it like an immature thing, or a lesser form of prayer?

This also helps us understand what the main outcome of our asking is all about. It is not our particular answer, but as Jesus put it, "This is to my Father's glory!" (John 15:8). John Piper rightly remarks that "The first function of prayer is to pray that people will pursue the glory of God." [3] But the glory of God is not just something we are asking for. Our very act of asking itself is to the glory of God. Our asking is the great means to the glorification of God. "Ask and I will do whatever you ask in my name ... so the Son may bring glory to the Father" (John14:13). The more asking then the more glory to God, not just from us but from Jesus Himself. Asking is the way we express our pursuit of His glory in all the earth, and the way we give Him glory. Was this not the entire point and purpose of Jesus's asking in His last hours? "Father ... glorify your son that your Son may glorify you" (John 17:1). In our theology of asking it is the fatherhood of God that is the premise for all assurance about the naturalness, the necessity, the liberty, the appropriateness, the expectation, the confidence of asking. The only limit on our asking is the limitation of our relationship with the Father.

The evidence of the New Testament is theologically conclusive and therefore persuasive about this. Asking of "the Father" is the essential expression of prayer. As we shall see, this is not to say that we cannot address the Son or the Spirit. The apostles and the early church did, and so do we. Asking is thoroughly Trinitarian, and is expressed by each person of the Trinity, as well as expressed by us to each member of the Trinity. We could describe our asking as 'Trinity asking'. Trust Paul to be so fervent in his asking that he manages to ask of and for all three persons in the same breath: "I kneel before the *Father*, from whom the whole family in heaven and earth derives its name. I pray that out of His glorious riches He may strengthen you with power through His *Spirit* in your inner being, so that *Christ* may dwell in your hearts through faith" (Ephesians 3:14-17). This is consistent with Paul's understanding of all communication with God: he exhorts the Ephesians to be "filled with the *Spirit*, giving thanks to God the *Father* in the name of our Lord *Jesus Christ*" (Ephesians 5:18-19). Asking of the Father was the normative address.

The fatherhood of God is the underpinning of the apostles' theology of asking. Just before he tells us that it is the Spirit who helps us when we do not know what we should ask for, Paul tells us that the most instinctive cry of the Spirit of sonship through us is "Abba, Father" (Romans 8:15, 26). Asking is the response of a son to the Father. It is what sons do all the time. How different is the asking of a son to what A.B.Simpson described as "the spasmodic cries of great emergencies rather than the habitual intercourse of a heavenly life." [4] The Apostle James understood that every thing that we ask for, including wisdom and every good and perfect gift, comes from the Father, the God he exhorts us to ask (James 1:5,17). When it came to asking, the apostles got it: "Since you call on a Father" (1 Peter 1:17); "We have an advocate with the Father" (1 John 2:1). Paul got it: "I keep asking ... the glorious Father ... For this reason I kneel before the Father" (Ephesians 1:17; 3:14). Like Jesus, and like the apostles, our asking is related to our assurance of God's fathering. The object of all asking and the consequent source of all answering is the Father. This was the bedrock conviction of the early church as it asked of God from the very beginning, when their asking of the Father in the upper room, imitative of Jesus's asking of the same Father for the same thing, received that commonly desired answer of the Father, the gift of the Holy Spirit.

The Father of Our Lord Jesus Christ

The most compelling evidence is that provided by Jesus Himself. It has been commonly noted that in every recorded instance of Jesus ever asking for anything, we hear Him asking His Father, with one notable exception. I say notable because there is little discussion as to why this is so. My conviction is that though at first this seems to be a contradiction to the pattern of Jesus's asking, it turns out to be a total confirmation, intensely powerful by virtue of the horrendous context for its utterance. The request in question is: "My God, my God, why have you forsaken me?" (Matthew 27:46) Jesus is directly quoting from Psalm 22:1. In "A Grief Observed" processing the death of his wife Joy through cancer, after much asking for healing and momentary signs of answers, C.S.Lewis asks, "Why is He ... so very an absent help in time of trouble?" [5] Jesus is not recorded as saying the remainder of that verse He quoted, but it is certainly implied: "Why are you so far from saving me, so far from the words of my groaning?" A few verses later in the Psalm we read: "O Lord, be not far off" (v19).

This is the last occasion in His earthly life that Jesus asks for anything. Here the horror of the nature of our sin that brought this separation between the Father and the Son is experienced and expressed, described by the psalmist as the Father hiding his face from the Son (Psalm 69:17). Jesus experienced this separation in every part of His physical, emotional, psychological and spiritual being moments before He died, not just concomitant with the moment of death itself. This is the ultimate loss of intimacy, the inability to ask of the Father who hears and answers the Son. We might say that Jesus's life ends with unanswered asking. This is the same Jesus who had earlier said to the Father "You always hear me" (John 11:42). But then Matthew and Mark describe what comes from his lips as "a loud cry" (Matthew 27:50; Mark 15:37). Luke and John give us further information: "It is finished ... Father, into your hands I commit my Spirit." What are we to make of this? Were both of these statements part of that final loud cry? It would seem that despite the fact that Jesus could not feel the presence of His Father in that agonizing asking "Why?", nonetheless, so incontrovertibly, indestructibly, eternally true and powerful and present is the fathering of God, that against all odds, against all sense, against all feeling, against all hope, against all abandonment, that inviolable truth is cried out by Jesus as loudly as His remaining strength of lungs allows. Despite the unanswered asking, there is a repeat of the Gethsemane experience, in that the unanswered asking in no way questions the holy integrity of the Father. So despite all that the eye sees on Golgotha, the Father yet hears and surely will yet respond. For Jesus, that response to what the Father heard was not the next day, or the day after, but it was "on the third day".

One other observation while we are at the cross. It is so significant that in Matthew's account the first words recorded by anyone following the death of Christ and the apparent unanswered asking by Jesus of His Father, are those of the Roman centurion. Similar to Peter's revelation at Caesarea Philippi, this was no less a revelation by the Holy Spirit. "Surely this was the Son of God" (Matthew 27:54). The new era, post-cross, is inaugurated with an incredible confession out of the mouth of a Gentile. Moved by the Spirit he declared Jesus to be the Son of God, which presumably means that God is the Father. If we are following the story, it means that despite what just seems to have happened to the Son, despite the hanging unanswered question of the Son, there will be an answer, precisely because God is still Father, and there will be more asking, because God is Father, and there is probably something going on here that has, as part of its purpose, the preservation and perpetuity of more sons and daughters asking of the Father.

There would be nothing more difficult for Jesus to explain than why, given His unanswered asking, He was still assured at that moment of abandonment that he had a loving Father. Where is there any evidence of fathering? Did not the cross cry out desertion and dereliction? Could there be any more acute theological and personal embarrassment? No son likes being embarrassed by his father. It creates a stinging relational distance, and is felt as deep shame. Scripture tells us that Jesus "endured the cross, scorning its shame" (Hebrews 12:2). Much has been written about the shame of the cross as it relates to that mode of dying with its attendant shame of nakedness and public humiliation. But there were other elements to that shame. Was Jesus not mocked: "He saved others but He could not save Himself." What He asked for others was answered but what He now asks for Himself, when He needs it most, is unanswered. The shame of forsakenness, of the appearance of fatherly forgetfulness, of unanswered asking is crippling.

Being shamed by a parent naturally separates, and the painful self-consciousness and potential feeling of betrayal, roots in the heart. Shame drives us to inward questioning of self, and away from outward asking of the father. Shame sets up the table for blame, and we cease to ask those we blame - accuse, maybe, but not ask. To ask implies trust as well as the trustworthy capacities of the one we ask to help us. Shame breeds fear, so fear of the other displaces faith in the other. Unresolved shame separates so many from the Father and convinces them that what once was, in trusting asking and answering, cannot be now or ever; that what was an unanswered request is where their life stopped, and cannot be restarted. There was shame for Jesus, or He would not have had to despise it, and disallow its power to affect His relationship with the Father.

If it is the shame of personal sin that is convincing us that we no longer have the right to ask the Father as a true son or daughter, then remember that Jesus took care of that shame as well, despising its power to keep us trapped in self-shaming and self-blaming. Shame is a real result of real sin, but its power over us is broken when in repentance we ask for forgiveness. Asking breaks the silence of shame and picks up again the dropped conversation of intimate asking and answering with the Father. The text says that Jesus "endured" the cross and "endured" the opposition, and in the same way we too can "endure" hardship, which may include like Jesus, the hardship of unanswered asking. But have you read Hebrews 12 recently? It immediately goes on to say that we may have "forgotten that word of encouragement that addresses you as sons" (v5). Although circumstance and feeling may have caused us to feel estranged from the Father, the relational change has been ours not His. The text admits that we are tempted to "lose heart" amidst difficulty, delay and discipline. "God is treating you as sons" which means He is still fathering us the best of all possible ways, though the best does not feel good. The ultimate purpose is not that all our asking is answered, but that as sons and daughters we grow in the family likeness "that we may share in His holiness." So in the same way that Jesus submitted and committed His spirit to the Father, with what he was asking for in the pending file, even so the writer of Hebrews urges us to "submit to the Father of our spirits and live!"

You can understand then why any lack of conviction or trust about God's fathering, whatever its source or root, is such a need for healing because it is such a hindrance to the confidence of intimate asking. Where there is no knowledge of God's fathering, it is not that people will not ask, it is just that they will ask of other "religiously approved" sources, like saints. "Not knowing God as a kind and willing Father, a God who brings us close, Luther found he could not love Him. He and his fellow monks transferred their affections to Mary and various other saints; it was them they would love and to them they would pray." [6] Any weakening of our sense of sonship, anything that subverts our assurance of His fatherhood and fathering, will be a weakening in our confidence to ask, or a redirecting of our asking from Father to other sources.

There are many who will religiously acknowledge the Fatherhood of God in a creational or creedal sense, but do not know God in a personal fathering sense, not because God is an absent uninvolved father, but because they have such distortions of fatherhood through injurious parental experience; or because, though spiritual sons and daughters, they are actually living as orphans or slaves in the Father's house. Let us briefly consider these possibilities and their effects on asking.

Why Sons and Daughters Don't Ask

So many key experiences in childhood have been identified that are like time-bombs waiting to explode with disabling force in the lives of adults. One might argue that the devastation of so many lives in childhood is precisely the devil's way to eliminate the safe and secure, dependent and devoted childlikeness that is a pre-requisite for intimate asking of God. It has been estimated that the roots of most personal brokenness are to be found in a pre-seven year-old experience. "Father-wounds" in particular have huge consequences for our asking. If assurance about the Father is the ground of confident asking, then any undermining of that confidence will subvert asking. In the early 1980's, Pastor Robert Frost (better known for his book 'Aglow with the Spirit') was part of the church community that I served and I was privileged to sit under his teaching. He was a pioneer in this area that I am now addressing and I am indebted to his pastoral insights. [7] There are many well-documented wounds that might be familiar to you in your own experience and ministry, but we need to apply their consequences in a way that explains their effects on sons and daughters who either fear to ask or refuse to ask.

1. **The fatherless child:** Whether so because of death, divorce, desertion, or because of the common experience of a father who is physically present but emotionally absent, the pains of absence make it hard to believe and experience the reality of Father God's presence. Asking assumes a present and responsive relationship, or else there is no trust in asking.
2. **The embittered child:** There are fathers that have goaded their children, whose practiced and habitual forms of response and behavior have engendered deep-rooted anger. The reluctance of such offspring to submit to God as Father can be understood if not excused. Where there is bitterness, the communication is marked by accusing, not asking.
3. **The ignored child:** So many develop a feeling of utter worthlessness, convinced there is nothing sufficient about them to attract attention, as they have no memories of endearment or affection, of tactile joy, from fathers who condemned their children in later life to performance without personality, seeking God's approval without expectation of His affection. If you do not think you have God's attention and attentiveness, you do not ask.
4. **The unwanted child:** Despair and self-loathing can beset those who have been branded an accident, either in birth, in gender, or in timing, whose life is just an impediment, one irregular smudge blot in the life of another. Many of these have an experience of fatherhood that leaves them asking: How can Father God be really interested in me? How can I be desirable to God? He is God so He has to love me but He puts up with me because I would not be

the child of choice. So God is now the reluctant father, technically loving because He is meant to be a loving God, but actually He is perceived as always disliking what He sees. They have been foisted on God by Jesus and God is stuck with it. For such, messages about heaven do not hold much joy, and there is no expectation to ask for anything for future happiness.

5. **The threatened child:** The threat of damnation and doom continues to linger for those who were the victims of anger, failures at obedience, and judged by parental legalism. For such, God is often the fearful father, who is never satisfied. Obedience and love have been divorced, and all that is left is command and coercion. The imperative quenches and suppresses the natural interrogative of a child who is genuinely asking and not seeking to countermand or question authority or disobey. If father always says 'No' or 'Shut up!' then why bother asking.
6. **The abused child:** Sexual molestation and the physical abuse of children is one of the most spiritually terrorizing scourges of the day. Beyond the physical abuse, there is also the emotional abuse that may have to do with rage on the one hand and neglect on the other. Children that are the victims of spiraling parental anger, children who remind their parents of past spouses, past relationships, past failures, often seem to believe that God is equally vindictive and arbitrary. Locked into fearfulness, withdrawal and self-destruction, they find it difficult to believe in a love that is clean and pure and a mercy that is just and fair. Why would you expect to receive what is asked for, if your only experience is that of having what is yours being taken from you? You do not ask of one you fear.
7. **The guilty child:** So many children whose lives were interrupted by the eruptions of family pain and division became punch bags for parental irreconciliation, or they were made the cause of parental disagreement, or were wrongly accused. Their tender but terrorized spirits took into themselves the grief and the guilt of the fall-out, as if they were the cause of what happened. But there are also those who bore an imposed guilt, whose father chose to never forget something, whose injured pride was incapable of nurturing forgiveness, of nourishing restoration and lovingly encouraging the

formation of the child. These were fathers whose own childishness, and immature self-protective sensitivities condemned their children to undeveloped emotions, leaving them stuck in this world of unabsolved guilt. Such feel no boldness to approach the throne of grace in time of need. How can such indoctrinated unworthiness dare to ask for grace and favor?

8. **The dominated child:** The expressions of frustration are myriad in those whose parents imposed false expectations on them as children to satisfy their own selfish concerns, who consequently condemned their children to believe that God's will was most likely to be an enforcement upon them that could not possibly bring fulfillment or freedom. Obedience with joy is hard to come by when fearful and resented compliance has been the order of life. What joy could there possibly be in asking according to Father's will or believing that you could ask for what you desired?
9. **The unloved child:** This is fundamental to everything already mentioned. So many who had to compete for their father's love and attention ended up resorting to other sources. The father-deficit is responsible for many ending up in addiction to pornography – the tragic search for feeling in contexts that can offer no faithfulness in relationship. For such it is hard to believe that God is interested in loving them, in embracing who they are, in treating them as the apple of his eye. If you doubt the love of God for you, why ask for that which only love would freely give?
10. **The pampered child:** Our culture is littered with indulgent children, who because indulged, think that fathers only say "yes" immediately to everything, so somehow God is nothing but a sugar-daddy. Their idolatries of self are rooted in being unhealthily idolized. It is hard for such to discover and develop a sense of responsible sonship and daughterhood. They feel confused when leanness and famine invade their experience and there is no blank check to supply the need. Asking does not work because Father God's answers are perceived as both inadequate and overdue.

Behind all these characteristics is a reservoir of pain and disfigurement. Now think of the sum total effect of all that on the heart of our heavenly Father.

What of His unrequited heart? Some observers have commented that 4 out of 5 radical dysfunctions in personhood can be put at the door of delinquent or absent fathering. Our attitudes to our earthly fathers can condition our attitudes toward God. Tremendous healing and deliverance ensues when the Holy Spirit reveals these roots, and exposes the lies of the enemy, not simply about God's fathering, but the lies about us that have resulted, that have now become our lies, and that have been the bricks of the walls of defensiveness that we have surely built but find it hard to acknowledge. These lies have stopped us being the sons and daughters we have always wanted to be, were made to be, but were denied to be. The enemy of our souls, but more particularly of God, will cede us any manner of relationships with God: working, serving, believing – just so long as we are not relating as a son or a daughter who can ask of the Father with both confidence and joy. The work of the enemy is to stop us asking, and therefore relating to our Father; to silence us by opposing the truth of our sonship and deceiving us into living, not as an asking son, but as a silent and sullen slave or orphan.

When Sons and Daughters Live As Slaves and Orphans

If there is a lack of assurance about God's fathering then we will be vulnerable to live as slaves or as orphans, and not as sons and daughters. Neither slaves nor orphans have the basis of relationship to be confident about asking. The slave has no rights to ask, because the predominant communication that governs the relationship is the command of the master and the enforced obedience of the slave. The orphan, if he thinks he has any rights at all compared to the slave, still knows they are very limited in their claims when compared to those who are related by blood, and who have an unquestioned expectation and a right, not only to ask for present provision but also for future inheritance. Once you understand the marks of a slave-spirit, or an orphan-spirit, you will realize why they not merely subvert our asking but silence it altogether.

Rooted in fear. "You did not receive a spirit that makes you a slave again to fear, but you received the spirit of sonship." Note what immediately follows: "And by Him we cry 'Abba, Father'" (Romans 8:15). The evidence of assured sonship is the asking of the Father based on an intimate knowledge of Abba.

It is because there is no trusting or loving relationship between a slave and his master, that fear is the order of the day. We are held in "slavery" by fear (Hebrews 2:15). It is fear not love that will primarily govern our responses, especially when the fear is rooted in lack of assurance about relationship with Father God, and about what makes for pleasing Father. The fear of the slave is a fear of intimacy. The binding of love is exchanged for the bondage of fear. If we are bound by fear-driven performance then we are not obeying out of love, the true mark of sonship, and we will have no need to ask because frankly, we are taking care of everything ourselves. Where there is no confidence in the Father because of fear, then our control of circumstance will take over. That is the choice: holy confidence or unholy control. We solve and resolve everything required without asking of the Father. Slaves have a fear of asking.

Dependent on false grounds for confidence: The slave spirit, in the absence of the assurances of sonship, will seek out counterfeit assurances and affections, and counterfeit forms of comfort and counsel. If we are not asking the Father, we will have to ask from some source or other. We will get our information and our inspiration from somewhere, from someone. The devil is ready to supply any number of counterfeit answers to our asking. Is not this how the scriptural record begins? To the implied question about why they should not eat "from the tree that is in the middle of the garden" (Genesis 3:3) there was a ready Satanic answer. The world is full of gurus and prognosticators, charlatans and false prophets, advisors and experts, coaches and mentors, available to be asked about the meaning of life and its stewardship. Where there is loss of confidence because there is no conviction or experience of God's fathering, then the need for counterfeit grounds for self-confidence will satisfy itself, and submit to the binding legalisms and demands of ungodly philosophies and methodologies and doctrines of demons. Counterfeit assurance does not ask.

In bondage to self: Father-consciousness of the son is replaced by self-consciousness of the slave. Where there is limited trust in the love of the Father, there will be independence, and independence does not ask. Where there is uncertainty about God's fatherly affections, there will be uncertainty about His response, and such uncertainty does not dare to ask. Where there is no safe relationship to acknowledge need, there will be self-reliance and there will be no need to ask. Where there is no sense of the Father's affirmation, no acceptance of the value with which the Father sees us, then there will a denial of holy self-worth and self-rejection, and if you are convinced you do not deserve anything, then you will not ask for anything. Usually, where there is no holy value of self, there will be a corresponding devaluing of others. It is only when you value others that you ask on their behalf. The self-consumptiveness of personal insecurity does not leave time or will for asking for others. It also produces an introspection that leads to a self-evaluation that in turn ends up as self-condemnation, and we know from the apostle John that condemnation runs interference with confidence in asking (1 John 3:21). There is a world of difference between serving as a slave by legal command, and serving as a son by loving consent. Slaves who have worked out a way to get on and get by on their own (self-reliant, self-motivated, self-driven, self-maintained, self-comforted, self-justifying) slaving alone in the field like the elder brother, do not ask.

Without future hope: Outside the cross of Christ, there is probably no description of greater dereliction and hopelessness than the one we find in Lamentations, portraying the fall of Jerusalem. The people described themselves as children who "have gone into exile, captive before the foe" (Lamentations 1:5). They had become slaves. They also describe themselves as "orphans and fatherless" (5:3). Is it any wonder that they said, "He shuts out my prayer" (3:8) or that they concluded that God had covered himself with a cloud "so that no prayer can get through" (3:44). Asking is in vain. It is impossible to believe there is any hope for the future. There is nothing to ask for, so no point in asking at all. It is only the reconnect with the fathering love and compassions of God that recovered the asking, so that later we read: "I called on your name ... You heard my plea ... You came near when I called you and you said: 'Do not fear'" (3:55). The slave has no hope for a change in their position, or their prospects. Asking for the future is disallowed. Servility destroys the human spirit and when hope is crushed, asking is futile. There are so many reasons that people get to this place, and become enslaved to disappointment, despondency, depression and despair. Future hope is not only lost, it can be abandoned when there is a loss of faith for the present. If hope is mocked or eroded, by whatever cause and for whatever reason, asking ceases. Other forms of communication like blame and complaint displace asking.

Increased hostility: For the slave, it is all about the assignments and the duty and the performance but there is no joy with it. The misery breeds resentments and envy, and treats as an enemy the one who would be Father, and of course, you don't usually ask for help from enemies. This hostility encourages the belief of lies about the Father: that He is capricious, or callous, or neglectful, or like the hard taskmaster in Jesus's parable of the talents. Such a one is not open to hear and listen to asking. If you watch the older brother in Jesus's parable, because of this spirit of a slave, you see how contempt and disdain for the father have come into his heart. His entire perspective on life and others' lives has been twisted so there is no discernment of the father's heart. It is impossible for a slave to enter into the joy of a son. He can only see the party as an insult because it seems to suggest the younger son's worth and value. Disdain for the other son is disdain for the Father, and disdain does not ask. If you envy another you will not ask on their behalf. Again, there is no asking here, only accusing, and increasing anger. The anger he expresses to the father is full of nothing but his own self-interest and self-deserving: "All these years *I've* been slaving ... You never gave *me* ... so *I* could celebrate." This is precisely the father's point in the story when he responds to this slave mentality (Luke 15:31). "My son, you are always with me." This is the intimacy of a father, not the intimidation of a master. "And everything I have is yours." This is the freedom to ask that comes from that assured intimacy. What is the father saying to the son who was choosing to treat the father as a master and to live like a slave? "All you had to do was ASK!" That's what sons do! But it is not what slaves do. The bondage gags the asking.

Hopefully, the point has been made. When there is a fracture in our assurance of our relationship with the Father, when we are tempted to live as a slave or orphan instead of a son, the external conflicts with circumstance and the internal conflicts with self will eliminate our asking. You do not ask of a source you have chosen not to trust. Anger and pride, hostility and hopelessness, fear and resignation, do not ask.

It is precisely because we are sons and daughters that we are free to ask of the Father. That God is our Father is the glorious truth that validates our asking; that nurtures and loves us as we wait in the answer-gap for the responses to our asking. What above all things assures our asking, and anchors our theology of asking? We can sum up these last three chapters about how our asking is validated: by the God who hears us, by the God who responds to us and by the God who Fathers us. In the words of Jesus: "Father, I thank you that you have heard me" (John 11:41). Jesus had a *Father* who *heard* and *responded*. Yours will too.

Asking and Jesus

"Go to the Blessed Master and ask him to enroll your names in that school; which He always keeps open for those who long to study the divine art of prayer and intercession." – Andrew Murray

"Prayer for Jesus is inextricably bound up with the work of God in the world. To pray is, at heart, to ask God to do what He has promised." – J. Gary Millar

8

He Asked

Strange as this may seem, I would strongly advise you to stop reading this book, and start reading a better one. I am suggesting that you get a Bible, sit down and slowly read through all four gospels – always an overwhelming experience – and focus on any and every reference either to Jesus's asking of the Father, or to His teaching about asking. Not surprisingly, it runs as a continuous and unifying thread throughout the narrative. Everyone would like to see the *interventions* of Jesus but fewer are interested in the preliminary *intercessions*. We would like to *act* as He did but we do not seem to be in such a hurry to *ask* as He did.

Asking Prefaced the Mission of Jesus

Every stage of Jesus' emerging and developing mission is grounded in asking. It is both the field and the fertilizer for the growth of the mission. The nativity story that opens the New Testament begins with Zechariah being told that his asking "had been heard" (Luke 1:13). The ensuing narrative provides one example after another of asking and its blessings and challenges, as the asking of Mary, Anna and Simeon undergird the unfolding story. Asking then preceded the moment of Jesus's acceptance of His divine vocation, when He went public in His messianic mission: "as He was praying … heaven was opened and the Holy Spirit descended" (Luke 3:21). Here is the nonnegotiable relationship between all mission and asking.

Asking prefaced Jesus's emergence in public ministry. It was after 40 days of asking and fasting in the wilderness that the public mission was launched (Luke 4:1). Private prayer preceded public proclamation; asking alone before God was the preparation for appearing in public before men. Again, it was about asking before acting. Asking preceded Jesus's assembling of His mission team: "Jesus went out to a mountainside to pray and spent the night praying to God." Next morning He chooses His disciples (Luke 6:12). It was asking before appointing - asking before acting.

Asking Was the Means for the Mission of Jesus

There are several code words and phrases for Jesus's asking of His Father.

- "**solitary place**" (Matthew 14:13). This is the code that describes the asking before the feeding of the 5,000. This phrase is littered through the gospels. Jesus "went off to a solitary place where He prayed" (Mark 1:35); Jesus "at daybreak went out to a solitary place" (Luke 4:42).
- **"lonely place"** "Jesus often withdrew to a lonely place and prayed" (Luke 5:16). This is contrasted with the preceding description (5:15) of a crowded place where He ministered: "crowds of people came to hear Him." The public platform of mission that engaged people always related to the private place of asking that engaged God. In Mark 1:45 He goes to a lonely place (to ask) because the mission drove Him there as He could no longer "enter a town openly." Asking preceded mission and mission provoked and promoted asking. Jesus was not just off to the next miracle-meeting with people but to the next prayer-meeting with His Father. He was not just acting and healing, but asking and hearing. So in the very first chapter of Mark's account of Jesus's life and ministry, the primary and foundational relationship is established between teaching, preaching and healing in public among crowds, and asking in private alone.
- **"mountain"** In John 6:15 we read that Jesus "withdrew to a mountain by Himself." Here is another code word for asking. The mountain was associated with prayer. So the mention of "mountainside" and asking is synonymous. In Matthew 14:23, it was after He had been "up on a mountainside to pray" that we then read "all who touched Him were healed" (v35). This is the same pattern already observed.

He goes from hearing God to healing people; talking to God to touching people; asking of God to acting for God.

- **"Mount of Olives"** He especially loved to go to the Mount of Olives, His favorite asking place and of course His final one. "Then each went to his own home. But Jesus went to the Mount of Olives" (John 8:1). This is a good example of His asking of His Father preceding questions asked by His enemies. Out of that asking of the Father came the answers that silenced the questions concerning the woman taken in adultery (vs. 8-11).

What is interesting throughout the gospels is the frequency with which His attempts to get time alone to ask are interrupted by the needs of the people who wanted Him to act. This emphasizes the necessity of our asking of the Father, before the needs of the world ask anything of us, but it also emphasizes the necessary privacy of much of our asking, compared with the public world of our active ministry.

Asking Is the Mark of the Public Ministry of Jesus

In His *teaching*:

- "Ask for those who persecute you" (Matthew 5:44). This is one realistic reason why asking and mission cannot be separated. If you are living for Jesus you will attract opposition and therefore you will need to ask for help and protection as well as for mercy and forgiveness for your persecutors. Lack of asking probably means lack of witness. Lack of witness means we do not need to ask for protection because no one finds anything about us that is different to them that needs to be opposed. Nothing about us threatens the rule of the enemy, which means that we may be more friends of the world than of Jesus. It is consistent witness that makes asking a lifestyle. Note what Jesus adds here: "that you may be sons of your Father in heaven." For Jesus, asking was the evidence of sonship. It is the way that our assurance as sons and daughters most naturally expresses itself.
- He taught on how to ask behind closed doors (Matthew 6:5).

- His exhortation is direct: "Ask and it will be given to you" (Matthew 7:7).
- He talked about the expectation that sons can have of Fathers: "How much more ... to those who ask Him" (Luke 11:11).
- Matthew 9:10 and Luke 11:1 give us His responses to the request for teaching on asking. Note that the disciples asked this question after Jesus had finished a private time of asking. It was Jesus's asking that provoked their question. Were they beginning to see the connection between His asking and acting? Had they realized that amazing things followed those asking times or that asking times followed times of miracle? The feeding of 5,000 is preceded in Mark 6:32 by "solitary place" and followed in Mark 6:46 by "up on a mountainside". His actions were preceded and followed by asking.
- Jesus's teaching about asking settles the issue. "Our Father ... Thy kingdom come" (Luke 11:2). This prayer is the model for all asking.
- In Matthew 12:39 Jesus talks about "The sign of Jonah." It could be argued that this is not just about the 3 days in the belly, as the sign of resurrection. It is also about what happened in the belly. What preceded the mission to Nineveh? "From inside the fish Jonah prayed" (Jonah 2:1).
- In Mark 9:29 Jesus makes clear that there is much in our mission that can only be accomplished through asking: talking of the mute spirit in the demonized boy, He says that this "comes out only by prayer." Interestingly enough, this is preceded by the transfiguration and we should not forget that this happened only after Jesus "went up on a mountain to pray" (Luke 9:28).
- Jesus's own experience and example of asking is conclusive: "Jesus looked up ... Lazarus come forth" (John 11:41). First He requested, then He raised. First intercession then intervention. First asking, then acting.
- Mark 11:29 notes the "house of prayer for all nations". The fact that the prophecy says that even the banned eunuchs and foreigners would have a place in that house because they asked for the nations, tells you the power and acceptability to God of our asking. This is how highly He rates it, that those who were excluded from the

place of His presence by the law were given a place by virtue of their asking.

- Jesus's teaching about asking is to be found in His parables: the friend at midnight ("he will get up and give him as much as he needs" Luke 11:8); the persistent widow ("always ask and not give up" Luke 18:1); the Pharisee and publican ("Two men went up to the temple to pray" Luke 18:10).

In His *personal asking*:

Whole books [1] have been written on the two main records we have of Jesus asking for something: the prayers commonly known as 'The Lord's prayer' (Luke 11:2-4) and the 'High Priestly prayer' (John 17:1-25).

In His *relationships and conversations*:

The exchange that Jesus had with the Samaritan woman at the well of Sychar in John 4:10 is pivotal. He told her that if she had known who was asking of her, she would have been urgent in her asking of Him. Here is a huge moment in the gospels for our understanding of asking. "If you knew *who it was that asks you* for a drink, *you would have asked Him* and He would have given you living water." Jesus is saying that there is an incredible cause and effect relationship between our relational knowledge of Him, and our asking. The more intimately we know who He is then the more intimate and expectant will be our asking of Him. The more we know Him, the more we will ask of Him. The paucity of our asking translates into a lack of intimate knowledge of Him. If we know Him, we will better know what He desires for us, so the better we will ask for that which we need most. We must grasp this. Asking is not primarily conditioned by what we know or think needs to be asked about, but primarily about what we know about Jesus – what He wants and wills, what He desires for us and requires of us. This opens up the heavens for our asking. Do we ask for physical water? Yes, if like the Samaritan woman, we only know Jesus as one who is capable of lowering a bucket and getting it out the well. If our physical needs are all that life is about then that will define the limits of our asking. But if we know Him as "living water" as He truly is, then we are going to ask for much more. There is asking and asking, depending on how well you know Him. If you do not know Him:

- *as savior* you are not going to ask Him for forgiveness for sin;
- *as teacher* you are not going to ask Him for counsel;
- *as healer* you are not going to ask Him for miracles;
- *as deliverer* you are not going to ask Him to break bondages;
- *as comforter* you are not going to ask Him for peace;
- *as the giver of living water* you are not going to ask Him for fresh infusions of the Holy Spirit;
- *as lover* you are not going to ask Him for deeper intimacy;
- *as light* you are not going to ask Him for revelation;
- *as the way* you are not going to ask Him for direction;
- *as the truth* you are not going to ask Him for instruction;
- *as the life* you are not going to ask Him for the resurrection of what is dead in your life.

Knowing Jesus unstops the wells of asking.

Asking Concluded the Earthly Mission of Jesus

We are establishing the importance of this foundational pattern in Jesus's life of 'asking before acting'. It was the characteristic of the means and marks of His ministry, of His message and miracles. Why would we expect anything different when all hell was let loose upon Him? If scripture tells us what we are called to, "because Christ suffered for you, leaving you an example that you should follow in His steps" (1 Peter 2:21) then we should take a closer look at what He especially exampled and exhorted amidst that suffering, particularly in the last week of His earthly life.

1. **Triumphal entry:** In one of the very rare "listen-ins" that we get to Jesus worshiping (Luke 10:21), the reason for His praise and joy is that the truth that is hidden from the "wise and learned" (the mature

in their own eyes) is revealed to "little children." The diminutive here does not invite us to diminish the capacities and abilities of a child. As we have already seen, it is child-like asking that becomes the primary context of extraordinary revelation of the mind and heart of the Father. Is this not the same equation that Jesus uses in one of His seminal teachings about asking? "If your *son* asks ... if you then ... know how to give good gifts to your *children*" (Luke 11: 11-13). God's responses to asking have as much to do with the fact that it is a child (a son) who asks, as it has to do with His heart to answer as a Father. How interesting it is that at the beginning of the last week of Jesus's life, after His entry into Jerusalem, the religious leaders ask "Do you hear what these children are saying?" (Matthew 21:15-16) The "children" were crying "Hosanna!" which basically means, "We are asking you to save us!" It is child-like asking for salvation that prefaces Holy Week. They were the only ones who got it. The asking of children assured the Messiah on the doorstep of His suffering. It was the asking for salvation by children that was going to be answered by Jesus before the week was over.

2. **Holy Week:** These cries that ask for salvation serve to inaugurate Holy Week, and set the pattern for what follows. Holy Week was dominated by asking, most particularly in the experiences and the explanations of Jesus. There is a little detail that is easily missed in the narrative. It is there in Luke 21:37: "Each evening He went out to spend the night on the hill called the Mount of Olives." We have seen that "Mount of Olives" is a code for asking. Is it not the asking of Jesus, recorded in His prayer that week that we know as the High Priestly prayer (John 17), that is foundational to all our understanding of asking? Here, yet again, is the nonnegotiable sequence: asking before acting, and in this case, before the consummate action of atoning. It is here that He is also doing the foundational asking for the entire mission of the church before the disciples even engaged it. "My prayer is not for them alone but for those who will believe in me through their message" (17:20). This is for all believers, so Jesus's prayer was asking for the success of our mission, whoever and wherever we are. We were included in this ask-list. We get an incredible insight into something else that Jesus

was asking for in that last week of His life. As if He did not have enough to ask the Father for, just for Himself, we read in Luke 22:32: "I have asked for you." He had been asking for Peter. There was a whole world to redeem, and the one who denied Him is foremost in His asking. How can we doubt that Jesus asks after us and for us.

3. **The Upper Room discourse:** Asking not only dominates Holy week but it is the major subject in Jesus's communication with the disciples at the Last Supper (John 14-16). (For the fuller treatment of this see Chapter 11.) There are no less than six mentions of this idea of "asking in His name" in the upper room discourse on the eve of Jesus's betrayal and crucifixion. Why the repetition? Last words are important, and of all the things that He could have focused on in these last moments, it is the subject of asking that is the main point of His communication.
4. **The Upper Room prayer of Jesus:** The last communication of Jesus before His betrayal is His asking of the Father recorded in John 17. Having spoken repeatedly about asking, it is as if His final instruction is by way of example, as He asks for Himself, for His disciples, and for the world. (See chapter 2 for Jesus' ask-list.)
5. **Gethsemane:** In Luke 22:39 we read, "Jesus went out *as usual* to the Mount of Olives." The first word He utters when they arrive there is "Ask" (v40). In Gethsemane we observe the greatest presentation of this relationship between personal, private asking and public, global mission. Here is the travail of asking before the triumph of atoning (Matthew 26:36; Luke 22:39). "He fell on His face to the ground and prayed." The few square inches of dirt in which His face was pressed in asking, became His claim on every square mile of the entire earth. And let us not forget that there is a great unanswered asking of Jesus here. He is experiencing overwhelming pain, poignantly and humanly expressed. All natural feeling and response protested what was happening. We are familiar with the circumstances of our lives that cause us to ask "Why?" as we fumble for a sense of the Lord's will in what to us seems to be unbearable and incomprehensible. Do not forget that in John 12:27 Jesus rehearsed this moment with foresight. Should He ask, "Father save me from this hour?" He answers His own question: "NO! It was for

this very reason that I came to this hour. Father, glorify Your name!" He shows us how to transform a question mark of personal woe into an exclamation mark of worship. So there was something that Jesus could have asked for but did not (for twelve rescuing legions of angels) and something that He did ask of the Father that was not answered (that the cup be removed from His lips).

6. **The betrayal:** It is telling that Judas knew exactly where to find Him. He "knew the place because Jesus had often met there with His disciples" (John 18:2). To do what? (Code word: "Mount of Olives.") It is interesting that the place of betraying was at the place of praying. This great subversion of Jesus's mission came to undo Him at the place of asking. If you can stop the asking you can stop the acting. The outcomes that are settled on the public battlefield are first settled at the place of private asking.
7. **The cross:** The asking does not stop in Gethsemane. Jesus is asking till the very end of His life on the cross. How raw and moving are the last two asking prayers Jesus ever uttered? *"Father forgive them"*: Jesus is in extremis asking for others (rather than for those 12 legions of angels for Himself). *"Why have you forsaken me?"* Jesus, infused with the Word, exhales the asking of Psalm 22, and is unanswered at this time.

Asking Is the Mark of the Post-Resurrection Mission of Jesus

You might think that after that third day, there could now be a rest from asking since the mission was now accomplished. But post-resurrection, Jesus seems to take up where He left off. Mark 16:9 tells us that "Jesus rose *early* on the first day of the week." Rising early "a great while before day" was his common practice. It was another code for 'asking' during His ministry. So often the records show it was early in the morning, a great while before dawn that he did what? Ask of the Father. The intercessory innuendos at the end of the gospels just cannot be missed. "The disciples went to *the mountain* where Jesus had told them to go" (Matthew 28:16). Yet again, another code. We are back on the Mount of Olives, the place of asking. I wonder what Jesus was doing while He was waiting for them to arrive? You have guessed it. Was He not asking for the nations as His inheritance (Psalm 2: 7-8)? How significant that this is where the foundational commission for mission is given. "Go and make disciples of all nations." The authority that Jesus said was given to Him was first an authority in asking and then an authority in proclamation and in practice. It was an authority to ask as well as act. How significant that His continuance of His asking is the foundational action for the resurrection experience, and for the resurrection message and mission of the church. It is what the new, young church immediately does in Acts (1:14). Are we surprised?

But it does not end there because the resurrected Christ ascended. The place of ascending was the place of asking, and the asking did not stop for a moment because now He is the glorified Christ and can you guess what He is still doing in the presence of the Father? "He is able to save completely those who come to God through Him, because He always lives to ask for them" (Hebrews 7:25).

Jesus and asking? I think so. If He always lives to ask, then it will be impossible for our experience of the living Christ not to include us in His continuing and continual asking.

9

A Story

Well, It's a Bit Like This

There is nothing like a story to make the point. A parable was Jesus's American Express card: He never left home without it. If you agree that Jesus is the One whose teaching we need, then read what follows in order to find out what He is saying about asking.

1 *One day Jesus was praying in a certain place. When He finished, one of His disciples said to Him, "Lord, teach us to pray, just as John taught his disciples."*

2 *He said to them, "When you pray, say: " 'Father, hallowed be your name, your*
kingdom come. **3** *Give us each day our daily bread.* **4** *Forgive us our sins, for*
we also forgive everyone who sins against us. And lead us not into temptation.'"

5 *Then He said to them, "Suppose one of you has a friend, and he goes to him at*
midnight and says, 'Friend, lend me three loaves of bread, **6** *because a friend of*
mine on a journey has come to me, and I have nothing to set before him.'

7 *"Then the one inside answers, 'Don't bother me. The door is already locked,*
and my children are with me in bed. I can't get up and give you anything.' **8** *I tell*
you, though he will not get up and give him the bread because he is his friend, yet
because of the man's boldness he will get up and give him as much as he needs.

9 *"So I say to you: Ask and it will be given to you; seek and you will find; knock*
and the door will be opened to you. **10** *For everyone who asks receives; he who*
seeks finds; and to him who knocks, the door will be opened.

***11** "Which of you fathers, if your son asks for a fish, will give him a snake instead?*
***12** Or if he asks for an egg, will give him a scorpion? **13** If you then, though you*
are evil, know how to give good gifts to your children, how much more will your
Father in heaven give the Holy Spirit to those who ask him!" (Luke 11:5-8)

There are three parts to this key section of Jesus's teaching, presented together by Luke since they have a common theme: asking. First, there is the disciple's prayer, which is essentially an exemplar of asking for: the essentials of physical and spiritual life, food and forgiveness, provision and protection. This rolls into a parable about someone asking for help from a friend which is then followed by another short parable, originally in a three-stanza poetic form, that was most likely addressed to the Pharisees as the primary audience, to opponents of the gospel - "you who are evil".

The parable called 'The Friend at Midnight' might be second only to the parable of the Good Samaritan in the questionable exegesis it has received. What is the point of this parable? What is Jesus telling us about asking here? Parables do not lend themselves to tailored, tidy points. Perhaps a little background would help. Although people traveled at night in many oriental regions because of the heat, it was less common in this geography because of the cool afforded by the elevations, so we need to understand that someone turning up at midnight was not a usual occurrence. This was out of the ordinary and presents an extremity of need. It was necessary and customary to offer a significant meal to the wayfarer in a manner that showed generosity and care. It was almost always over the top, and more than the guest could ever possibly consume. This was no 'late-night-snack-from-the-fridge' deal. It was deemed a very special occasion and required the works.

And this was not just any stranger. This was his friend, so how much more were the motivations and obligations to bless and provide. To give a guest a broken loaf was a terrible insult, and brought shame on the host, so it had to be a whole loaf. There has been much discussion about why so many loaves and it has been well argued that it would probably have been to serve the guest, the host, with one left for the angel, according to rabbinic tradition. Whatever the case, it speaks of the commitment to provide plenty, more than enough. And lest you think it was just bread he needed, the parable says that he had "*nothing* to set before him" (v6). The bread, in so many cultures, is the equivalent of a utensil. It is used to dip into the common dishes of meat or sauce and is the mode of transport to the mouth. So the host is first asking for the bread, but the implication is that he needs everything else as well. Was he going to visit other houses in the village to get the rest of the meal? Talking of the village, it also needs to be understood that whenever a guest came to someone's home in the village, they were seen as the guest of the entire community. Hospitality was not simply a private affair but a communal one, thus his asking had a community component.

The parable opens with a question: "Suppose one of you has a friend and…?" (v5) Here is the gist of it. "Could you ever imagine a friend showing up at your place, really late at night, and finding yourself having to go to another friend to borrow some bread to bail you out, and all he does is palm you off with some ridiculous excuses about his door being locked and his kids being asleep? Well, hello? They should be asleep, shouldn't they? Now, could you ever imagine that happening and being treated like that by your friend at a time of great need?" The parable is set up by Jesus to solicit a negative response to that question. What the disciples should all be thinking is: "Absolutely not … we could never imagine that happening in a month of Sabbaths … no way … not in a million years … over my dead body … you've got to be kidding." It was absolutely impossible to think that this scenario Jesus was suggesting could ever happen.

The entire description of the first stanza is not about a faint possibility that any aspect of what is being described did happen or could ever possibly happen. The needy host's request was backed up by socially acquired and required reasons for having to ask. Given these social protocols there were no possible acceptable reasons for the friend to refuse to respond. It was not going to happen. No way! Equally, we could never entertain the idea that our answer would ever be "Yes" to the possibility that God would be reluctant to give, to respond, to answer our asking. There is absolutely no way that He would deny, devalue or dismiss our asking. So basically, the first part of the parable is telling us what cannot possibly happen when we ask the friend.

How Shameless!

The second part of the story then tells us what will happen when this asking takes place. It is here that the interpretation gets challenging. It all has to do with the translation of one word in v8, translated variously in different versions of the Bible as boldness, as importunity, as persistence, as standing your ground. There is much disagreement about this among scholars. Most good commentators will at least admit that this is a very challenging linguistic matter. It is certainly one for the experts, one like Professor Kenneth Bailey, an excellent scholar and professor of Middle East New Testament studies, whose work on the parables of Luke in particular has been landmark, drawing on linguistic scholarship and supported by the deep cultural knowledge of Arab and Palestinian commentators.[1] If the common translations are correct, it would suggest that the main point of this parable on asking is that if we holler long enough, beat the door hard enough, nag long enough, such dogged determination will eventually be taken seriously and our asking will receive a response, albeit a reluctant one.

Is there any truth in the idea that persistence is meant to be a component of our asking? Yes. Jesus Himself told another story in Luke18:1-8 to "show them that they should always pray and not give up." The widow went on and on asking the judge for justice against her adversary. She is described as the persistent widow. Jesus approves of those who likewise cry out to God "day and night." This implies a long time of asking. Yet He also says that they will get what they ask for "quickly". The waiting will seem short-lived compared to the thoroughness of the answer. Indeed, Jesus affirms, extols and advocates persistence in our asking, feeding our trust and hope in God's timely deliverance, His "in the fullness of time" answer, His "on time" delivery.

But where in our parable is there a ground for this idea of persistence? It is only in the word used to describe the quality of the man. But which man? It would seem to be a description of the needy host, would it not, given how this is commonly translated? So here lies the problem in two parts, for Aramaic scholars like Bailey. First, there is an issue with the Greek word that is translated into English as *"boldness"* or *"persistence"*. Which is it? Can you be persistent without being bold or bold without being persistent? Yes. They are not necessarily co-existent. What we know about this particular Greek word that is used as a translation of the original Aramaic is that it developed two meanings in its usage, one positive and one negative. The positive meaning is indeed "persistence" but there is also a negative one. Don Carson, an eminent New Testament scholar, has acknowledged that the meaning of the Greek word is disputed: "Literally 'anaideia' means shamelessness and some assign this shamelessness to the man at the door." So the negative meaning is "shamelessness" or literally "without any shame." However, in most translations it is the positive meaning that is emphasized. Like Bailey, Carson concludes: "This is almost certainly incorrect." [2] Many would argue that this translation is influenced by the different and separate parable that follows where the commands to ask, seek knock are in a tense which describes a continuous action. Ask and keep on asking. That sounds like persistence to anyone. It could be argued that this has influenced how 'persistence' has been read back into the previous parable. However, what is interesting, and is well documented by scholars, is that there is no example of this Greek word ever being used in the first century to mean persistence, nor does it have this meaning in the preceding seven centuries in any classical Greek literature. This is overwhelming evidence that cannot be ignored. The common meaning was the one perceived as negative, namely "shamelessness".

So Who Is Shameless?

Perhaps it was hard to understand how it could be possible that a figure in the parable could be shameless. You can argue that the host is in fact "shameless" (in the way that word has meaning for us), simply in the way that he throws cautions and concerns to the winds and wakes up someone at midnight. How shameless! Have you no respect for civility and decency, my man! But the problem here is that shame would not have been attached to this action by anyone who knew the need that had necessitated it. It would have been shameful *not* to provide for your visiting friend and *not* to make the effort, no matter how demanding and extreme it was to satisfy the need. In Jesus's culture, there is no way that the host was losing face by borrowing from his friend, even though he may have been possibly embarrassed by having no supplies. On the contrary, it would have been shameful if he had not done this.

And there is another thing. If indeed the host was acting shamelessly, and therefore shamefully, or trying to shame his friend, do you think that he would even hope that he would ever be given a loaf, let alone three, from a really annoyed guy who had been yelled out of bed by a friend (some friend!) who would not take "no" for an answer? "Hey, here's the bread, you loafer – scram!" But the text says that the friend gives him "as much as he needs." As Bailey argues, he got the dip as well as the bread and probably a jug of wine thrown in for good measure.

Are you following this? We have this problem about the meaning of the word in the context of the story. We should ask if there is in fact any evidence of the need for "persistence" in the asking in our story. I agree with those like Bailey and Carson who argue not. There is no knocking. The story says specifically that he "calls" – it is just a spoken voice. And there is arguably a reason for that. He was a friend. It was only strangers who knocked. The friend knew the voice of a friend, so he knew exactly with whom he was dealing. There is an established relationship here. They were intimates. Another point: when the needy host has finished his asking, the friend inside answers immediately so no persistence was needed. In any case, Jesus taught elsewhere against vain repetitions, and that we were not just heard for our much speaking. He also taught elsewhere about importunity.

Furthermore, the friend who was wakened knew all about what was good and right in a circumstance like this. He knew what was normal expectation. Though the need of the host was pressing and even critical, there was nothing out of the ordinary when it came to responding to a need like this in that culture. This was what you did. The friend would have been shamed if it had taken persistence to persuade him to do the right thing. There is something else to consider if you are still feeling persistent! When the descriptive and poetic structure of the second stanza of the story is literarily examined, scholars point out that every reference is to the friend who had been sleeping. The whole stanza is about him, every line of it. He is the subject. So why in the third line would the reference suddenly switch to the needy host? Listen to it: "though *he* will not get up because of being a friend of *his*, yet because of *his* ———— *he* will arise." This leads to two possible conclusions. First, this word is not describing the host but the friend who was awoken. The main point of the parable hangs on the response of the man inside the house, not the man on the outside. Secondly, this word cannot be describing persistence. It is most likely that it meant exactly what it meant in every other context it appeared: shamelessness. The Greek word used is not referring to shamelessness in a western sense, describing folk who could not care less if they brought shame upon themselves or others. "The way forward comes from recognizing that in Greek, 'anaideia' can mean shamelessness in a slightly different sense … in Greek 'shameless' people can be those whose conduct ensures that they will avoid shame; they act in such a way that they are literally 'shame-less', utterly innocent of any shame." [3] This means that the word used here is referring to the man who is inside the house, not the one outside the door doing the asking.

All of this makes perfect sense. Why? In oriental culture, a sense of shame is understood as something positive. It is only understood negatively by a western mind. To have a sense of shame, or to know what has to be done not to lose face, is a virtue. The avoidance of shame was in fact the same as the retaining of honor. In other words, what is emphasized here, which is absolutely in keeping with things scripture teaches elsewhere about asking, is that the emphasis in this story is not actually on *the nature of the need* being asked about, but on *the nature of the friend* who was asked.

Who's Your Friend?

This brings us back to relationship and intimacy again. The confidence of the needy friend to ask was premised on that friendship. Why would we be surprised then that a few verses further on from encouraging the disciples to "ask" in order that they would receive (John15:7), Jesus says to them "I have called you friends" (John 15:15). What was absolutely certain to get the sleeping friend to rise and respond was his character that would not and could not be shamed by responding wrongly or inappropriately to the one who was asking. It was because of the friend's honor and shamelessness (i.e. having no presence of shame or anything shameful) that his friend could trust him with his asking and have an assurance that brought confidence in his approach. It was not about who the asking friend was, that was the most compelling reason for him to get up and help him. It was all about who he, the answering friend was, who acts to maintain the quality of his honor, the integrity of his name and character, and the commitment of his relationship to his friend. Do any of us ever feel assured about our merits when it comes to this asking business? Are we expecting our Friend to stop His world and answer us because of who *we* are? Is our voice so commanding, our need so demanding, our character so righteous, our pleading so persuasive that there is sufficient clout to overcome any reluctance on the part of the one being asked (the friend), or any other mitigating circumstance that would interfere with the desired response (the needs of other children)? I think not.

The point in Jesus's stories in Luke 11 is all about "how much more". If this is true of the sleeping friend to the calling friend, if this was true of the father, who gives his children fish and eggs for breakfast, not snakes and scorpions, how much more do you have a father and a friend. Our God is a "how much more" Father and an "as much as he needs" friend. This conviction is foundational to our confidence in asking.

The Takeaway

What encouragement can we take from this? We are not all in the same place when it comes to asking. Some have more need than others. It may range from a wish to a want, from a minor lack to a major loss, from a crinkle to a crisis. Are there any helpful applications here? Let's face it. Everything was against that host. Yes, the unexpected happened, and yes it was threatening to his peace because yes, he did not have the resources to meet the situation, and yes, the doors were locked. Oh, and yes it was the midnight hour. Could it get any worse, or any darker? But this is not a story about a 24-hour convenience store but about a God who is a 24/7 friend. God hears and responds at the midnight hour, at the limit of our extremity.

God is an honorable friend. He will never answer in a way that is ever inconsistent with His honor or His character. There is another aspect of this embedded in the story. He acted honorably to save his friend's honor, in the face of the other friend-guest. The lie of the enemy to us, so often, is that we have lost face, or we will lose face. One of the great enemies of intimacy and trust is shame, and that is the enemy's garment of choice for us, to cover up our own sense of need, or spiritual nakedness. We end up feeling deeply dishonored and one reason for that is the fear or the anxiety that we will not be answered. God is zealous for His honor and for our honor too, before Him and a watching world. If there have been dishonorable responses in our hearts to our circumstances, then there is forgiveness for our sins and covering for our shame, but we cannot be silenced by the shame and cease to ask boldly of the Lord, our friend, for the provision we need in order to recover our capacity to live without shame, and without loss of face. The worst thing we can lose is our pride. Let us lose it. In any case, we cannot ask of Him with pride or self-righteousness, or a sense of our own desserts.

Talking about lies of the enemy, there is another one that arises from the context of this story. In answer to the question, "What is the answer that God will give to me?" the demonic answer is "snakes and scorpions." There are many things in our lives that shrivel faith and hope, and that reduce request to resignation. The enemy of our souls sponsors the lie that we are kidding ourselves if we think it could be about the fish and eggs. The devil sponsors a determinism that assassinates asking and convinces people that God will serve them up with something that will have a sting in the tongue, like a snake, or a sting in the tail, like a scorpion. Whether up front now or down the road later, something will not work out, something will go wrong, the goodness of God will not be all that it is dressed up to be. So what is the use of asking?

There have been many over the centuries who have been captured by the teasing reference in the story to the God who rises to meet us in our place of need, our place of death, the place of our spiritual and physical incapacities and insolvencies. We come to the risen interceding Christ with confidence. After all, He died and rose to gain for us the inheritance that God has promised to His sons and daughters. But the fact is that so much of our asking is in a place of indebtedness and death. We are asking to be raised. There is an honest humility that confesses that we too have "nothing to set before" our guests. Our asking often comes out of a deathly shame, not least the asking for cleansing, but the host in the story has got to the place of desperate necessity and is unashamed to confess his shame. This is important because this tells us that the boldness here is not brashness or presumption, like 'name it and claim it'. It is a boldness born in brokenness. He has died to self-respect; he is dead to self-sufficiency; he is dead to the opinion of others; he is dead to social propriety, unless someone rises to raise him. His boldness is not an expression of self-assertiveness but of powerlessness and dependence and weakness. But the boldness is also rooted in a trust of the friend's character. He can trust that he will do the right thing. Note the number of times the word *"friend"* is mentioned: four times. It dominates the story. When we ask of God, it is always as a friend, of a friend. His capacities for friendship are not in question. Are we friends of God? Like Abraham, our father in the faith, is our faith the evidence of our friendship? Or is the friendship with the world that James describes the thing that keeps us from our heavenly friend's door. In our asking, we come to the Lord as a trusted friend and likewise, we can trust He will do the right thing. It is impossible for him to do anything shameful or to be shamed.

Please note that the friend does not sleep as some consider God asleep in response to their asking. God is not coming up with reasons not to answer us. God is not more concerned with other children than for us. Are we accusing God of sleeping on the job? Is that another lie? The parable tells us that this is unimaginable. Are we accusing God of being more concerned about His other children than us?

No matter what aspect of asking that we deal with, we end up in the same place with the same conclusion. Our parable is no exception. What is first established is not what our posture should be before God, but what His posture is towards us. As we continue to say, this matter of asking is all about first knowing His nature, before it is ever about knowing our need. Why did Jesus repeat six times that we should ask in His name? He did so because His name is the sum of His nature, His character. Maybe we need to imagine that we are literally and physically in Christ when we ask of the Father – in Jesus, asking in His name.

It's Not Just About Me

Before we leave this brilliant "asking" story, note its community implications. The friend in need was not just asking for himself but for another when all was said and done. Has our asking broken through beyond the barriers of personal need into the passion to see the needs of others met by Jesus? This is in accord with the plural address of the Lord's Prayer that preceded it. Asking is a community business. Talking of community, it is impossible to read Luke 11:13 about asking the Father for the Holy Spirit without thinking again of the next time we actually hear that being done, in the Upper Room in a community ask-meeting. The Holy Spirit seems to be Jesus's favorite thing to ask for (John14:6). It seems that this just might be where the parable was perhaps leading: to ask our Father and Friend for His Spirit. The Christ who has risen, meets us in our death, and by the power of His Spirit, His never-to-be-shamed character, He delivers us from our shame and gives us the Holy Spirit of grace. This was the message of Peter at Pentecost. We should ask this Friend right now for the fresh infusion of His Holy Spirit that we need.

The burden being expressed here in this parable is about the free expression of asking, the abandonment of fleshly protocol, as with Hannah when she ended up being accused ofbeing drunk. This is hardly a dignified description for one desperately asking of God, more a shamed one. It is interesting that this was the same "shameful" impression the bystanders got of the disciples after all their upper room asking. When all is said and done, never forget that it is always more about our Friend, the God we ask, than about who we are as needy hosts, and about the things we ask for. He hears us, He is the rewarder of those who diligently seek Him, and He is the Father who is also our friend, who can never shame Himself, who for His honor's sake, will do what is right by His children. Now well supplied, and free of shame because his kind friend would not be shamed by his request or appear shamed in being unable to meet it, our host makes his way back home to give away what he has just received. His answer becomes the answer for another.

A Three-Loaf God

Did it dawn on him that the Godhead, Father, Son and Holy Spirit, was a 'three-loaf' outfit? Would he not have understood the intimacy that is wrapped up in the old saying, "A jug of wine, a loaf of bread and thou"? Do you not think that the taste of that eucharistic bread and dip was a savor that remained with him? Had he not tasted and seen that his Friend was shamelessly good? To the questions, "Will He ever ... will there ever ... can it ever ..." may the answer of Jesus come afresh to us: ask whatever, whenever for whoever. In our asking we need Him to be more than our butcher and baker and candlestick maker, more than our broker and banker – we simply need Him to be our Friend.

I wonder, given all his asking, if the host stopped for a moment before he served his late-night guest, and raised a glass of recently supplied wine and proposed a toast? *"Cheers! Here's to desire born out of desperation; here's to boldness born out of brokenness; here's to request born out of relationship; here's to friendly answers from confident asking; here's to new loaves where there was no flour; here's to restored provision where there was poverty; here's to renewed intimacy where there was intimidation; here's to holy shamelessness where there has been shame. Here's to asking of a friend!"* Asking changes things. Cheers!

"I hope you have a place like Bethany that you can go to when you are struggling with unanswered prayer … Bethany is a connection point that reminds you of something you once knew for sure: that God can do immeasurably more than all you ask or imagine … when there's little evidence of it in your situation … Bethany is the kind of community or the kind of family where you can sometimes still smell the perfume of God's presence." – Pete Grieg

10

A Miracle

Asking For a Sign

John's gospel is structured around seven great events in Jesus's ministry, each of which are presented, not as random miracles, but as intentional signs. The emphasis is on what they tell us about Jesus. Regardless of what miracle was performed, or what problem was confronted, these signs can only be understood if we discern what they are pointing towards. They are not attracting attention to their immediate wonder and relief, but they are pointing away from themselves to something else. The first of these event-signs is found in John 2:1-11 where Jesus turned water into wine. What a divinely brilliant but holily mischievous way to launch the messianic ministry. How gratuitously extravagant was it to miraculously cask over 1800 gallons of a wine that would even stretch the enological sensibilities of the world's finest sommelier. This was followed by: the healings of the official's son in Capernaum (4:43-54), and the invalid at the pool of Bethesda (5:1-15); then the feeding of the 5,000 (6:1-15); the walking on the water (6:16-24) and healing of the blind man at the pool of Siloam (9:1-41). That brings us to the final one, which is presented as the climactic sign of Jesus's entire ministry. It marks the end of the road for Jesus but the beginning of the highway of holiness for us. It is the story of the raising of Lazarus and perhaps you can find it in John 11 before you read any further.

It is a story about asking and acting: man's asking but God's acting. You cannot read John's gospel without watching the tightening of the screw and the rising hostility of the Judean authorities towards Jesus. Although all the gospel writers chronicle this increase of temperature, it is John who gives particular details about what was stoking the furnace for an intended funeral pyre. You need rewind no further than the previous chapter. Jesus's comments about being the good shepherd who gave his life for the sheep did not win the "pastoral message of the month" award. "At these words the Jews were divided ... He is demon-possessed and raving mad" (v19). The very next incident recounts Jesus going for a meditative walk in the temple through Solomon's Colonnade, and He is interrupted as He is asked, "How long will you keep us in suspense? If you are the Christ tell us plainly" (v24). He replied, "I and the Father are one" (v30). We then read, "Again the Jews picked up stones to stone him" (v31). "The Father is in me and I am in the Father" (v38). Again they tried to seize Him, but He escaped their grasp (v40). In other words, Jesus had to take evasive action to escape violence against Him.

This is a time of heightened duress and antagonism. Jesus is approaching the end, so it is interesting that in order to lie low, He chooses to slip away to the part of the Jordan near where He had been baptized right at the beginning of it all: "the place where John had been baptizing in the early days" (v40). No doubt He drew succor from the memories of the Father's affirmation of Him there: "You are still my Son in whom I am still well pleased!" He was still fathered by God. He was still founded on the prophetic words of scripture about God's purposes for His life. He was still filled with the Holy Spirit and empowered for the same task at hand now as then – nothing less than the taking of the kingdoms of darkness God's way. What is so amazing is that despite all the reasons for Him to isolate Himself and focus only on His own need for replenished resources, the text reads: "many people came to Him ... and in that place many believed" (41-42). Despite the extremities of the conditions, whether the scorching hate of His enemies or the chilling intimations of His death, He remained faithful and fruitful. So this is the set-up for our story in which John describes nothing less than an extraordinary preview of a drama that was yet to be staged. The earlier words of Jesus take on a spine-shivering resonance: "The hour is coming and now is, when the dead will hear the voice of the Son of God, and those who hear will live."

Reading Between the Lines

It was late in the afternoon when the messenger arrived with the news that Jesus' dear friend Lazarus was gravely ill (John 11:3). Some commentators remark that this was just a friendly message about Lazarus' state: "We just thought you might be interested, seeing you are friends and all that ... just thought you might want to include him in your evening prayers." It was nothing of the sort. It was not that kind of note. Do not think that just because the interrogative is not obvious that there is not a huge bit of ASKING going on here. One of the ways we sometimes know our asking is desperate is that we drive through all the speed limits imposed by asking the question the right way and accelerate at God with nothing but statements about the problem. "This is an awful and painful mess and there is nothing that anyone can do about it!" (Except you! Implied.) But the statement begs an answer no less than the direct question. The text says, "The sisters sent word to Jesus, the one you *love* is sick" (v3). Did Mary and Martha ask, "Anyone got nothing to do ... O good, Joel, run along and find Jesus and mention what's going on here with Lazarus, just so He doesn't hear it from someone else ... there's a good chap!"

Make no mistake about it. Desperate asking is going on here by two sisters who are staring death in the face. Why am I so sure? Because the ensuing text makes it absolutely clear that they believed that if Jesus had responded then all would have been answered. "If you had been here" is repeated by both of them (vs.21, 32). If the person you ask is Jesus, and you know He is the only one in the universe that can possibly answer the request, and you already know He is not only able to provide the answer but should be motivated to do so ("the one you love"), then you are confident in your asking and assured of what the outcome will be. There is no way you are not going to get the information to Him as fast as possible so He can answer immediately, since an immediate answer in this situation is the only one that will do any good. It would appear this was all perfectly reasonable. Not so.

Martha says to Jesus: "I know that even now God will give you whatever you ask" (v22). "Whatever you ask"? Is this not a familiar phrase by now? Their confidence in asking Jesus was because they were confident in His asking of the Father. God will listen to Him. If we convince Him to make our need His need, then we are in for a miracle. It proves that asking has something to do with relationship. It was precisely because of the relationship between the Son and the Father that Martha was assured about the asking and answering between them.

Answering It 'Slant'

The response that Jesus gave to this hand-delivered message seemed at first to be reassuring. "This will not end in death and through it I will be glorified." That is exactly the answer they wanted. Marvelous! Everything is going to be fine so back to paddling in the Jordan. Not quite. The next two verses (vs5-6) make two points:

- Jesus's love for Mary, Martha and Lazarus was not only affirmed by them, as in the message of v3, but by other witnesses. It was crucial to establish this relationship of unquestionable love.
- Jesus could not now plead ignorance of the problem being asked about. He heard the message and He understood it. The Godhead had heard and "yet" (v6). YET! When you want a divine "YES!" this is the last word you want to hear. Can we hope this is a divine lisp? There is almost controlled disbelief, certainly muffled and muted surprise, in the acknowledgement that even though Jesus now knew Lazarus was really ill, that he decided to stay where He was.

So we have two foundational points here for our asking.

1. **The God we ask LOVES who is asking.** That love is inviolable, unbreakable, unquenchable, incorruptible, durable and unshakeable. In a word, it is eternal. This is important because it means that regardless of what happens next, or regardless of how it seems or appears or sounds, or ends up, or regardless of how it IS according to our experience of its reality and its consequences - the answer to the asking, or the lack of one, cannot be separated from His love, cannot be inconsistent with His love, and cannot be contradictory

to His love. Whatever happens cannot be bad fathering by God, bad brothering by Jesus or bad comforting by the Holy Spirit.

2. **The God we ask HEARS what is asked.** Have we not established the truth about God's nature that "He hears" and that it is foundational to our theology of asking? You cannot deny that Jesus heard what was being asked.

If we think the disciples now had enough information to settle their concerns, we would be wrong. The conversation about going to wake Lazarus up did not happen until they were on the road later. The disciples were then relieved because if he was sleeping that was a good sign, because it meant he was resting, the fever had broken and "he will get better" (v12). The only thing Jesus had told them was: "This sickness will not end in death." Contrary to all expectations, this is not going to be the death of him! (Ah, you cannot fool me, you can hear someone say. It all depends what you mean by death, doesn't it?)

My Grief – His Glory

The worst we are asking about is not going to be the death of us either, not in terms of the life that Jesus is about to talk about and demonstrate. "It will be the death of him." It is a saying in our vernacular. "The boy will be the death of her." What a curse from hell, what a spirit of death. What an assassination of godly trust and hope and faith. What a robbery of life and joy and purpose. Did not Jesus say that the devil was a murderer and a robber? Your pangs will not be unto the ultimate death of that hope, or that vision, or that promise, or that purpose. "It is for God's glory so that God's Son may be glorified through it." In other words, our understanding of the outcomes of our asking just got completely re-arranged.

We are asking for an answer for our grief and He is answering that it is about His glory. We are asking about what needs to be resolved for us, and He is answering about what needs to be revealed about Him. We are asking for a natural response for a natural need (like continuance of my life as it is now) and He wants a supernatural answer for a supernatural life (perpetuity of life with Him forever). We are asking for our mortal dying nature to be shored up and He wants our nature to be transformed into His likeness. We are asking about solving the new crisis and He is answering about saving my old character. We are asking for the obvious while He is answering about what cannot yet be conceived or imagined. We are asking for temporal relief and He is answering for eternal redemption. We are asking for one, usually for me, sometimes for him or her, or them but usually not so desperately, but He is answering for a multitude that no man can number.

In our story, Martha wants Lazarus raised for this life (she thinks she is kosher with the doctrine of the resurrection of the dead) but Jesus's answer was not about life in Israel then, anymore than it is primarily and only about our life in our present circumstances now. We should perhaps be shocked about the percentage of our asking that actually concerns that which is only temporal. In the same way we should be shocked at the denials people will endure, the disciplines they will accept for temporal gains, through exercise or savings or study, and yet God forbid that we would volunteer to do an ask-fast for a day for another's need, let alone ours. We ask much of ourselves for that which perishes, and little of God for that which endures forever, which moth and rust will not decay. It is as if most of our asking is immediately about us and ours and now, but the answer He has prepared is ultimately about Him and His and then!

Interestingly enough, was this not also the message of the very first sign that Jesus did in Cana of Galilee when He turned water into wine? It had nothing to do with the Jewish-mother thing. Mary was asking for her reasons, all of them good and kind and serving. Her outcomes have to do with a nice wedding, happy guests, a happy couple, and no possibility of shame for the family that ran out of supplies. It seems that Jesus did not respond to that asking for those laudable reasons because we know why He did the miracle: "He thus revealed His glory." Is this not what He says again here? "It is for God's glory so that God's Son may be glorified through it" (v4). Please understand this. When Jesus talks of being glorified, His answer is answering something way beyond anything that is going to happen to Lazarus. The glorious outcome that this is all unto is His own death and His resurrection, the climax of the entire volume of history no less. In the light of "the fullness of time" there was actually no delay, no deferment in getting to Lazarus. The train of God's grace was exactly on time.

We need our mundane, pragmatic, functional, mechanical, dull view of asking to be lasered by the light of this revelation of glory, of the knowledge that we can serve this glory through our asking of God's will. Our asking, as weak, helpless, mumbling, diffident, tremulous, and even doubting as it may be, is nothing less than the pursuit of His glory and all that this glory purposes that is guaranteed to be true and pure. This asking of ours is another opportunity, not primarily for us to get through, but for God to come through. In a twinkling, our demand for His answer on our terms becomes our delight in His disposal on His terms. We have to relate our understanding of God's will to His glory! Just hearing people say the phrase "the will of God", you would think it was a sentence of death. Jesus said that the only thing He did was the will of the Father. "I have brought you glory on earth by completing the work you gave me to do" (17:4). The will is the glory! Asking according to the will of God is asking for the glory of God. The most pathetic, inconsequential and seemingly frivolous little but needful thing we could ask for finds its greater meaning to the extent that it's smallness is enlarged by the grandeur of the possible outcome of the glory of God, not least in our glorification of Him, in our worship and thanksgiving, in our submission to His will and in our surrender to His sovereignty. The darkness of our emotional, spiritual, intellectual or material need that we bring to Him in our private asking chamber is iridescent with the glory of the throne to which we come in our time of need. Beginning our asking at a place of isolation, we are invited to offer it to be part of a larger answer beyond our parochial dreams.

In Search of 'Amen!'

There are thousands of requests that we will yet have to make of God for a thousand possible people or situations. Will we choose to remember that every asking prayer goes somewhere? Where does it go? It goes to the bowls of incense that are the prayers of the saints that are in the throne room, in the presence of the Lamb who is holding the scroll of the destiny of our lives. Though that asking of ours is important to us at the time, it can seem discouragingly and hopelessly insignificant in the big scheme of things. That asking prayer that at first seems so specific and particular to us in our earthly walk can seem tangential and even random in the light of eternal destiny. What is our need among so many, and what is our life among so many? Yet the fact is that it takes its place in the bowl of intercessions that will indeed be poured out at the right time. Their fulfillment may not be yet, but their necessity is for now, so ask. This is why no godly asking prayer is redundant or wasted. In this heavenly context, it is probably incorrect to talk about unanswered prayers. We should call them unfinished prayers. It is asking that is still awaiting God's "Amen" – His creative word, "Let it be", that speaks things that are not into being. Someone who discovered this in the throes of terminal cancer wrote this: "Prayers we think of as directed to the present, are in fact being stored up to be answered in the final day." [1]

We await those divine 'Amen's' to our asking. But the answers can only be properly understood if we see *where they come from* – from a context where the glory of God is the over-riding reason for everything – and if we see *where the answers are going*, what the answers are ultimately for – the glory of God that would cover the earth as the waters cover the sea. As we began to ask, all we were thinking about was our local request. This is overwhelming, that God would glorify our asking for the purposes of glorifying Him; that our words of request would be like an incense that He would not be ashamed to use for His glory, in us and in our circumstances and our lives when appropriate. Who would ever have thought that the asking of a breathless messenger by the side of the Jordan, on behalf of the asking of two distraught sisters in Bethany, would become the prelude to an answer that would glorify the Son in the highest of all possible ways, namely the triumph of the cross and resurrection that was about to be foreshadowed at Lazarus' tomb.

The Vacuum of Unanswered Asking

But there is still that word "YET"! Despite them being His best and beloved friends; despite it being a need in extremis; despite all the evident effort to get the message to Him; despite the appropriate response that He should have given being obvious to everyone: "YET ... He stayed where He was two more days." Did a cynical mind recall the incident when Jesus had first showed up in Bethany and been invited to supper by Mary with no warning for preparation, thus precipitating all Martha's angst? Is God ever on time? If he arrived too early at the first meeting, this was looking like a case of arriving too late.

We can work out the chronology. Given Jesus's first statement about this sickness of Lazarus not being unto death, the disciples would have assumed that Lazarus' was going to recover. The fact is that he was most likely already dead by the time Jesus got the message. It took the messenger a day's journey to get to Jesus, He stayed an extra two days, and it would have taken him a day to get to the tomb and we know that Lazarus would have been buried immediately after death. He had been dead for four days (v39) when Jesus got there. You do the calculations. What was being asked for had in fact now changed. A healing touch to restore Lazarus to everyday life was now off the asking list. Interestingly enough, as cultural traditions would have it, four days dead was accepted as the real thing when it came to death. There was a folk-belief that the spirit re-visited after 3 days to see if there was still any fighting chance so if you were dead four days, even the spirits had given up on you.

Here is the vacuum of unanswered prayer – the vortex of apparent divine unresponsiveness. From Mary and Martha's point of view these two days after Jesus received the message were marked by one main thing: the absence of God in the person of Jesus. To use C.S.Lewis' famous words after his wife died of cancer: "Why is He so very absent a help in times of trouble?" [2] And if you think two days is long, how about the 430 years that elapsed before this: "God heard their groaning and remembered His covenant" (Exodus 2:24). There is a deep darkness in the delay of unanswered asking. It is threatening: to faith and future, to present peace, to future fulfillment. "If it is possible, take this cup from me ... My God, my God, why hast thou forsaken me?" Even Christ was not spared the temporary experience of unanswered asking as a part of His human experience as Son of Man. He had no more to go on, shocking as this may sound, than we do. He only had the Word of God, the character of God, and the promise of God.

YET! There are these two days, that become three. In his book about unanswered prayer entitled "God on Mute" Peter Grieg writes: "Unanswered prayer can be used to craft the greatest answers to prayer." [3] Citing that out of context does no justice to the quote, because it sounds like a cute "mind over matter" jingle, but if you read Grieg's story, you know that this was a conviction borne out of a deep experience of suffering, doubt, testing and a life and death struggle. There is nothing jaunty in it at all. It comes out of the furnace of affliction. It turns out that this was exactly what was happening in our story at Bethany.

Delay Can Be Life-Threatening

The clock is ticking on Lazarus' life and Jesus seems to be acting as if there is all the time in the world. And so it was that He and His disciples stayed on together at the Jordan, journaling the time as "conversations and conversions" until Jesus woke up on the third morning and said, "Let's go back to Judea." What? Judea? How vague is that? You have had a specific request and you are giving the most general of geographical intentions. Not even Bethany? The mystery of God is one thing but at what point does mystery feel like sheer vagueness? But then why did He need to go to Bethany if he said Lazarus was not going to die, or if in fact Lazarus was already dead? It would not be the first time His Word had resulted in distance-healing.

What are some of the possible consequences of this potentially dangerous delay? Well, there is a serious threat to Lazarus' well-being, and possible death will change your way of life. What about the disciples? If we are right that Lazarus was already dead, and Jesus already knows that he is dead, then we are heading for a potential problem. This is going to raise more than eyebrows among His followers. Jesus would not come out of this looking very good. Not to answer the sisters was certainly not good publicity for friendship, or for the healing ministry. A tarnished reputation, moral ambiguity and the loss of trust were all possible serious consequences from this divine delay. It seems that Jesus could neither spare others the grief, the pain, or the perplexity consequential to the delay, nor spare Himself from being maligned, impugned, doubted, even disbelieved.

If you have ever ordered anything online, you will know that you get a series of communications. The first one is "ORDER RECEIVED". At least you know that what you asked for has registered – it has been heard. So far a theology of asking is holding good. Then you get another note telling you that it has gone to "FULFILLMENT", an interesting use of the word. There is fascinatingly deceptive psychology in that because although it may have reached their 'fulfillment center' your request is still not fulfilled until you get what you asked for. The final communication lets you know it has been "SHIPPED". But it still has not arrived. Where on the delivery track is the answer to prayer? Was it received? Is it being fulfilled? Has it been shipped? When will it arrive? What if it arrives too late or not at all? Is there someone named Lazarus staffing the complaint desk?

But It Does Not Feel Like Love

Do not forget how this story began. Love was the premise of these relationships between Jesus and the Bethany siblings and consequently of all these decisions, regardless how they looked. This love was responsible for this unanswered asking. We have to say that love not merely allowed it but purposed it. God's love is always the first thing that is questioned by unanswered asking which is why it is so important that it is established here. Jesus's delay in answering had nothing to do with a lack of love or concern. So how did He appear to them when He delayed and did not show up? Less than helpful, less than responsive, less than caring – which for most people would translate into less than loving, at least as we expected to be loved in the circumstances. How does He appear to us when His timing is not our version of timeliness, when all we want is His immediate YES and all we seem to get is the same word of our text: "YET Jesus stayed another two days." Two weeks, two months, two years - what does it matter? Too late is too late, and the delay now feels like two life times. And do not forget that this delay is arguably more culpable because it lasts until Lazarus is way beyond resuscitation.

The Bethany crowd would not be the last ones, would they, to accuse God of being too slow, too neglectful, too distracted with other concerns? (By the way, it is not that Jesus did not have life-threatening concerns of His own.)

What about the accusation of divine lack of involvement? Is omniscience not impugned by this charge that He has overlooked something? Is His omnipotence questioned given that there is no response? At a time when Jesus appeared to love less, He actually demonstrated that He knew more. Writing of this incident, Saint Augustine summed it up like this: "It is sufficient that Jesus knows." [4] Maybe it is not comfortable or comforting, but it should be sufficient. It is interesting to note that on the three occasions in the gospels when Jesus is strongly urged to do something, it is always the persuasion of a close friend or family member, the very hardest of people to turn down. We are all His kin who ask of Him as His followers are we not? When asked who His mother or brethren were, Jesus replied, pointing to His disciples, "Here are my mother and my brothers. For whoever does the will of my Father in heaven is my brother and sister and mother" (Matthew 12:49). The closeness results from the desire to do His will in the first place, but it is this same desire that brings us to places where it is not just about our asking of God, but His asking of us. When our desired answer runs the risk of not being what His will desires, will our close relationship continue to be sufficient a desire for us to be able to accept an unwanted answer, or no answer at all?

Not All bad, Not All Good

This delay was not bad for everyone. The later conversation lets us know that the disciples were more than happy for Jesus to stay put, because any move toward Bethany was trouble for Him and therefore them. When they did eventually leave for Bethany the last word was spoken by Thomas as they hit the road: "Let us go that we may die with Him" (v16). Forget Lazarus' death! What about ours? Now that is something to worry about. This delay is the full deal. If Jesus does not answer the asking and stays by the Jordan, it tests the faith of the sisters; if he does answer and goes to Bethany it tests the faith of the disciples. One man's answer may be another man's asking. We always assume our answer could not but be wonderful for everyone. Many of our requests are just not filtered through the needs of anyone but ourselves.

As we have seen, this delay is so long that it actually strikes the original request from the list of future possible things to ask for. Asking for Lazarus' healing will never be asked for again. The grand irony here is that the delay turns this incident into a story about things you do not ask for, should not ask for, and could not possibly ask for. "If you had been here my brother would not have died." So if Jesus is present He can take care of some things, but if He does not answer according to our scheduled need and timing then He is powerless to deal with the consequences? So it is good to have Jesus around when you are dying but not when you are dead? Is this suggesting that we have come to believe that there are some things not worth asking for, not possible to ask for, too embarrassing to both God and to us to dare to ask for? "If you had been here ... But I am ... here." So we expect some things that we ask about to change, but not everything, and we get to decide which and what?

Remember that the disciples were concerned about another attempt on Jesus's life, following a recently failed attempt at stoning Him. They were evaluating the cost to Him to respond to the request. Indeed, how can we ever forget what it cost Him to answer our asking? The base price for every good and perfect gift was nothing less than His life laid down. There is therefore no such thing as a cheap answer. We do not consider the cost to divinity of our deliverance, anymore than Mary and Martha thought for a moment that the saved life of their brother might be at the expense of the life of the healer. He would be walking knowingly into the inferno of hatred that would burn Him. When we have done our asking, we really need to trust this One who loves us, for the miracle that has the greatest and most glorious outcome *for Him*.

Our Delay – His Day

Jesus says something interesting here about timing. "Jesus answered, 'Are there not twelve hours of daylight? A man who walks by day will not stumble, for he sees by this world's light. It is when he walks by night that he stumbles, for he has no light'" (11:9). We are now well-used to John's sayings which carry more than one meaning. You cannot hear about light in this gospel without knowing its cumulative meaning and relation to Jesus, the light of the world. Jesus is simply saying that as long as it is day (i.e. as long as the time is given by God for His work) then the disciples' fears for Him are groundless. God's timings, God's purposes will be fulfilled and Jesus will finish the work He was given to do. We say, "It's delay." Jesus says, "It's still day." This is a very different view of time passing while waiting for an answer. There is something for us to learn here. Often the desperation of our asking-need can throw us off balance, out of sync, and precipitate pre-emptive actions on our part, and presumptuous, reactive decisions out of fear. In the absence of the answer we want we are tempted to take things into our own hands and force the issue. We end up leaving places where we should have stayed, agreeing to things we should never have considered, giving in to demands we should have rejected, accepting offers and invitations we should have refused, succumbing to temptation when we should have fled, going through a door when we should never even have been near that room, arriving at a destination when we should never have been on that road. If we walk in the light we can trust the timings of God and wait.

He then tells them that He is indeed going to respond to what was asked of Him and go to Bethany to wake Lazarus up. The humor here is welcome after all the intensity. Sleeping? Wonderful. Sleep is exactly what a sick guy (not a dead one) needs to recover. Then comes a wry (except it is not really funny at all) read-my-lips moment: "Lazarus is dead." Try not to think now of the Monty Python "this is an ex- parrot" skit, in which the store owner who sold the dead parrot was arguing that it was resting, stunned, or pining.[5] Nor was Lazarus resting, stunned or pining. This was the ex-Lazarus who was not traumatized, mesmerized or paralyzed. He was dead. Now what has happened to our asking?

Our Asking and Two Realities

Our asking must be informed by two realities: the true nature of our problem and the true nature of Jesus's power. They convince us of why we have to ask. There is absolutely nothing we can do in our own strength to spiritually enliven ourselves, yet amazingly we still try to do so, and we hail these dead works as the essence of what life is really about. Of course, we like to believe that our problems and the consequences of our sin, as the disciples hoped for Lazarus, will be just like a passing touch of flu, a minor lapse, a momentary hitch, a fleeting shadow, a tiresome inconvenience, a bad dream that will be gone with sunrise. However, millions of people will discover too late, when the night that Jesus spoke about does fall and when men do stumble, that all the positive-thinking, stress-management, die-hard determination, actualization techniques and new-age hocus-pocus, with everything techno thrown in for good measure – cannot raise the dead. We can beautify the coffin but we cannot raise the corpse.

Lazarus was dead. Without Christ he would remain so. We are dead. Without Christ we will remain so. This is what needs asking about. But was that not the strangest thing for Jesus to say? Was it tactful in the circumstances? "I am glad I was not there ... for your sake ... so that you may believe" (v14). How glad is Lazarus about this? All that weeping going on at what appeared unanswered asking and Jesus found reason to be glad in it? All that the askers saw was the bereavement – and all Jesus saw were the benefits. He does not come to help people who ask Him to manage their wakes, to help them just to exist in a living death or a dying life; to relieve their dying hope with temporary anodynes or smelling salts. He comes to connect our asking with His timely glorious will no less, the will of Him who is the resurrection and the life. Come, now is the time to ask for this one to act.

Or Maybe Not Because It's Just Too ...

No doubt it was a subdued bunch of disciples that approached Bethany. They had already missed the funeral. Martha is coming toward them, and there is no Mary in sight. Perhaps she was just too disconsolate to be able to talk to Jesus. Maybe she was making a point about her disappointed hope in His response. So what would Jesus say to the grief-stricken Martha? "Sorry I'm a little late dear ... How did the memorial service go?" Thomas, the natural depressive, no doubt braced himself for the awkward greeting. What now follows in the story presents the differences between human and divine responses to the same situation. However, there is a strange similarity between the reactions of the characters to the unanswered problems, and the practiced reflex reactions of our own self-defense systems, whenever we are presented with the undeniable reality of the decomposition of our spiritual life, or the decay and mess that is the result of our sin, or the death of our hope. These similar reactions to our need serve to equally silence our asking.

- **It's too dangerous**: (v8) Walk away from it, abandon any hope because to engage the problem now, to deal with the consequences now, is to court disaster. It is going to cause too much trouble. Preserve the peace. Resign yourself. Let it be. Don't ask.
- **It's too difficult**: In any case, the problem is too far-gone now, and there is no point in asking for anything else. This is not one of your straight-forward "spit in the blind man's eye" jobs. This is past the point of rescue or resuscitation, so why ask?
- **It's too embarrassing**: There is a feeling of discomfort in all this. There is almost a sense of shame. The unanswered asking has left everyone feeling a bit naked, a bit exposed and there is not enough condolence to clothe the self-consciousness of it all. Asking is just a bit too awkward now.
- **It's too distressing:** (v20) Mary is staying at home which seems to speak for the hopelessness. Hiding her sense of sorrow for Jesus's apparent lack of response, she is giving the impression that there is nothing more to talk about, thus no reason to go and meet Jesus for a depressing conversation. Or maybe she had removed herself so much into a place of isolation that she just never heard the news that Jesus had eventually been sighted up the road. She was cloistered away surrounded by friends who were trying to comfort her (v31). It is strange that we too can get so engaged by our sorrows that we fail completely to discern the Christ who waits for us to come to him. So we do not ask.
- **It's too disappointing:** This is the response from the nameless crowd. It was even seen as disappointing for Jesus. "See how He loved him" (v36). They could not discern more than a feeling, since faith had long since been displaced. "Could not He who opened the eyes of the blind man have kept this man from dying?" (v37). "You'd have thought wouldn't you…?" This captures the tone of the gossip, the questioning and doubt about who Jesus really was. "Such a shame… and we thought He was his friend…" Maybe they took some satisfaction, some sense of superiority in the fact that they had arrived there to comfort the sisters long before He did. There was clearly genuine puzzlement and disappointment at this failure of Jesus to intervene. They asked for Jesus; He could have done the

miracle; He did not answer and there was no miracle. In the absence of the answer all we are left with is the unanswered asking. No need to add to the crippling disappointment and add insult to injury by asking again. Except the asking does not stop but it is now less the interrogative that is asking God, and more the interrogation that questions God.

- **It's too bad:** What might have been: "...my brother would not have died" (v21). There is genuine regret here but that is the way it goes for everyone. You just have to accept it and live with it. Hopefully, life will limp on. We tried the asking but no need to do it again because it does not work.
- **It's too late:** "If you had been here" (vs. 21, 32). Maybe something could have been done. If you had answered then, or in that way, then it could have happened back then. Circumstances were better back then. I had more faith and hope back then. I could ask back then, but not anymore.
- **It's too good to be true:** "Your brother will rise again" (v23). Would you have winced if you had been a disciple and heard Jesus say this in these circumstances? A public relations problem just got immeasurably worse. Thomas was scrambling for his anti-depressants. But wait. Of course, Jesus was being thoughtful and pastoral, reminding them of the resurrection at the last day. Martha treats it as a word of well-meant consolation. "I know he will rise again at the resurrection at the last day" (v24). I get that Jesus. The only problem is that good and true doctrines still have a way of sounding a bit hollow at a time like this, and still do not help to provide a late explanation to the unanswered asking. Martha is not denying the truth of what Jesus seems to be saying. She is just not connecting with it. As we have already noted, it is true but it does not have anything to do with the reality of her world of unanswered asking.

Have we ever been there? We have done our asking, and then we have ceased our asking. It is too dangerous to go back to it, because it will stir up too much trouble and pain. It is too difficult anyway. It is too disappointing, and too distressing to think about other undesired and undesirable possibilities, especially when hope has taken a beating. It is embarrassing to be unanswered. We were bold in our asking and now we look and feel stupid. We are feeling shame in our unresolved situation and circumstances. The faith we once had is looking irrelevant right now. It is too bad, too late, and any other possible good outcome is too good to be true. We know the doctrines; we actually believe them, really, but we are having a hard time connecting with them right now, or should we say, they do not seem to be connecting with our reality. These are the responses of everyone standing there by Lazarus' tomb. So what about Jesus? What were His responses?

Our Asking – God's Answering

Into this tangle of groans and moans, this ruin of remorse and regret, this wreckage from the asking that hit the wall unanswered, comes Jesus. Like surgical scissors, His responses cut through the Gordian knot of unanswered asking's grief.

- **He repeats A PROMISE: "Your brother will rise again"** (v23). He had already said that this would not end in death. He keeps His Word to do what is best for us in every situation. He must see and know something that we do not, and desire something that we have long since given up on. The promises of God, though seemingly un-cashable at the moment of deepest debt, and unhelpful at the time of greatest need, still remain non-negotiable and the sure basis that the one who saved us will give us all we need for life and godliness and will procure for us the needful provision for what His will has prepared for us to do and to be. The promises of God remain foundational for our assurance and succor. He is a present help in time of trouble. He is present at the graveside of this buried hope. He did promise that He would never leave us nor forsake us. The promises were not about make-believe but make-better. He said whoever came to Him would not be turned away, especially if they came in a coffin. It seems that the clearer we are about our inability to save ourselves the more He likes it. Our death does not contaminate Him. His presence decontaminates us. He does not come to bury with empty promises.
- **He makes A PRONOUNCEMENT: "I am the resurrection and the life"** (v25). The promise is followed by a pronouncement,

a proclamation if ever there was one. This was not resurrection wrapped up in the wording of a doctrine, of a catechetical statement, of a line from a liturgical creed. This was not resurrection as a proposition but as a person. "I AM..." Suddenly the issue has less to do with what I know about my problems (my death, or my sin, or my prison) but about how much I know about who He is in relation to it (savior for my sin, deliverer from my prison, life for my death). Where the doctrine did not relate, where the theologizing failed, He insists on relating personally and presently. It is almost amusing, certainly unexpected, but at this point Martha delivers a volley of apparent belief. "I believe that you are the Christ the Son of God, who was to come into the world" (v27). Yes, she is still definitely orthodox but still there is no connection between professed creed and present crisis. Her doctrine was in great shape but just did not seem to have the stamina to get her where she needed to be. The formula was not quite the stuff of faith. Despite appearing to be in the ozone layer, Jesus was actually the only one in touch with reality.

There is one lovely little touch. Jesus notices Mary's absence. The text says that Martha goes back to tell her that Jesus is asking for her. Not asking after her, but for her. While we are sitting around mourning our losses and bewailing the possibilities that His love for us is somewhere between questionable and quizzical, it is precisely the unchanging love of Christ that initiates and asks that we still keep coming to Him –that we keep on asking. Would to God that our responses to His invitation were as speedy as Mary's. "When Mary heard this she got up quickly and went to Him" (v29). His equal need for her to be there with Him is unabashed. Jesus did not move, did not do another thing until she came to Him. Her first words are the repeat of Martha's: "Lord, if you had been here ... When Jesus saw her weeping, and the Jews who had come along with her also weeping, He was deeply moved in spirit and troubled" (vs. 32-33).

- **He gives A PROOF: "Where have you laid him? ... Come and see Lord"** (v34). It seems that Jesus loves to engage others in the answer.

He did some asking of His own. He asked the obvious. He still does. He seeks our confession, our admission, and our invitation. His question and their answer cut right to the heart of the matter. Where is the problem? Where is the source of the grief? What is the loss of joy, loss of worth, loss of personhood, loss of integrity, loss of dignity, loss of hope, loss of direction, loss of calling, loss of love, loss of meaning ... loss of life? Right here Lord. Maybe we could have argued that this was the time for Jesus to do one of his "say the word from a distance" kind of miracles. Civilized distance would be preferable – does He have to reveal the corpse, the source of sorrow and hopelessness, defeat and despair? Do we really want answers that get our hands this dirty? Do we want answers that require that we face the effects of all this: the consequences, the realities that are better left where they are, out of sight all the time and out of mind some of the time. Asking is one thing but answering this way?

The preface to the concluding action was simply "Jesus wept." No wonder. It is as strong a word for grief as you can find. They thought His tears were proof of His love for His friend, but they were evidence of the heartbreak and righteous anger at the unbelief that had caused the death of all hope and faith. It not only communicates the depth of His passions and compassions but also the divine anger in His confrontation with the work of Satan. No wonder He was so troubled by the sea of despondency and resignation around Him. He stands there, in-between, in the no-man's land of grief between man and God, between good doctrine and bad despair, between what is and what might have been, between a dreaded finality and a hoped-for future. Surely He was bearing already the crushing weight of our infirmities and iniquities.

The text tells us that Jesus "came to the tomb" (v38). He does not come to read the inscriptions or simply to leave flowers. His interest is not to beautify our gravesite or give us a veneer of respectability. This is such moving footage of the way that Jesus insists on approaching the off-limits of our desolation. Then the unbelievable, impossible to anticipate instruction: "Take away the stone!" Notice again that there is no abracadabra here, no 'hey presto!', of the kind we always want in our answers. Human volition, human choices to participate and co-operate with Him were necessary for the answer to be effected.

Who Is Delaying Now?

At this point there is a delay of a different kind. Ironically, this time it is Martha doing the delaying, having once accused Jesus of being responsible for tardiness. Well might she step in between Jesus and the problem. "By this time there is a bad odor." No kidding. So how badly do you want God's answer to your asking? The consequences of our dead works and our dead sins do have an after-smell, an after-taste. Having commented upon the divine "YET", here is its companion it would seem: "BUT LORD!" We can all relate to this in our past, and maybe for some it is in the present. That root of bitterness, that chronic attitude, that secret sin, that intractable bondage, that unresolved anger that withheld forgiveness – they should not be exposed to sunlight. We ask for healing and joy and peace and direction ... but Lord! Equally and eerily familiar are the interventions that block His healing progress, His delivering intent in answer to our asking. And then there are the wretched stones that He insists on being moved simply because they obstruct and hinder His engagement. What are our stones that impede His answering to what we ask for? What deceit, what fear, what avoidance, what denial, what suppression, what hypocrisy, what delay? As Martha stands with her arms outstretched barring Jesus's way toward the tomb, she is defending life as it is. The truth is that she ends up defending death as it is.

But thankfully and gloriously, there seems to be a simple principle at work here. If we do the rolling, He will do the resurrecting. His answering asks something of us. Our confession, our invitation, our rolling of the stone surrenders access to Jesus. Others may be shocked by what is revealed. The delay served to reveal the decay. The crowd may draw back but Jesus never flinched, averted His gaze, or held His nose. So that brings us to the enacting of the answer to the asking, the proof of his promise and pronouncement.

What An Answer!

What follows is presented with an incredible economy of detail.

- **"Take away the stone ... they took away the stone"** (v39-41). He works best in the light. Is this not how John's gospel opened? He was "the light of men." You cannot illuminate your own darkness, but let Him in and where He is, light is, and the darkness cannot put it out. His answers to your asking will expose some things.
- **"Did I not tell you that if you believed you'd see the glory of the Lord?"** (v40) Earlier Jesus had asked, "Do you believe this?" Nor will He spare us the question about our state of belief. We asked but did we believe? We asked as if we trusted but did we really have faith in Him? Our confession of belief is so important. We must take responsibility for our response to Jesus. He simply asked people to believe His word. Do we believe this when we ask?
- **"Then Jesus looked up and said, Father, I thank you that you have heard me"** (v41). That sounds like such a short asking on Jesus's part for He seems to go straight to the Amen! The outcome Jesus was after is mentioned in His prayer: "that they may believe that you sent me." Jesus's concern was that any answer to the asking would not simply spotlight who He was as the Son, but would center-stage the Father who sent Him. Beyond a miraculous answer of bodily resurrection, He wanted them to see the desired outcome of all asking: the glory of God in the answer.
- **"Jesus called in a loud voice, Lazarus come out! ... the dead man came out"** (v43). You have to love that loud voice, the rehearsal for the loudest cry of our salvation that was to come, "It is finished!" You have to love the fact that He does not even address death, or the problem, but speaks Lazarus' name. It is the person, not the problem itself, that Jesus is really after. You have to love that He does not bother with the grave-clothes. This is strange when you think about it. Why not take them off then do a number on the body? But the body is not the heart of the problem. It is a picture of the truth that if you free the spirit, the grave-clothes will follow suit and be loosed. There is no point in the answer picking at the packaging

of the problem if it is our wounded heart that needs healed, or our bound spirit that needs to be freed from its present idolatry. Are we ready for this when we ask?

- **"Take off the grave-clothes!"** (v44) The answer comes with an instruction to the community. There is a vital community component to our asking, and equally, a necessary community sharing in the answering. If one suffers we all suffer. The asking of one becomes the asking of many. In the same way that we get involved in another's asking, we are invited to share in each other's answers of deliverance; not just in the joys of it, but also in the process of healing and restoration itself. Jesus commits others to participate in His answering work. He commits Lazarus to a wider network of care and attention, loosing and freeing. This is God's answer to the asking!

Responding to the Answer

In conclusion, please note that there are two responses to the answer. Of one group it said, "they plotted". The fuse had been lit that would explode in Passion Week. There are some who are tempted, once they see how He answers, to eliminate His presence lest He comes too near again, lest it gets too raw, lest it challenges too radically the status quo of accustomed life.

Of the other group it says, "they put their faith in Him." They set off for a memorial service and ended up at a welcome-home party. Their response was to embrace Jesus and the evidence of His saving work in their brother Lazarus; to accept His answers according to His will, His timing, His purposes, and His outcomes. There is no cookie-cutter template here, but there are truths that are sure. He does love, He does hear, He does answer, He does act in accordance with the greatest answer for the greatest glory.

Asking In Our Bethany

Indeed, Bethany is still a place to go to when we are struggling with unanswered asking; when all we want is an immediate 'YES' and all we seem to get is 'YET'. But Bethany is still a place that gathers those who trust the Lord for the answer to their asking that most manifests His ultimate glory. May the Lord's will be revealed in our Bethany's, in the answers that are according to His knowledge of what is needed, when it is needed. May it be a place where we express the rigor of the asking as well as experience the relief of the answering; a place where the brokenness of our asking, will become the breaking open of our answers.

If we are serious and desperate enough, humbly needy of His intervention enough, honest enough about the death we cannot raise, we will simply ask of Him, and connect our asking to His glory. He knows how many hours there are in our day; He knows our times and our timings. He said He loves us, He hears us and He knows us. We must not stop praying our unfinished asking until we know that God has spoken His 'Amen'. There is no past due date on asking. That is why we ask and keep on asking because at the end of the day, there is no end of the day, if our asking is essentially about His glory and His eternal work and purposes in us.

If, in our Bethany, we are still mourning over the "if you only had been there for me..." routine, and no longer asking, then like Mary, we need to come to Him again, and ask again in His Name and thank Him that His daily intercession of the Father continues on our behalf at the throne of God. He is still saying, "Father I know that you hear me." Maybe in all our asking for this and that, it would be helpful for us to ask Him what He is asking for us that is most needful for Father's glory and our resurrection of faith and hope and joy. Maybe?

"Everything in prayer depends upon our apprehending this – IN MY NAME." - Andrew Murray

"Asking in Jesus's Name - that is our passport!" - E.M.Bounds

"'The name of Jesus gives my prayers royal access. They get through. Jesus isn't just the savior of my soul. He is the savior of my prayers ... My prayers come before the throne of God as the prayers of Jesus." - Paul Miller

"The spirit of prayer in Christ's name is the true child-spirit." - P.T.Forsyth

"Christ as Mediator sends His own to His Father to ask supply of their wants, and allows them to tell that He sent them, as one recommends a poor body to a friend. So to pray in the name of Christ is to go to God as sent by the poor man's friend." - Thomas Boston

"To pray in the name of Christ is to pray as one who is at one with Christ, whose mind is the mind of Christ, whose desire are the desires of Christ, and whose purpose is one with that of Christ." - Samuel Chadwick

"We have the heart of God as soon as we place before Him the name of His Son." - John Calvin

"The glorifying of the Father in the mission of the church will be the fruit of intercession offered by the church in the name of Jesus." - Leslie Newbiggin

11
Asking in Jesus's Name

It's All In the Name

"Ask in my name." Of all that Jesus taught about asking, this is one of the most important things to understand and to do. It would seem that we have registered this, given the high percentage of prayers that end: "...in Jesus's name. Amen." But what does this mean? Surely it is not just a liturgical ending that politely but religiously lets everyone know we are done, and they are now free to pray. It is not a rubber stamp or a hopeful affirmation that makes up for the lack of faith that might be latent in what has just been asked for. It is not a spiritual sounding 'abracadabra'. As Donald Bloesch commented, the idea that the mere repetition of the name of Jesus somehow "has automatic efficacy is more akin to magic than biblical belief." [1] What we can say is that this truth cannot be complicated or difficult to comprehend if God is so eager that we ask of Him. If He paid the highest price in the sacrifice of His Son, Jesus, so that we could ask of Him as a son and daughter asks of their father, then He is not going to make it unduly difficult or impossible to do so, for His sake, not just ours. Asking is not the obstacle course that some have made it out to be. He really wants us to ask.

By His death, Jesus "destroyed the barrier, the dividing wall of hostility", atoning for the sin that separated us from God, thus providing "access to the Father by one Spirit" (Ephesians 2:14-18). All three persons of the Trinity work together to allow us to have an asking relationship with Father. "Therefore since we have a great high priest who has gone through the heavens ... *let us approach* the throne of grace with *confidence*" (Hebrews 4:14-16). "Therefore, since we have *confidence* to enter the most holy place by the blood of Jesus, by a new and living way opened for us through the curtain, that is His body ... *let us draw near* to God with a sincere heart in *full assurance* of faith" (Hebrews 10:19-22). If the grounds of our *assurance* are challenged, we will lose confidence to *approach*, and not avail ourselves of *access* and consequently cease to *ask* in Jesus's name. The enemy of our souls will do everything in his power to booby trap and obstruct our assurance, precisely because that stops us approaching (either because of false condemnation, or true but unheeded conviction) and that means that if we do not access we will not ask. But Jesus wants us to ask, and to ask in His name. How is that for confidence?

Where Does This Phrase Come From?

There are no less than six occurrences of this idea of "asking in His name" in the upper room conversation on the eve of Jesus's betrayal and crucifixion. It is interesting that Jesus does not give any explanations about what this means, perhaps because a Jew would be familiar with what was represented by "the name." In His last recorded asking before Gethsemane, Jesus says to His Father "I have revealed your name" (John 17:6). Earlier, Jesus had made the equation between believing "in the name" (John 3:18) and believing in Himself, the Christ. A Jew understood that "the name" was the concise compendium of all that a person was: their character, personality, work, reputation – anything and everything about them. There are over 150 ways that Jesus is named in the New Testament alone, so there is no end to what is "in the name".

Why the repetition? Clearly, Jesus's insistence is pointing to its importance. It is almost as if He is doing His own "asking and keep on asking." Some, like Andrew Murray, see it as an evidence of "how slow our hearts would be to take it in." [2] It is puzzling, given this repeated emphasis on asking at the Last Supper, that so many commentaries on the text say so little about it. The context is important for our understanding of its meaning. He is about to go to the cross and finish the work the Father gave Him to do, and the main thing He seems to want to talk about is asking. The entire backdrop to the asking that Jesus is talking about is the work of redemption that He is going to complete through His death, resurrection, ascension and glorification. We should therefore assume that this asking has something to do with asking for what Jesus died for.

Here are His references:

John 14: 13-14: "And I will do whatever you *ask in my name,* so that the Son may bring glory to the Father. You may *ask me for anything in my name,* and I will do it."

John 15:16: "You did not choose me, but I chose you and appointed you to go and bear fruit—fruit that will last. Then the Father will give you whatever you *ask in my name.*"

John 16:23, 24, 26: "In that day you will no longer ask me anything. I tell you the truth, My Father will give you whatever you *ask in my name*... Until now you have not *asked for anything in my name.* Ask and you will receive, and your joy will be complete ... In that day you will *ask in my name.* I am not saying that I will ask the Father on your behalf."

Asking As the Sign of His Presence

We have observed how much Jesus taught about asking and how His entire life and ministry were grounded in asking the Father. Last words are important, and of all the things that He could have focused on, the final extended conversation about asking in the Upper Room was the way He drew attention to its absolute necessity for the lives of the disciples, present and future. Jesus makes it quite clear to the disciples that He is going away but that when they see Him again (after the resurrection) an entirely new era will have begun which will bring them into a totally new experience of prayer. Until now, they had been asking things of Jesus, and they had been praying their Jewish prayers. But after the resurrection, an entirely new way of asking would be inaugurated. Asking 'in His name' would be one of the characteristics of the new age. It is worth noting that post-resurrection they go from doubting questions to bold asking, circumstantial evidence for the resurrection that is seldom, if ever, mentioned (John 16:23). Jesus will be physically absent, but by asking in His name they will continue to experience

His presence. This is an extraordinary revelation. Asking becomes a sign of His presence. Asking becomes this vital link with Jesus. It is almost as if asking replaces sight. Blessed are those who have not seen yet believe, and we know that those who believe, ask.

Post-resurrection asking is about to go heavenly, and go global. "Christ Jesus, who died – more than that, who was raised to life – is at the right hand of God and is also *asking for us*" (Romans 8:34). "Because Jesus lives forever, He has a permanent priesthood. Therefore He is able to save completely those who come to God through Him, because He always lives to *ask for them*" (Hebrews 7:24-25). What is it that will be the new key to prayer? Simply, they will now *ask in Jesus's name*. And did they ever! In Acts 1:14, "They all joined together constantly in asking." The story of the church begins with the disciples asking the Father in Jesus's name in an upper room after the resurrection and ascension, for the very same thing that Jesus asked for in an upper room prior to the cross – and the answer was the day of Pentecost and the birth of the church, and our birth.

Too Good to Be True?

We have been trained to believe that if it sounds too good to be true, it probably is, which then makes it bad and not good at all. "Anything?" "Whatever?" C.S.Lewis asked if this was truth in advertising. Do Jesus's promises about asking not sound a bit over the top, and would hearers not be forgiven if they thought them somewhat exaggerated or extravagant? Do these repeated promises deliver? They sound very open but are there any conditions that will just whittle away at the promise until it only applies to a few things and a few people? Yes, this is problematic if we understand these promises as only having to do with our personal wishes. No, these promises do not cover anything we want. They are only relevant to the life that is in Christ, the vine, and to the production of fruit. Andrew Murray understood the matter:

> The promises of our Lord's farewell discourse, with their wonderful six-fold repetition of the unlimited 'anything' and 'whatsoever', appear to us altogether too large to be

> taken literally and they are qualified down to meet our human ideas of what appears seemly. It is because we separate them from that life of absolute and unlimited devotion to Christ's service to which they were given." [3]

The promises do not come without the pruning. The "woodiness" of the self-life that would resist or seek to avoid pruning, cannot be served by asking. Jesus makes an inseparable link between asking and the fruit that only grows because of the pruned branch. It is only in the context of bearing fruit that we will ask, and it will be for more fruit that we will ask. In his excellent exegesis of John's Gospel, Don Carson makes clear that the fruit that Jesus refers to in John 15:5 "is the consequence of prayer in Jesus's name ... The means of the fruitfulness for which they have been chosen is prayer in Jesus's name." [4] So are these promises to act upon our asking just too good to be true? How can they be if they are the words of Jesus? But it is too bad, if the abiding relationship that He describes as the context for asking is not true of us.

So What Does It Mean?

What do we need to understand about that phrase "in my name"? A simple illustration may help. This is a version of one that was used by many great preachers, especially R.A Torrey. He defined asking "in His Name" like this: "It means simply this, that you ask the thing that you ask from the person of whom you ask it, on the ground of some claim that the person in whose name you ask it has upon the one from whom you ask it." [5] If I go to your Bank with one of my personal bank checks and try and cash it, I am going to have a problem. Why? It is because they are going to ask me if I have an account with them. It is clear from the Bank check that I have passed to the teller that I do not. Nothing in fact that I present to them *in my name* will produce anything because my name has absolutely no claim against the bank. However, if you write me a signed check against your account in that bank, and I present that to the teller, then I am in the money. I will receive the amount asked for if your name is on the check because you have legitimate grounds for the claim. Here is the principle. You can ask confidently in someone's name if that someone has a claim on the one being asked. As Torrey put it: "It means we can go to the bank of heaven, on which neither you nor any other man on earth has any claim of his own, but upon which Jesus has infinite claims."[6]

We have no claims on God. We have done nothing that makes Him obliged to us, or that makes Him our debtor. God does not owe us anything and thus He is not beholden to us. We cannot argue our merits. If we think we do have some grounds for claims on God, including thinking that God owes us some explanations for unanswered asking, then we are asking in our name and not Jesus's name. We can only pray in the name of Jesus if we know that we have absolutely no claims on God, no rights. The right that we are given, that we are graced with, is the right to ask in Jesus's name when we have no right to ask in our own.

The Grounds of Asking

When we ask, we do so on the grounds of Jesus's claims on the Father. We do not have the ground to stand on, but He does. Centuries before, Daniel foresaw this when he said that the people did not present their asking to God "on the ground of our righteousness but on the ground of your great mercy" (Daniel 9:18). The risen Christ can claim His redemption rights. So what are some of those "infinite" and righteous claims? He has His claim on us as His inheritance, promised to Him through His obedience unto death even the death of the cross. He has a claim on that which He has fully purchased. He can claim the right of access to the Father. He can claim on the basis of His relationship with the Father. He can claim upon the will of the Father because He only ever does what Father wills.

When I ask in the name of the one who has the claims on the one being asked, when I ask in the name of Jesus of the Father, when I am allowed as it were to sign my asking with His signature, then I am heard and my asking is acknowledged, received and responded to. Jesus gives us the right and the authority to use His name to access the resources of the Father and make our claim, as if He was the one doing the claiming. This is why we can ask boldly, and why we can ask for great and precious things.

This means that we can never ask anything in Jesus's name without being worshipfully conscious of the fact that Jesus Christ is our mediator. There is absolutely no room here for self-confidence or self-congratulation, for presumption or for arrogance, for a sense that we have personal rights or that we are owed, for parading our sense of worth or experience, or assumed faith. We can never forget that the Last Supper, on the eve of His death, was the context for Jesus's teaching about asking. As Donald Bloesch defines it:

> To pray in the name of Christ means to pray in the awareness that our prayers have no worthiness or efficacy apart from His atoning sacrifice and redemptive mediation. It means to appeal to the blood of Christ as the source of power for the life of prayer. It means to acknowledge our complete helplessness apart from His mediation and intercession. To pray in His name means that we recognize that our prayers cannot penetrate the tribunal of God unless they are presented to the Father by the Son, our one Savior and Redeemer. [7]

It is only through Jesus the Mediator and only because of the price that He paid, that we can ask. Our asking is premised on the fact of Jesus's finished work of salvation. Warfield states it bluntly: "For sinners the atonement of Christ lays the only basis for real prayer." [8] Our asking can only become His asking if we come to God "through Him, because He always lives to intercede" (Hebrews 7:25). Whenever we ask in Jesus's name we are proclaiming in our praying that Jesus is the only way for us to come to God. Writing over two hundred years ago, Thomas Boston urged this truth on his congregants in Aberdeen.

> We must take hold of the Mediator and come in at His back, who is the Secretary of heaven ... No prayers are heard and answered but for the Mediator's sake ... He is the only Mediator of redemption, so He is the only Mediator of intercession." [9]

All asking in Jesus's name is founded and grounded on the finished work of Christ. If it is "in His name" then as Craig Keener affirms in his commentary on John's Gospel, our asking can only be "predicated on His merit alone." [10] A.B.Simpson echoed this conclusion: "Asking in Jesus's name, therefore, is asking that for which Jesus has suffered and died, and which He has freely, fully purchased for all His own." [11] Oswald Chambers repeated this truth in his devotional writing, that God answers our asking "on the ground of redemption and no other ground" and that our asking is heard "not because we are earnest, not because we suffer, but because Jesus suffered." [12] What does this then mean for those of us who ask? If our salvation was the great outcome of His submissive asking of the Father, then, as Professor James Houston rightly deduces, anyone who asks in Jesus's name will "co-operate in that task: dying as Jesus died, being raised from death as Jesus was raised by the Father." [13]

The Gospel of John begins by telling us that Jesus "came from the Father" (1:14) to give to those who receive Him "the right to become children of God" (1:12). When talking to the disciples about their future asking, He said that "*My* Father will give you whatever you ask in My name" (16:23). But four chapters later, after the resurrection, He says, "I am returning to My Father and *your Father*" (20:17). This serves to make the same point, that God is only *our* Father as a consequence of the saving death of Jesus, the only basis for being "born again" and becoming a child of God who can ask of their Father. In the upper room, Jesus knew that once He fulfilled the will of the Father, once He had drunk of that cup, then the floodgates of asking would be opened for all. "In Jesus's name" is therefore no cheap slogan. And it cannot be an assumed imprimatur on just anything we want to ask. Does the "whatsoever" we ask for pass the test of what Jesus died for; of what He obtained for us by His salvific and mediatorial work on the cross?

So What Does This Mean For Us?

This is where it gets awesome. In a sense, we are Jesus's representatives. We are His ambassadors. He has given us a passport with His name and insignia on it that gives us unquestioned spiritual diplomatic access to the heavenly throne. When we ask in the Name of Jesus it is as if we are asking in His place. It is as if He is personally doing the asking. He makes our asking His asking. As Calvin put it, we are asking "as it were at the lips of Christ." [14] Professor Houston puts it this way: "Our prayers are no longer our prayers, made from our point of view, but are made from Jesus's point of view within us." [15] All of who He is, all of His titles, all of His character and nature, all of His personhood, all of His works, all of His words are applied to what is being asked for. This is the biblical understanding of what "the name" signified. It represented total identity, and functioned as a complete summary of personhood and character. In a theology of asking, to ask in Jesus's name is to request something of the Father, believing that all asking is founded on Jesus's finished work and grounded in His own revelation of Himself. This entirely explains why we can be bold and confident.

To be His representative and able to ask personally for ourselves in His name, it means that we can only ask what is concordant with His will. *We will ask for what He wants.* We can only ask for what He Himself would ask for: "His good, pleasing and perfect will" (Romans 12:2). Richard Foster explains it like this: "It means that we are making the kinds of intercessions He would make if He were among us in the flesh." [16] It is like saying that when we gather to ask, it is what Jesus would ask for if He were there with us in the prayer meeting. When Jesus says, "Ask what you will", it is already based on the assumption that our will, like His will, is only to do the will of the Father. So when we say that our asking in His name is as if He is doing the asking, that is true because the only asking that He could possibly do would be according to the will of the Father. Asking out of our own willfulness does not carry the promise of being answered. So asking in Jesus's name is about: having a *full assurance* of His saving work for us, and being in *full accord* with His will for us.

What a Name

This means that "whatever" or "anything" (John 14:13-14) is in fact conditioned by whatever is within the scope of His will and His work, by anything that is His desire and will for us. Samuel Chadwick was the saintly principal of Cliff College in England, and much quoted on prayer. "Prayer is endorsed by the Name when it is in harmony with the character, mind, desire and purpose of the Name." [17] Basic to understanding Jesus's words about asking "in His name" is knowing His will, expressed by us in our loving obedience to His commands, and in our abiding in Him, our living on the vine. We have noted that so much of Jesus's teaching about asking was at the Last Supper, so this holy context makes it perfectly clear that this is not an "anything goes" deal. There are stipulated conditions: intimacy (14:23); abiding (15:7); indwelling word (15:7); believing (14:12); loving and obeying (15:9-10); being solely motivated for the glory of God as the outcome (14:13-14). The old saints used to reduce these asking passages to two basic questions. *Who* gets what they ask for in His name? That question is answered by these conditions: believing, loving, obeying, abiding, glorifying, word-filled, Spirit-guided people. How do they have to ask in order to get what they ask for? That answer is "in His name".

Knowing His Name Before Knowing Our Need

We have already noted that our asking is not primarily determined by how well we know ourselves, and our needs, but simply by how well we know Jesus. The difference between godly and fleshly asking is intimacy with Jesus. We cannot ask "in Jesus's name" if we are not first in Jesus, abiding and remaining "in Him". The same conversation at the Last Supper that invited the disciples to ask in His name, again and again, is the same passage that repeats "in Me". Before Jesus told the disciples that they could ask in His name, He called them friends. Why? Because everything He learned from the Father He had made known to them. It is intimacy that is the context for learning the heart and will of the beloved, which means we know what to ask for. Thus it is a committed, intentional and deep relationship with Jesus that will always be asking in His name.

Intimacy will express itself in intercession. Our abiding will overflow in asking. Love for Jesus will fuel our asking of Him, and love for others will fuel our asking for them. Friendship with God tutors us in "the master's business" (to use Jesus's phrase) that informs us of His will, and inspires our asking for the holy success of His business. It is because asking is a fruit of intimacy that Jesus says that we ask so that our joy may be full. It has nothing to do with the answers yet. The joy is not conditional on the answers. All the fulfilled conditions for asking produce joy. It was when Jesus laid down the pre-conditions for our asking, love and obedience, that He said: "I have told you this so that My joy may be in you and that your joy may be complete" (John 15:11).

To ask in His name is essentially to be in union with Him, to be one with Him, to be so identified with Him, and He with us, that we share the same name. So if there is any acceptable use of the word 'level', Chadwick employed it: "Prayer reaches its highest level when offered in the Name which is above every name, for it lifts the petitioner into unity and identity with Himself." [18] His name becomes our name for the purposes of accessing, approaching and asking. His ID is ours and it is not identity fraud.

Summary: Asking In Jesus's Name

Here is a summary of some things that are operative when we ask in the name of Jesus:

- **Advocacy:** Jesus's last act on earth before entering the heavens was to raise His hands in the posture of asking and bless His disciples. Those hands were nail-pierced, reminding us that He would continue to exercise that high-priestly ministry on our behalf as He "entered not into a holy place made with hands ... but into heaven itself, now to appear before the face of God for us" (Hebrews 9:24). Indeed, "we have an advocate with the Father, Jesus Christ the Righteous" (1 John 2:1-2). He becomes our authoritative, advocating asker before the Father, presenting the claims of His righteousness as the ground of our appeal when we ask in His name.
- **Association**: We are identifying ourselves with Jesus as the Son of the Father, and accepting our identity as sons and daughters of the Father. We are not outsiders but family. How closely are we associated? We are "in Christ." Jesus has put His name upon us. D.M.McIntyre, in his classic on the prayer life of Jesus, wrote: "Praying in Jesus's name we are set free in our inner selves to take on our identity in Jesus as the Son of God." [19] We share a common cause in our asking. We are invited to ask on His account, and draw

on His account. He is asking us to ask for Him, on his behalf as it were, and not just for ourselves. Our name is not on it. "Jesus will associate Himself with us in our requests when our requests match what He wants for us." [20] So close is this association, it is as if we have Jesus's asking-nature in us, and we cannot but be lovingly welcomed, as Jesus Himself is loved. He asked that the world would know that the Father loved His disciples "as you love me." It should be understood that this association is more than just 'dwelling' with Him. He 'indwells' us so that His very spirit is within us, expressing our asking to the Father.

- **Access**: We have access to the Father by the blood of Jesus. We have access in His name. Without this access we are left with our own independence. Where there is no dependence there is no asking.
- **Approach**: Because Jesus is the great High Priest who has gone before us, we not only have access, but we have the invitation and authority to boldly approach the throne of grace itself. To get into the White House is one thing, but to get into the Oval Office is quite another. It is one thing to have the code to get into a place where we have no personal authority or leverage, and another to be able to walk the corridors to the very inner chambers of the operation. The name of Jesus is our security pass and assures us of both access and approach. You cannot be given access but denied approach. We are all in the inner circle of His love and power when it comes to our asking in Jesus's name.
- **Acceptance**: We know that the only ground of our acceptance is "in the Beloved" (Ephesians 1:6.) The acceptance of our asking is not assured by the legitimacy of our needs or requests, or even the sincerity of our affections. Because we are in the beloved, we have acceptance and we ask in the beloved's name.
- **Assurance**: It is because of who Jesus is, that His name is the confident calling card for all our asking. There is no confidence in our own name, or in the reasonableness and righteousness of our petitions. We have no leverage of ourselves. We have no persuasive credentials or communications in which we can be assured. As John put it so clearly, our assurance is our belief "*in the name* of the Son of God" (1 John 5:13-15) and in asking "according to His will." It is this

knowledge that assures us, and that now produces the "confidence we have in approaching God" assured that He hears us and will answer us. Blessed assurance, Jesus is mine, and He has set His name upon me, so when I ask, it is by His name that I am known. Is it any wonder that in a timeless treatise on assurance published in 1654, Thomas Brooks would conclude: "Usually the most praying souls are the most assured souls." [21] Our assurance in His name persuades us to ask, and as we do so, our asking becomes a sluice gate for the assurance that is both the premise and the product of our asking in Jesus's Name.

- **Appropriateness**: Obviously if Jesus's name is on it we cannot be asking for something that is not in keeping with who He is. This is a sanctifying effect on our requests.
- **Agreement**: Foundational to the agreement that invites us to ask in His name, is our agreement with everything that Jesus says about Himself, and everything scripture reveals about Him, in which we fully believe. We also live in agreement with His commands and obediently love Him. His name is inseparable from His will so to ask in His name is to ask in agreement with His will and His word. It is only possible to ask for the same things that Jesus would ask for. The nature of what we ask for will conform to Jesus's nature. Our need for ourselves, or anyone else, will be His need. Asking in His name will be in agreement with His purpose and His passions. Asking "in His name" will always be "for His sake." When we ask in agreement with Jesus, according to the Father's will in heaven, then we draw on an unquantifiable resource that is more than sufficient for any and every possible thing we could ever ask for.
- **Authority**: There is authority in Jesus's name recognized by angels as well as demons. Jesus has authorized us to be His representatives, so we have assurance that we will be recognized by the Father as those who are authorized users and agents of that authority.
- **Audacity**: Although this has become a pejorative term it actually has to do with boldness. Asking in the name of Jesus gives us the same boldness that Jesus Himself has. Precisely because asking acknowledges personal limitation, asking in His name has the

courage to go to the limit, to ask all the way, realizing that God invites us to test Him, though He is not thereby tested.

- **Approval**: To ask in Jesus's name is to have approval for what we request. In John 6:27, talking of Himself, Jesus said: "On Him God has placed His seal of approval." Jesus is approved of God, so His name carries that approval. We seek His approval in our asking, looking for His "Amen" not just ours. We also need to know that what we ask for meets with His approval. D.M.M'Intyre wrote: "As a man will not lend his name to any enterprise which does not approve itself to his mind, so our Lord Jesus grants His name only to those causes with which He Himself is identified." [22] We can only endorse our asking with His name if it is consistent with all that the name stands for. So important is this hallowed and reverential relationship between the character of His name and the content of our asking, that one commentator [23] reports Calvin's conviction that to by-pass asking in His name was tantamount to "a profanation of God's name." [24] We cannot ask Jesus to "pass on" through His intercession anything that does not accord with His name, and thus meet approval.
- **Anticipation**: Our confidence in the advocacy of the Holy Spirit when we ask is sufficient to heighten our anticipation. But furthermore, we have an understanding of how the Father feels about receiving our requests. The anticipation is shared. Together with us, the Holy Spirit is assured, to quote Houston, that "the Father's love is already eagerly anticipating those requests." [25] But there is another aspect to this sense of anticipation. The reason we are asking in His name is because He is not physically present to ask. That means that every time we ask in His name, there is a reminder about two things: where He is, and from whence He is yet to return. Whenever we ask in His name we are reminded that although we are engaging the purposes of God for this present world, we are equally anticipating what all this is unto, the world that is to come. What this means is that our asking in His name is a sign that a day is coming when all our asking for now will give way to nothing but adoring Him forever. As McIntyre put it: "Until then, all our petitions express themselves as a sigh for His appearing."

> [26] Asking "in His name" is thus both the *sign* and the *sigh* for His return. Of course, this quickens the importunity and the intensity of our asking.

It is all about advocacy; association; access; approach; acceptance; assurance; appropriateness; agreement; authority; audacity; approval; anticipation. It is all about who Jesus is, what He desires, and especially what He asks for us that He wants us to ask for too. We cannot ask in our own name any more than we can do anything spiritual in our own name. It is often the case, when the names of men seem more predominant than the name of Jesus, and when more attention is drawn to the ministry of men than the ministrations of the Holy Spirit, that you will find more public acting than private asking. If we knew what asking "in the name of Jesus" meant, our own names would not be up in lights, and there would be no opportunity for there to be glory for any other than Jesus, the name above all names.

We are agreed then that to ask in Jesus's name is not to use a magic mantra. In both Jewish and Roman tradition there were magicians who used the names of deities (secret names of God in the case of Jewish charlatans) to invoke the power for magic. We see an example of this in Acts 19 where Jews, including the seven sons of Sceva "tried to invoke the name of the Lord Jesus over those who were demon-possessed" (v13). At the time of Jesus, the Romans would say their prayers in the name of any number of gods, in the desperate hope that one of them might come up trumps. How wonderful that we ask confidently in only one name, because "there is no other name". We are also agreed that to ask in His name is not to use a rubber stamp or engage what commentarian Bruce Milne calls a "pedantic formality." [27] Because of all that the name represents, it can never be a vague slogan to endorse generalized non-specific prayers. We can be *very specific* about the *very specific* characteristics of Jesus that are summed up in that name, that we are asking to be applied to the *very specific* situation that we are asking about. What is it that we actually need Jesus to be and to do in the circumstances that we are asking for? Let us ask in His name for specific characteristics and provisions of that name to be operative in all that we ask for. In Jesus's Name. Amen.

Asking and the Holy Spirit

"How clear the two great truths stand out: where there is much prayer there will be much of the Spirit; where there is much of the Spirit there will be ever-increasing prayer. So clear is the living connection between the two, that when the Spirit is given in answer to prayer it ever wakens more prayer to prepare for the fuller revelation and communication of His divine power and grace." - Andrew Murray

"It is right, then, that the doctrine of God should precede that of prayer and that we should deal with prayer in the context of pneumatology, for the Spirit alone enables us to pray and gives us strength to do so." - Wolfgang Pannenberg

12

Never One without the Other

Ask In the Name of the Father, the Son and ...

Having seen how God the Father and God the Son are so intimately related with each other through asking, and with us through asking and answering, we should not be surprised that God the Holy Spirit is also equally and totally involved in our asking and in the communication of the Godhead among themselves. We cannot make the two essential confessions, "Jesus is Lord" and "Abba", without the Holy Spirit revealing and enabling. "No one can say 'Jesus is Lord' except by the Holy Spirit" (1 Corinthians 12:3). "You received the Spirit of sonship. By Him we cry 'Abba, Father!" (Romans 8:15-16) So what is the relationship between the Holy Spirit and our asking? In many textbooks of Christian Theology, the chapters that deal with the Holy Spirit usually have disarmingly little to say about the relationship between the Holy Spirit and prayer. Illustrative of this is a 255-page text I have in my library that focuses only on the theology of the Holy Spirit and yet has not a single page on prayer. Perhaps this was because the author observed that the Holy Spirit's ministry in prayer is "mentioned infrequently" in scripture. [1] How can this be? As John Stott put it: "The general ministry of the Holy Spirit in prayer is much neglected." [2] Rightly, he went on to affirm: "The Holy Spirit's inspiration is as necessary as the Son's mediation if we are to gain access to the Father in prayer." We should begin by affirming that there is a non-negotiable and non-replaceable relationship between the Spirit's work and our asking. All asking is not just "by the Holy Spirit' and "with the Holy Spirit" but also "in the Holy Spirit." There is no asking that is not attributable to the work of the Holy Spirit in us and through us. The revelation of the Father in the Son, revealed to us by the Holy Spirit, determines that our asking is 'Trinity asking.' Bloesch concludes: "The Holy Trinity is the basis of true prayer as well as its goal. Prayer, as biblical faith understands it, is made possible by the triune God and is directed to this God." [3]

"The prayer of a righteous man is powerful and effective" (James 5:16). This is one of the most commonly cited verses on prayer. Something is "working" but what, and who is working? There seems to be a conditioning of the possible effectiveness of asking by the designation of the asker as "righteous." Unrighteousness does not make for effective asking. But as true as that is, it will not do to read this verse as though effectiveness ultimately has to do with our state of righteousness while we are asking. We know where this can lead, as affirmed by Jesus's parable of the Publican and Pharisee. The problem is with the use of the word 'effective' (NIV, NRSV), particularly as it is commonly used now, having to do with results and getting things done. However, the emphasis here is not on *what* needs to be done according to our asking, but on *how* it is being done and *who* is ultimately doing it. For certain, it is not the righteous asker. The translations that use the word 'effectual' (AKJV, KJ21) help us to get nearer the meaning, and nearer to the subject of this chapter. The Greek word used (*energeo*) explains itself in the key contexts in which it is used. It conveys the idea of something "working in" or to put it another way, something "inwrought". This is how Paul describes faith (Galatians 5:6), the Word (1Thessalonians 2:13), and grace (Ephesians 3:7) in believers' lives. They have been "inwrought" and if not by them, by whom? What is this "inwrought" power of Ephesians 1:19 but "the working of His inner strength"? Paul makes this clear in another decisive statement about asking: "Now to Him who is able to do immeasurably more than all we ask or imagine, according to His power that is *at work in us*" (Ephesians 3:20). That which is "inwrought" in us when we are asking, the power that is effectual, and that consequently makes our asking effective, is exactly what Paul has just talked about and asked for: "I ask that out of His glorious riches He may strengthen you with power *through His Spirit* in your inner being" (3:16). Paul and James are totally agreed. So are the asking saints, like E.M.Bounds, who knew that our ability and our power to ask was "dependent on the measure of the Holy Spirit received by us, dwelling in us and working through us." [4] There is no effective asking without the "inwrought" working of the Holy Spirit. Asking and the Holy Spirit? They are inseparable because of what is "inwrought" in the asker by the Spirit of asking.

A Spirit of Grace and Asking

One of the great descriptions of the Holy Spirit in the Old Testament is: "a Spirit of grace and asking" (Zechariah 12:10). The prophet foresees the outpouring of the Holy Spirit at Pentecost after which it was not fear or timidity but the experience of grace that both initiated and inspired asking. It follows that wherever there is asking you will encounter the gracious work and ministrations of the Holy Spirit. In Acts 4 the believers "raised their voices together" to ask for help in a wonderfully Trinitarian prayer: "*Sovereign* Lord ... You spoke by the *Holy Spirit* ... through the name of your holy servant *Jesus*" (vs. 24-30). The asking was under "threats" but they asked for more boldness for preaching and for more signs and wonders. Is it any surprise what this kind of asking attracted? "After they asked, the place where they were meeting was shaken and they were filled with the Holy Spirit" (4:31). The Spirit of asking came upon them so should we be surprised by the outcomes? "With great power the apostles continued to testify ... and much *grace* was upon them all" (v33). Here is grace-asking. If we know that our asking is dependent on the Spirit of grace then we will never be able to be mistaken about any answers that we receive having anything to do with our merits or our rights. We will not be able to think that because of our assumptions about our needs, our insights, our obedience, our faithfulness, that we have any cash-in or cash-out rights that we are able to put in a layaway account that obliges God to answer by giving us what we want – or what we think we earned. We will not be able to make a fleshly thing out of our own asking as if somehow we have perfected what it is all about.

We need to grasp this. Where there is a Spirit of asking there will be great grace, because that is how the Holy Spirit comes to us. Grace is what He brings with His presence, and that is what we need when we are asking. We need to be convinced of that grace, and experience it. We need that grace to make us gracious in our submission of our requests to God, and not petulant or demanding or belligerent. We need that grace to trust Him for

His gracious responses. We need that grace to wait patiently, if need be, for answers. It is grace we are asking for. Is asking not an expression of need and dependence? Is it not to the "throne of grace" that we direct our asking? And what does scripture tell us that we can expect to find when we do so? Our asking will "find grace to help us in our time of need" (Hebrews 4:16).

It can equally be said that where there is the Spirit of grace, you will find much asking as a manifestation of that Spirit. Where the grace of God is operative, asking will be a gracious operation of the Spirit. As Spurgeon taught: "No grace, no prayer ... There can be no hair where there is no skin, and no true prayer where there is no grace. A prayerless soul is a graceless soul." [5] Where there is no grace there is no gratitude and ungrateful people are ungraceful and do not ask. Is it not true that the more you realize the great grace in which you stand, the grace of the gospel, the more there is an inevitable response to ask and keep on asking for that grace to be both personally experienced and expressed but also preached and received by everyone, in every nation. A mere knowledge of the doctrines of grace will not effect this. We must know the Spirit of grace and asking. Why was Paul impassioned and insistent about asking the churches to ask God for him in his international mission (Colossians 4:3; 1 Thessalonians 5:25)? The answer is because he was passionate about "the grace that is reaching more and more people" (2 Corinthians 4:15). If you are not moved by the grace of God you will not ask for much, well not for much that God desires. The Spirit of asking is a sanctifying Spirit and the very process of asking, in what it asks of our spirits, is a means by which we "grow in the grace" (2 Peter 3:18). Thus asking is a non-negotiable and necessary constituent element of discipleship.

It is worth noting that the first words recorded in scripture that were spoken by the apostle Paul, were not teaching people but asking God. "Who are you, Lord? Saul asked" (Acts 9:5). Paul's spiritual life was birthed in an asking room. Asking was the context for his deliverance. Benjamin Warfield, one of the great Reformed theologians of his day, used to teach Sunday-afternoon classes at Princeton Seminary for over thirty years. In one of these he spoke about "prayer as a means of grace". He drew the students' attention to Acts 9:11 that describes what Ananias heard in a vision about Saul of Tarsus: "for he is praying." Warfield went on to use this passage to show that prayer is indeed a means of grace. "The reason is that Paul is now prepared for the visit. And the preparation consists of two items: that he is praying and that he has seen in a vision Ananias coming ... The passage thus represents prayer as the state of preparedness for the reception of grace; and, therefore, in the strictest sense, as a means of grace." [6] Why would we be surprised that the Spirit of grace would be the means for both the preparation for grace, and the provision of grace? Warfield described the effect of this work of the Spirit upon a soul like Paul's as "like the flower turned upwards towards the sky and opening for the reception of life-giving rain." Asking, by this Spirit of grace, becomes "the very adjustment of the heart for the influx of grace." The Spirit of grace and asking then direct us and connect us to the God of all grace. The only means to receive grace is to employ the means that God has given – ask for it.

Holy Spirit-Asking In the New Testament

Whenever there is a move of the Holy Spirit, you will find a lot of asking: before it, during it and after it. Lack of asking, prayerlessness, must therefore be an absence of the Spirit before it is an absence of prayer. Pre-upper room, in the upper room, post-upper room, and the history of the early church establishes this *expectation* and *experience*. A.B.Simpson understood this: "Every new Pentecost has had its preparatory period of supplication." [7] Equally, the relationship between asking and the Holy Spirit is established in the *explanation* of New Testament teaching. Our asking is "in the Spirit ... in the Holy Spirit" (Ephesians 6:18; Jude 20). There is nothing that is spiritual that is not "in" or "by" the Spirit. Our entire life depends on the Spirit by whom "we put to death the misdeeds of the body" (Romans 8:13). This means that our spirit is now alive because of righteousness (Romans 8:10) so the only way that the asker in James 5:16 can even be "righteous" is because of the Holy Spirit's work. That work has qualified us to ask. All of our worship is by the Spirit (Philippians 3:3). Our entire life is lived "by the Spirit" (Galatians 5:16) and since we live by the Spirit, our entire walk with God is "in step with the Spirit" (Galatians 5:25). This is to say that all of our asking is in this context of the Spirit's life and work. When we ask, we are in step with the Spirit, energized by the Spirit, and our asking is first "inwrought" before it is spoken out.

Writing to the Philippians, Paul makes the assured connection between their asking on his behalf and "the help given by the Spirit" (Philippians 1:19). And of course, the Holy Spirit is a constant object of asking: "I keep asking that … the glorious Father may give you the Spirit … I ask that … He may strengthen you with power through His Spirit" (Ephesians 1:17; 3:16). When Paul is in a "struggle" and needing to be "rescued" (Romans 15:30) his appeal to the Romans to strive in their asking of God on his behalf is "by the love of the Spirit." The loving character of the Holy Spirit is what he expects to both energize and inform their hearts to ask. Jude understood this too, as he presented asking in the Spirit as a vital means for keeping us in the love of God. Those who ask are secured in His love. Those who are secure in His love cannot but ask. What a partnership! Spurgeon's comment on Jude v20 was direct: "Mark the grand characteristic of true prayer—in the Holy Ghost." [8]

Asking assumes we have access, but without the Spirit's work, that access would not be possible. *"Through Him (Jesus)* we both have access to the Father *by one Spirit"* (Ephesians 2:18). Working together with the Son, the Holy Spirit enables our access to the Father so that we can ask. Our asking is the means by which we receive the Spirit, and the Spirit is the means by which we ask for anything. The Spirit is the context, the content and the communicator for our asking. Any way you look at it, asking and the Holy Spirit are hand in glove.

So Who Are We Asking?

We have established the basis of a scriptural template for asking. It is to and of the Father (Matthew 6:6), in the name of the Son (John 16:24), by, through and in the Holy Spirit (Jude 20). Many ask if it is possible to ask of all three persons. As three-in-one, most certainly when we ask of God, who always is Father, Son and Holy Spirit, distinctive in persons, one in personhood. Scripture asserts that God is one (John 17:22) but is three divine persons (John 6:27, Hebrews 1:8; Acts 5:3-4). This oneness is not simply the collaborative or co-operative of three independent beings. (This is called 'tritheism'.) Each 'person' of the Trinity is presented with an identifiable individuality that has no traits of independent individualism.

For example, they are all presented as distinct communicators with each other within the Trinity and with us, yet they all speak the same thing with one voice. For each person, what is 'his' or 'mine' is always 'theirs' (John 16: 12-15). Like nothing else, it is asking that draws us into the interpersonal, 'intratrinitarian' relationships of Father, Son and Holy Spirit. It is asking that becomes the means by which we learn about the divine economy of love and labor shared by all three, but then acted out as one.

In his excellent treatment of Christian Spirituality, Alistair McGrath writes: "The concept of *perichoresis* (co-inherence, mutual interpenetration) allows the individuality of the persons to be maintained, while insisting that all three persons share in the life of the other two ... Each person, while maintaining its distinctive identity, penetrates the others and is penetrated by them." [9] Propositional argumentation and discussion about the nature of the Trinity is necessary, but without prayer to Father, Son and Holy Spirit, it is unknowable in the fullest biblical sense of 'knowing'. Our asking personally responds to their personal speaking, and despite the philosophical and theological challenges that this doctrine has fueled, despite the charges of some that it is 'incomprehensible', it is the intimately relational expression of our asking that 'penetrates' the Trinity in a way that is reflective of, but subordinate to, the manner in which all three persons have been described as intimately 'penetrating' their own respective and distinctive identities. It is persuasive that it is in the context of His Last Supper discourse about the interrelationship of the Father, the Son and the Holy Spirit and His explanation of how they relate in-person-in-unity, that Jesus talks repetitively about asking as the means of our relational access and intimacy. That particular indwelling (interpenetrating if you will) work of the Holy Spirit that helps us to ask, clearly presents how the interrelationship of Father, Son and Spirit works to draw us into their familial community. There is no gain in writing a brilliant thesis on Trinitarian theology and remaining an 'orphan' in Jesus's terms (John 14:18). As we have seen, it is a son by the Spirit of sonship that can ask of the Father.

There are clearly scriptural grounds for asking directly of the Father. Jesus did it, exhorted us to do it, and exampled how we should do so. There seem to be scriptural grounds to ask of Jesus. However, there is not a single example in scripture of anyone ever asking directly of the Holy Spirit, though it may be inferred. It has been argued that the "Lord of the harvest" we ask (Matthew 9:38) is the Holy Spirit, the sender, the appointer of overseers, and the equipper with gifts, and the empowerer for mission. The reason that attention is not focused on the Holy Spirit is because He does not bear witness to Himself, but is always directing attention away to Jesus, who in turn always directs attention to the Father. The pattern of asking that is to the Father, in the name of Jesus the Son, by the agency and power of the Holy Spirit, is the spiritual norm. Again, asking cannot happen without Trinitarian collaboration. By the way, this does not invite some judgmental legalism or theological particularism that denounces our asking as ineffective if we do not adhere to some particular formula. That has more to do with superstition, fear and doctrinaire nit-picking than it has to do with supplication and faith.

The fact is that as we pray in the Holy Spirit, and with the help of the Holy Spirit, we should not be surprised at the way our asking is led and guided in an appropriate direction. There is nothing wrong when someone, rightly identifying the work of Jesus, or the work of the Spirit, should invoke their ministry with words like "Come Jesus" or "Come Holy Spirit." After all, *"Veni sancte spiritus"* has been a liturgical cry for the presence of the Holy Spirit in the church for centuries. Having affirmed the rightness of asking of Jesus, Packer affirms that "prayer to the Spirit is equally proper when what we seek from Him is closer communion with Jesus and fuller Jesus-likeness in our lives." [10] Where one goes, they all go, and what one does, they all do (the doctrine of 'appropriation') and there is more than sufficient humility within the Godhead for no theological umbrage to be taken, if in our holy desire, we asked the first one whose sense we were most aware of at that moment. In any case, even if we were to get it wrong, we have already seen that the Father knows well how to translate the prayers of an asking child by the agency of His Spirit. The asking of God for His loving answers is never denied on a technical or grammatical point.

Asking In the Name of the Father, the Son and the Holy Spirit

Once we get over how amazing this is, and how validating this is for our asking, how could we not commit to a life-time of asking, given this kind of endorsement and encouragement, this kind of initiation and invitation, this kind of example and experience. Consider it this way. Jesus said, "where two or three are gathered", right? Whenever we ask, it is like walking into a prayer meeting in which three persons are already gathered in unity, and we already know that this is a really good set-up for a sense of presence and agreement (Matthew 18:20). Well, is there ever presence – the presence of God in all three persons! They are so glad to have us join them in their three-fold commitment to our need to ask, to their need that we ask, to our need for answers and to their desire to answer. Origen understood this trinity-partnership that enables our asking: "The discussion of prayer is so great that it requires the Father to reveal it, His first born Word to teach it, and the Spirit to enable us to think and speak rightly of so great a subject." [11] It would only seem right to conclude with some 'trinity asking'. The following prayer is one from the collection of Puritan prayers compiled by Arthur Bennett. [12]

> O *Father,* thou art enthroned to hear my prayers; O *Jesus,* thy hand is outstretched to take my petitions; O *Holy Spirit,* thou art willing to help my infirmities, to show me my need, to supply words, to pray within me ... O Triune God ... Thou hast commanded me *to ask* ... Let me live and pray as one baptized into the threefold Name.

"We shall receive from the praying Spirit, and commit to the praying Christ those petitions which are of divine birth." - D.M.M'Intyre

"However powerful the initial coming upon us of the Spirit may be, if this does not find expression in a life of prayer, the blessing will soon become a fading glory." - Arthur Wallis

"I have never found anyone who prayed as well as those who had never been taught how. Those who have no master in man have one in the Holy Spirit." – Madame Guyon

13

According to Jesus

Jesus Settles It

Jesus is the best person to go to if we want to learn about 'asking and the Holy Spirit'. Since He is a Trinity insider, He will give us the best possible understanding of the Spirit's role, not only in the asking within the Trinity's relationships, but about our asking of the Trinity. Jesus knew personally about the relationship between asking and the Holy Spirit. "As He was praying, heaven was opened and the Holy Spirit descended on Him" (Luke 3:21-22). Jesus's baptism marks His public acceptance of His holy vocation and the inception of His public mission. Foundational to this was His asking of the Father and the consequent coming of the Holy Spirit.

Andrew Murray put it succinctly: "The whole ministration of the Spirit is governed by one great law: God must give and we must ask." [1] *Jesus the Son* said, "How much more will the *Father* give the *Holy Spirit* to those who *ask* Him" (Luke 11:13). More than what? More than an earthly father knows how to give good things to his son. Our assurance about our asking for the Spirit is based on our assurance about the nature of the Father. This sure word of Jesus promises the sure response of the Father and the sure answer of the gift of the Holy Spirit to those who ask. E.M.Bounds described the Holy Spirit as "the Father's greatest gift for the child's greatest need." [2] You cannot be more assured about the work of one person of the Godhead than another. Full assurance of each Person is contingent and dependent on full assurance of the Others. What confidence this gives to our asking of God, and what assurance to our submission to their co-operative work, and our expectation that they will respond and landscape the answers for which we ask, in a way that is best for all. We have already seen that our asking accesses the Father and the Son but what about the Holy Spirit? It is no surprise that through our asking we access and appropriate the work of the Holy Spirit, because the Spirit accompanies us in our asking. We can never say that we ask alone, or that we do not have an asking-partner. That prayer-partner is the Holy Spirit.

Before we ever asked for the Holy Spirit, it was asked for us within the Godhead. Jesus the Son told the disciples, "I will ask the Father and He will give you another comforter to be with you forever – the Spirit of Truth" (John 14:15). The relationship between this asking of Jesus for the Holy Spirit, and the teaching about our asking in His name that He then gave with such repetitive emphasis, cannot be ignored. Jesus is establishing the inviolable relationship between our asking and the work of the Spirit. Without the Holy Spirit, the asking that He is talking about will not and cannot happen, because it is a spiritual exercise and expression, a response of the human spirit to God that can only be effected by the agency of the Holy Spirit. Everything that Jesus says about the work of the Holy Spirit is in this context in which He is also teaching primarily about asking (John14:16). He is telling us what the role of the Holy Spirit will be in our asking. His last teaching to His disciples is not about how to address the world in their preaching but how to address God in their asking. Jesus has written the chapter on 'Asking and the Holy Spirit.' For every one of His declarations about the work of the Holy Spirit, there is a command or invitation to ask. That the same discourse has an emphasis on the Holy Spirit *and* asking has to be regarded as significant. There are some helpful footnotes that are added later, especially by Paul, but Jesus did not leave us with too much left to ask about 'asking and the Spirit'. We have never had a moment of our spiritual lives when our asking was not related to the Holy Spirit. From the moment of being born again, we received the gift of the Holy Spirit, and since then, every baptism, every infusion of the Holy Spirit has expressed itself in more asking and asking for more. Just as we have seen that our asking is Father-asking, and Jesus-asking it is also Holy Spirit-asking.

So how will the Holy Spirit be involved in our asking? If we note all the specific things that Jesus says will characterize the "Spirit of grace and asking", then we will know what we can expect to experience when we are asking in Jesus's name.

1. The Holy Spirit will help us to ask

Jesus said, "I will ask the Father and He will give you another helper (14:15; 14:25; 15:26; 16:7) ... to be with you" (14:16). Until now, Jesus had been their "paraclete" (Gk. *parakletos*), the one who was physically and intimately alongside them to help them, especially by answering their asking. This is Jesus's self-description and one that John repeats in his epistle when he describes Jesus speaking to the Father in our defense, helping us as an advocate would (1John 2:1). But all this was going to change. Jesus told them that He would no longer be physically present with them, and this would mean that they would "no longer ask me anything" (14:19; 16:23). Was that the end to asking? How could it be if He said, "I will come to you" (14:18). Jesus promised that He would send them "another paraclete" (14:15) who would be the equivalent of His presence. Our ability to ask will be effected now by the Holy Spirit. Though the world "neither sees Him nor knows Him" Jesus says that the disciples would know Him and the Holy Spirit would "live with you and be in you" (14:17). The presence of the Holy Spirit is the presence of Jesus so asking can continue as if He was physically present to ask face to face.

It is because of this assurance of Jesus continuing to be intimately with us by His Holy Spirit as our continuing ever-present paraclete, that we always have someone alongside us to ask. If there was no Holy Spirit, there could be no asking. But because Jesus said that He will be "with you forever" there is no limit set on our asking, either because there is no one to ask, or because time has run out. "Forever" means we can ask and keep on asking. Our asking is the evidence and the sign of the Holy Spirit's presence. Andrew Murray wrote: "Prayer on earth, whether as cause or effect, is the true measure of the presence of the Spirit of heaven." [3] It is because of His presence that we can ask about "whatsoever ... forever". It is the nature of need to create feelings of distance and separation and to heighten self-consciousness.

However, we never have to ask without the conviction of His presence and His closeness, and without as real a Jesus-consciousness as if He was up close and personal. Thus our asking is provoked more by His presence than our problem; more by the presence of the provider than the need for provision; more by the presence of the savior than the consequences of our sin; more by the presence of the healer than the pain of our sickness; more by the presence of the deliverer than the oppression of our bondage; more by the presence of the enabler than the debilitation of our disability; more by the presence of the giver than the poverty of our lack. This assurance of a paraclete, forever, secures our asking.

The fact is we need help from the outset, and this is why John Bunyan described the work of the Holy Spirit as putting us into an asking "frame of mind." [4] The Spirit draws us into asking, because as our helper, He knows where we will find the source of needed help. A lack of asking is an indication of an insensitivity to the Holy Spirit and possibly an early-warning of a possible hardening of our hearts. Interestingly, an evidence of back-sliding, of "those who turn back from following the Lord", is that they "neither seek the Lord nor inquire of Him" (Zephaniah 1:6). We need help because we have "no confidence in the flesh" (Philippians 3:3) and therefore cannot help ourselves. All self-confidence is an enemy of asking. Our confidence to ask is the antithesis to this false confidence. However, there are many weaknesses that seek to rob us of this confidence, as Paul would later teach about. But he repeats the assurance of Jesus, that the Spirit will be our helper when we do not know what to ask for, and will help us to ask despite the weaknesses.

We must grasp two things about the place of asking:

- **It is the work of the Spirit to do whatever it takes to help us to *get there*:** to get to the place of asking by prompting and prodding us, inviting and inspiring us, preparing and propelling us. It is always the work of the helping Spirit, whether our asking comes out of conviction of sin or confidence in supplication, or whether out of a sense of unholy despair, or holy desperation and desire. If our asking is of God and to God, it is not crisis but Christ that has brought us to ask Him by the enabling of the Holy Spirit. It is the Spirit of God that has drawn us near to ask, not the spirit of the times or circumstances that forced us to do so as a last resort.

- **It is the work of the Spirit to do whatever it takes to help us to *stay there*,** once having counseled, convicted, convinced and conducted us to the place of asking. If this asking began in weakness and we needed the Spirit's help because of it, then it is clear that strength has to come from somewhere to pursue it, and to persist and persevere in it. If we are without strength, then our asking can only be "without ceasing" because of the Spirit's empowering and fortifying help. Bunyan knew this: "As the heart must be lifted up by the Spirit, if it pray aright, so also it must be held up by the Spirit when it is up, if it is to continue to pray aright ... None knows how many by-ways the heart has, and back lanes, to slip away from the presence of God ... unless the Spirit of supplication be there to help!" [5]

2. *The Holy Spirit will teach us what to ask for*

Jesus said, "The Spirit of Truth (14:17) ... The counselor will teach you all things (14:26) ... All that belongs to the Father is mine ... the Spirit will take from what is mine and make it known to you (16:15) ... He will testify about Me (15:26) ... what He hears He will tell you" (16:13). When Paul said that the Spirit "asks for us" (Romans 8:26) he was applying the teaching of Jesus. When it comes to asking, the Holy Spirit does two things for us that you would expect any good legal advocate to do: give us the words so that we can ask and plead effectively for ourselves, and ask and plead for us Himself on our behalf. The Holy Spirit briefs us, prompts us, and scripts us. There is such solace in this helping work of the Holy Spirit for our asking. Spurgeon spoke of the occasions when "the beclouding of the soul is dense." [6] This is probably a spiritual way to say that we get totally befuddled at times. He went on to say, "We see the disease but the name of the medicine is not known to us." Lack of knowledge and lack of earnestness to ask are serious problems that require the Spirit's help. But even if we are moved and motivated to ask, we still need help. Earnestness in itself does not resolve our ignorance of things, when we have no handle on a situation, or are uncertain about what needs to be asked about and asked for. To use Spurgeon's image, we need the knowledgeable help of a physician to instruct us about the right medicine to ask for that needs to be dispensed as the divine answer for the conditions and circumstances we are asking about.

Jesus told us that the helping Holy Spirit would come to us as the teacher of our asking. He will inform us of the 'what's' and instruct us in the 'how's'. In a sermon entitled 'The Holy Spirit – the great teacher', Spurgeon said: "There is no college for holy education like that of the blessed Spirit, for He is an ever-present tutor. We only have to bend the knee, and He is at our side, the great expositor of truth." [7] Asking, the 'bending of the knee', is one of the key contexts for a disciple's learning, and one of the primary expressions of a disciple's character. As J.I.Packer put it: "I believe that prayer is the measure of the man in a way that nothing else is." [8] The sad truth is that so many of the questions and issues that are raised for people by the fact of daily living, never end up being directed and processed in our asking of God. We do not transfer to Him what is troubling to us. We have been programmed for the immediate not the intimate, and we want quick resolutions and solutions. We want our answers now. Thus, we continue to live with so much presumption and so many unproven and unspiritual assumptions. It is asking with the Holy Spirit's instructional help that actually teaches us about the true nature of our needs and what we should ask about them.

There is an important point about our asking that is couched in Jesus's promise that our Helper will tell us and teach us what He hears. The Holy Spirit is "in the know". As Paul later put it to the Ephesians, He is a "Spirit of wisdom and revelation" (Ephesians1:17-18) and it is in this capacity that Paul asks for the Spirit to enlighten them to "know the hope" to which they have been called. That includes every aspect of our hope, including our future "blessed hope". The Holy Spirit is not just the helper for the delivery of present requests, but also the one who reveals and inspires what we should ask for the future, for the fulfillment of God's will concerning things that we may never live long enough to see the answer. "We pray through the guidance of the Spirit, who teacheth us what to ask, for many things that come to pass in after ages." [9] It is likely that the deeper you grow in intimacy with the Father, the more your asking will relate to these future purposes, the more your tears will be stored in a bottle, and the more your intercessions will be added to the incense bowls holding the prayers of the saints (Revelation 5:8).

It has been observed that the sheer magnitude of what God does when he winds up history as we know it, will be an answer to the stored asking of those hope-full saints. The unknowingness of the future, far from provoking us to fear, promotes faith as we ask. We do not need to surmise, or speculate – but ask. Scripture has already given us plenty of teaching about what will be ("nation will rise against nation"); about what to expect ("because of the increase of wickedness the love of most will grow cold"); about what to spiritually budget for ("the wise however took oil in their jars ... therefore keep watch"); about what it will cost ("You will be handed over to be persecuted"). There is plenty to ask about: for the nations, for community, for the church, and for personal life and discipleship. If the Spirit is helping our asking, and He is teaching us by telling us what He is hearing, then expect to do a lot of future-hope asking and not just here-and-now asking.

No wonder the repeated message to the churches in Revelation is to "hear what the Spirit says" because as Jesus said, He will tell what He hears, we will thus be taught by it, and our asking will then reflect what we have learned. Consider how far into the future Jesus's asking went in John 17. "I ask for those who will believe in me through their message" (v20). That included you and me centuries before we were born. Paul's asking reached forward beyond the mission he was engaged in to nothing less than the time when "all Israel will be saved" (Romans 10:1; 11:26). This is purpose-asking in that it is related to the as-yet-unrealized, but surely to-be-answered purposes of God. These kinds of asking have been described by Murray as "the indicators of the movement of the wheels of providence." [10] If you want to know what God is saying to the church, listen to those who are asking and listening to what the Spirit is teaching them about what He has heard, and what He is teaching them as they ask according to the Word. We need fewer self-appointed charismatic prophets, and more of those whose knowledge of the Holy Spirit is at the place of asking.

So when you are asking, expect the teaching of the Holy Spirit to be manifested in the three ways that Jesus described:

- ***The Holy Spirit will "remind" you (14:26).*** The Holy Spirit will teach, not only by reminding us of what we should be asking about, but also by bringing to our remembrance the things that we need in order to ask aright: key scriptures that will influence and inform our asking, the names of people who should be asked for, situations that need to be asked about, precedents of God's actions in the past, in His ways and works and wonders (Deuteronomy 8:2; Psalm 77:11) that embolden our asking and give further grounds for more of it. It is the activation of remembrance that is a great trigger of so much asking by the psalmists. When the psalmist "remembered" his spirit "inquired" (Psalm 77:6). The 'reminding' help of the Spirit blows on the embers of our asking, likened by Spurgeon to "a live coal from off the altar into our soul." [11]
- ***The Holy Spirit will "convict" you (16:8).*** The Holy Spirit will teach by bringing conviction as we ask. First, is the conviction of sin, both our sins and the sins of others, and of nations. He will convict us if there are hindrances to our asking (see chapter 5). Through such conviction He will be teaching us about God's righteousness and what we need to ask to be established in the lives and circumstances that we are asking about. But He will also bring us the kind of conviction that teaches us about the need to ask, and the need to persevere in it. As He convicts and teaches us of the power of God's will and word, we will be stirred and faith and fervency will be strengthened.
- ***The Holy Spirit will "guide" you (16:12).*** "Those who are led by the Spirit of God are sons of God" (Romans 8:14). So those who ask 'Abba' will be guided in their asking. Having given us traction in our asking, the Spirit will now keep us on track, away from distractions. The guidance will be experienced as directed asking, both to specific needs as well as to specific requests for those needs. John Calvin had no experience of a GPS, but when it came to the need for direction, he knew that the Spirit served us as our prompter:

> "No one can succeed in praying as he ought without prompting of the Spirit of God." [12]

Again, note the full engagement of all persons of the Trinity in this asking process, Holy Spirit-style. What Jesus has received from the Father, He has given to the Spirit, which the Spirit will then teach us. Does not this tutor us about the DNA of our own asking, that this divine process would continue, so that we too, having received what we asked for, would give it away to others in Christ's name? What confidence this gives to asking. Note too how Christocentric this is. The instruction is all about the application of Jesus's word and the implementation of Jesus's will. Paul said that the Spirit asks for us "in accordance with God's will" (Romans 8:27). Our helper is the executor of Jesus's will and is committed to instructing us so that we know what to ask for from our inheritance. The Spirit helps our asking to be truthful, and to bear witness to Jesus. Our asking will always be reflective of the character, commands and concerns of Father, Son and Holy Spirit. Trinitarian asking will not allow us to be focused on our needs only.

3. *The Holy Spirit will assure us that we can ask as sons and daughters*

Jesus said, "I will not leave you as orphans (14:18) ... you will realize that I am in the Father and you are in Me and I am in you" (14:20). Jesus is addressing the feelings of bereavement that they were experiencing, that would seek to convince them that things could not be the same again. Jesus would not be there to be asked about or for anything. In an earlier chapter we have already addressed this most crucial of truths, when we spoke about why orphans do not ask in the way that sons do. Essential to the Holy Spirit's role in our asking is the truth that the Spirit who is our helper in asking, our teacher about asking and what to ask for, is the "Spirit of sonship" (Romans 8:15). In the words of an early church Father, Cyprian of Carthage: "None of us would dare to venture on in prayer unless He (the Father) Himself had allowed us thus to pray." [13] Similarly, Calvin wrote: "None dares to call God Father unless the same Spirit put the Word in us." [14] We can ask as assured sons and daughters because when we do, it is by the Spirit "we cry 'Abba, Father.'" The Spirit relates us to our Father and why would we be surprised that as His sons we speak His language? 'Abba' is our natural and native tongue. Does it not make sense that the Spirit would help sons to relate to their Father?

This means that when we ask of the Father, we can be assured that we are acceptable to Him, but also that what we ask for must be acceptable to Him. That we ask is more important to the Father than how we ask. With fondness, I remember the scrawly notes from my kids on Father's Day, when they were learning to write. I did not grade their written notes like a language teacher but I read their hidden hearts, as a father. This suggests that one of the ways that the Spirit of sonship helps our asking is to assure us that despite our inarticulacies, He will not only be the mail carrier of our asking, but will make sure that it arrives in good form. Even our groanings will make sense, as we will see in the next chapter. The weakness of our presentation ceases to be an obstacle to being heard. It is as if the Spirit improves the quality of our asking, when it feels and sounds unqualified on our terms. Once he adopts our asking as His own, it is as if He adapts it for our good. Peter Masters, one of Spurgeon's successors at The Metropolitan Tabernacle, described the Holy Spirit to his congregation as the one who helps our asking by "taking on all our mistakes and polishing them up, adding emotion, perfecting them and making them acceptable." [15] We know exactly what he meant. The Spirit assures us that God is our Father, and that He is not going to respond to us as failed or failing language students.

4. The Holy Spirit will seek God's glory in our asking

Jesus said, "He will bring glory to me" (16:14). The Holy Spirit's relationship with our asking will always ensure that the outcome is God's glory. Asking that is helped, instructed and guided by the Holy Spirit will bring glory to the Father. He will only further the desire of Jesus, which is the glory of the Father. When Jesus asks, we hear Him say: "Father, glorify your name" (John 12:8); "Father ... glorify your Son that your Son may glorify you" (John 17:1). Was this not the prominent and pre-eminent thing that Jesus taught us to ask for too? "Our Father, Hallowed be your name" (Luke 11:2). It has been argued that the first three things asked for in this 'Lord's prayer' were specifically and obviously concerned with God's glory, and thus in the light of that, even the next three that appear to be specifically more focused on human need, require (to use Calvin's words) that we "seek nothing for ourselves without the intention that whatever benefits He confers upon us may show forth His glory." [16] We can take no pride in our asking, no satisfaction in our prayer movements, no pleasure in even apparent effectiveness or answers, as if it was somehow our bent knees that achieved what only His raised right arm could do. How we ask, how long we ask, who we ask with, what we ask for are all important, but together they give us no grounds for boasting. Prayer can become a self-righteous work just like all other spiritual works. Even if we are not asking for ourselves, but for others, there is still no basis for our gratification in that. That would oppose the glorification of God. At the end of the day, all our asking is for the glory of God, that His glory will cover the earth as the waters cover the sea. We "do it all for the glory of God" (1 Corinthians 10:31).

The Answering Spirit

It should encourage us that we can ask, helped by the Holy Spirit, in a way that all the outcomes will be as Spirit-infused as our asking was. We want to ask in a way that invites Spirit-soaked answers. There is a story told of a minister in the Welsh revival, who preached a particular message that drew hundreds to Christ. Inevitably, someone asked him, "Where did you get that sermon?" "There!" he said, pointing to the place where he had knelt before the window. "I cried for power ... and the answer came not." He described how he kept asking and asking as the Holy Spirit helped and instructed him, as the sky turned from grey to silver to purple to gold. "Then the sermon came and the power came." The Spirit that helped the asking was the Spirit that was the answer. Is there any answer we receive but we do not still need the continuing help of the Holy Spirit to landscape it, to nurture and nourish it, to help ensure that it is stewarded rightly, to rouse gratitude and thus incite increased faith and more asking? What confidence for our asking, that we are assured of the Holy Spirit's help, instruction, direction, and His glorification of the Father, exactly as Jesus said. What motivation for our asking that the Holy Spirit's ultimate purpose is to ensure that the ultimate outcome of our asking will not be the satisfaction of human need but the satisfaction of the Father. The more Holy Spirit-assisted our asking is, the more will be the fulfillment of what Jesus loves to do most: "I will do whatever you ask in My name so that the Son may bring glory to the Father" (John 14:14). The Holy Spirit helps us to ask Jesus for our answers, which brings glory to Jesus, and the answers given by Jesus become a means by which He brings glory to the Father. Our asking of Jesus is how we adore Jesus, and His answering is how He adores His Father. This is why there is no boundary between our asking and our adoring. Prayer and worship will always be together. So no matter how alone we feel in our asking, we are partnered by the Holy Spirit. No matter how self-conscious we may feel as we ask about our need, we are in fact participating in a massive God-conscious exercise. No matter how grieved we may feel about the burdens we bear, we are being drawn into the gravitational pull of the glorification of the Father and the Son. The Holy Spirit who helps us as we ask about the worst of things, is committed to have that "worst" transformed into the worship of God. Let this possibility of the glory of the Father and the Son being effected through your Holy Spirit-assisted asking motivate you and move you to ask! And again we say, ASK!

"Unless He (the Holy Spirit) intercedes, our prayer is not true prayer." - Donald Bloesch

"The Holy Spirit loves to be petitioned. And those who ask most will always have most of His influence." - Bishop Ryle

"One of the most remarkable inconsistencies in studies on Paul is that thousands of books exist that search every aspect of Paul's thinking, while only a few seek to come to terms with his life of prayer." – Gordon Fee

14

According to Paul

Apart from Jesus, we have more insight into Paul's asking than any other person in scripture. [1] It is extraordinary that Paul, who had so much to say about asking, and whose epistles are filled with his personal practice of it, is first described by Ananias before his conversion as one who was committed to persecute "all who call on your name" (Acts 9:14). His life pre-Christ was antagonistically anti-asking of Jesus, yet as we have seen, his life turned on some asking: "Who are you Lord?" (Acts 9:11) Is it any surprise that he has so much to say about it?

Paul Was Always Asking

If there is one thing that marked the spiritual life and ministry of Paul it was his asking, his calling on the name of Jesus "night and day ... earnestly ... continually ... constantly... always ... joyfully ... thankfully ... at all times ... on all occasions ... have not stopped ... first of all" (1 Thessalonians 3:10, 5:17; 2 Thessalonians 1:11; Philippians 1:4; Colossians 1:3; Romans 1:10; Ephesians 6:18; Colossians 1:9; 1 Timothy 2:1). Most of Paul's epistles begin by him assuring his readers that he is asking God for them. "I remember you in my prayers all the time; and I pray that now at last by God's will the way may be opened for me to come to you" (Romans 1:10). Given that Rome became the place of his martyrdom, we are reminded that we are not always aware of what we are asking for. If he was thankful for people, he asked for them: "We always thank God for all of you and continually mention you in our prayers" (1 Thessalonians 1:2). If he asked for them, he was thankful for them: "We always thank God ... when we pray for you" (Colossians 1:3). If he remembered them, he asked for them, thankfully and joyfully: "I thank my God every time I remember you. In all my prayers for you I always pray with joy" (Philippians 1:3-4). If you want to become more thankful, more joyful, ask more for others, which is a relieving deliverance from self. The relationship between thanksgiving and asking is cemented in Paul's thinking. Giving thanks is usually an expression of gratitude for an action done, so when Paul urges us to ask with thanksgiving (thanks before we even get an answer) he is ensuring that it is impossible for us to ask God to do anything without being reminded that He is the God who acts, and who has already acted on our behalf. The God who acts in His world (thus our continual thanksgiving) can be trusted to act again as He so determines. As we have seen (chapter 3) asking and thanksgiving are always spiritually one. They work together.

Paul was always asking others to ask for him and with him. Herein is the expression of humility. Sometimes he begins by thanking them for their asking for him and he reports "the gracious favor granted us in answer to the prayers of many" (2 Corinthians 1:11). He understood that asking the Lord for each other was the strongest and most effective way to identify with others. "I urge you ... to join me in my struggle by praying to God for me" (Romans 15:30). "Pray that we may be delivered from wicked and evil people" (2 Thessalonians 2:3-5). "In their prayers for you their hearts will go out to you" (2 Corinthians 9:14). Arguably, the largest part of his recorded prayer is asking for others. "My heart's desire and prayer for Israel is ..." (Romans 10:1). "Our prayer is that you may be fully restored" (2 Corinthians 13:9). "I pray that the eyes of your heart may be enlightened" (Ephesians 1: 15-23). "I pray ... that you may be filled to the measure of all the fullness of God" (Ephesians 3: 14-21). "This is my prayer: that your love will abound more and more" (Philippians 1:9-11). Asking for others like this is a very effective way of maintaining strong relationships, of dealing with irreconciliations or anything that interferes with unity in relationship. No wonder Jesus said, "And when you stand praying, if you hold anything against anyone, forgive them" (Mark 11:25). Have you noticed that you do not ask for people you are out of relationship with? Asking restores and deepens relationships.

At other times, Paul includes a prayer report in the body of the letter (e.g. Ephesians 3:14-21) and when he does this, it is his way of showing that whatever is being asked for is of absolutely vital importance to his readers. [2] That he asks is sufficient to emphasize the truth that he is teaching. He is always concerned to relate his apostolic teaching and pastoral appeals in a way that become the fuel for asking. So often, he opens things up and wraps things up by either asking God directly for his readers, or by leaving them to take what they have just heard and go and ask the Lord about it. Both Paul's personal asking and his exhortations about asking, serve as example and encouragement for most of what we need in order to mature in our asking. Any study of Paul's prayers will draw attention to the truth that asking is wrought by the Holy Spirit and is ultimately the evidence of the indwelling Spirit, the proof that we have been born again and are truly sons of the Father. It is this work of the Holy Spirit that is the distinctive factor about Christian prayer.

Paul knew that this Spirit was the Spirit of grace and supplication and that our capacity to ask is a grace-gift of the Spirit, and therefore its efficacy is not derived from any human merit or might. Writing to the Thessalonians he makes clear the basis for any effectiveness in the asking he has just expressed on their behalf: "We pray this ... according to the grace of our God and the Lord Jesus" (1 Thessalonians 1:12). Notice again that our asking is a Trinitarian work. Do not forget that Paul was a former graceless Pharisee who was in captivity to law, and that law expressed itself in the same kind of lifeless praying as that which Jesus described in His parable of the Pharisee and the Publican. If anyone knew the difference that the Holy Spirit made to prayer it was Paul.

The Holy Spirit and Asking

Nowhere does Paul make the relationship between the Holy Spirit and our asking clearer than in these words to the Romans: "In the same way the Spirit helps us in our weakness. We do not know (the) what we ought to pray for, but the Spirit himself intercedes for us with groans that words cannot express. And He who searches our hearts knows the mind of the Spirit, because the Spirit intercedes for the saints in accordance with God's will" (8: 26-27). By saying "in the same way" he is telling us that whatever is being said here about asking "in" and "with" the Spirit is linked to what has come before. You can argue that the entire chapter is about the work of the Holy Spirit in the believer's life. He empowers us to put to death the works of our flesh (8:13); He affirms and witnesses to our sonship by which we cry 'Abba!" (8:15); He inspires our hope of what is to come (8:18); He helps us in our weakness to ask of God (8:26).

It is important to note that although Paul is going to say some things about the very specific role of the Spirit in our asking, he is not presenting the Spirit just as an aid, though we are clearly aided. Paul is aware of this function of the Spirit's work precisely because he understands that ALL of our asking is of the Spirit. To those who think that the Holy Spirit only adds "a little something to our prayer" or comes along to complete what we are asking about because we do not ask "very well", Jacques Ellul's response is emphatic: "That is quite incorrect ... It is the entire prayer which is the prayer of the Holy Spirit." [3] All of our asking is Spirit dependent – that is what makes it spiritual.

There is another linkage in the repetition of "groaning" which suggests that we especially need the Holy Spirit in a context where we experience trial and trouble amidst the grit and grind of daily life, and cultural, environmental and cosmic threat. In the text, creation groans, the church groans and the Spirit groans in harmony with us. In the same way that all the preceding works of the Holy Spirit in us and on our behalf serve to sustain and maintain us and guarantee that we will obtain what has been promised, the work of the Holy Spirit to help us in our asking is absolutely crucial for our normal spiritual lives. We should not be surprised that this word about the assurance of sonship would be followed by the assurance that even in challenging times when we cannot work out what to ask, or how to ask our Father, like any knowing father, He can understand the inarticulate noises of a needy child. The Spirit of sonship is the Spirit that helps us to ask.

Help to Know What to Ask For

So what are some of the things that Paul tells us about our asking and the work of the Holy Spirit? Is his answer familiar? Paul provides important confirmation about the helping role of the Holy Spirit in our asking, first spoken about by Jesus. "We do not know what to ask for" (Romans 8:26). I thought Paul knew everything. This is why we need help to even begin our asking. Did he not tell the Corinthians that whatever we communicate is because "God has revealed it to us by His Spirit" and that it is the Spirit that "searches all things" and that "no-one knows the thoughts of God except the Spirit of God" (1 Corinthians 2:10-13). But we have received "the Spirit who is from God." This is why we can now know what to ask for. Ignorance is our problem but the extraordinary truth here is that because of the Spirit's work we are not silenced in our asking. Just because we know nothing about what to say, does not mean we have nothing to say. It is the work of the Spirit, according to Jesus and Paul, to teach us; to revive us and quicken our desires and longings to ask; to reveal to us the knowledge we need to ask aright. Not knowing what to ask is never a hindrance to asking. The Spirit's strength trumps our weakness; the Spirit's help trumps our hindrances; the Spirit's knowledge trumps our ignorance; the Spirit's articulate groans trump our inarticulate griefs.

Paul knew that there is great pain when there is difficulty in intimate communication. His emphasis in this text is not on the activity of asking. That is assumed. It is on the particularities of what to actually ask for. In the Greek there is a definite article before 'what': "we do not know **the** what." Thus we are wordless, but that just means we are unable to ask with words – our asking is expressed differently, but nonetheless surely, because of the Spirit's work. Before we have our needs and requests, we have His Spirit. Writing in prison in 1662, John Bunyan wrote: "It is the Spirit only that can teach us so to ask ... Without which Spirit, though we had a thousand Common Prayer Books, yet we know not what we should pray for as we ought, being accompanied by those infirmities that make us absolutely incapable of such a work." [4]

Help For Our Weakness

Like Bunyan, Paul knew all about those "infirmities". "The Spirit helps us in our weakness." It is important to note that the word Paul uses for 'help' here is only used one other time in the New Testament, by Martha when she is appealing to Jesus to get Mary to help her in the kitchen by sharing the burden (Luke 10:40). Martha is not asking for Mary to take over the whole cooking operation but to come alongside to assist in the execution of the meal. We cannot manage the whole asking operation. Think of your request and need as something bigger than you can lift by yourself. The Holy Spirit takes 'the other end' as it were, to ensure it gets lifted to the Father.

The Spirit is helping us by giving assistance, sharing the burden, but not doing all the work. He is our asking-partner. He works with us, not instead of us. We are not given a pass from asking as if we have handed over our crumpled and unwearable needs to a dry-cleaner who will now do all that is needed to return to us our sense of perfectly pleated circumstances, to our answered satisfaction and provision. The Holy Spirit is presented as acting on our behalf, while we continue to ask, since He is groaning and expressing what needs to be really asked for, in and through us, when the words fail us. But we are thoroughly involved in this, as our desires and longings are giving rise to the groanings, so this text cannot be manipulated to defend passivity and a failure to ask. Nor is it saying that a grunt and a groan is better and somehow more spiritual than the normal verbal articulation of a need. After all, it is God himself who instructs His people: "Take words with you" (Hosea 14:1-3).

By definition, our asking is the evidence of weakness in some shape or form, in that it is acknowledging that there is needed help that only God can give. Paul is clearly not thinking here about a self-serving laundry-list of personal 'likes' that we want given to us and personal dislikes that we want gone from us. This is about debilitating infirmities and weaknesses, about which Paul had a lot of experiential knowledge, that reduce us to being wordless. How do we deal with these weaknesses? More to the point, how do we ever get to say with Paul, "I glory in my infirmities ... I delight in weaknesses" (2 Corinthians 12:9-10)? The same way Paul did: by presenting every weakness to God "by asking" (Philippians 4:6) or, when words cannot articulate the need, by entrusting the asking to the Holy Spirit, for us and through us. The weakness here is this inability to express what needs to be asked. That may be because we are just totally overwhelmed, or just do not know what to ask for. Paul did not know what to ask for: to stay or depart (Philippians 1:23)? Even Jesus, in a dress-rehearsal for Gethsemane, asks about what is the best thing to ask for Himself: "Now my heart is troubled and what shall I say? Father, save me from this hour? No, it was for this very reason I came to this hour" (John 12:27). Paul discovered that his prayerful longings were not just acceptable when he was weak, but they turned out to be really effective. Thomas Goodwin also discovered that: "The strength of prayer lies not in the words, but in that it is fitted to prevail with God." [5] Paul understood the work of the Holy Spirit as the one who does the "fitting" of the kind of asking that seems very "unfit" to us.

It is so interesting that he identified the primary fruit of such asking as: "the peace of God which transcends all understanding" (Philippians 4:7). When we are dealing with things that incite great anxiety, asking in the Spirit is the antidote, because we can ask until we experience peace. This is precisely the same thing that Jesus said would be characteristic of the work of the helping Holy Spirit when we asked: "Peace I leave with you, my peace I give you" (John 14:27). If you are short on peace you should get long on asking. Despite the pressure or the pain, the anxiety or the need that we are asking about, (whatever is our infirmity or weakness) we can know the undergirding buoyancy of that peace. It comes and fills the empty spaces of ignorance and misunderstanding. For Paul, there were some weaknesses that never left him. Arthur Wallis wrote: "The weakness is perpetual only that we might be perpetually dependent on the Holy Spirit." [6] Because of the strengthening work of the Holy Spirit we are not even the best judges of our weakness, or what is possible when we are weak. One is reminded of the experience of Jacob who in his wrestling with God "struggled ... wept and begged for His favor" (Hosea 12:4). Yet the verdict on the outcome is clear: he "overcame."

How Does the Spirit Help Us to Ask When Weak and Wordless?

It makes perfect sense that Paul would describe the Spirit that helps us in our asking as "groaning". Thomas Goodwin observed: "It is the meaning of the spirit that God looks unto, more than the expressions; for the groans there are said to be unutterable." [7] Much of our asking is wordless, like Hannah's: "her lips were moving but her voice was not heard" (1Samuel 1:13). We are invited to be volubly silent. The psalmist describes how intensely he asked God to hear him, and he just "groaned" and "was too troubled to speak" (Psalm 77:4). When Hezekiah describes how he asked God to heal and deliver him he says that he "moaned like a morning dove" (Isaiah 38:14). Asking can be unintelligible to human ears, but always understood by a hearing God, even if it is just tears.

David is buckling under the pressure and pain of his asking as his "bones are in agony" and his "soul is in anguish". He is "worn out from his groaning". He describes how he wet his couch with tears and flooded his bed with weeping. Asking is noisy and irregular and does not always conform to socially acceptable manners. Anyone standing outside the door and listening would not have had a clue what this was actually about. Yet David concludes the psalm with these words: "The Lord has heard my cry ... the Lord accepts my asking" (Psalm 6:8). God knew exactly what it was about, to the letter. Sometimes Jesus's asking of the Father before a miracle would be expressed like this: "He looked up to heaven and with a deep sigh said..." (Mark 7:34). At Bethany His asking of the Father was tear-stained. "During the days of Jesus's life on earth, He offered up prayers and petitions with loud cries and tears" (Hebrews 5:7). So much asking comes "out of the depths".

The prayer of Jabez no doubt derives its power and potency from the fact that he was born in sorrow and pain (1 Chronicles 4:9). It was asking that had been tested and proven over years. Yes, the Spirit assists us in our weakness but His identification with us is such that He agonizes, and is able to express what we are struggling to even know or feel. In the words of Job, even when we cannot communicate, we can commit our cause to the Lord (Job 5:8). The Holy Spirit ensures that our desire is met. A seventeenth century German hymn-writer, Paul Gephardt, picks up this thought: "To him commend thy cause, His ear / Attends the softest prayer." [8] Softest? How about inaudible? How about unintelligible because wordless? The great thing about old hymns is that they were basically poetic sung versions of the biblical text, as in these words by James Montgomery in 1818 that comment on our text: "Prayer is the burden of a sigh / The falling of a tear / The upward glancing of an eye / When none but God is near." [9]

If there were no other reasons for both needing and desiring the gift of tongues, this would be it. Usually, those who are committed to asking of God for everything, in all circumstances, would admit their need and appropriate the provision for the Spirit to ask through them in an unknown tongue, when personal articulacy is spent, whether for words or for strength, and yet there still needs to be expression. It is an amazing gift for our asking and hard to imagine asking without it. It is a singular help of the Holy Spirit in weakness. Sometimes the Lord can use the gift through another when help is needed. Once, I was in my study grappling with some deep truths, preparing to teach and preach them, but I felt powerless, such was the weight of them, such the consequences of receiving or rejecting them, such the challenge to do justice to the heart of God in it all. My phone rang, and I instantly recognized the voice of a dear "spiritual mother" of mine who without any conversation, proceeded to ask God for me, praying in tongues, followed by an interpretation. The entire interpretation was about the very issue I was preparing to teach. I slumped in my chair under the loving touch of the hand of the Lord, but when it was over, I sat up as if every burden had been lifted, knowing that I would experience the Lord's strengthening answer in the message I was about to pen. Only the Spirit of God, my helper, could have prompted her to call me at that very moment, to ask through her in a way that I could not, and she could not. The Holy Spirit and asking? O how he helps you and me in our weakness.

"My mind wanders: I chatter like a crane; I roar like a beast in pain; I moan in the brokenness of my heart, but oh, my God, I know not what it is my inmost spirit needs; or if I know it, I know not how to frame my petition aright before thee ... It is in such a plight as this that the Holy Ghost aids us, and hence He is a 'very present help in trouble.'" [10] This was a confession from no less than Spurgeon who, like Paul, knew his weakness but knew the help of the Holy Spirit amidst it. The Spirit helps us to ask about these "inmost spirit needs". When things are challenging, it is natural to ask for things that we think will relieve us of the problem. It makes sense to ask for things that seem good to us, but those good things may not necessarily be good answers. We need help to ask as we "ought". We need to mature in our spiritual ability to discern the difference between what our nature is wanting and what the Spirit is prompting. It is helpful to write our own list of why we need help in our asking of God. Our list may include: help to be stirred to ask in the first place; help for lack of desire and sense of need, or concern for others; help for apathy and lethargy; help for empowerment to ask; help for inspiration; help for holy affections; help for reliance and trust; help for fervency and faithfulness; help for faith and endurance; help for ignorance and inarticulacy; help because overwhelmed or desperate; help for perplexity and complexity; help for disappointment or resignation. None of us need to be persuaded that we need help for our asking and in our asking. None of us should need to be persuaded that help to ask is present and available.

The Holy Spirit Is In the Know

Paul was always in awe of "the Spirit of wisdom and revelation." What Paul is saying to the Romans here is mind-blowing when you really feel like your mind is already blown. God reads the script of our hearts when we ourselves cannot read it out loud as it were. "Search me O God and know my heart; test me and know my anxious thoughts" (Psalm 139:23). In Jeremiah 17:9-10 we read: "The heart ... who can know the heart? I the Lord search the heart." When you are in the midst of struggles and do not know 'the what', when you do not know how to present yourself rightly to God, there is a comfort, described by Stuart Briscoe as a "comfort in knowing that even the unspoken prayer of the unformed opinion springing from an uninformed mind is valid when prompted by the Spirit who steps in and invests the sigh with significance and the tear with meaning." [11] 'We sighed' replaces 'we said'. These moments of spiritual illiteracy receive the help of the Holy Spirit, who makes our groans His own. He takes all our disconnected, unpronounceable emotional and spiritual phonetics and presents them to the Father Himself, and precisely because our God is our Father, like a good father, He can listen to the noises and grunts and groans of the child who is not speaking sense, and He can perfectly discern the true passions, longings and needs that provoked them.

We can hardly read our own minds, given the pressures and the pains, the desires and the demands, and yet the Holy Spirit is our helper so that God hears what the Spirit expresses, and God who searches the heart, and can read both its intent and its content, knows the mind of the Spirit, when our own mind is not so clear. By the time the Spirit gets hold of our longings, it is almost as if He rewrites them in an intelligible form that aligns with the will of God for us. Our inarticulate desires for God's will are presented by the Spirit's groans in a way that is perfectly articulate to Jesus. Is this not exactly what Jesus said the Holy Spirit would be – our advocate. Paul is telling us about a particular manifestation of this advocacy. Have we not noted that a good advocate gives us the words to say, and if we cannot do so, represents us himself?

It is nothing but self-pity to ever think we are alone. We have no less than two intercessors: the intercession of Christ in the heavenly sanctuary (Hebrews 7:25) and the intercession of the Spirit in the sanctuary of our own heart. They both address the Father for us. Lonely in our asking? No way! It involves the Father, Son, Holy Spirit and you and me.

Grieve Not the Holy Spirit

Given our dependence on the Holy Spirit for our asking, it is important to Paul that we do not "quench" or "grieve" the Spirit and thereby quench asking. It is tragic when there is so much talk about the Holy Spirit, yet a failure to discern His personhood in our asking. It is painful irreverence when anyone is either dismissive of the Spirit's personality, or overly familiar, treating the Holy Spirit like a domestic or valet, subject to our 'beck and call'. It is grievous to hear people talking about the Holy Spirit as if He was a quantifiable juice, or essence, or liquid, or vapor. It is grievous when the work of the Spirit is dishonored because unrecognized when we ask. The Holy Spirit is a person, not an influence or an atmosphere. As a person, the Spirit can be lied to ("You have lied to the Holy Spirit!" Acts 5:3); can be resisted

("You always resist the Holy Spirit!" Acts 7:51); can be insulted ("How much more severely do you think a man deserves to be punished ... who has insulted the Spirit of grace?" Hebrews 10:29). You cannot hurt a power, a principle, or a proposition but you can hurt a person. Those most familiar with charismatic renewal need to heed this as much as those who oppose the gifts of the Holy Spirit. There can be a hurt Spirit even where there are gifts manifested, for there is nothing worse than a proud gift user. Is there grief to the Spirit concerning our asking, or lack of it? "Do not grieve the Holy Spirit ... Do not quench the Spirit" (Ephesians 4:30; 1 Thessalonians 5:19). How may we grieve the Holy Spirit in our asking? Let me suggest some ways.

1. ***When we fail to recognize His personal role in it:*** I have just referred to the way that we can treat the Holy Spirit as less than He is by either ignoring His role or idolizing it. Given all that Jesus has said about the availability of the Spirit for our asking and the indispensability of the Spirit's ministry to us in asking, let us not grieve the Spirit by our unfamiliarity, or our ignorance of His necessary work, and fail to avail ourselves fully of it, especially by not asking.
2. ***When we fail to remember His purpose:*** The purposes of the Spirit in helping our asking are to draw us to ask of the Father, for the fulfillment of His desires in us and in His world. His purpose is to sanctify us now, ensuring that we are "sealed for the day of redemption" and therefore asking for that which is to come in a way that is preparing us for it. Let us not grieve the Spirit by overriding these purposes with our own self-occupied temporal agendas.
3. ***When we fail to realize His presence:*** Jesus told us the Spirit would be with us, so it is grievous when there is no sense of His presence in our asking, and no asking in His presence. When we ask, we should expect manifestations of that personality, particularly in His gifts. Acknowledgement and gratitude for His presence can be verbalized. It is grievous when this is neglected. That is when we take the Spirit's help for granted and treat Him as we would an unnoticed housekeeper.
4. ***When we fail to respect His purity:*** How can we forget that He is the HOLY Spirit. Let us not grieve Him by hindering His help of our asking through our unholiness. We have noted elsewhere the

sanctifying affects of the Holy Spirit's work in and through our asking.

5. ***When we fail to respond to His promptings:*** Let us not grieve the Holy Spirit by avoiding or resisting His conviction or His leading, or resisting His nudges to ask of God in response to His promptings.
6. ***When we fail to receive His provision:*** Jesus told us that the Spirit would give to us what was His, making available all that Jesus has received from the Father, to fuel and foster, encourage and empower our asking. Let us not grieve the Holy Spirit by not availing ourselves of that provision.

If the role of the Holy Spirit is to help us in our weaknesses when we are asking, how foolish is to weaken our asking by grieving or quenching that help?

We are so used to thinking of the church as a "house of prayer." But what about us? "Do you not know that you yourselves are God's temple and that God's Spirit lives in you?" (1 Corinthians 3:16) Is our body that kind of house or temple in which the Holy Spirit can ask His heart out for all nations? Bunyan wrote: "The Spirit of God uses the nature of the believer as a temple in which He offers His prayer of intercession." [12] Are we available as an asking-room for the Godhead? If He needs a place to ask and seek and knock, will He find room in us, as He did in the life of Paul, undeterred by weakness, because totally convinced about the Holy Spirit's relationship with his asking?

Effectual Asking

"Prayer is not mere wishing. It is asking with a will ... Bible searching and searching prayer go hand in hand. What we receive from God in the Book's message, we return to Him with interest in prayer."
- P.T.Forsyth

"I seek the will of the Spirit of God through, or in connection with, the Word of God." - George Mueller

"The petition is half God's will. It is God's will inchoate." - P.T.Forsyth

"Dear God, Your will – nothing more, nothing less, nothing else."
- Anonymous prayer

"It is silly to say that God can do anything. But it is scriptural to say that God can do anything He wills to do." - Tozer

"Through God's Holy Word ... and through God's Holy Spirit ... we will learn to know that our petitions are according to His will."
- Andrew Murray

"The aim of all our petitions must be the alignment of our own will with the will of God." - J. Burnaby

"It is well for us in the beginning of our supplication to direct our hearts towards the Holy Scriptures." - D.M.M'Intyre

"Asking arises more out of God's word than our need." - P.T.Forsyth

"To have prayed well is to have studied well." - Martin Luther

"God demands reciprocity. He demands that we listen to His word before He listens to our prayers." - R.A.Torrey

15

Asking According to His Will and His Word

This Is How You Should Ask

"This then is how you should pray ... Your will be done" (Matthew 6:10). This is what asking is all about and consequently this has determined all catechesis when it comes to prayer. "Prayer is an offering up of our desires unto God for things agreeable to His will." [1] The primary, practical instruction on asking that Jesus gave to His disciples, establishes that it is God's will that we ask, and that we ask according to His will. Here are some considerations.

It Is God's Will That We Ask.

Paul affirms this: "Ask continually ... for this is God's will for you in Christ Jesus" (1 Thessalonians 5:17). The very moment we begin to ask we are both engaging and expressing His will, which is "done" even before we go on to ask for it to be "done" specifically in the things we are asking about. It is done "even as the creature calls and presses and prevails upon it to be done." [2] It is God's will that our will willingly responds to His request that we ask. "The will to pray, we say, is Thy will ... He wills to be entreated ... When we entreat we give effect to His dearest will." [3] His will invites us and commands us to participate in what He wills. Any theological construct that renders asking superfluous or of no influence in the enacting and effecting of God's will, may be consistent with its own philosophical concepts about providence and predestination, sovereignty and immutability, but it will be at odds with biblical teaching if it discourages people from asking specifically with an expectation of equally specific answers. "Given the Bible's exhortation to pray, any thinking that leads us away from this is wrong reasoning. No true theology can be a disincentive to pray." [4] It is almost as if our asking is the means by which we go on-line with God's will, and in doing so become an intimate part of whatever He is working on, especially as it relates to what we are asking Him about. Asking becomes the primary context for our co-laboring with God, who incorporates our asking in a way that furthers divinely intended outcomes, or as someone has put it, "moves things along in the direction of His purpose." [5] Jesus does not present asking as one of many possible spiritual electives, only dependent on our willing choice. He *exhorts* it (John 14:24), He *expects* it (Luke 11:2), and He *examples* it (John 17). Because it is God's will that we ask, our asking is not self-determined and self-directed so much as it is God-responsive and God-required, and the failure to ask is therefore treated not as a matter of oversight but of disobedience. Your will be done!

It Is Our Will That We Ask.

Because our love for God is expressed in our obedience, we are obediently willing to ask as He wills, and joyfully expectant about the outcomes. Lest this sounds too easy-going we must emphasize that because our asking is about embroilment with the will of God, then we put everything into it. "Prayer is not mere wishing – it is asking with a will. Our will goes into it." [6] Many have commented on the misunderstandings of the will of God, "as if what God wills must inevitably come to pass" [7] in a manner that does not require our asking. Striving to communicate this relationship between God's will that we ask and our will to ask, Murray wrote: "He has left it to prayer to say where the blessing is channeled. He has committed to His believing people to bring the living water to the desert places. The will of God to bless is dependent on the will of man to say where the blessing goes." [8] In our asking we want to agree with the psalmist, and more particularly, with Jesus's own use of this verse as a self-description of His will's response to His Father's will: "I desire to do your will, O my God" (Psalm 40:8). Your will be done!

Asking Seeks the Will of God and Submits to It

"The surrender in prayer is not so much servile submission as seeking to bring our will into accord with His will. It is willing with God and thereby aiding God's will, becoming one with His will." [9] Thus it is that when we ask we are to discern and know that divine will: *accepting* it (1 Peter 4:2), *apprehending* it (Ephesians 5:17), *approving* it (Romans 12:2) and *applying* it (Matthew 7:21). "In asking this (God's will to be done) we renounce the desires of our flesh, for whoever does not resign and submit his feelings to God, opposes as much as he can God's will ... In consequence, *our wish* is that he may render futile and of no account, whatever feelings are incompatible with *His will*." [10] Before asking, one's heart must have "no will of its own in regard to a given matter." [11] This does not mean that we will desist in strongly expressing our most longing desires, or passionately pleading the most earnest of our requests based on the extent of present perception and knowledge. Such expression is the way that we actively seek His will, a process in which we wrestle, in which our insights jostle with God's revelation, in which our longings nestle in His love. When we ask we do so submissively to the limit of our understanding and we push in as far as we are able to go, in what may sound like acceptable interrogatives one minute, and unacceptable interrogations of God the next. Do we not encounter this seeking and submitting as Abraham intercedes for Sodom, as Moses pleads against the destruction of Israel, as Jonah prays in the belly of the fish, as Daniel petitions for Jerusalem, as Jesus asks about the cup, as Paul asks about his thorns. It is in our asking, more than any other context, that we experience this extraordinary co-operation of wills, and alignment of will, the conforming of our will to His will. We ask, acceding to His will. Your will be done!

We Can Ask According to His Will

We ask according to His instruction, not our insight. Our desire is that our request is in line with what His revealed will both desires and determines, and we will be bold in such asking. However, so much of our asking is because we are not sure what that perfect will might be, but that should not cause any delay in the asking. We can freely ask because we trust God's ordering of our needs and desires, the certain as well as the confused ones. Regardless of how they are formulated or how they arrive, our requests are received and registered. Admittedly, we would prefer our answers by next-day delivery rather than sea-mail. Our asking, if it is according to His will (whether past, present or future), is not initiating anything. The exciting thing about asking according to His will is that we are joining a work already in process and progress and "we can be sure He is already operating towards the end we pray for." [12] It is particularly in and through our asking that we grow in our understanding of our role, our contribution, and our participation in the work that God wills. Asking therefore strengthens our sense of the meaningfulness of our lives. Asking according to His will is an antidote to meaninglessness. For George Mueller, this was one of his conditions for prevailing asking. "This is the confidence ... If we ask anything according to His will He hears us" (1 John 5:14). Lack of assurance about the will of God produces diffidence not confidence. We can ask boldly according to His will. Your will be done!

Asking Trusts God's Will and His Willingness to Respond.

John Bunyan argued that good asking needed a good understanding, not only of the will of God but also of His willingness to respond. It is not the will of a detached and impersonal deity but the Father's will, whose will for us is not propositional but paternal. It is not the expression of an exacting law but of an extravagant love, that wills what is good and pleasing and perfect for us (Romans 12:2). His is not a reluctant will but a responsive one. Your will be done!

"Lord here I hold within my trembling hand
This will of mine – a thing that seemeth small;
And only Thou, O Christ, canst understand
How, when I yield Thee this, I yield mine all.
It hath been wet with tears and stained with sighs
Clenched in my grasp till beauty hath it none.
Now from thy footstool where it prostrate lies
The prayer ascendeth, Let thy will be done." [13]

Your Will Be Done: A Warning About Usage

"Your will be done." It is easier said than done! It is noteworthy that for Jesus, these words were uttered in extremis. There is nothing jingoistic or blasé about this declaration. The process of submission to that will is often not without struggle and duress, sacrifice and pain, trouble and trial. It is not without trust in the truth that you believe but maybe not feel. It was Agabus who brought a prophetic word of the Lord, "The Holy Spirit says" and went on to predict that Paul was going to be arrested by the Jews in Jerusalem and handed over to the Gentiles. Understandably, those who loved Paul started weeping and pleading with him not to go, because they sensed this was going to be the death of him. Luke writes: "When he would not be dissuaded, we gave up and said, 'The Lord's will be done'" (Acts 21:14). Even though they had heard the Lord's Word by way of a supernatural manifestation of the gift of prophecy, it was a heart-breaking process that got them to accept it according to the will of the Lord.

"If it be your will" can so easily become a shallow lip-service to a vague deity; a camouflage for ignorance and unbelief; a deceptive masquerade of submission and obedience to the divine will; a passive acquiescence or a spiritless resignation to the way things are; a dogged resolve that has more to do with pagan stoicism or a pietist fatalism than with biblical faith. *"Your will be done"* cannot be a cop-out from what is required by an active pursuit of God's will. Nor can it be used as a bail out, or as convenient religious language to cover up a pre-emptive readiness to accept the present circumstances as God's will. "The popularity of much acquiescence is not because it is holier but because it is easier." [14] It is certainly legitimate to say "if it be your will" as a possible expression of a genuine lack of knowledge but that does not mean it is said with a lack of genuine faith.

His Will and His Word

To ask according to His will assumes a knowledge of that will. If we do not know what the will of God is but we are required to ask according to it, then our asking has a problem. How else do we know how to ask, when to ask, what to ask for, and why we ask? How will we avoid being "unwise" in our asking? Paul goes on to immediately give the answer: by "understanding what the will of the Lord is" (Ephesians 5:17). This raises two immediate questions:

1. Where do we get that understanding?
2. How do we get that understanding?

The answers to these questions are respectively: the Word (both eternal Savior and written Scripture) and the Spirit "of wisdom and understanding ... of wisdom and revelation" (Isaiah 11:2; Ephesians 1:17). The Holy Spirit is the 'match-maker' between the Will and the Word of God. Jesus is the perfect embodiment of both Will and Word: "the Word became flesh ... I have come to do your will" (John 1:14; Hebrews 10:9). The Son and the Spirit embody, express, example, explain and exhort the will and the word of God. Without this understanding there will be no substance in our asking.

According to Your Word

It is no surprise that the psalm that is most consumed with life "according to the Word" (Psalm 119) happens to be the longest prayer in that collection. That is an explanation for why those whose life in the word of God is limited or negligible have a prayer life to match. Jesus said, "If you abide in me and my *words* abide in you, you shall *ask* what you will and it shall be done" (John 15:7). The abiding Word inspires us to ask according to the Word. Our asking increases exponentially when we ask according to the Word and then apply that Word in our lives. We have to hear God speak before we ask. The words with which we ask will be responses to the Word that we have in us. God is the first one to say: "Give ear to me!" before we ever ask Him to listen to us. Asking according to what He has already said, according to His Word, then becomes our way to get the ear of God. This is why we have already described our asking as answering. How wonderful is it then, and how confident can we be to ask Him to do what He has already pronounced, promised, prophesied, prescribed, pre-ordained and prepared. According to your word! In Psalm 119 the asking that is offered according to the Word is described in two ways: as according to "your precepts" (v15), and as according to "your promises" (v41). What surer ground do we have for our asking than to ask according to God's Word in which His will is revealed to us.

There are many biblical characters whose asking is preserved for our instruction and encouragement. In every case, the power and the persuasiveness of the petition is grounded in the Word of God. David prays "for the sake of your word and according to your will" (2 Samuel 7:21). Josiah's response upon the discovery of the Torah was, "Ask of the Lord for me ... concerning the words of this book" (2 Chronicles 34:21). When he died, a record was made of his "acts of devotion according to what is written in the Law of the Lord" (35:26). Ezra asks on the basis of "the commands you gave through your servants the prophets" (9:10-11). Nehemiah asks according to the Word that had been read to the people every day for a week and confesses in response to the "commands, decrees and laws" (9:14). Daniel records: "I, Daniel, understood from the Scriptures, according to the word of the Lord ... So I turned to the Lord God and pleaded with Him in prayer" (Daniel 9:2). Our most compelling example is Jesus Himself, the one who taught us to ask that we not be led into temptation, who showed us how asking triumphs: "It is written" (Luke 4:4). It is no surprise that the thing that Jesus considered to be the most important use of His time post-resurrection was opening His disciples minds "so they could understand the scriptures" (Luke 24:45). Equally, we should not be surprised that the Acts of the Apostles records the asking of the early church, according to the Word, as they pray Psalm 2 (Acts 4:25), no doubt one of the "Psalms" referred to by Jesus.

From those days on, the story of the church has been peppered by the accounts of those who asked according to the Word. George Mueller could not ask until his mind had been steadied and stayed on a particular text of scripture "so though I did not, as it were, give myself to prayer, but to meditation, yet it turned almost immediately more or less into prayer." [15] He argued that nine-tenths of the difficulties we have with asking are overcome when our hearts are ready to do the will of the Lord, but such readiness came from meditating in the Word. The Word and asking will always be found together. The lack of the Word among professing believers explains the lack of asking, or the dominance of a selfish asking according to personal want and not according to divine will. John Bunyan put it bluntly: "Prayer ... is blasphemy or at best vain babbling, when the petition is unrelated to the Book."[16]

Word-Asking According to the Bible's Prayer Book

The collection that we know as the Psalms is the Prayer Book of scripture, and out of the asking of God comes the adoring of God. As in the New Testament, petition and praise are inseparable. The great strength of the psalms is that together they bring the whole range of physical, mental, emotional and spiritual reality into the presence of God. Is that not what prayer essentially is: bringing the truth and reality of our lives to the truth and reality of who God is? Is that not precisely why we identify so readily with them? They give legitimacy to our own voices with the variety of tones that reflect the variety of emotions that we need to express in our asking, whether we are in clover or in crisis.

Though the prayer manual for the Old Testament and the Jew, there is an inviolable relationship between the Psalms and the New Testament, between the Psalms and Jesus and between the Psalms and the church, which makes them the prayer manual of the New Testament and the Christian. There are over 125 direct quotations from the Psalms in the New Testament but arguably hundreds of cross-references and inferences. No Old Testament book is quoted more, and by every New Testament writer, with references to 103 of the 150. They are cited in the gospels as a vital part of their persuasive presentation of who Jesus is.

Indispensable as the guide to asking, they were recited in the monasteries 24/7 and the continuous exposure to them was maintained in the Western church that recited all 150 psalms in a weekly cycle; it was every two weeks in the Eastern Church. By the 4th century this usage had seeped way outside monastic and seminary walls, far beyond the church pulpits and doors, and there are so many references to the psalms being sung by farmers in their fields and by the common man. It became the key biblical text to help people know how to speak to God, how to know him, how to ask of Him and for Him. Not surprisingly, it was the single most significant influence on worship and prayer in all cultures.

What we must observe is how the editors chose to introduce this asking manual. Psalms 1 and 2, originally a single psalm, are brilliantly and strategically placed together at the beginning of the psalter. They are a custom-made opening, an overture as it were. Interestingly enough, they are neither prayers nor songs. "They get us ready to pray ... They put our feet on the path that goes from the non-praying world in which we are habitually distracted and intimidated, into the praying world where we come to attention and practice adoration." [17] How significant is it that the asking manual of the Bible opens with a 'torah' psalm that is all about the power of the Word of God, about its wisdom for our lives, about our response to it, and about the results that will be determined by the nature of that response. The word for "torah" is explained like this: "The noun 'torah' is built from the Hiphil (causative verb in Hebrew) fork of the verb 'yarah' which means 'to shoot' ... but means as well 'to teach'. When one man teaches another he shoots his ideas from his own into another's mind. But in so doing he reveals what is in his own." [18] This explains why Eugene Petersen puts it this way: "The word that hits its mark is the Torah. In living speech, words are javelins." In other words, God's Word, His Torah, is like an arrow and our heart is the intended target. This is why God's word can never simply be regarded as one deems a passive library book. Does this ring any bells? "For the word of God is alive and active. Sharper than any double-edged *sword*, it penetrates even to dividing soul and spirit, joints and marrow; it judges the thoughts and attitudes of the heart" (Hebrews 4:12). This is Torah. So the psalms are for those whose hearts are open to be pierced by the word, to be willingly pinned by the precepts. The Torah is not just about commands but includes all the teaching of God. The greatest of the Torah-psalms, 119, is as much about the promises of God as about the precepts, as much about the consequences of obedience, as about the commands to obey.

The other key word that must be understood is the one that describes our relationship with this powerful Torah. It is the word "hagah" translated "meditate". What kind of images come into your mind when you hear that word or the noun form "meditation"? It has become way too tranquil in its modern meaning to catch the activism, the actions of this relationship with God's Word. It does indeed mean to meditate in a contemplative sense, but it has other amazing meanings and nuances that fill the backdrop and sneak into the sound system. Yes, any good Hebrew lexicon will tell you it can mean: to meditate, devise, muse, imagine, but it also carries the idea conveyed by these words: to moan, growl, utter, mutter, to roar, groan - very physical, almost animal words. Isaiah uses the word in Isaiah 31:4 to describe the noises a lion makes when it is salivating over its kill. Have you ever made funny noises when you are eating something good? Have you ever listened to kids eating something 'yummy'? From the earliest age they make incredible noises as they chew and swallow. You can understand why one of the images commonly used to explain meditation is the one of the cow chewing on the cud. The idea here is of something being masticated; breaking it down, working it in – yum, yum, yum! It is a brilliant way to capture the process of our engagement with God's Word which does not always go down easily. Here is the foundation for all the asking that is to follow in the psalms. It is going to be according to the Torah, the Word.

Against the *insight of the world* ("the counsel of the wicked ... the way of sinners ... the seat of mockers") is set *the instruction of the Word*. That which shapes your thinking shapes your asking. If your thinking is shaped by the word of God, your asking is going to be Word-soaked, Word-instructed, Word-directed. Once the wicked (who only have each other to ask) have been identified in terms of their associations, it is interesting that the only relationship that is presented for the godly man is with the word of God, not as a disembodied communication, but as the voice of a person with whom he has an intimate knowledge, and of whom he can ask. It is a later torah-psalm (Psalm 19) that develops and extols the sheer joys of the Word of the Lord. It is this delight in the Word that makes asking according to the Word an equal delight. As someone has put it so well, you cannot go any further into the psalms, into this asking manual, without tripping over the enormous roots of this tree in verse three.

Are you, or will you be, a meditator in God's word in order to be an asker according to that Word? Jesus's teaching is premised on the same truth. He said, "Take heed how you hear." Not any hearing will do. Not any relationship with God's Word will do. Fruit, according to Jesus (Matthew 13; Mark 14), only comes from the kind of Word-hearing that *preserves* (not just initial but continual joy), that *perseveres* (does not quickly fall away), that *produces* (hear the word, accept it and produce a crop). The difference between mature and immature asking is a meditative knowledge of the Word.

So What Has Psalm 2 Got To Do With It?

Here is the great asking of the Son by the Father, asking Him to "ask of me!" Having established in Psalm 1 the necessity for life according to the Word, we are here presented with asking as God's essential and non-negotiable means for engagement with His purposes in the nations. The personal meditation in the Word that is encouraged in Psalm 1 is followed by an invitation to public mission in Psalm 2 by way of asking. In other words, God's Word in us is for God's world. The most common reason that so many believers are not acting believers is because they are not asking ones. Right at the beginning of the introduction to the Psalter is this massive invitation to ask for huge things, for transformations that defy the imagination and challenge faith. Herewith is the agenda of faith: the call is to speak out in prayer what needs to be spoken, God's Word, and what cannot be silenced by the world's mocking, raging and raucous unbelief. What is the strategy to take the nations? Asking is the strategy that overcomes. We inquire, then find that we acquire nations as our inheritance. Who would ever have thought! And whoever would have thought that the meek (humble askers) would inherit the earth? Here is an invitation to bold asking in a world that threatens us and would think it has the right to push us around and mock the choices of the congregation of the righteous. The tumult of the nations in the first stanza looks unchangeable, unstoppable, invincible. What is the use of hoping, of opposing, of praying about it? It is too much, and it is too late, so too bad. But suddenly the asking Son is installed, and He is invoking the Father. He still is, as He ever lives to make intercession for us. Now He invites us, His anointed ones, to join His asking of the Father.

Asking according to the Word is our public service, what Petersen insightfully describes as our "sustained act of patriotism". It is our secret service, as our secret asking is powerfully linked by the Spirit of God to the public domain of kings and rulers. Asking of God in the private places (living rooms, sanctuaries), not of politicians in the Senate chamber, remains still one of the greatest ways we influence the public square. It is those who meditate on the Word, whose minds are informed by the will of God, and whose hearts are infused by the passions of God, who you will find in prayer meetings that are asking for God's mission in the world. You rarely find someone who is passionate about the Word who is not passionate about asking. Word-less people are prayer-less people.

Psalm 2 is quoted no less than 8 strategic times in the New Testament, and is singled out as *the* example of the early church asking for God's Will according to God's Word (Acts 4: 25-26). There are two keys here to the apostles' triumph in trouble that we need to get a hold of for our asking.

- They were saturated in scripture. They could quote and pray Psalm 2 because they knew Psalm 1 and were rooted meditators in the Word. They had been on an intensive biblical meditation course with Jesus for 40 days. They were saturated in the Word's truth, encouragement, instruction, guidance, power, and authority. It was hidden in their heart. It was the sap in their trunk. It was the springboard for their appeal to ask God. It was foundational for their faith and their trust. They knew how to ask (Psalm 2) according to the Word (Psalm 1).
- By doing that, they recalled and remembered the truth of Psalm 2 and they asked for the application of this Word for their own situation, a thousand years after it was written. It was still a living word of truth for their circumstances. They remembered that God remains the sovereign in crisis. He is bone dry above the flood. His laughter is heard above the shouts of the enemies. He is in control of the crisis that would threaten to unravel life. What had happened? The representatives of nations, the Jews, the Romans, and the Gentiles were seeking to silence the message about Jesus. Why were the apostles emboldened despite the turmoil? Why did they have hope that their call to the nations, their commission from Jesus, would not be silenced or snuffed out? What is the turning point in the possible slide to despair? Peter prays the Word and quotes Psalm

2. This is often referred to as 'the Acts 4 prayer meeting'. It should be called 'the Psalm 2 prayer meeting'. No matter what, they were going to ask for the nations. With the nations raging against them, this is how they were able to rise above it all. By standing on Psalm 2, they were able to reconnect with the God who was enthroned above the tsunami of need and despair and trouble, and they received a fresh revelation of the greatness of God, despite the limitations of their situation, and of their resources. Listen to what they asked for. They asked that God would embolden their mission. They asked to be even more effective, and they asked God to stretch out His hand and heal – they asked God to do mighty things in the nations. The place where they asked was shaken. The Holy Spirit invaded the place. I guess God approved! How changed were their expectations, on the basis of asking according to the sure Word that was Psalm 2, about what God could accomplish through them.

Asking According to His Unchanging Will and Word

This word is as true for us today. Amidst the realities of CRISIS we need a revelation of the anointed one, the CHRIST. Don't think crisis – think Christ. Don't think threat – think throne. Don't think the enormity of the TASK – think ASK! This has always been the revelation to those who are besieged. This was the revelation that John had as a prisoner for the gospel on Patmos while the rest of the world was going to hell and the church was being pounded with persecution. He could have only heard the terrifying sound of the waves that crashed on the rocks at his feet that imprisoned him there but he heard the voice of Christ, and the Word that He spoke. He could have only seen the lamp-stands of the churches with all their problems and persecutions and with all the threats that were about to extinguish their light but he saw the Christ who walked among the lamp-stands. He could have seen only the iron fist of Rome but he saw the iron rod in the hand of the Son. He saw "One like the Son" as Daniel's friends saw in the fiery furnace (Daniel 3:25). This was the same Son of Psalm 2 that David saw. When you ask according to this Word you see the Son. Have you seen this Son? Do you know this Son? What do you see in crisis when you ask? Do you only see the problem, the pain, and the misery? Do you see the Son? Do you see the Fourth Man? Where are your allegiances and dependencies and securities and affections? So while the questions are flying around our heads about God's involvement, His timings, His provisions, His interventions, His delays, these words of Psalm 2 should be ringing in our spiritual ears: "Blessed are those who take refuge in Him!" This is the safety for those who ask according to the Word.

The Word of this psalm, if we meditate in it, will strengthen our roots, and give us stability in turbulent times. Is it any wonder that it carried such meaning for the persecuted church? As the world raged about them, their trust was in the anointed one. They may be incarcerated but he was installed, and the end of their lives was not the end of the story. You should really get this psalm into your spirit because it a "last days" psalm, as Revelation makes clear. The end times as described there are the same as in the psalm: the anger of nations (11:18); the political conspiracies against God's truth (19:19); the demonstrations of the Messiah's rod of iron (2:27; 12:5; 19:15).

Psalm 2 begins with a hurricane. But as you know, in the center of every hurricane there is a still and quiet center. Jesus the Son is that center. The Psalm is reminding us of what someone had described as "the quiet sovereignty of God". It is calling us to the place of asking where we accept our anointing to be God's agents in this raging world as His sons and daughters: asking for the nations and for the peoples and refusing to cede them into the hand of the enemy. We are asking for outcomes according to God's Word and Will, not man's words and will-to-power.

We have to accept this anointing for our asking for the Will of God according to the Word of God. As followers of Jesus we are now called His anointed ones. This Psalm is about all His anointed ones, all who bear the Father's name and DNA and are sent out into this unruly mess, in towns and cities, schools and offices, campuses and corporations, slums and IFDP camps all over the world, in apartment complexes and garbage dumps, in downtown offices and street-side poverty, in poor projects and affluent suburbs. As Teresa of Avila used to say, what is the point at looking at all that is raging around us and crying "the devil! The devil!" when instead, on our asking knees we can proclaim "God! God!" So when we are getting pounded, wearied, disheartened, tested, and when our hearts are groaning 'how long?' it is then that we need scriptures like Psalm 1 and 2 that fuel our asking afresh. Our asking is according to the Word that it may be for the world. We meditate in the Word, we imbibe the ways, the works and the wonders and will of God and we ask, ask, ASK ... according to the will of God as revealed according to the Word of God.

"Gathering all generations to pray for all nations, asking God to do what only He can do, and doing whatever He asks of us." - Mission statement of ASK Network

"I have seen many men work without praying, though I have never seen any good come out of it; but I have never seen a man pray without working." - James Hudson Taylor

"To pray to the Doer must help us to understand what is done ... Can we pray in earnest if we do not in the act commit ourselves to do our best to bring about the answer?" - P.T.Forsyth

"Prayer must involve the courage of unilateral action ... Action receives its character from prayer ... Prayer bestows upon action its greatest authenticity. It rescues action from activism ... It is from prayer that one expects action to take its value." - Jacques Ellul

"In prayer we tempt God if we ask for that which we labor not for; our faithful endeavors must second our devotion." - Richard Sibbes

"Prayer does not stand alone. It is not an isolated performance ... To pray well is to do all things well." - E.M.Bounds

"The best help in all action is to pray; that is true genius." – Kierkegaard

"God is asked to act, and the petitioner makes himself available as secondary cause through whom God can act." - Vincent Brummer

16

Asking And Acting

To Ask Is to Act ... to Act Is to Ask

Asking is the most necessary and normative act of the spiritual life. Asking is acting. It is the act out of which all other actions will flow. Jesus has been described as the one who "was mightiest in His action for men, not when He was acting on men, but acting on God ... Prayer is faith in action." [1] It can be argued that what makes any work specifically Christian is that it is derived from and dependent upon asking of God. It is not enough that asking is the first act that is then displaced by other actions. To the extent that consistent and persistent, constant and instant asking ceases to be the maternity ward, the holy think-tank, the laboratory, the conference room for ministry, then other actions will perhaps continue as religious works but not necessarily spiritual ones. In order to emphasize the inseparability of our acting from our asking, the actions that have ceased to be asked for, regardless of their activity or activism, have been described as "only idleness if this true and proper work is not done." [2] To ask is to act. To act is to ask. "Asking is ... behind all movements ... empowers all agencies." [3]

Keeping It Together

The failure to ask is the explanation for the failure to act. It is also the clearest reason for the ineffectiveness of the actions that we do engage. Asking and acting are one. Asking has been described as "the most intimate and effective form of Christian action." [4] But it is also in the context of asking that we discover and recover what God wills for our actions. The reason that Shane Claiborne and Jonathan Wilson-Hartgrove were effective in their just actions is that they understood just asking: "Prayer is not so much about convincing God to do what we want God to do as it is about convincing ourselves to do what God wants us to do." [5] What God has put together, let nobody put apart. Not only are they not separate, they are not mutually exclusive as some think. We cannot choose which of the two, asking or acting, we would rather specialize in. The story is told of a man who could not swim and who was heard to ask God, as he dived into the waters to rescue his drowning child, "O Lord could you teach me to swim?" This certainly illustrates the necessary co-existence of asking and acting. However, it is not enough just to say that they "go together". Jacques Ellul understood that there is an order of value. He chided those who agreed to spontaneous action and then said prayers as an additive. "The order is the reverse of that, namely, to pray, and then to act because of having prayed, as a function of that prayer." [6] If asking does not precede acting, our acting will pre-empt asking.

Asking of God is a relational engagement by which one is *changed*. When you ask according to His will, you discover that this will is not a passive thing, which can be responded to or not. Talking of passivity, there are those like Bloesch who rightly take issue with the description of prayer by the mystics as "holy passivity" or "holy inactivity." [7] It is impossible to engage the intimacy of God in a way that satisfies our hearts, and not in that exchange, discern the things that weigh on His heart, that invite us to co-work with Him in the world that He so loved at such cost to Himself. Many treat God's will as if it is His wish, in a way that it loses its decisional desire. His will is pro-active not passive, which is why the failure to respond to it is disobedience, not an oversight. It is commanding and demands obedience. "I'll give it some thought ... perhaps ... maybe ... let's revisit this ... there's an idea ... there's always tomorrow ... whoever would have thought of that ..." are not responses that the will of God invites. Jesus told a story (Luke 12:42-48) about a servant who knew the master's will. Jesus comments: "That servant who knows his master's will ... and does not **do** what his master wants will be beaten with many blows." Our knowledge of the divine will, according to which we are asking, assumes our acting upon that will, as the servant in the story did.

But asking of God is in itself an obedient response to God's will and is therefore already a holy action of engagement. It is right to talk about the labor of asking. That does not make it laborious, or labored, but it does make it spiritual work. It is understandable that Ambrose saw the asking-manual of the Psalms as "the gymnasium of the soul ... a stadium for all the virtues." [8] Asking is first a personal 'work-out' in which we 'work-in' the truth of God's will, but then it calls us to 'work-out' what God's answers are asking of us. By definition, to ask according to His will is to further engage us in this call to actively join what God is both revealing about what needs to be done, as well as about how those needs can be met. Many of our actions are often stimulated by external appeals, whether others' cries for help, or the persuasive legitimacies of the need. The problem with this is that we act only when **challenged** to do so, like "fair-weather" believers, wind and weather permitting.

Often this is reduced to responses to external crisis, rather than being the response that is rooted in an internally consistent obedience to the eternal Christ. We need to be changed not just challenged. It is impossible to ask according to God's will, and not be changed by the acceptance of that same will, that then inspires us to serve and obediently do that will. Asking is what determines the value and the veracity of the acting. But acting will determine the biblicality and the integrity of the asking. Acting will often lose its direction and distinctiveness as it is influenced by its context, unless asking keeps its hand on the rudder and keeps it tracking according to God's navigational instructions. Staying with the sailing image, Luther presented the inevitable exertion of asking as "comparable to that of a ship going against the stream." [9] It really is holy work. Asking will lead to acting, and acting will then lean on more asking. "If a person thinks of prayer as a way of not getting involved, of not acting, of avoiding risk, if he supposes that prayer lets him escape fatigue and danger, assures him of tranquility and a good conscience, gives him all-round protection, then we can say ... that he has not understood the reality of prayer." [10]

Seeing Action

Asking is not without its danger for it does not go unopposed. In arguably the most decisive spiritual action, the most strategic offensive operation of all time (the ransacking of death and hell no less), namely Jesus's engagement with the will of God in His choice to act as mediator, we find Him asking. We have noted how that asking grapples with the will of God in Gethsemane, and how the acceptance of that will determined how He would then act. But we also get that glimpse of Jesus, with enough of His own needs to think about, choosing to ask for Peter. "Simon, Simon, Satan has asked to sift you as wheat. But I have asked for you" (Luke 22:31). Given His knowledge of this satanic version of asking, Jesus acted by asking for Peter, and because we know the end of the story after his denials, we know that Jesus's asking was answered. Jesus turned back Satan, and Peter did turn back and strengthen his brothers. The nature of the spiritual warfare, of "seeing action", pitted the asking of Jesus against the asking of Satan. Asking of the Father was Jesus's instinctive and intuitive response to the demands of acting out the Father's will. As we have seen, that asking continued to the very last seconds of His life. The naming of Satan by Jesus here leaves us in no doubt about the nature of the terrain of this battle. That is why asking is 'seeing action', what Ellul calls "a decisive combat and a final commitment." [11] When we ask about something, we are not "going to bat" before God for the matter, so much as "going to battle." That is seeing action!

WDJD

This is not about what WOULD Jesus do but what DID Jesus do, about which there can be no doubt whatsoever. The WWJD bracelets are cute but remain theoretical. We have seen (in Chapter 8) the pattern in Jesus's life that has Him going from hearing God to healing people; talking to God to touching people; asking of God to acting for God. These are all single and seamless manifestations of His private and public life, His worship and His work, His ministry to His Father and His mission to the world. Jesus's demonstration of the relationship between public acting and private asking was confirmed by His teaching of His disciples. His final communication to them before his death is clear. "You may ask ... and I will do ... I will do ...

whatever you ask ..." His acting, for them and through them, was contingent on their asking of Him. This principle is the DNA of discipleship. If we ask for forgiveness, it will be necessary to act upon that and offer forgiveness to others. The failure to act will render our asking null and void. Ask for forgiveness and act forgivingly. Ask and act.

We have already gleaned much about asking from the Upper Room discourse (Chapter 11) but listen again: "I tell you the truth, anyone who has faith in Me will do what I have been doing. He will do even greater works than these, because I am going to the Father. And I will do whatever you ask in My name so that the Son may bring glory to the Father ... I chose you and appointed you to go and bear fruit – fruit that will last. Then the Father will give you whatever you ask in My name" (John 14:12-13; John 15:16). There is a point that is easily missed. Did you detect the common denominator in those two passages? In the first passage we read *"works"* and in the second passage we read *"fruit"*. In both passages we read *"ask"*. Jesus is telling them that two things are going to mark the new era, that together will constitute kingdom life: we will be acting in His name (doing greater works and bearing fruit that will last) and we will be asking in His name (He will do whatever we ask). These two things are inextricably linked in Jesus's mind. The *acting* of God (the works and the fruit) is related to the *asking* of the disciples (in His name). The continuity of Jesus's actions is going to be through continuous asking. It is not our wants, not what we want to do or what we want done that is fueling the asking here, but what He wants to do, because it is about His acting. As Murray put it, we ask in His name "as His representatives *while about His business.*" [12] Is it any wonder that where there is little asking there will be little acting. The asker is the worker, and the worker is the asker. Great works require great asking - no great asking, no great works.

If you have a desire to do Jesus's works, to be fruitful, you will ask in His name. Note again the sequence: "He will do ... I will do ... ask" (John 14:12-13). It is after Jesus tells His disciples that they will do what He is doing, act as He is acting, that He immediately says that His future "doing" will be in response to their asking. So what can we assume dominates our asking? It will not be asking for what we need for ourselves, but asking for what we need in order to do the work of Jesus; not just asking for things, but asking for people. "Ask the Lord of the harvest ... to send out workers" (Matthew 9:38). This is all about asking for the work of Jesus to be manifested and multiplied. This is about asking for what we need in order to bear fruit that will last. Is this what dominates our asking or do our prayers never get out into God's world beyond our own front door step? There was something other than asking that was also dominant in Jesus's communication to the disciples at the Last Supper. There is no passage of the Bible where more reference is made, not only to asking, but to *"the world"*. There are about 40 references. It was on Jesus's mind. Asking in His name is the vehicle, the means, the bridge, the fuel, the script for acting in His name, in and for the world that His loving Father asked Him to redeem through His answering redemptive actions of obedience.

This asking, given the immanent crucifixion, is hardly a "Bless the missionary" kind of prayer. It is battlefield-asking. It is as if asking is the troop carrier that gets us to the action, the means by which we engage the battle, but once there, it is like a 'transformer' and it becomes a tank, since asking is an action which brings the kingdom of God and our Christ into the places where the kingdom of this world previously ruled. The asking of Jesus on the Mount of Olives that is recorded in John 17 is fulfilled in the acting of Jesus on Mount Golgotha in John 19. Jesus's asking of the Father in Gethsemane that was premised on the will of God, is expressed in His saving action on the cross, taking on death and hell, reconciling the world that was asked for, to Himself. For Jesus, asking and acting were contiguous and continuous, and Murray understood this: "Whoever wants to do the *work* of Jesus must *ask* in His name." [13] Again, that is why you will find that where there is little asking, there is little doing. And those who do not work much for God, do not ask for much. Some, like Lovelace, have put this in polite missiological terms: "Mission cannot be effectively pursued without prayer." [14] To put it bluntly: NO ASK – NO TASK!

Let us put this another way so that we understand how powerful our asking really is. When we ask in His name, we are actually empowered by the Holy Spirit so that He can then act through us. We ask through Him, and He acts through us. The Lord said, "You ask and I will act!" The answers were not first about us getting something for ourselves, but about us being able to do something for Him. The answers were about divine necessities for His work, not just about personal needs being met for our private welfare. Our most effective asking is going to be for those things that make us effective in serving God's kingdom purposes in the world. Fortunately, there are some who grasp this: "Prayer not only strengthens one for work – work teaches and strengthens one for prayer." [15] Murray is arguing that you cannot miss the interplay between asking and acting as they inform, inspire, and invigorate each other.

The Asks of the Apostles

The Acts of the Apostles could have been called 'The Asks of the Apostles'. It is as much a text about praying as preaching, about asking as acting. It is a marriage made in heaven. Did the apostles not insist that they needed to give their priority to asking (Acts 6:4)? The recurring motif in the story of the early church is the relationship between persistent asking and powerful acting, in the name of Jesus. "Surely," argued Murray, "of all the gifts of the early church for which we should long there is none more needed than the gift of prayer." [16] You cannot separate asking and tasking. You could do no better than put this book aside now (I seem to suggest that a lot – you might never finish it!) and spend a significant amount of time marinating in Luke's account of the early church. In chapter after chapter, incident after incident, when asking is expressed in private, power is exhibited in public actions. "In one accord they devoted themselves to asking" (1:14). At the outset, it is extended asking that is the prelude to the outpouring of the Holy Spirit at Pentecost that results in power through passionate preaching and compassionate personal ministry in Acts 2. When the authorities seek to stop the proclamation and demonstration of the gospel, the response of the church is decisive: "they raised their voices together in asking" (4:24). As we have already seen (Chapter 15), asking according to the Word for their world threw them right back into the action despite threatened reprisals. Again, here is the relationship between dependent asking and empowered acting.

In Acts 6, it is not outside antagonism but internal dissension that threatens the continuing acts. The apostolic antidote is to reaffirm the call to asking: "We ... will give our attention to asking" (v4). The result was that "the word of God spread" and "the number of disciples in Jerusalem increased rapidly" (v7). Acts 10 is a huge hinge in the history of the church for it describes the inclusion of the Gentiles. If you are not a Jew, this should be sufficient argument for asking a lot, because it determined your inclusion. The chapter actually begins with a description of Cornelius' life of asking of God and his acting mercifully to the poor. God found this asking and acting to be irresistible. He responds by sending him an angel no less, and telling him how to find Peter. Cut to Peter. He is on a roof-top. Why? The text tells us: "Peter went up on the roof to ask" (10:9). The most significant world-shaking development for the expansion of the Christian mission is premised again on asking. Peter ended up in Cornelius' house, the Holy Spirit fell as at the beginning because as the angel said to Cornelius, "God has heard your asking!"

In Acts 12, there is yet another attack on the mission as Peter is imprisoned. We know what is coming next: "But the church was earnestly asking for him" (12:5). There is a demonstration of divine power and the acts continue. That brings us to Acts 13 that explains why Antioch is known as the maternity ward of New Testament missions. Why? "They fasted and prayed ... and sent them off" (13:3). Thus was launched the first missionary journey. It is important to observe that it is in the context of asking that there is empowerment for the acts of the apostles. The word 'mission' is a perfectly good word but it allows us to think too easily about task, about the actions that need to be done. Sadly, the tasks can be done without asking and consequently without power. Mission is but the power of God in action, in response to the asking of the missioners. That is the unavoidable message of Acts of the Apostles, and that is why John Wesley concluded that God does nothing but by asking for it. In that case, given the little asking that takes place, what is actually being done? This may explain the lack of fruit. That is why you will find that where there is much asking, there will be much evidence of the activities of the Holy Spirit, and the just acts of the saints. Acts of the Apostles is a persuasive text, the gateway to the history of the church, that will not let us pass any further without being convinced about this inviolable relationship between prayer and power, between asking and acting.[17] Acting without asking results in programs without prayer. Running programs replaces requesting God.

Asking and Acting In the Rubble

The story of Nehemiah's restoration of Jerusalem is a tremendous illustration of the interrelationship between acting and asking. Nehemiah's experience tells us that it was the preparation of the heart of the one asking that was so important to the transformational action that followed. His story is an example of how we can recover asking that engages us in godly acting.

Before he begins to ask of God, we hear him inquiring of his brothers about the situation in Jerusalem. "He questioned them" (1:2). If we do not ask about present need, we will not ask for future deliverance. Asking of others leads to more asking of God. The more we ask about the circumstances of our lives, of our neighbors, of our communities, of our nations, the more we have things to ask God about and for. We ask our way into the action. As we begin to look and listen something begins to happen to Nehemiah. First of all, he is overwhelmed by what he discovers, the sheer extent of the need with its despair and desolation. One of the reasons there is often no asking is simply because there is no burden. We must have a burden. We have to be broken by that which is breaking the heart of God. As much as this situation was going to require supported action and strategic conversations with the king, the weight of this burden sank Nehemiah to his knees, took away his appetite, and broke his heart: "for some days I mourned and fasted and prayed before the God of heaven." When the questions we ask about the earth bring bad answers, we need to ask heaven for the good answers. Chapter 1 of Nehemiah is an encouragement to recover asking when the need for action dawns on us.

There is a sequence of responses that chart Nehemiah's journey.

- It is about initiative: he invites the burden (v2)
- It is about information: he gets the burden: (v3)
- It is about intercession: he asks about the burden: (v5)
- It is about identification: he shares the burden: (v6)
- It is about involvement: he acts upon the burden (v11)

The mainspring of this process is asking, and when it is sprung, the acting follows. So what are some of the necessities that fueled his asking to become acting?

The Necessity of Facts

"I questioned them" (v2). Nehemiah moves beyond self-interest to actually find out what was going on and what was needed: "great trouble ... disgrace ... walls broken ... gates burned with fire" (1:3). This does not make for a cute prayer list. General observations suddenly become personal confrontations, and he is undone by the needs arising from sin's consequences.

He needed a baptism of reality. "Prayer is bringing reality into the presence of God." [18] The paucity of prayer is an indication of the lack of spiritual reality in people's lives as they carry on disconnected with God's world. There is nothing to stir them to ask, nothing to be desperate about. In his study in Nehemiah, Alan Redpath noted: "You are never used of God to bring blessing until God has opened your eyes and made you see things as they are. There is no other preparation for Christian mission than that." [19] What kinds of facts should awaken us? How about the fact that life is utterly destructive outside the will of God; that the wages of sin is death; that the soul that sins will die; that there is a hell; that there is a judgment; that we will give an account of our stewardship; that there is salvation in no other than Jesus; that there is an end to all things; that the kingdom of God is at hand. Do these ring any alarm bells? Does this remind you of anyone who asked a lot and acted a lot?

Nehemiah recalled: "when I heard these things I sat down" (1:4). Maybe we need to sit down before we go anywhere. We have to stop and let it sink in. Maybe we need to remember what it was like to be lost without Christ and without hope. Maybe we need to absorb the shock of it all so we can get desperate, get dependent and get determined. Stopping and sitting down resulted in something, and it was not an armchair prayer meeting. "For some days I mourned and fasted." For some of us, we never asked and acted until we were affected. It has been said that no one can build the ruins they have not wept over. We will not *face* it if we do not *feel* it. The heart needs to be stirred before the hand can be stretched. If we have no sense of the price exacted by sin, we will not understand the price paid for the sinner. The facts of sin are not functional and dispassionate statistics. It is not just another virginity lost; another abortion performed; another divorce settled; another porn website visited; another body bleeding; another needle stuck; another affair consummated; another child abused; another lie deceived; another race slandered; another parent rejected; another bitterness harbored; another rumor started; another tumor discovered; another character assassinated; another government toppled; another life and soul lost. Perhaps like Kurt in Joseph Conrad's 'Heart of Darkness' we need to be hung over the abyss in order to utter the same response, "O the horror!" [20] Why should the screams of the sinner and the sinned against be louder than the intercessory cries of the saints? We should take a long look and then sit down and first mourn our indifference. What affects us? To the extent we are affected we will ask and act. The truth is that if there is no engagement with the reality of life without Christ, there is probably little reality in engagement with God.

This is not just about the facts of what God *sees*, and requires that we see, but about the facts of what God *says*. We must understand the connection between cause and effect according to God, most specially the connection between my sin and the cross. To ask, we cannot ignore or sidestep the necessity of facts: about God's character, about the condition of life without knowing Him personally, about the content of His instruction and commands about what to do about it, about the consequences of sin, but also about what He can and will do about it. Where we ask is not hermetically sealed from what we ask about. This is not 'barracks room' asking but 'battlefield' asking. I appreciate Shane Clairborne's description of one of his favorite asking places, an abandoned row-house next door that was reached by a secret passage. "Sometimes as I prayed there, I'd notice the traces of the old world, like an empty heroin bag in the corner of the chapel." [21] This is why we ask "on site with insight".

The Necessity of Faith

Faith here is the rightful response of our will to who God is and to what He says to do about it. It is the exercise of complete trust in God's will and God's

Word. It is the conviction that believes and the commitment to behave in a way that is consistent with that belief. The premise of asking is not our request but His revelation. It is not first about our prayer lists or prayer techniques but about a revelation of God that assumes two responses of faith: a relationship with God and a responsibility to discharge faithfully what we now know. Nehemiah was not reacting to Jerusalem's crisis, but first relating to God, out of which came, not reacting, but real acting; not just a program, but a prayer.

The Necessity of Feeling

Reconnecting with God's affections rekindles ours. It is worth studying, not only Nehemiah's responses, but also those of Abraham before Sodom. The identification with the feelings evoked, and owning them, provoked boldness and pleading. Feelings arising out of intimacy with God and love for what He loves, will get you talking to Him – fast and furiously. It will be intense, urgent, confident, compassionate, but it will perhaps seem pushy, and feisty and even irreverent. Abraham, more than once, asked God not to be angry with his persistent, passionate asking. There is no virtue in tears for their own sake, but Nehemiah was not being sentimental but spiritual. Sometimes our asking is only borne in tears. Our asking should be arising from the same things that caused Jesus to weep. Do we remember those occasions for the Redeemer's tears? At Bethany outside Lazarus' tomb, He wept at the refusal to accept His *revelation* as the Resurrection and Life. He wept over the Rich Young Ruler and His refusal to accept His *requirements*. He wept over Jerusalem and her refusal to accept His *relationship*. In asking, we engage the grief that God feels; the grief that God requires; the grief that God responds to.

What is the point here? The asking of Nehemiah connected him with the actions that God desired, and that God intended to empower Nehemiah to do. The relationship between asking and acting is indivisible.

- **Between our asking and God's acting.** God answers and acts because He is asked. Asking is often a condition of God's acting. As has been observed, asking is a necessary but not a necessarily sufficient reason for God's actions. What we are affirming is that the very act of asking of God presupposes that God can, and indeed will provide answering acts in response to our asking for those acts.

- **Between God's answering and our acting.** Our asking so often reveals what needs to be enacted, and how we need to be the actors, but it is in our asking of God that we most often hear what God is asking of us. We ask God to interfere divinely in a situation and He asks us to apply our intercession with godly intervention. The heart that is moved to ask is then moved to act.

Let Jesus have the last word as we read again His words: "I tell you the truth, anyone who has faith in me will do what I have been doing. *He will do* even *greater works* than these, because I am going to the Father. And *I will do* whatever you *ask in My name* so that the Son may bring glory to the Father ... I chose you and appointed you to go and bear *fruit* – fruit that will last. Then the Father will give you whatever you *ask in My name*" (John 14:12-13; John 15:16).

A Pastoral Postscript

One might argue that Jesus is still bearing the burden of personal unanswered asking: specifically, His pre-cross prayer that "they be brought to complete unity" (John 17:23). The history of community-wide, city-wide, nation-wide church-based outreach (whether for evangelistic crusades or justice campaigns) is littered with the fallen and tangled infrastructure of attempts to build cohesive, reconciled, relational unity. A few years ago, undone by the limited progress in reconciled relational unity in our city, I got an appointment to meet with the pastor of a black congregation that had a publicly acclaimed history of proclaiming the gospel of reconciliation and promoting unity. I was graciously received as I presented my 'asking' need. My proposal was hardly a new program. I asked if our respective communities could team up to invite others to join us at a Communion service, where we broke bread together, shared the cup, adored Jesus and asked of Jesus together, upper room style, how He wanted us to engage our city together. My request was met with surprise, followed by complete disinterest. I was asked, "Why would our people want to do that? We're happy with our worship." I was then told of all the city-programs that the church was directing and I was invited to send volunteers, preferably with monetary gifts. It was another disappointing experience of the primacy of tasking as the only means for 'getting together.' Unity ends up being defined by tasking, not asking. Of course it is not an either / or but there is a desperate need to put the 'ask' back in the 'task'. Far from being an avoidance of action, or an interruption of existing action, it is the very maternity ward for new and renewed corporate and communal life and action. Why? Because we are not getting our marching orders and our call-up papers from co-operating pastors, but from a solo commander, a commanding God. Our relationships seem to be as deep and wide as our commitment to ask God together for the task. "The communion of prayer is the very first form of communion that belief takes. It is in this direction that church unity lies. It lies behind prayer ... Prayer for church unity will not bring that unity; but that which stirs, and founds and wings prayer will." [22] P.T.Forsyth got it right. May the 'asks' of the apostles once more be the 'acts' of the apostles in our communities. May 'standing in the gap' to ask become the 'healing of the gap' in our ask-based acting. May the revelation of God's will at the place of asking become the restoration of the broken walls at the place of acting on the instructions and directions received. At the end of the day Oswald Chambers came to the right conclusion: "Prayer does not fit us for the greater work; prayer is the greater work." [23] Ask and task!

"Prayerlessness is an injustice." - P.T.Forsyth

"He will respond to the prayer of the destitute; He will not despise their plea." - Psalm 102:17

"The moment social action is based on prayer, then that action can take on a lively versatility." - Jacques Ellul

"We have the right of declaring war in prayer on every leader on earth who violates the will of God by oppressing the poor, denying civil rights and deforming society." - Richard Lovelace

"My plea is just." - Psalm 17:1

"The just man does not desist from praying until he ceases to be just." - John Chrysostom

"Prayer in the Spirit is socially revolutionary because it prepares the way for the advance of the gospel in society, and the gospel carries with it new social values that contain the seeds for a new society based on the righteousness of the kingdom." - Donald Bloesch

"When we throw our hands up at God and inquire, 'Why do you allow this injustice?' we have to be ready for God to toss the same question back to us." - Shane Claiborne and Jonathan Wilson-Hartgrove

17

Just Asking ... Justly

Clasping the Issue

"To clasp the hands in prayer is the beginning of an uprising against the disorder of this world." [1] Doing justice must include just asking, the means by which we recover and discover the will and word of God for His creatures and for what makes for shalom on God's terms. It is not for lack of programs but for lack of prayer that so many remain unengaged in God's just action. Asking is not only "for justice" for those "out there" who are suffering injustice. It implicates the one who is asking and requires that they be accountable to be just. It has long been acknowledged that the pursuit of public justice without the equally passionate pursuit of private and personal just-ness, is destined for long-term failure though there may be apparent short-term gains. The kind of transformation that is required to deal with the roots of injustice is one that must be established in the human heart. It is at the place of asking that the blade of God's word turns over the hard clods of our hearts.

Jesus's parable about the persistent widow in Luke 18:1-8 is usually used to draw attention to the character required of the one who is asking. They have to be persistent. However, it might be good to note what is actually being asked about, which in turn may explain exactly why importunity was so essential, given the intractability of the subject matter. "Grant me *justice* against my adversary." This is asking about injustice. Both the Old and New Testaments draw our attention to this kind of asking that attracts God's attention. The common and repeated message is that God hears the asking of the victims of injustice, whether the destitute of Psalm 102:17 or the unpaid harvesters of James 5:4.

Given the necessary and overdue emphasis among Christians on matters of justice, it would be helpful to affirm that we are not only about "just asking" but also about "asking justly" in order to "act justly". We have established that there can be no separation between asking and acting; there is no disconnection between intercession and intervention. We should be heartened by the renewal of emphases both on justice-mission as well as on prayer in recent years. However, sadly and wrongly, they tend to emerge as distinct and unrelated movements. There has been a tremendous renewal of prayer and fasting in our generation. Prayer organizations and national prayer-movements proliferate, topic-focused or generation-sensitive. Equally, justice missions abound, locally and globally, and many of them were born in Christian concern and gospel passion. Problematically though, we end up with prayer-movements that are unengaged in just mission, and justice missions that cease to ask of God. The prayer-movements that begin with a credible prayer agenda for the national life, end up being more concerned to pray for the preservation of that way of life and for a social stability that favors personal security. God's main concern is not to protect our economic stability or provide a middle-class revival. These movements often degenerate into self-serving nationalism, supporting the status quo and predominantly ending up as the hand-maiden of Christ-less conservative politics. Few who stand for the republic understand the dynamics of a kingdom. Meanwhile, many justice missions end up losing their spiritual zeal and fire and degenerate into Christ-less, secular humanitarianism, becoming syncretistic, and ending up theologically universalist. They certainly may have a theology of good works, but they often get politicized and seduced by the funding they get from non-Christian sources. They have ethics without supernaturalism and end up as arms of the secular social services. This loss of gospel distinctiveness has overtaken many formerly Christian organizations, and the pressure to cave in to cultural, secularist intolerance is common. The societal activism may continue but the spiritual action is quenched. It does not need to be an either/or. It must be a both/and: asking and acting, intercession and intervention, passionate prayer and compassionate mission.

Swords and Trowels

Richard Lovelace, in his classic treatise on the dynamics of spiritual renewal, rightly argues that there is a necessary link between personal renewal and social reformation. He sets out to prove "that authentic spiritual renewal inevitably results in social and cultural transformation; that no deep and lasting social change can be effected by Christians without a general spiritual awakening of the church; and that evangelicals must stress more than evangelism and church growth if they are to duplicate the social triumphs of earlier periods in their own tradition." [2] The history of evangelicalism illustrates the struggle with this issue, particularly since liberalism, in its abandonment of the message of the cross and the necessity of personal salvation, appeared to have cornered the market when it came to justice. The social had clearly displaced the spiritual. It was maybe an understandable response that conservatives dug in to defend their soteriology, but in the process, they lost a "social-minded ethical consciousness." They had a soteriology but not a sociology.

In a stunning passage in 'Screwtape Letters', C.S.Lewis captures the problem for the Christian, when it comes to matters of personal justification and social justice. Having failed to subvert the new convert through the flesh and the world, Wormwood is advised by Screwtape that "the best point of attack would be the border-line between theology and politics." [3] The old demon remarks on how many "Christian-political writers think that Christianity began going wrong, and departing from the doctrine of its Founder at a very early stage." This begins yet another search for "the historical Jesus" that invariably exalts humanity over divinity. Screwtape wryly comments that these searches for the real historical Jesus, that seem to come every 30 years or so, "all tend to direct men's devotion to something which does not exist, for each 'historical Jesus' is unhistorical ... The 'historical Jesus' then is always to be encouraged." He observes that 'the Jesus' who ends up being presented is the result of the suppression or exaggeration of certain points. The old demon is right. Jesus emerges as a crusader but not the Christ. He is a humanitarian martyr, not a holy Messiah. He is just but not the justifier. The crusade of social action displaces the cross of salvation. Screwtape reminds Wormwood that the earliest converts were "converted by a single historical fact (the resurrection) and a single theological doctrine (the redemption) operating on a sense of sin which they already had." The demons want to subvert that foundation and "make men treat Christianity ... as a means to anything – even to social justice. The thing to do is to get a man at first to value social justice as a thing which the enemy demands, and then work him on to the stage at which he values Christianity because it may produce social justice."

This is profoundly simple and simply profound in its analysis. Social reformation ends up not requiring a spiritual revelation. The justice program does not require Jesus's presence. The emphasis becomes the organization of available natural means and a denial of the supernatural. We end up really believing that we can save the planet unaided. The reason Lewis emphasizes all this is because he knew that once you can "coax humans round this little corner" you are taking the first steps towards disaster – new versions of Christianity are formed and forged and the journey from orthodoxy to heterodoxy, to heresy and to apostasy has begun. Making a good society ends up having nothing to do with the work of the Spirit, to applying the cross of Christ that alone can make men good on God's terms, nor does it require anything to be asked of God.

This is precisely why asking is such a significant indicator of the spirituality of a mission, particularly a justice mission. By definition, asking-prayer is the confession that it has to be God's work not ours. Asking is the expression of humility about our ability. People do not ask, not because they are prayerless, but because they are proud. If there is no asking, as we have seen, the only assumption that can be made is that we are capable and do not need God. Asking of God is the non-negotiable vehicle that prepares us for mission, that propels us into mission, that powers us in mission, that preserves us in mission, and that produces fruit in the mission. Just as there is little worship among those who reduce Jesus to the poster-boy for justice, so there is little prayer. These vital evidences of supernaturalism are missing, most particularly, the supernaturalism of the Holy Spirit who helps our asking. Nehemiah gave us a graphic image of what makes for a balanced mission, as he describes how the people "did their work with one hand and held a weapon in the other, and each of the builders wore his sword at their side as they worked" (Nehemiah 4:18). When Paul mentions the sword of the Spirit ("which is the word of God"), he immediately pleads: "Pray in the Spirit" (Ephesians 6:18). A just war requires just weapons: asking justly directed by a just Word. It is about the sword and the trowel.

Just Asking a Just God

There are over 1200 scriptural passage that address issues of justice-mission, of intervention. But what is the relationship between acting justly and just asking? There must be clarity about God's justice in our *heads* (biblical conviction), in our *hearts* (emotional compassion) and in our *hands* (practical commitment). By the time you have finished reading this chapter, thousands of young girls and women will be coerced into sexual acts in brothels, where they are permanently enslaved, including in the USA. But good theology and godly ministry cannot sufficiently be based on an argument about human need, as empirically attested as it is. Why not? Because we are not always moved by human need, so we are not always responsive to it. It is not a sure enough guarantee of our commitment or compassion. As evident and in-your-face as it is, it does not of itself have the inevitable power to capture our attention or elicit our response. In fact, sometimes it stymies us and freezes us because we get overwhelmed, caught in the headlights, and fear it and submit to our ignorance about how to respond - so we don't.

Like the priests and Levites in Jesus's parable of the Good Samaritan, there are any number of reasons why we may walk by the concentrated explosions of pain, the mini-holocausts of violence, the shrapnel of injustice, the human debris of oppression – for the same reasons they did: to get on with the Lord's business as we understand it to be. Whatever that priest or Levite thought was the more pressing demands of their religious worship, there is an irony in the Samaritan's oil and wine – both sacrificial elements in Jewish worship. But the Samaritan could not worship in their temple. So the question leaks out of the story: what does God regard as true worship? It would seem that it has something to do with the oil and wine's relationship with justice.

Like all other scriptural necessities, this matter of justice is rooted and earthed in something more persuasive and way more demanding and commanding than the *need of man*, as crucial as it is that we ask and ask again for those needs to be met. As we have argued from the beginning of this book, it is anchored non-negotiably in the *nature of God*. Like asking itself, it is God himself who validates it. If it is God's purpose by His Spirit to reproduce His life in us, then whatever is concordant and consistent with His personhood will be conspicuously manifest in us, His children, His spiritual DNA. Justice is not therefore a relative matter – it is rooted in the absolute of God's truth and God's order, God's character, God's design and desire. Working definitions are sometimes hard to hone but suffice it to say that biblical justice is about first, a right relationship with God's *person*, and secondly, about a right relationship with God's *purpose* for His creation, including not only people but the animal world and the environment and the land. Whatever violates God's intention, should command our attention. Justice is when things are simply as they are meant to be on God's terms; when any and all exercise of authority and power is in submission to God's authority and therefore God's plan and purpose for how things should be; when an acknowledgement of divine dominion renders null and void any expression of human domination. But given the overwhelming flood of injustice that drowns our capacities to process and respond, how do we retain any buoyancy, any hope that anyone can be rescued?

Read the Book

Gary Haughen, founder and President of International Justice Mission, records how he retained hope after witnessing so many atrocities: "I hope in the Word of God ... It is through His word that God reveals His character, and it is God's character and God's character alone, that gives me hope to seek justice amid the brutality I witness." [4] Response has to be rooted in our response to God's Word, not only to human woe. Mission is therefore rooted in prayer, in asking according to that Word. If this spiritual communication with God is not the context for our social conversations arising out of our perceptions of what is needed, then what understandably happens is an immediate pursuit of effective programs that sadly and inexcusably bypass the necessary asking of God and asking for God. We find a way to feed the hungry without having to fast ourselves. Intercession, our asking, gets disconnected from our intervention, our acting.

Our orientation to just mission must be directed by our theology of just mission, which means that it must be grounded and rooted in the nature of God before it is ever about the need and nature of man. The mission of our hands will be limited to the extent that it is disconnected from the mission of God's heart, on His terms. To ask justly, we have to be convinced and convicted by the just character of God. Only such a revelation will fuel our asking and stir us to ask what His justice seeks and requires. Four things should convince us to ask justly.

1. **The Character of God:** "The Lord is a God of justice" (Isaiah 30:19). He does not leave this to our observations or deductions but states it personally so there is no doubt about it. "For I the Lord love justice. I hate robbery and iniquity" (Isaiah 61:8). "Let him who boasts boast about this: that he understands and knows Me, that I am the Lord who exercises kindness, justice and righteousness on the earth, for in these I delight" (Jeremiah 9:23-24). "I (wisdom) walk along the paths of justice" (Proverbs 8:20). "He (Josiah) defended the cause of the poor and needy. Is that not what it means to know Me" (Jeremiah 22:16). But when His spokespersons do get in on the act, their testimony is equally unequivocal. "All His ways are just. A faithful God who does no wrong, upright and just is He" (Deuteronomy 32:4). "The Lord loves justice - those who love violence His soul hates" (Psalm 11:5-7). "God is a righteous judge who expresses His wrath every day" (Psalm 7:11). "The Lord will be exalted by His justice" (Isaiah 5:16). "Righteousness and justice are the foundation of your throne" (Psalm 89:14). "A scepter of justice will be the scepter of your kingdom" (Psalm 45:6).
2. **The Concern of God:** "To deprive a man of justice - would not the Lord see those things" (Lamentations 3:36). "The Lord ... does not ignore the cry of the afflicted" (Psalm 9:9,12). "The cries of the harvesters (unpaid!) have reached the ears of the Lord Almighty" (James 5:4). "The Lord works justice for all the oppressed" (Psalm 103:6). "He will be a spirit of justice to him who sits in judgment" (Isaiah 28:6). "The Lord abhors dishonest scales - just weights are His delight" (Proverbs 11:1). "They caused the cry of the poor to come before Him so that He heard the cry of the needy" (Job 34:28).

"Do not encroach on the fields of the fatherless for their Defender is strong; He will take up their case against you" (Proverbs 22:28). "In their affliction He was afflicted" (Isaiah 63:9). "You God do see trouble and grief. You consider it to take it in hand" (Psalm 10:13-14). "Because of the oppression of the weak and the groaning of the needy I will arise says the Lord" (Psalm 12:5). "I know that the Lord secures justice for the poor and upholds the cause of the needy" (Psalm 140:13).

3. **The Command of God:** "Follow justice and justice alone so that you may live and possess the land" (Deuteronomy 16:20). "Do not deny justice to your poor" (Exodus 23:6). "Maintain justice and do what is right" (Isaiah 56:1). "Seek justice, encourage the oppressed; defend the cause of the fatherless; plead the case of the widow" (Isaiah 1:17). "He has showed you O man what is good and what does the Lord require of you? To act justly and to love mercy and to walk humbly with your God" (Micah 6:8). "Administer justice every morning" (Jeremiah 21:12). "Administer true justice; show mercy and compassion to one another. Do not oppress the widow or the fatherless, the alien or the poor" (Zechariah 7:8).
4. **The Condemnation of God:** The expressions of God's emotions toward manifestations of injustice and to the perpetrators of injustice and inhumanity cannot be down-sized or diluted. "I will pour out My wrath on them" (Ezekiel 22:31). "My wrath will break out and burn like fire" (Amos 2:7). "So the Lord Almighty was very angry" (Zechariah 7:12). "Woe to you Pharisees ... you neglect justice and the love of God" (Luke 11:42). "All who have an eye for evil will be cut down: who with a word make a man out to be guilty; who ensnare the defender in court; and with false testimony deprive the innocent of justice" (Isaiah 29: 20-21). "Woe to those who join house to house" (Isaiah 5:8). "Woe to those ... who covet fields and seize them, and houses and take them, and defraud a man of his home, a fellow man of his inheritance" (Micah 2:2). "The Lord enters into judgment ... the plunder from the poor is in your houses. What do you mean by crushing my people and grinding the faces of the poor" (Isaiah 3:13)? Incidentally, we should be outraged by the way that so many so-called Christian TV ministries essentially

> prey on the poor. "Woe to those who make unjust laws, to those who issue oppressive decrees, to deprive the poor of their rights and withhold justice from the oppressed. What will you do on the day of reckoning" (Isaiah 10:2)?

Did you notice the zoom lens moving in with increasing definition and demand? Not surprisingly, the passion for justice, for its establishment and maintenance, the call to confrontation with injustice, for its exposure and defeat, the call to rescue and save the victim and the violated, are equally the DNA in scripture of all that which is of God. Thus justice is intrinsic to the messianic hope and the mission and the ministry of Jesus. "I will put my spirit on Him and He will bring justice to the nations ... In faithfulness He will bring forth justice ... He will not falter or be discouraged till He establishes justice on the earth. In His law the islands will put their hope" (Isaiah 42:1-4). "Seek first the kingdom of God and His righteousness" (Matthew 6:33). "The Spirit of the Sovereign Lord is on me ... For I the Lord love justice" (Isaiah 61:1, 8). The gospel is to the literal poor and to the sexually abused and enslaved, and was readily received by such. This DNA is in the witness of the church that sought justice for those who were both within and without the community as instructed in Deuteronomy 15, eradicating injustice within and alleviating it without. Is not this the religion that God our Father accepts as "pure and faultless ... to look after orphans and widows in their distress" (James 1:27). "Selling their possessions and goods they gave to anyone as he had need" (Acts 2:45). "There were no needy persons among them" (Acts 4:32). Deacon ministry has lost its meaning in the church. It is not about building management but about administering a mandate for social justice. In Acts 6:1-7 when the necessity to appoint deacons is described, it was a response to the need for both intercession (led and exampled by elders) and intervention (led and enacted by deacons). Given all the things for apostolic leaders to talk about in a young and growing Christian movement, Paul himself tells the Galatians that all that was asked of them was that they should continue to remember the poor (Galatians 2:10). It is salutary to note that Paul came to Jerusalem to bring offerings for the poor, and it was as a result of that justice mission that he was arrested, and a process began that ended eventually in his martyrdom.

What They Don't Tell You at Spiritual Leadership Conferences

Not surprisingly, this DNA of God's character was expected to characterize spiritual leadership. To be "just" (Titus 1:8) is a qualification of leadership. You will be hard pressed to find a book on Christian leadership that has a chapter on this. You will find chapters on: team development, vision forming, leadership culture, reproduction, change agents, conflict management and on and on, but nothing on the call to just ask and act justly. If justice is not a passion for leaders then it will be no surprise that churches are inward and self-satisfied with internal growth. Proverbs 31:8 is a word to leaders: "Speak up for those who cannot speak for themselves for the rights of all who are destitute. Speak up and judge fairly; defend the rights of the poor and needy." Is it not "by justice" that "a king gives a country stability?" "His mouth should not betray justice" (Proverbs 16:10). And talking of leaders who have earned the right to be heard, these words were among David's very last: "He who rules over men must be just" (2 Samuel 23:3).

When we are asking God for peace in our nations and communities, we must understand that this matter of justice is fundamental to the whole biblical understanding of Shalom – of peace on God's terms – for every dimension of personal and public life. It is fundamental to the covenant. From Genesis to Revelation it is the theme of God's heart and the call and passion of God's men and women. In Genesis 18:19 God describes Abraham, why he chose him, and what he chose him for: "to keep the way of the Lord by doing what is right and just." He was a qualified leader – our father in the faith no less. Immediately God speaks of the outcry of Sodom which we read about in Ezekiel 16:49: "Now this was the sin of your sister Sodom: she was arrogant, overfed and unconcerned; they did not help the poor and the needy. They were haughty and did detestable things before me. Therefore I did away with them." Not surprisingly, one of the earliest records of intercession in scripture is of Abraham just asking but asking justly for God to spare and rescue an unjust city. In Revelation 19:1,11 we read: "Hallelujah! Salvation and glory and power belong to our God for true and just are His judgments ... With justice He judges and makes war." These Bible book-ends, Genesis and Revelation, tell the beginning and the end of it all.

Intercession and Intervention

What is the first thing we think of when we hear the phrase "stand in the gap"? Probably intercession? Such a response is an incomplete response to the biblical phrase, and will result in unfinished business if the intercession is not accompanied by intervention. Just asking must be asking that is just, that asks for what is the equitable, peaceable, pure and saving will and work of God to be accomplished.

It is not my purpose to examine key passages in detail but let us mention some that will encourage us to just ask and ask justly.

- **Isaiah 56** opens with: "Maintain justice and do right ... Blessed is the man who does this." This chapter speaks of the inclusion of eunuchs and foreigners who would not be familial covenant-insiders, but were considered so by God because they "choose what pleases me and hold fast to my covenant". They are allowed to enter the "*house of prayer*" for "*all nations*", the central place of asking. The answered prayers, are linked with justice and the keeping of the sabbath, the supreme sign of deliverance from trade and material acquisitiveness. There is a relationship between intercession (asking) and intervention (justice).
- **Isaiah 58** presents the inconsistency of asking "for *just decisions*" (v2) yet persisting in *unjust practices* that require intervention, not just intercession. Without the motivation of justice, fasting can degenerate into a self-seeking, self-satisfying, self-affirming practice, and thus become a religious work. Indeed, fast the food, but face the facts. God's response is all about the ongoing practices of injustice: "you exploit all your workers" (v3). The kind of asking that God has chosen was not only asking for just decisions but for just actions: "To loose the chains of injustice and untie the cords of the yoke" (v6). Ask and act for loosed chains and untied cords – the freeing of the individual. But also ask and act for the breaking of the yoke – the freeing of the communal and the corporate, for the breaking of the systemic influence of principalities and powers in the societal structures of governance and organization. This

requires Spirit-empowered asking. There is a relationship between intercession (asking) and intervention (justice).

- **Isaiah 59** presents God looking for someone. Who and why? The opening charge and summary of the people's sin is clear: "No one calls for justice ... there is no justice in their paths ... justice is far from us ... we look for justice but find none ... justice is driven back ... the Lord looked and was displeased that there was no justice" (4-16). The sins of injustice were both public and private: "your hands are stained with blood" (visible as a result of public acts) but also "your fingers with guilt" (emphasis on close private personal contact). When God is looking for someone who is different "He was appalled that there was no one *TO INTERVENE*". Being an intermediary is clearly part of the call to ask, but such mediation involves more than intercession – it involves intervention. There is a relationship between intercession (asking) and intervention (justice).
- **Ezekiel 22** is the other key chapter in which God looks for someone: "No one calls for justice; no one pleads his case with integrity" (v4). The advocacy of the Spirit that works through us in our asking, that pleads the cause with God, is matched by the social advocacy that pleads the case with men. Like Isaiah 59, the context is one of horrendous injustice. The call to "stand in the gap" (v30) is again the call for an intermediary, an intercessor, though the call is not just to ask but to act justly: "to build the wall". What wall? The walls of just order that have been torn down and breached by the injustices that have been identified in the chapter. Most people can quote 2 Chronicles 7:14. (Go ahead and prove I am right!) Yes, there is a call to be humble and to ask, but the emphasis is on what needs to be heard, what needs to be forgiven, what needs to be healed in the land. Why is the land so sick and diseased? The defilement of the land is related specifically to the denials of justice in every part of national, societal and personal life. Ezekiel 22 gives a comprehensive list. Note that it is addressed to the "princes" (v.6), to the leaders and is about how each one "uses his power". Do you need an ask-list? Here is a graphic one, as you read through the list of what the people are doing:

- o **Destroying** (2, 12) - *"shedding blood ... accept bribes to shed blood"*
- o **Defiling** (3, 11) - *"making idols ... defiles his daughter-in-law"*
- o **Defaming** (7) - *"treated father and mother with contempt"*
- o **Despising** (8) - *"despised my holy things"*
- o **Desecrating** (8, 26) - *"desecrated my Sabbaths ... teach that there is no difference between the clean and the unclean"*
- o **Debauching** (9-11) - *"commit lewd acts ... violate women"*
- o **Dishonoring** (10) - *"those who dishonor their father's bed"*
- o **Defrauding** (12, 29) - *"you take usury and excessive interest and make unjust gain from your neighbors by extortion"*
- o **Devouring** (25) - *"they devour people"*
- o **Defying** (26) - *"her priests do violence to my law"*
- o **Deluding** (28)- *"false visions and lying divinations"*
- o **Demeaning** (29) - *"oppress the poor and needy and mistreat the alien"*

Sound familiar? This is the context in which God "looked for a man." You will find the same pattern and theme, the same call to just ask and act justly wherever you go in the prophets. The intercession of Amos in chapter 7 cannot be separated from the calls and commands of God about justice that have preceded it. Are you available to be found for this kind of asking and acting? Could you take on this ask-list for your own community and nation? There is a relationship between intercession (asking) and intervention (justice).

All these passages bring asking into the death chambers of injustice, affirming the non-negotiable relationship between intercession and intervention, affirming the basic call of 1 Timothy 2:1-4 that "first of all" we need asking that pursues public and social peace on God's terms of shalom, of His justice.

It is not enough, however, to state the effects on intervention where there is no intercession. There are effects on intercession when there is no just intervention. Go back and check out again those reasons given earlier (Chapter 5) for God choosing not to hear asking because of a refusal or evasion of His just requirements.

Just Jesus

But a greater than the prophets is here. Of this one it was said, "He made intercession for the transgressors" (Isaiah 53:12). The cross was the ultimate "standing in the gap", that unbridgeable chasm and breach between man and God, that "great gulf fixed" (Luke 16:26). Here is yet another presentation of Jesus's ministry of.intercession for our injustices. The cross was the ultimate union of intercession and intervention. In His death Jesus fulfilled the divine requirements for justice and satisfied the judgments of the law that decreed and demanded that the unjust soul should die. The intercession and intervention of Jesus were undivided. Just acting will always be found with just asking.

When Peter told his readers that Jesus was the "example that you should follow in His steps" the context was not a comfortable 'discipleship 101' course. The context is all about "unjust suffering." The just asking of Jesus got Him into this unjust mess. Jesus, the just one, then died for the unjust (1 Peter 3:18). When we engage injustice in Jesus's name and for His sake, it will be highly likely that unjust suffering will be inflicted on those who seek justice for the afflicted. Incarnation sometimes means incarceration. Freeing the violated means facing violence. It is not only the trafficked who end up traumatized but also the rescuers. What's the point? There is an asking of the Father that we have already heard in the mouth of Jesus, at the place where the cross-coordinates of intercession and intervention met. It was asking in extremis, about the forsakenness of soul while redeeming the forsaken. Lest we sound too glib about just asking, we desperately need to be able to ask as Jesus asked, with a just sense of injustice in extremis. Why, you may ask, given that there was no answer. Because though there was silence, He still had a Father. "Father, into your hands I commit my spirit" (Luke 23:46). The just asking remained His means of communication, when all the field-phones had their wires cut. Part of the "example" that Jesus set was to continue to offer "asking with loud cries and tears to the one who could save Him from death" (Hebrews 5:7). His asking amidst unjust suffering was a means by which He "learned obedience from what He suffered" and was thus empowered to stick with the mission. Just asking against the odds enabled Him to act justly against those odds.

Practicing the Presence - Justly

There is much talk these days about experiencing God's Presence and rightly so. But everyone desires the feelings, the atmospherics, the awe, the visceral sense of presence, but few have considered what God actually says when He is present. Outside the transfiguration of Christ, is there a more awesome experience of Presence than that of Moses on Sinai where God revealed Himself for Moses to see His glory? But have we read recently what God actually communicated in that holy Presence? How about the *10 commandments*: 1-5 - duty and justice to God; 6-10 - duty and justice to others. Or how about the *Book of the Covenant* – the justice mandate with specific problem-solving examples (Exodus 22-23). You seldom hear these texts expounded at 'Presence' gatherings. It is interesting that the two dominating features of Moses' communication were: his relaying of God's concerns for justice, and his prayers to God. Intervention and intercession were the two main motifs – asking for justice.

From Dietrich and William

This is how Dietrich Bonhoeffer believed that a person's relationship to God and to others would be revealed: "Our being Christians today will be limited to two things: prayer and doing justice among men." [5] *That sounds like just asking and acting justly.* How do we stand on those two things? William Wilberforce was such an example of this. His explanation for the success of his mission was simple: "By hearty prayer." [6] He was part of a community of faith where every member asked of God for 3 hours a day. Is there any wonder that their asking fueled an acting that shook and changed the life of nations, and literally broke the chains and the yoke of slavery? As Richard Lovelace kick-started us, I will let him wind us down. He observed: "The small quality of intelligent intercessory prayer in most congregations is part of the short-circuiting of missionary consciousness among the congregants." [7] No wonder our enemy seeks to divide asking and just mission, so that we have intercessors uninvolved in practical justice and justice workers who do not intercede.

If the actions of our life that did not depend on our asking were removed, what would be left that we do? If the programs of churches that did not depend on the prayers of the congregation were removed, what would remain? Neither scenario is just on God's terms. I know what is meant when we talk about 'being the answer to our prayers' but I am not sold on the phrase. We cannot be the answer to everything, even if we have every resource and gifting needed. Many who subscribe to this truism have no conviction about the need for supernaturalism in the endeavor, and while they acknowledge the prayer, believe that the answer will be more their intervention than God's. This condemns us, to use Paul's terms, to remain "looking only at the surface of things". Unfortunately, in most injustice, we are not fighting "against flesh and blood" which is why the constructs of injustice are so institutionally evil and personally demonized, and why we need to know the full picture of what we are standing "against", and know how to strategically "wage war" (2 Corinthians 10:4-7; Ephesians 6: 10-12). Of course we will be the answers to our prayers but it may be more helpful to see our prayers as the answer to what God was asking of us all along, especially as He knew that if He could get us asking, He would get us co-acting. By seeing it this way, it is impossible to forget the primacy of God's initiating engagement.

Talking of spiritual warfare, in the same way that we have a plethora of prayer-movements that do not engage just asking, the brigades of spiritual-warfare camps that rhetorically shout what we are against, often do not really show what we are for. Is it just words, all this prayer and prophetic proclamation? If they are biblically 'just', then just words will produce a harvest of just works. Those who take the camouflage off the unjust enemy should put on the battle fatigues of justice. Spiritual warfare will bring a recovery of social welfare. Just asking will be integral with acting justly. Intercession and intervention will be our clasped hands and the open hands of God. Just asking ... and asking justly ... and just acting ... and acting justly.

Postscript

While writing this chapter, I happened to be reading 'My Bright Abyss' by the American poet, Christian Wiman. He describes how he went to a chapel near his office to pray, and while doing so a man came and sat across the aisle from him, though the entire church of empty pews was available. The man was a fidgety distraction. "When I finally got up to leave," writes Wiman, "he stood immediately to face me." Clearly, he was homeless and needy, bearing "the skeletal clarity of long addiction and that vaguely aggressive abasement that truly tests the nature of one's charity." Wiman was chagrined that this man had "preyed upon the praying." But as he thought about this "nagging" moment in the days that followed, he felt chastened and convicted. At that juncture in his life he had been "wondering how and why and to whom" he prayed. Let the last words of this chapter be his: "I felt almost as if God had been telling me, as if Christ were telling me (in church no less): get off your mystified ass and *do* something." [8] No 'assing' – just asking and acting justly.

"What various hindrances we meet
When coming to the Mercy Seat."
William Cowper

18

What makes for Effective Asking?

A Qualifying Word from James

In one of his discourses on the Sermon on the Mount, John Wesley dealt with the discouragements and frustrations that attend the efforts to live righteously and witness engagingly. After suggesting some ways to respond he said that there was "yet another remedy left; and one that is frequently found effectual when no other method avails ... ask and it shall be given you." [1] We should never be ashamed to state the obvious. To be effective in your asking you first have to be "effectual" by just asking! You only learn to ask by asking.

A righteous person's prayer is "effective" (James 5:16). What is meant by 'effective'? In our mind, the word implies that something is successful because it is working. Translators have argued and disagreed about the participle *'energoumene'*. Is it to be understood in the middle voice as *"is able to do"* or in the passive voice, *"is enabled to do"*? Is the emphasis on what we do to make it effective, or on what we are enabled to do to make it effectual. Whichever the case, what is clear is that the end result is a powerful prayer, most likely because a righteous person is operating in the will of God, including of course His will that they live a holy life. Why is this important? Because we are not using the word 'effective' here in a way that implies that because we do certain things we can guarantee the effectiveness of our asking, and thus make a work out of it, or think we have the means to assure its success. Nothing could be further from the truth. The word *"effectual"* is perhaps better, even though less used now. It suggests a different nuance, in that it is usually used of inanimate or abstract things that attain a desired result. This puts the emphasis less on what we do to make asking effective, and more on the idea that asking is a means for someone else's desire to be effected. Furthermore, the root of the word that James uses is the one employed by Paul to describe the workings of the Holy Spirit, which utterly accords with what we have already discovered about our asking being the evidence, not primarily of our formulations, but of the Spirit's utterance; not the result of a few prayer techniques that we have mastered in order to be a really effective asker, but of the Spirit's help and instruction. Our effectiveness has to do with the power that works in us and therefore enables us to ask powerfully, not with our ability to develop a method and means to ask effectively in our own strength and wisdom. In any case, did not James begin his epistle with the need to ask for wisdom from God in order to ask aright for anything?

The Friends of Asking

We have noted the many scriptural reasons for why God chooses not to listen to what we ask, or chooses to refuse to hear what we ask, as unwelcome as this feels. It follows that to ask effectively we should ensure that we are heard and that none of those exclusions apply to us. (It might be helpful to go back to Chapter 5 and review some of these.) Yes, there are many possible hindrances and interferences to asking, but there are also many godly factors that help our asking to be more effective. If you want to get more effective at something, you have to engage it, and start doing it. You can read all the books you like about tennis but you will never have an effective volley if you never get onto the court and get to the net. All the books in the world about prayer may be encouraging, but if you are not asking personally they are ineffective. So what makes for effective asking? Asking and continuing to ask.

Asking activates the context in which so much is matured and changed in our lives, precisely because it relates us to God, and in that relationship we are nurtured and nourished, taught and touched. Asking forces us to stop and think about what we really want for life and godliness, and thus purifies our future asking. Yes, it convinces us how much we need, and how far we are from asking effectively, but that revelation in itself is a tremendously effective first-fruits of asking. Just asking becomes a bondage-breaker: breaking the silence, breaking the fear about asking specifically, breaking the deception that we can get by without it, breaking the pride of our independence. As Forsyth put it, just the act of asking serves to "relax the tension of our self-inflation." [2] Asking is a holy end in itself, before it is ever about answers. So if you are asking, you are on your way to effective asking.

However, there are some considerations, and perhaps conditioning factors, that we should be aware of when we come to ask of God. We keep referring to these in different ways throughout this book, but it might help to get these on the table in a single serving, by way of a summary. When we pay heed to these, we will find that our need and desire to ask becomes such a contribution to our maturing godliness and discipleship. Asking is what disciples of Jesus do, and as we ask the Father, because it is such a means of grace, we will find ourselves in the classroom of the Holy Spirit, learning of Christ, and we will continue to receive the blessing of something that Paul asked for disciples: "I keep asking that the God of our Lord *Jesus Christ,* the glorious *Father,* may give you the *Spirit* of wisdom and revelation, so that you may know Him better" (Ephesians 1:17). Is that not the learning (to know him better) that discipleship is all about? We will continue to note that all three persons of the Godhead are actively involved every time we ask. How can we feel short of help? What follows are some scriptural encouragements for your engagement in effectual asking.

Knowing Jesus As Personal Lord and Savior

"Believe me when I say that I am in the Father, and the Father is in me ... I tell you the truth, anyone who has faith in me will do what I have been doing ... And I will do whatever you ask in my name." (John 14:11-13) The promise to respond to asking is made especially to those who put their faith in Jesus. He is answering Philip's question here, asking Jesus to "show us the Father." The "way" to the Father is Jesus, thus our asking of the Father can only be through relationship with Him. We are confident in our asking, because our confidence is in Jesus Christ. Because we have acknowledged Jesus as our

Savior, as the one who bore the penalty of our sins, then we who were once separated from God and incommunicado, can now draw near and ask, not as strangers, but as sons and daughters of His Father, because as an earlier verse in John's gospel says, "all who received Him, to those who believed in His name, He gave the right to become children of God" (John 1:12). Do you know Jesus as your personal Lord and Savior? Have you confessed your sin to Him, repented of your sin and received His forgiveness, received the gift of the Holy Spirit and committed to live submissively and obediently to His Lordship? **Knowing Jesus Christ as Lord and Savior makes for effective asking.**

Knowing God's Acceptance

"... so that you may know that you have eternal life. This is the confidence we have in approaching God ... that if we ask" (1 John 5:13). We have been forgiven and cleansed by the blood of Christ, which gives assurance about our acceptance and therefore our access and our asking. Our asking is accepted because we have been made acceptable to the Father through Christ. "We know that we are children of God" (1 John 5:19). Where there is acceptance there is assurance. Where there is assurance there is access. Where there is access, there is asking. **Knowing we are accepted and acceptable makes for effective asking.**

Confessing Sin

We know that "iniquity in my heart" (Psalm 66:18) is a barrier to asking, thus choosing to live a life that keeps short accounts with God makes for effective asking. James 5:16 is explicit that the asking of a "righteous" man is effectual. The debris of unconfessed sin blocks the spiritual arteries, and silences asking. It is the confession of sin that restarts asking by first asking for forgiveness. "Until known sin is judged and renounced,' wrote Oswald Sanders, "we pray and plead in vain." [3] I do not think it is without significance that John's first epistle that begins with: "If we *confess* our sins He is faithful and just to forgive us our sins" (1:9), then tells us that "if our hearts do not condemn us we have *confidence* before God and receive anything we ask" (3:21), and concludes: "If we know that He hears us – whatever we ask – we know that we have what we asked for" (5:15). Confession is heard by God and responded to with forgiveness, opening His ear, freeing us from condemnation and restoring our confidence to ask again. **Confession makes for effective asking.**

Humility

Asking that is a true confession of need requires humility. If people will "humble themselves" then God says that He "will forgive their sins" (2 Chronicles 7:14). "But the tax collector stood at a distance. He would not even look up to heaven, but beat his breast and said, 'God have mercy on me a sinner' ... this man went home justified" (Luke 18:13-14). The pride of the Pharisee at prayer and the prideful asking of Herod before Jesus are met with silence. "Stubborn pride" encounters heaven that is "like iron" (Leviticus 26:19). Asking will not be answered. "All God's thrones are reached by going downstairs."[4] "He hears the cry of the humble" (Psalm 10:17). Humility asks and pride does not. We often talk about prayerlessness as if it was the lack of a particular kind of activity. No, it is the lack of a particular attitude: humility of heart. Prayerlessness, the failure to ask, is therefore to be defined not as the lack of prayer, but as the presence of pride; not as a passive ignorance but as active arrogance. If we do not ask in humility then presumably we are either too proud to ask, or we consider that we have no need to ask. Meekness qualifies our asking. The poor in spirit are rich in asking. They have nothing with which to commend themselves to God apart from their great need of Him. **Humility makes for effective asking.**

Believing

"Whatever you ask for, believe that you have received it" (Mark 11:24). "If you believe you will receive whatever you ask for" (Matthew 21:22). "He who believes in Me, the works that I do shall he do also ... Whatever you ask in My name, that will I do" (John 14:12-14). "When he asks, he must believe and not doubt, because he who doubts is like a wave of the sea, blown and tossed by the wind. That man should not think he will receive anything from the Lord" (James 1:6). William Carey, the father of modern mission, said: "Believing prayer lies at the root of all personal godliness." [5] **Believing makes for effective asking.**

Faith

"According to your faith be it unto you ... If you have faith as small as a mustard seed ... if you have faith and do not doubt ... Have faith in God ... whatever you ask ... Increase our faith" (Matthew 9:29; 17:20; 21:21; Mark 11:22; Luke 17:5). Our personal faith is not in our asking, but in the One we ask. Our discipleship is about our fitness to ask and the faith to ask. "The best thing in prayer is faith" commented Luther.[6] At the end of the day, it is our asking that is perhaps the clearest way that our faith presents itself. Forsyth put it like this: "Petition is the form your faith takes ... Faith is what turns need into request. It is what moves your need to need God." [7] We may be tempted to stand in fear before our needs, but faith gathers those needs from the basement of helplessness, and instead of allowing them to fester and decompose the soul, presents them to God in our asking about them all. "Let us draw near to God ... in full assurance of faith" (Hebrews 10:22). Fear is the antithesis of faith and will silence asking. Faith takes every individual request of "I need this" or "They need that" and rewrites all these chits into a single request: "I...we... need God!" Faith always asks, when founded in a conviction of the Word of Truth, fired by a confidence in God's will, and fueled by the concerns of Jesus Christ. The faith that asks is the faith that now needs to persevere in what happens next – or does not happen. The great pioneer missionary to China, J.O.Fraser, observed that, "The real battle begins when the prayer of faith has been offered." [8] **Faith makes for effective asking.**

Abiding in Jesus

"I am the vine, you are the branches ... If you abide in me ... ask what you wish" (John 15:5-7). This proves that asking is all about relationship. The invitation to ask is not unconditional here. It is not about anything we want, any way we want it, any time that works for us. It is conditionally premised. Asking is the fruit of abiding, the manifestation of our union with Christ. Does this not make sense of our experience? Is it not when spiritual intimacy with the Lord wanes that asking evaporates? Where intimacy is limited, so is intercession. Where abiding is shallow, so is asking. Thus asking is both a gift and goad to a closer walk with God; it is a premise and a product. At the moment we think our asking is our invitation to God to move, to get involved, to do what we want or need, we find that it is His invitation to us to a deeper, more faithful, pleasing, expectant, intimate, abiding relationship with Him. It is His invitation to be changed into His likeness, before it is about our need for our circumstances or needs to be changed. The changes effected by our asking will always be secondary to the changes effected in us. **Abiding in Jesus makes for effective asking.**

Forgiving

"And when you stand, if you hold anything against anyone, forgive him" (Mark 11:25). Why were they standing? That was the posture for prayer. Jesus is speaking directly about what needs to be taken care of before we ask about anything. Usually, we find this first requires us to ask forgiveness for ourselves, given the delay in forgiving others, or for the contrary attitudes and feelings that have hardened in our hearts. **Forgiving makes for effective asking.**

Knowing He hears

"And if we know that He hears us, whatever we ask, we know that we have what we asked of Him" (1 John 5:15). We have acknowledged that sometimes there are reasons that God refuses to hear, but that does not mean He does not or cannot hear. (See Chapter 5.) Questioning His hearing is often a cover for questioning ourselves. When we are waiting for an answer, God's silence is not an inability to hear. John's argument is simple and clear. To know He hears is to know that everything consequent to our asking is in His hands, because it is in His ears. If we are not sure that He hears, then everything is unsettled and uncertain. **Knowing that God hears makes for effective asking.**

Knowing His Word

"Preserve my life according to your Word ... Strengthen me according to your Word ... May your unfailing love come to me according to your promise ... Be gracious to me according to your promise ... Direct my footsteps according to your Word ... May my cry come before you O Lord; give me understanding according to your Word" (Psalm 119: 25, 28, 41, 58, 133, 169). "If ... my words remain in you, ask whatever you wish" (John 15:7). The psalmists' asking is totally Word-based. The precepts, the promises, the proclamations and the prayers of the Word are the premise for all asking. The Word tutors our asking, giving us the matters to ask for, and giving us the very words to use. "Furnish thyself with arguments from the promises to enforce thy prayers, and make them prevalent with God .... The mightier any is in the Word, the more mighty he will be in prayer" (William Gurnall). We pray the Word. **Knowing His Word makes for effective asking.**

Waiting and Listening

"Those who wait on the Lord will renew their strength" (Isaiah 40:31). This is perhaps the best-known verse about waiting but it is addressed to people who are tempted to give up asking and waiting for an answer: "My cause is disregarded by God" (40:27). The idea here is of someone bringing their case to be heard but having it continually dismissed. It is the end of their asking. But then God asks them over twenty questions. In a strange way, these divine questions are God's answer. He is not asking in order to add to their despair, but as the God of hope He asks them to think about what He has done, so that they recover their lost faith in who He is and their lost confidence in asking. Just like us, when we need our answer now, all these people can see are the problems that demand an answer, but as they wait, they are told to see something else. "*See*, the sovereign Lord comes in power ... *See*, His reward is with Him ... *Lift your eyes* and look to the heavens" (40:10, 26). All the people can hear are the sounds of war and the cries of helplessness, but they are told to listen to something else: "A *voice* of one calling ... Have you not *heard*? The Lord is the everlasting God" (40:3-4, 9, 21, 28). If all you see and hear is the present reality as you perceive it to be, then you have failed to see and hear what is happening on God's terms. You will not discern the answer, you will stop waiting and you will stop asking. The hope that keeps asking effectively is rooted in a revelation of the character of God. The time of waiting that follows our asking is a time to listen to truth about who God is.

Time passing need not be the enemy of our hope, because "those who wait upon the Lord shall renew their strength." By the way, was not Jesus's last word to the disciples before His ascension, "Wait" (Acts 1:4)? And was not that waiting a time of asking? "They all joined together constantly in asking" (1:14). Waiting on the God of hope and listening to what He says to us while we are waiting will strengthen us to keep on asking. "I wait for God my Savior; my God will hear me" (Micah 7:7). **Waiting and listening makes for effective asking.**

Asking in Jesus's Name

Refer back to Chapter 11 for the details, but suffice it to say by way of summary that asking in Jesus's name is an expression of assurance. We have been given His name so we are *accepted* by Him. We have been *appointed* as His name-bearing representative to ask the Father. We have been fully *authorized* by that name and given all the rights of access and claim that He has. Again, no wonder we can be bold and expectant. **Asking in Jesus's Name makes for effective asking.**

Not Depending On Our Own Understanding

To ask is to acknowledge that we do not have it all together. Asking ensures that we do not "lean on our own understanding" (Proverbs 3:5). It is precisely our lack of understanding that should provoke us to ask: "If any of you lacks wisdom, he should ask God, who gives generously" (James 1:5). As long as we are asking we are not claiming that we have the measure of everything. A knowledge of the Holy One is understanding (Proverbs 9:10), so if asking is primarily the pursuit of intimate knowledge, then asking is a key to understanding. It was Jesus's intimate knowledge of the Father and therefore of the "Father's business" that gave Him such understanding and such "answers" (Luke 2:47). In the parable of the sower, Jesus explained that the one who "hears the Word and understands it" (Matthew 13:23) is the one who is going to be fruitful. But the one who is fruitful will be the one who asks (John 15:16). By spending 40 days post-resurrection opening the disciples' minds to "understand the scriptures" (Luke 24:45) Jesus laid the foundation for their asking. Our asking is "in the Spirit" so whenever we ask, we are engaging the "Spirit of wisdom and understanding" (Isaiah 11:2; Ephesians 1:17). Asking for understanding was one of Paul's major concerns: "We have not stopped praying and asking God to fill you with the knowledge of His will through spiritual wisdom and understanding ... I pray ... so that you will have a full understanding of everything good" (Colossians 1:9; Philemon v6). Daniel's experience illustrates all the moving parts. It was because he "understood from the scriptures" that he was moved to "plead with Him in prayer and petition". The outcome was the understanding that he needed: "I have come to give you insight and understanding." (9:2-3, 23) **Not leaning on our own understanding makes for effective asking.**

Fasting

"When you pray ... When you fast" (Matthew 6:5, 16). Jesus teaches asking and fasting as related subjects. Scripture describes them as a combined action, both in the Old Testament (Ezra 8:23) and in the New, as practiced by the early church (Acts 14:23). In scripture, turning from food was always representative of turning to the Lord, and asking of Him. Asking with fasting is one of God's means to encourage us:

- **To be heavenward**: "He answers him from His holy heaven" (Psalm 20:6). There is such a focus and consciousness of heavenly presence and purposes, and a deliverance from earthly distractions (Nehemiah 9:6). The asking-fast called in Joel (1:14; 2:15) brought a revelation of God on His "holy hill" (3:17) and what was going to take place in the heavens (2:29-30).
- **To be holy**: "They stood and confessed their sins" (Nehemiah 9:1-3). The sense of heavenly presence brings conviction of sin: "Our sins are higher than our heads and our guilt has reached to

the heavens" (Ezra 9:6). As a result of a "chosen" asking-fast "your righteousness will go before you" (Isaiah 58:8).

- **To be humbled:** "I humbled my soul by fasting" (Psalm 69:10). "I proclaimed a fast ... that we might humble ourselves before our God" (Ezra 8:21). It is the clothing of humility that acknowledges that there is no other ground for sustenance other than asking for intimacy with God.
- **To be heard:** "So we fasted and petitioned our God about this, and He answered our prayer" (Ezra 8:23). "They declared a fast ... He had compassion and did not bring upon them the destruction He had threatened" (Jonah 3:5-10). "Declare a holy fast ... Let them say 'Spare your people' ... The Lord will reply to them" (Joel 2:17-19).
- **To be helped:** The loss of natural energy through fasting is a picture of the desperate need for the Lord's help to supply what is needed, as human resource has failed. In response to asking-fasting God said, "You will call and I will answer" (Isaiah 58:9) and this is affirmed by the avalanche of active verbs that describe His response: "I am sending ... I will drive out ... I will repay ... I will pour out ... I will gather ... your light will break forth ... the Lord will guide ... He will satisfy ... you will be like ... you will be called ... you will find ... I will cause you to" (Joel 2-3, Isaiah 58).
- **To be healed:** Asking with fasting is sometimes necessary for healing and deliverance. "Your healing will quickly appear" (Isaiah 58:8). "This kind can only come out by prayer and fasting" (Mark 9:29).
- **To hear:** Daniel pleads with God: "In prayer and petition, in fasting" (9:3). He asks to be heard: "Hear the petitions of your servant ... Give ear O God ... O Lord listen" (9:17-19). But while he was asking he heard an answer. "As soon as you began to ask an answer was given, which I have come to tell you" (9:23). Kierkegaard articulated the need here: "The true relation of prayer is not when God hears what is prayed for, but when the person praying continues to pray until he is the one who hears, who hears what God wills." [9] Asking with fasting is not just in order to be heard by God, but to hear what God is saying.

Fasting makes for effective asking.

Desiring

"May He give you the desire of your heart ... May the Lord grant all your requests" (Psalm 20:4-5). "Whatsoever things you desire, when you ask ..." (Mark 11:24). "My heart's desire and prayer to God ..." (Romans 10:1) There is a relationship between desire and asking, affirmed by David, Paul and Jesus Himself. Notice that in every case, the expression of asking is preceded by the experience of desire. All the logistics of asking (when we ask, why we ask, what we ask for) are evidence of the longings of the heart, most particularly, the desire for God. Catherine of Siena taught that effective asking was "not attained by the use of many words but through the affection of desire."[10] Augustine understood that "God wishes our desire to be exercised in prayer."[11] John Piper is succinct: "Asking reflects desire."[12] If we are not asking much for spiritual things then it is evidence that we do not desire much. "Desire is the soul of prayer, and the cause of insufficient and unsuccessful prayer is very much to be found in the lack or feebleness of desire."[13] **Desire makes for effective asking.**

Seeking His Will and Submitting to It

"If we ask anything according to His will He hears us" (1John 5:13). This is best exemplified by Jesus in Gethsemane, at the moment of His greatest need to have God answer what He asked for: the cup of judgment to be taken from Him. He was not answered according to His need but according to God's will. How effective was this? The outcome was not that He was personally saved from the cup of judgment but that the whole world would be offered the taste of the cup of His blessing. It is one thing to seek God's will and another to submit to it. Seeking and submitting are two constituents within a single response. It is one thing to ask for His will to be done, and another to act upon that will. "Your will be done" (Matthew 6:10). "He listens to the godly man who does His will" (John 9:31). **Seeking and submitting to His will makes for effective asking.**

Loving the Believers

"If our hearts do not condemn us we have confidence before God and receive from Him anything we ask because we do His commands ... and this is His command ... to love one another as He commanded" (1 John 3:21-23). John's memory of Jesus's last words was clear. Jesus, after giving the disciples the new command that they love one another (John 13:34), goes on to talk about them asking in His name. Not to live with love for other believers is not a lack of affection so much as it is disobedience, which runs interference with our asking. This is a contradiction between our requests and God's requirements. How much asking is eliminated if there is no motivating love for those we are called to ask for? **Loving the believers makes for effective asking.**

Unity in Agreement:

In John 17 Jesus asks His Father "by the power of Your name – the name You gave Me – so that they may be one as we are one" (17:11). Jesus and His Father have the same name, so Jesus asks that His disciples will experience the attribute of that shared name - unity. The name of the Lord means oneness. Not surprisingly, the declaration that is the foundation for the central act of asking in the Jewish faith, the Shema, is: "The Lord is one" (Deuteronomy 6:4). It is the unity of the Father and Son, of whom we ask, that calls for the unity of those who ask of them. "If two of you on earth agree for anything that you ask for, it will be done for you by My Father in heaven" (Matthew 18:19-20). We are asking together of the Father, in the unity of sons and daughters, consequently now brothers and sisters, agreed about each other's request but also about who the Father is. Do we anticipate Trinity disunity in the answering of what we ask for? Why would our unity in asking be any less? It is interesting to note that the two or three who are gathered are not praying for unity. The key to that experience of unity was the asking. Paul knew the power of this united agreement of brothers: "I urge you, brothers ... to join me in my struggle by praying to God for me" (Romans 15:30). **Agreement and unity make for effective asking.**

Boldness

"We may approach God with freedom and *confidence*" (Ephesians 3:12). "And this is the *confidence* that we have in Him, that if we ask" (1 John 5:14-15). "Having therefore *boldness* to enter the holiest by the blood of Jesus" (Hebrews 10:19). Charles Wesley understood it: "Bold I approach the eternal throne!" The Greek word used for 'bold', *'parrhesia'*, was the word used to describe how Jesus talked about His Father (John 16:25) and how He walked about the country (John 11:54), so much so that on one occasion Peter tried to *"rebuke"* Him for it and tone Him down (Mark 8:32). Not surprisingly, it is the word that describes the early church in its preaching (Acts 2:29; 13:46) and in its praying (1 John 5:14). Is it surprising that boldness was something they asked for and received (Acts 4:29-31)? The word describes confident asking of God, convinced announcing of the gospel, and conspicuous godly acting in the public square. It is a word that originally had political usage, describing the freedom of speech of those who were citizens and did not need to fear when they shared their convictions. It is the word used to describe how we approach God when we ask (Hebrews 4:16, 10.19; 1 John 5:14). This word is so important for our asking, with all its nuances: simplicity, straightforwardness, frankness, without reserve, daring, not holding back, not avoiding difficulties. When we ask we are never speaking out of turn so we need not be self-conscious in His presence, but bold. The scepter has been extended to us in the throne room, so we can come with a firm tread, not mistaking humility for servility (Esther 5:2). John Newton wrote:

> *My soul, ask what thou wilt*
> *Thou canst not be too bold*
> *Since His own blood for thee he spilt*
> *What else can he withhold?* [14]

Boldness makes for effective asking.

Knowing God As Our Friend

We have noted from the context of the parable of the 'Friend at Midnight' (see Chapter 9) that Jesus tells us that God's fatherhood is a reason for our boldness (Luke 11: 2-13). But He speaks of God's friendship. "Suppose one of you has a friend, and he goes to him at midnight." For anyone who thinks that a father *has* to give to his asking child because that is what he is obliged to do, Jesus affirms that our Father is also our Friend, assuring us that His response is not reluctantly paternalistic but freely and kindly altruistic, a response not only rooted in kinship and obligation, but in character and loving free choice. Friendship gives a boldness to asking, with its assurance of being loved and cared for, and with its expectation of a responsiveness that does not require argument and persuasion. When it comes to asking for help, a friend will always be on the front foot of response, not the back foot of reluctance. **Knowing God as Friend makes for effective asking.**

Expectation

"Ask and it shall be given you" (Matthew 7:7). It is Jesus's teaching about asking and His invitation to us to ask that is foundational for our expectation. Again and again, He invites His followers to ask with the expectation that what they lack they will receive, that what is lost they will find, that what is closed to them will be opened. This same expectation is taught by Paul. "To Him who is able to do immeasurably more than all we ask or imagine" (Ephesians 3:20). Follow Paul's trail of expectation here. He is able to *do* ... He is able to do *what we ask* ... He is able to do what we ask *or think* (before it even gets expressed in asking) ... He is able to do *all* that we ask ... He is able to do *more than all* that we ask ... He is able to do *abundantly more* than we ask ... He is able to do *vastly more than more* than we ask. Melanchthon wrote of Martin Luther that he insisted on the promises in the Psalms "as if he was sure his petitions would be granted." [15] Is that how we ask? According to E.M.Bounds: "The reason why we obtain no more ... is because we expect no more." [16] **Our expectation makes for effective asking.**

Experience of the Holy Spirit:

"According to His power that is at work within us" (Ephesians 3:20). The context describes the person who will experience God doing more than they ask. They will be: empowered by the Holy Spirit (v16); indwelt by Christ (v17); established in love (v17); filled with the fullness of God (v19). If we are not living in this place of fidelity, surrender, obedience and empowerment, God's working in us to "do more than we ask" is limited. All asking is both 'in' and 'with' the Holy Spirit as we have seen, thus it follows that in order to ask effectively, we need the work of the Holy Spirit in our lives. Without that reception, asking will be just a recitation. Our asking cannot be a spiritual work unless it is energized by the Holy Spirit. "Would we pray efficiently and mightily?" asked E.M.Bounds. "Then the Holy Spirit must work in us efficiently and mightily ... Would you pray with mighty results? Seek the mighty workings of the Holy Spirit in your own spirit." [17] It is impossible to witness the beginning of Jesus's public ministry and follow the beginnings of the public life of the church on the day of Pentecost, without being convinced of this relationship between asking and the activity of the Spirit. Bounds continues: "We must seek the Holy Spirit by prayer ... The measure we receive of Him will be gauged by the fervor of faith and prayer with which we seek Him." [18] The measure we receive will be evident in the manner in which we then ask. The relationship between the Holy Spirit and prayer is inviolable. We ask for the Spirit and then we ask in the Spirit. This is not complicated, though some make it so. Bounds concludes: "How simple and direct is our Lord's direction — ASK! This is plain and direct." [19] So when it comes to asking "according to His power" let us ask for the Holy Spirit. When it comes to praying in the Holy Spirit, let the Spirit ask through us. Any which way, ASK! **Our experience of the Holy Spirit makes for effective asking.**

***Pleasing Him With Uncondemned Hearts*:**

"I will do the very thing you have asked because I am pleased with you" (Exodus 33:17); "If our hearts do not condemn us, we have confidence before God and receive from Him anything we ask, because we obey His commands and do what pleases Him" (1John 3:22). Where there is no condemnation, John says that our hearts will be "at rest in His presence." Condemnation, like a dripping tap, erodes our sense of being qualified to ask. It sidelines us and we feel spiritually benched, excluded from the huddle that asks about life on the field of play. Its nagging accusation subverts assurance and therefore boldness. Freedom from condemnation is basic to our confidence in asking boldly and effectively. **An uncondemned heart makes for effective asking.**

Importunity

"Ask and keep on asking ... knock and the door will be opened ... to show them that they should always pray and not give up" (Matthew 7:7; Luke 18:1). According to Jesus, the only possible alternative to persistent asking would be to quit altogether, to "give up". Jesus encouraged persistence in His teaching (Luke18) and in His practice (Luke 22). He was importunate in Gethsemane. Asking persistently is the antidote to losing heart. There is no half-way prayer house here. It is interesting that in this context Jesus asks if He will find faith on the earth when He returns, possibly suggesting that persistent asking will be the evidence of faith and increasingly the order of the last days, pursued by fewer and fewer believers. The asking will rise as faithfulness falls. Bounds taught that, "Our praying needs to be pressed and pursued with an energy that never tires, a persistency that will not be denied, and a courage which never fails." [20] This has been called "a theology of audacity" [21] that requires confident humility. This is about asking that is consistent, insistent and persistent.

The willingness to see how far we can go in our pursuit of God's will is vital, but it will feel uncomfortable, as it did for Abraham, who asked again and again for Sodom against ridiculous odds. This is the kind of asking that goes all the way. He says, "Now that I have been so bold as to speak" (Genesis 18:27). Is this precocious, or presumptuous? It is not treated by God as such. On the contrary, God co-operates with his persistence and renegotiates the terms of Sodom's salvation. Twice Abraham asks, "Let not my Lord be angry ... What if?" Asking is not for the faint-hearted who do not wish to be troubled by the interplay between their will and the divine will. Such people will not wrestle like Jacob and insist on their request for blessing being answered. The will of God that pronounces particular judgments is not questioned in our asking, but our asking will persist in importuning Him to stay His hand and remember mercy.

There is a kind of submission to the will of God that appears as active obedience, but is more like a passive acquiescence. Paul's statement about the sufficiency of the grace of God may sound like a mellow and passive state of peace and calm, but we know that it came from a place of desperate need and that he got to this place of contentment after great persistence in his asking, by bringing his anxieties to God while feeling he was in extremis (Philippians 4:12). Obediently, he submitted to God's ordained outcomes. If asking is all about relating to God, then you can understand why the saints have always understood persistence as simply driving us deeper into Him, and further into His will. This is not commanding God or thinking we can force His hand. We are submissive in heart but not necessarily in tone. It feels like we are resisting His will. ("If it's alright with You, it is not alright with me!") But it is our ignorance that persists in pursuing His knowledge about the matter; our continuing hopelessness that persists in pursuing His help; our continuing pains that persist in asking for His poultices of healing and deliverance. The persistence has its own rewards other than that which is sought after, as importunity purifies our own nature, provoking sanctifying changes in us that bring us to a place of preparedness where the answer is now possible, or not possible. Persistence has been likened to a ripening process of the spiritual nature until the time comes when it is ready for the answer. **Persistence makes for effective asking.**

Unceasing

"Give him no rest" (Isaiah 61:2). "Pray without ceasing ... Prayer was made without ceasing" (1Thessalonians 5:17; Acts 12:5). The asking that is needed to be instant (Romans 12:12) may also have to be constant (Romans 1:9). Our persistence is serial – there is a time component. There is no passive or lazy waiting for answers. We are not persistent just because we regularly repeat a request. Our persistence needs to be unceasing. Forsyth called unceasing prayer "the bent of the soul." [22] The gap between our asking and God's answering is more asking. This is neither filling time (as if life stops until we are answered on our terms) nor doing time (as if the waiting was an imposed limit on our freedom). The Greek word for asking (*ektenes*) that describes the early church's praying, means extended, really stretched out. You know that if you stretch you feel the pressure of working against something. You feel resistance. It makes demands on your strength. Asking is literally a stretch, in two senses: in that it requires extended time and effort, but also in that it seems to be beyond our capacities and capabilities, and a stretch for us to do. But this is the same word that is used to describe Jesus's asking in Gethsemane (Luke 22:44). He was stretched to the limit of comprehensible tautness of spirit and intensity of emotion. No wonder we need the Holy Spirit as our helper when we ask. As we have already seen, the Holy Spirit that gets us to the place of asking also helps us to stay there. To ask unceasingly is, for Piper, to "have the spirit of prayer continuously." [23] It was said of Origen that his life was "one unceasing supplication." But unceasing asking is not just for that which is not yet received. The pursuit of asking is ceaseless beyond the point of the answer. A poem of Alan Redpath's reads: "The victories won by prayer / By prayer must still be held / The foe retreats, but only when / By prayer he is compelled." [24] Unceasing asking is also necessary for those situations in which we can no longer continue to act, having engaged them at one time. Paul planted the church in Thessalonica but he could not stay there to grow it. Instead, he continued to nurture it by watering it with his unceasing asking "night and day asking exceedingly for you" (1Thessalonians 3:10). **Incessant constancy makes for effective asking.**

Personal Holiness

We cannot ask God for His name to be hallowed if there is no place for holiness in our lives. Asking (as in the Lord's prayer) is a frisk test for discipleship. Asking fails "when the desire and effort for personal holiness fails." [25] "The asking of a righteous man is powerful and effective" (James 5:16). There is a symbiotic relationship between asking and holiness. Not only does unholiness hinder and impede our asking but Wesley noted: "The neglect of this (asking) is a … grand hindrance to holiness." [26] Pere la Combe, the Spiritual Director of Madame Guyon, was attributed with this maxim: "He who has a pure heart will never cease to pray, and he who will be constant in prayer shall know what it is to have a pure heart." [27] **Personal holiness makes for effective asking**

Being Specific

"*What* do you want me to do for you?" (Luke 18:41) Our specific asking is what Jesus asks of us. Though his blindness was obvious to all, Jesus wanted the blind man to acknowledge his personal and particular need, and confess his desire for Jesus to answer him. There is often an evasion, even a dishonesty, possibly a cover-up, in our vague and generalized prayers. As the old saying goes, 'We aim at nothing in particular and hit it every time!' We confess sin in general but do not ask for forgiveness for anything in particular. We pray for everyone in general but no one by name and need. We ask God to bless the world but do not engage the nations. Hedging and fudging are what we do best.

This may be an indication that we are not as zealous for God's work, or as desperate for ourselves or others as we should be. "It is most proper in prayer, to aim at great *distinctness* of supplication." Spurgeon went on to talk about all the prayers that are uttered that contain "a great deal of very excellent doctrinal and experimental matter uttered, but *little real petitioning*, and that little in a nebulous kind of state, chaotic and unformed. But it seems to me that prayer should be *distinct*, the asking for something *definitely and distinctly* because the mind has realized its *distinct* need of such a thing, and therefore must plead for it. *IT IS WELL NOT TO BEAT ROUND THE BUSH IN PRAYER*, but to come *directly* to the point." [28] If you are hungry you will ask specifically for food. Nothing else will do. Our asking must be definite and explicit. Spurgeon always emphasized this: "We greatly need to be more *definite* in our supplications than we usually are. We pray for everything in such a way that we practically pray for nothing. It is good to know what we want". [29] Asking brings the facts as they are, fearful or challenging as they are, into the presence of God. When we ask in broad brush strokes, it is no wonder that we are skeptical about the answers some people get that are the finest of bristles: the exact answer needed, at the exact time. One reason that specific asking begins to decline is simply because busyness has overtaken our time to meditate, reflect, consider, and inquire about what is going on, and specifically needs to be asked about. A sound-byte world reduces our asking to the same shallowness. If we are ignorant of God's will, if we are distanced from God's heart, it is unlikely that we will be specific, especially about what God Himself specifically cares about. We can and should ask 'straight-out' and 'all-out'. If our assurance about asking is wavering, we will be less sure and less direct in our asking, and because there will be a lack of boldness, assurance will give way to ambiguity and uncertainty. According to John Rice, "Where there is no *definiteness* in prayer ... there is no burden, no urgency, no heart desire." [30] Spurgeon taught against what he called "indistinct generalizing prayer" which "fails for lack of precision. It is as if a regiment of soldiers should all fire off their guns anywhere. Possibly some-body would be killed, but the majority of the enemy would be missed." [31] Nor is Murray: "Our prayers must be a *distinct* expression of *definite* need, not a vague appeal to His mercy or an in-definite cry for His blessing." [32] **Being specific makes for effective asking."**

Hopefully, at the end of the day, it is clear that every conditioning factor mentioned conditions the **specificity** of our asking and its effectiveness. We could do no worse than to take each of the above points and make them our asking-list. Ask for each of these characteristics to be distinctive and definite in your asking, the motivation and the means to effective asking.

When Asking is Unanswered and Answered

"Our God is able to … but if not …" - Shadrach and friends

"Prayer is request. The essence of request, as distinct from compulsion, is that it may or may not be granted. And if an infinitely wise Being listens to the requests of finite and foolish creatures, of course He will sometimes grant and sometimes refuse them."
- C.S.Lewis

"If we got all we asked for we should soon come to treat Him as a convenience or the request as magic … No true God could promise us an answer to our every prayer. He is the Father of mankind … The rain that saved my crop would ruin my neighbor's." - P.T.Forsyth

"Sometimes I thank God for unanswered prayers …
That just because He doesn't answer doesn't mean He don't care"
Lyrics of 'Unanswered prayers' by Garth Brooks

"Unanswered prayer is only a problem for those of us who truly believe." - Peter Greig

"Every war, every famine or plague, almost every death-bed, is the monument to a petition that was not answered." - C.S.Lewis

"The only prayer that can be unanswered is prayer that is uncertain of an answer, so that it is not calling upon the true God." - Karl Barth

"Giver of good, so answer each request
With Thine own giving, better than my best."
- Annie Johnson Flint

19

When Asking is Unanswered

It All Depends What You Mean By...

There is much asking that seems to go unanswered, but there are divided opinions about how this should be perceived and understood. The truism that there are no unanswered prayers, because the answer is always 'yes, no or maybe' is not a helpful place to start. No jaunty jingle will serve to provide healing balm or resolution for an unanswered asker who feels caught in the no-man's land between the request and the response. The longer the answer is in coming, the more that space is marked out by emotional and theological barbed wire. Although silence is at first the mark of a good listener, the protracted silence to asking raises some questions: was the phone off the hook, was the phone picked up at all, was it just a recorded message, was it heard, did it register, will there be a return call, is the line cut?

Given the nature of these challenges, it is tempting to avoid them altogether, and refuse to admit that there are any possible problems. Or one can adopt the approach of 'bumper-sticker' theology that shouts things like 'Let go and let God' – peppy cheers delivered from the sidelines of another's pain. Another temptation is to try to impose a fool-proof, fear-proof, mystery-proof template on all the confused and contradictory thoughts and feelings that arise, and come up with a one-stop explanation. When things do not make sense to us, we try and rationalize what is happening as best we may, in the hope that some coherence will emerge from our confusion that will make us feel better about ourselves and more pointedly, about God. We want a system that will provide some order, that will be comforting enough to distract our attention from the jagged-shaped thoughts and concerns that cannot be accommodated. It is not that the scriptures are short on counsel, but we have to resist the temptation to take all that they do say, and force it into a construct that rationalizes and systematizes everything to our satisfaction. The bottom line is that there are still going to be some things missing that we just do not know, and some things present that we just do not understand. "A determination to know what cannot be known always works harm in the Christian heart ... We dislike to admit that we do not know what is going on, so we torture our minds trying to fathom the mysterious ways of the Omniscient one. It's hard to conceive of a more fruitless task." [1] I do not think A.W.Tozer meant that we do not try to seek understanding - we should do so. But it does mean we are not going to be tortuous in trying to explain everything that seems to be torturing us. We are not going to call something a 'mystery' as a convenient cover-up for not engaging the truths and realities of a situation, nor are we going to try and rationalize what is indeed a 'mystery'. In all our asking, there will be times when we need to discern the boundaries of our questioning an unanswering God. Oswald Chambers put it more strongly: "Our insistence on being answered means we are always off track ... The purpose of prayer is that we get ahold of God not the answer." [2] But as Spurgeon said: "There is no fanaticism in expecting God to answer prayer ... There can be no reason for praying if there be no expectation of the Lord's answering." [3] So, can we have a godly expectation that does not become an ungodly insistence?

"What do you mean by 'unanswered'?" This is a reasonable question. The most obvious unanswered asking is simply that which was never asked in the first place – sadly. But the way we most generally define 'unanswered' is the silence of God, the absence of His apparent response to something that has been asked to be effected on our terms and our timing according to the needs of ourselves, or others as we perceive them best. By 'our terms and our timing' I am not suggesting a selfish view of things but simply the nature of the need as best understood by us. Given that our perceptions are not necessarily complete or even accurate, our asking is unanswered to the extent that the fullest presentation of our request, with the strongest expectation possible, remains unfulfilled. Reasons why our presentation may have been inadequate or why our expectations were possibly unfounded are open for discussion, with the proviso that such an exchange is conducted with neither an offensive posture towards God, nor a defensive posture towards oneself.

What's Up With This ... What's Up With You?

When it comes to asking about asking, there are certainly some challenging questions and none more so than those raised when asking is unanswered. Ask the psalmist: "When my prayers returned to me unanswered I went about mourning as though for my friend or brother. I bowed my head in grief as though weeping for my mother" (Psalm 35:13). In order to capture the disorientation and the sheer depth of the pain, he likens his emotions to those of loss of the most intimate relationships in his life. If, as we have argued, our asking is an expression of intimacy, then the apparent failure of that communication, when it becomes one way, when it becomes all asking and no answering, is akin to the silence of a death, an abandonment or a betrayal. Of course, the One whose silence we are struggling with is not without His own experience of this: "When I called, why was there no one to answer" (Isaiah 50:2)? He is at least touched with this infirmity, but frankly, another's shared experience of the same pain does little to allay it for us, when our asking is still needing an answer.

Unanswered asking, in some shape or form, is a universal experience without a universal answer. We all have our stories. We have all been moved to ask in response to things that are unfaceable, unacceptable, undoable, unthinkable, insuperable, unbearable, unconscionable, and not received an answer. We have been equally inspired to ask for what is inoperable, impossible, unimaginable, inadmissible, immoveable, unable, inconceivable, and found ourselves in a waiting room at the 'prayer clinic'. We are familiar with the unanswered asking that seeps into the spirit like a slow toxic leak, and the kind that leaves you feeling as if you have been hit right off your faithful feet by a tsunami of helplessness. There are the unanswered requests that are small on the grand scale of need but nonetheless deeply meaningful, and there are those that loom large, loud and breathless, given all that is riding on them.

Sitting at my study desk one afternoon, I was suddenly provoked to ask for a very serious and urgent situation, which had been the subject of much asking by many people for some time. The more I asked, the more my emotions were roused and rallied by the need, and I came to myself with the sound of my own hand smashing down on the table, with the consequent pain that shot through my arm, and with the crying words coming out of my mouth: "What's up with you?" I was taken aback by this irreverent-sounding question that expressed the frustration of my asking. There was no anger in me towards God, but it was expressive of any number of consternations. I could have shouted: "Why is this such a big deal for you to respond to? Is it really that hard for you? You could do it in your sleep! It makes sense to everyone, so why not to you? What attention this will draw to you? Just do it!" The commands and the interrogatives punch each other in the fight to get a hearing. And then there are the other unanswered requests that attract a variety of responses from a resigned sigh to a mumbled reiteration of the need. But surely, if He is God, the God who asked Abraham "Is anything too hard for the Lord?" then should there not be a zillion less unanswered prayers to dissuade the cynical laughter of Sarah erupting from our mouths and corrupting our hearts? How hard is it? What's up with this? What's up with You?

Galaxies? One Star Will Do

Talking of Abraham, it seems that his experience of extended unanswered asking was going to be the family lot, as generational infertility aggressively called into question the promises of God. How strange it is that the history of redemption hung by the frayed threads of unanswered asking, time and time again, including 400 years of unanswered Israelites crying in Egypt, right up to that really long silence of 400 years that at very long last, was broken by the words of Gabriel - words that every unanswered asker had been waiting for: "Your asking has been heard" (Luke 1:13). Was it helpful to Abraham, with no answering baby's cries in the tent, to be repetitively told by God that He would "greatly increase your numbers", that he would be "the Father of many nations" (Genesis 17:1-17)? Enough of these continuing references to "descendants" and "the generations to come." Sarah gets a bad rap for laughing behind the tent flaps, but she was neither the only one, nor the first one to laugh. After God's longest and most detailed re-statement of the covenant promise, Abraham's response was not belief like the first time (Genesis 15:6). "Abraham fell facedown; he laughed." Understandably, with no desired answer in sight, it was time to ditch the waiting and go to Plan B: "If only Ishmael may live under your blessing?" When covenant-waiting wears thin, we can always contract another solution. Of course we identify with the patriarch, our father in the faith no less. It seems we are his children after the flesh as well as the faith. When God shows us a galaxy of future promise while our asking remains unanswered, we are less than encouraged. It is not as if we are asking for some future Milky Way. Right now, just one star of answered asking will do.

The Long and Winding Garden Path

For many, unanswered asking brings unanswered pain. It is hard to remember that though the storm did not stop, Jesus was still in the boat (Matthew 8:24). "What chokes every prayer," wrote C.S.Lewis, "and every hope is the memory of all the prayers H and I offered and all the false hopes we had. Not hopes raised merely by our own wishful thinking; hopes encouraged, even forced upon us by false diagnoses, by X-ray photographs, by strange remissions, by one temporary recovery that might have ranked as a miracle. *Step by step we were led up the garden path.* Time after time when He seemed most gracious, He was really preparing the next torture." [4] Much unanswered asking cannot but be taken very personally. If an answer make us feel accepted, then no answer is often felt as rejection. So many other feelings and attitudes get aroused by unanswered asking: sadness, disappointment, discouragement, disillusion, deception, anger, betrayal, bitterness, contempt, loss of faith, loss of trust, loss of hope. An unanswered Bunyan described himself "in my fits of agonies of spirit." [5] It matters not whether the garden path is short and straight or long and winding. A quick dashing and smashing of hope when unanswered about something that is time-sensitive can be as toxic as the unanswered asking of years. Two kinds of weakness emerge.

- **The weakness of God**: Something is wrong with God. Where is His strength of arm when I need it? I thought "the arm of the Lord is not too short to save, nor His ear too dull to hear" (Isaiah 59:1)? Three things are called into question: His *affection* (His love and care); His *ability* (His power and sovereignty); His *attention* (His attentiveness to detail, His parental eye upon us). This leads to more asking but of the wrong kind: what's the use? This can lead to a diminishing, a down-sizing of God.

- **The weakness of self**: Something is wrong with me. This may be the self-condemning weakness that comes from allowing oneself to be misled by the 'false advertising' of asking. It may be the weakness that comes from a sense of unworthiness in not being answered, and from the sheer physical and psychological exhaustion from ineffective efforts to be heard or to be sure enough of God's will, or patient enough, or faithful enough. In these situations, when folk come along who tell us there will be a reward for our faithfulness (Isaiah 49:4), we feel worse not better, and perhaps may end up despising ourselves that it is not some uncertain reward that we want but the specific result of our asking. Unlike Paul, many do not feel they are strong when they are this weak. Gethsemane was the place of the olive press, the place of crushing. To many observers, Jesus did not look very messianic or triumphal there.

It is often our pain and need that drives us to ask in the first place, and thus "We pray for the removal of pain, pray passionately, and then with exhaustion, sick from hope deferred and prayer's failure." [6] Forsyth goes on to argue that there is a "higher prayer than that ... It is a greater thing to pray for pain's conversion than for its removal." True, but this is easier said than done at a place of suffering. However, it is worth considering that the very fact that we are asking about what pains us, serves to take that situation out of the arena of the devil's gladiatorial assault, and bring it into the gravitational pull of God's grace, not to mention bringing us into closeness with Him. This sacralizing of our pain through our asking about it, robs the enemy of our souls of a means to impugn God through it, or to turn it into a weapon to beat us further into bondage to despair, doubt and unbelief.

So much of our asking tends to go straight to the final outcome of what we want. We are hoping that our answers will be served immediately in front of us, as a vase of flowers whose scent vanquishes the odors of need. We neither want nor expect a 'garden path', a journey that requires a longer search for the requested blooms in the garden of provision. We do not consider the process to get there, to effect it, for those of us who are asking, for those being asked for, or for the One being asked. We are not usually ready to discover how the continuation of the walk up the garden path serves the purposes of God in sanctifying us and glorifying Him. When there is pain in the asking and then pain in the waiting, this walk does not always feel voluntary. Rather, like C.S.Lewis, we feel led, perhaps even misled, up the long and winding garden path.

When Silence is Ferrous

There is a saying that "silence is golden". This gives silence a good press. One of the scriptural images used to present an unanswering divinity describes the silent sky above the Israelites, not as gold, but "like iron" (Leviticus 26:19). Nothing seemed to be getting through. We do not do well with the discomforts and embarrassments when our asking is met with silence. Eventually, we are going to take it personally. Awkwardness becomes restlessness, disappointment becomes distance, frustration becomes anger, giving time becomes giving up. We can agree that some asking, especially about difficult things, may warrant measured and considered answers, but does God really need that long to figure it out? The period of acceptable, understandable even bearable silence gives way to a different kind, to a silence that begins to speak fear and fatalism. This is not the silence of being still in the presence of the Lord in a posture of trust, at a place of peace, feeling quiescent and acquiescent (Psalm 37:7; 46:10). This is the silence that is associated with those in scripture who are asking for answers that are slow in coming, like the psalmist: "When I was silent and still my anguish increased ... my bones wasted away" (Psalm 39:2; 32:3). The silence spells the demise of hope and confidence. It is the graveyard of trust and faith, and there are many who make bad vows about never trusting again, or who just take their leave of faith. There seems to be a choice. We can allow the silence to silence us, because we lose faith and like Zechariah, experience dumbness and numbness because we did not believe the "words which will come true at the proper time" (Luke 1:20). Or, we can choose, bravely and brazenly, to continue to ask in the silence and challenge the silence of God. The psalmists knew both options: "I would soon have dwelt in the silence of death … O God do not keep silent; be not quiet, O God, be not still." (Psalm 94:17; 83:1). They did not "go gentle" into the silent darkness of their unanswered asking.

Closed Doors

'Open doors' is a perfectly good and true scriptural image that relates to asking, describing both physical doors that were opened by asking like the doors of prison (Acts 5:19; Acts 16:26); like the metaphysical doors of faith (Acts 14:27); like the doors of opportunity (1 Corinthians 16:6, 2 Corinthians 2:12). Jesus used it: "Knock and the door will be opened to you" (Luke 11:9). It was His euphemism for answered asking, so it is reasonable that a 'closed door' would be the picture of unanswered asking. The truth is that none of us reacts well to closed doors. It always feels up-close and personal when doors are closed "in our face." To knock and get no answer when you know there is someone in there is the ultimate frustration: so close yet so far away. Our response produces bruised and beaten hands, broken prayer toes and scuffed asking shoes. We wonder why Jesus did not say, "Ask, seek, kick"! There may well be closed doors, but they may not be the final word. Spurgeon quoted an old divine who said that fervent prayer "like a cannon planted at the gates of heaven, makes them fly open." [7] The point is that it has become so easy to use this phrase, 'closed doors', in a way that perhaps too quickly accepts the lack of an answer. Paul faced closed doors everywhere he went but did not attribute all of them to God's failure to answer his prayers. His response is clear in his words to the Colossians: "Devote yourselves to prayer … and pray for us that God may open a door for our message" (Colossians 4:2). The fact is that "what He shuts no-one can open" which is why we have the wonderful gift of the Holy Spirit to help us to discern whether we accept the shut door as the answer we did not originally anticipate, or whether we keep knocking and kicking until the 'unanswered' shut door is 'answeringly' opened. The Puritan, Jeremiah Burroughs, had a wonderful exhortation: "We have waited a long time. Well, but yet know that you are at the right door."

Cloudy Skies

So what about the weather forecast of cloudy skies? "You have covered yourself with a cloud so that no prayer can get through" (Lamentations 3:44). In the previous chapter these people described themselves as being "covered ... with the cloud of His anger" (2:1). They are sitting alone "in the silence" of unanswered asking. "Even when I call out or cry for help, He shuts out my prayer. He has barred my way with blocks of stone" (3:8-9). At least clouds sound more hopeful than stone. It is a catalogue of woe. In fact, outside the crucifixion of Christ, there is no darker presentation of dereliction in scripture. This is unanswered asking of a kind that is second only to the unanswered asking of Jesus on the cross.

However, there is something for us to learn here. The silence of unanswered asking elicited some responses that many can identify with: "He has walled me in ... He has weighed me down ... I have been deprived of peace ... my soul is downcast." The lack of an answer that wears you down becomes the loss of much else: "My splendor is gone and all that I had hoped for from the Lord" (3:19). All the unanswered asker can do is "remember my affliction."

A Lesson Despite Lament

The challenges of unanswered asking are not in question. However, there are three things in the Lamentations text that teach us how to hold on and be held up.

1. We do not have to succumb to accusing God sinfully, even though we feel that we are somehow being sinned against by the silence. They do not accuse God of being deaf, dumb and blind to their unanswered state. They know that He hears their asking: "Do not close your ear to my cry for relief" (3:56). They know He can still speak other things to them and is not mute: "You said, Do not fear" (3:57). They know He can see their situation: "See O Lord how distressed I am ... Look O Lord ... You have seen the wrong done to me" (1:20; 2:20; 3:59). The answer they want may not have

appeared but the need is apparent to God and He is not absent. He is very much present.

2. When the prophet remembers the affliction concomitant with the silence, he chooses not to limit his remembrance to the immediate only: "Yet this I call to mind and therefore I have hope." What makes the difference here in what has already been described as a hopeless circumstance? "Because of the Lord's great love we are not consumed, for His compassions never fail. They are new every morning; great is your faithfulness" (3:22). The well-known hymn that we sing, inspired by these words, is not the confession of worshipers at joyful ease with their lovely lives. It is a classic example of the kind of praise that is forged in the furnace of affliction, in the prison cell made with those "blocks of stone" he was talking about. There is no unanswered asking that can keep out the shafts of truth about the character and nature of our God, unless we choose to refuse their remembrance, and in the process of dealing with what seem to be God's denials of us, we become deniers of Him.
3. These acts of remembrance have a knock-on effect. They renew their asking by inviting God to join the remembrance review: "Remember O Lord what has happened to us; look and see our disgrace" (5:1). There then follows an iteration of all the terrible things that require an answer, but this time, it does not end with a focus on their unanswered plight. It is not that they are suppressing anything because in the middle of their Godward affirmation ("You O lord reign forever") the pained frustration unashamedly breaks through again without mincing the words: "Why do you always forget us? Why do you forsake us for so long?" (5:20) But here is the point. Despite the awful facts of their predicament, they are not asking for all the things on the unanswered asking list to be taken care of so much as for the relationship to be recovered with the unanswering Answerer: "Restore us to *yourself,* O Lord … renew our days as of old" (5:21). Precisely because it is the sense of relational intimacy that is affected by unanswered asking, especially the longer it drags out, it is what becomes the greater subject of renewed asking. They were clear what they were after but was this what God was really after all this time? Their desire for Him was

> now more than their need for their answer. The things they wanted had been trumped by the Person they needed, even though they were still struggling with the fear that they may have been rejected.

Thus in these times of unanswered asking, closed doors are not necessarily the final word when the lubricating oil of the Holy Spirit is applied to their hinges. It is not inevitable that the sky will be as iron. Cloudy, almost certainly, but as Lamentations shows us, they ultimately cannot stop us getting through, or stop shafts of God's light getting through to us. But we still remain 'unanswered.

A Mute Moot Point

'God on Mute' [8] by Peter Grieg is a personally poignant but biblically integrous book about "engaging the silence of unanswered prayer". Its front cover-photo of a mouth that is taped shut may be a deliberately problematic image. Is God silent because He is gagged? Did he muzzle Himself or are there other external factors that have gagged Him? Or has His silence now muted our asking? We know He cannot be silenced against His will, which means He can voluntarily, for whatever reasons, choose to be silent and withhold answers. We know He cannot be mute in the strict sense of that word, because He has not, and cannot lose His power of speech. At the moment we think that God has gone silent on us, all around us the created order "pours forth speech" (Psalm 19:2). I have dealt elsewhere (Chapter 5) with the many scriptural reasons as to why God has said He will not hear what is asked of Him. That is a silence that is about the refusal to hear, not the inability to answer.

Is it possible that God often does answer but in a way that we do not hear, or want to hear, and therefore we deem Him silent on the matter? Is our hearing selective? Just as there are griefs that interfere with our perspective on things and our ability to discern what is really happening (Mary's tears in the garden obscured who Jesus was), so also there are many possible things that can jam our spiritual frequencies when it comes to listening to God. God's 'muteness' may be our 'deafness'. We are all familiar with the mute button on our devices. The characters on the screen are mute to us, but they are in fact still speaking. We have chosen not to listen. Is it possible that we press the mute button on some of God's answers and then claim to be unanswered? Just asking.

What is true is that any discouragement and pain has a muting effect on our spirits and thus on our communication. Being mute is as much a possible description of our condition as it is of our perception of God.

Deaf, Dumb and Blind

When asking goes unanswered, God is subject to three consistent questions. Are you deaf? "Do not turn a deaf ear to me" (Psalm 28:1). Are you dumb? "Be not silent" (Psalm 35:22). Are you blind? "Open your eyes O Lord and see" (Isaiah 37:17). To accuse God of being deaf, dumb and blind is essentially to equate Him with an idol, given that these are the three obvious attributes of a false God. An idol cannot hear: "Shout louder" (1 Kings 18:27). An idol cannot talk: "their idols cannot speak" (Jeremiah 10:5). Idols cannot see: "their eyes are plastered over so they cannot see" (Isaiah 44:18). It is easy to understand how God gets impugned with being false in His nature, or false to Himself because He is being perceived as false to the unanswered asker. Perhaps we could argue that the fact that God is reduced to the equivalence of a deaf, dumb and blind idol, may mean that there is a DNA of idolatry in the asking, not in the one who is being asked. If there is idolatry in the asking (in matter or manner) does that reduce God to an idol, to being expected to be false to Himself in answering what is required of Him? Just asking. Because He is always true to Himself, He will not respond in any way that is false to His character, His will, His Word, or His compassions for all. He is not deaf, dumb or blind.

Closing the Gap

Is it possible to close the gap between our asking and His answering; between our actual speaking and His assumed hearing; between our wanting and the waiting; between what we expect and what we experience; between what we are hoping for and what is actually happening? What bridged that gap between Abraham's childlessness and the Pleiades and Orion? On starry nights was he tempted to stop looking up? It seems that he found a way to keep staring at stars: "Against all hope Abraham in hope believed" (Romans 4:18). Does that settle everything for us? We do not want to accept specious rationalizations as to why our asking is in the pending tray, if in fact it even made it that far. But is it not reasonable to at least ask about some possible explanations for the "gap" that might help close it somewhat? Can we look for some possible reasons?

"We pray and pray and no answer comes ... Why? Perhaps we are not spiritually ready for it ... A time comes when we are ready for an answer ... Nothing would do more to cure us of a belief in our own wisdom than the granting of some of our eager prayers."
- P.T.Forsyth

"The apparent limitation to answered prayer is in effect a gracious act of love." - J. Oswald Sanders

"How is it possible at one and the same time to have a perfect faith ... that you will get what you ask and yet also prepare yourself submissively in advance for a possible refusal?" - C.S.Lewis

"Unanswered prayers have taught me to seek the Lord's will instead of my own." - J.O.Fraser

"God does not delay to hear our prayers because He has no mind to give; but that by enlarging our desires, He may give us the more largely." - Anselm of Canterbury

I thank Thee, Lord, Thou wert too wise to heed
My feeble prayers, and answer as I sought,
Since these rich gifts Thy bounty has bestowed
Have brought me more than I had asked or thought.
- Annie Johnson Flint

20

When Asking is still Unanswered

Heaven, We Have a Problem!

Since the movie 'Apollo 13' the phrase, "Houston we have a problem" has passed into the vernacular. When it came to asking, C.S.Lewis not only described it as the form of prayer "that raises a problem" but saw it as "a problem without an answer." [1] Heaven, we have a problem! Was he right about this? As he recounts in 'A Grief Observed' his asking during his wife's fight with terminal cancer did not leave him feeling alright. Like many before him and since, he was perplexed by what appeared to be two contradictory and inconsistent types of asking. The first he called 'Pattern A', in which "thy will be done" seemed to modify what is asked for, making it conditional, so that there is no surety of the desired answer. The second, 'Pattern B', was when "whatever you ask in my name I will do" appears to be unconditional. So how do these two relate? Does the offer that we shall receive whatever we ask, really mean that we shall only get what we ask if it happens to be what God has in mind to give? Can I ever expect a sure relationship between what I wish and what He wants? Lewis was concerned that 'Pattern A' might end up being a cover for someone of little faith, who then will not "receive anything from the Lord" (James 1:6-8). He described 'Pattern B" as resting on "embarrassing promises". [2] Herein lies the perplexity. "I am not in principle puzzled by the fact of the refusal; what I am puzzled by is the promise of the granting." The problem raised by Patterns A and B was that "the real assurance that we shall receive" seemed to be "incompatible with the act of preparing ourselves for a denial."

In a nutshell, the problem was "not why refusal is so frequent, but why the opposite result is so lavishly promised." How was it possible to have "a perfect faith" or a "perfect confidence" if being refused was a real possibility? Does not confidence assume that you will not "take refusal into account"? So where does that leave us, Jack? "For most of us the prayer in Gethsemane is the only model. Removing mountains can wait." [3]

Did Lewis resolve this problem raised by his asking about asking? The crowd's mockery at the foot of the cross was not lost on him. "He saved others; Himself He could not save" (Mark 15:31). Lewis admitted to feeling a bit of mockery himself in all this: "of goods being a little larger in the advertisement than they turn out to be. Not that we complain of any defect in the goods; it is the faintest suspicion of excess in the advertisement that is disquieting. But at present I have got no further ... How am I to pray this night?" [4] Lewis avoided facile answers, as we all must. He spoke of his "discomfort" with a presentation of God who will grant us what we ask by faith, but will only give the required faith if we ask for what He has determined to give. However, he was convinced by both the command and the example of Jesus to ask of the Father. He believed that asking was God's gracious way of including us in His purposes. "He seems to do nothing of Himself which He can possibly delegate to His creatures." [5] Most important was his conviction that asking could only be understood as a relationship between God and us. He argued that our assurance, when we ask something of a friend or a wife, is our personal relationship with them. It is all about knowing them and them knowing us. It is that intimate context that makes sense of how we ask, what we ask for, and how we are answered. "Those who best know a man, best know whether, when he did what they asked, he did it because they asked." [6] It is interesting that Lewis did mention a friend or a wife, but not a father. He spent most of his life pained and troubled by the lack of intimacy in his relationship with his father, who died without Lewis feeling any sense of reconciliation. Given that Jesus relates our assurances about asking almost exclusively to our relationship with our heavenly Father, perhaps it was the seriousness of that lack of closeness with his earthly father, that was a burden that tested his assurances about asking, thus adding to 'the problem'. At the end of the day, with such characteristic humility and humor, Lewis refused to back down in the face of the 'problem' and wondered if we should not see the Pattern B guys as "the true Christian norm and ourselves as spiritual cripples." [7] There was nothing lame about Lewis' convictions on asking, or his practice of it, despite the problems that it presented.

He wrote: "I have no answer to my problem, though I have taken it to about every Christian I know." However, although he felt that part of the problem was perhaps his lack of faith, this did not leave him skeptical or cynical about asking. Why? Because he did not actually believe that the refusal of asking, the unanswered asking, was the main issue, as there were so many other possible reasons for unanswered requests. [8] There is one thing that remains true. The very first truth we established in our 'theology of asking' (see Chapter 5) was that God hears. No asking is unanswered because He does not hear. When God chooses not to hear, His hearing is not impaired. Murray wrote: "There is still another question - that of the multitude of apparently vain and unanswered prayers ... As little as we can comprehend we can comprehend this, one of the most blessed of His attributes, is that He hears prayer ... The Holy Spirit can enable us to believe and rejoice in it, even where every question is not yet answered." [9]

Looking for Reasons

Once again, are there enough reasons to close the gap between our asking and the lack of an answer? What 'reasons' would Lewis have been open to consider? He did mention two: asking for what is not good, and asking for something, the granting of which, would involve the refusal of another's request. Whatever other reasons he would have accepted, there would have been a proviso. In his typical self-effacing way he offered a throw-away line at the end of his essay on the efficacy of prayer, expressing his own weakness, but gently yet firmly warning about being too dogmatic about any area that we cannot fully fathom, or about legitimate tensions that we cannot resolve but have to keep taut in order to get the whole picture. Though a permissible discussion, there were not enough reasons for Lewis to close the gap completely. "Meanwhile," he wrote, "little people like you and me, if our prayers are sometimes granted, beyond all hope and probability, had better not draw hasty conclusions to our own advantage." [10]

If a friend either refused to respond to our request, or denied it altogether, we would want to ask questions and seek reasons for it. Similarly, we look for reasons for unanswered prayer in order to make sense of things and to make sense of relationship with God, in the same way that Lewis did, but with the same cautions. God is not threatened by this endeavor. Thomas Goodwin, writing in the seventeenth century, suggested that: "If God doth not grant your petitions it will put you to study a reason of that His dealing: and so you will come to search in your prayers and the carriage of your hearts therein to see whether you did pray amiss." [11] Indeed, James does confirm that we can ask "amiss" (James 4:3). Oswald Sanders conducted "a post-mortem on unanswered prayer" and concluded that "behind every unanswered prayer is a reason, which we must discover for ourselves." [12] Peter does advise us that there are things that "hinder our prayers" (1 Peter 3:1-7) and we have already seen the many other scriptural reasons for unanswered asking that are accounted for by the reasons that God refuses to listen.

What should we make of this? Goodwin's Puritan encouragement to "study" and "search" in a way that checks one's own prayers, cannot but help our own personal growth in asking. Who knows but in that process we may discover some things that will influence an answer. However, though I agree with Sanders' thought that there is a reason for every unanswered prayer, I do not believe that they are all discoverable, or even that it is necessary to discover them. The faith that we need to ask is the same faith that we need to be operative when an answer is not forthcoming. Reasons alone will never close the gap.

That agreed, what follows is a *descriptive* but *not prescriptive* attempt to point out some of the possible ways of ordering our understanding of unanswered asking. This is not an inflexible classification or an exhaustive systemization. This would be neither possible nor desirable.

Disqualifications: Not Listened To

Jesus's prayer in Gethsemane was not answered, neither because it was unheard, nor because it did not qualify as a legitimate request. In not being answered and not having the cup taken from Him, and in not being saved

Himself, God's answer saved the entire world. What is being referred to here is the kind of asking that is not answered by God because it is not listened to by God at all, for the disqualifying reasons already given in Chapter 5. To be fair, not everyone is accepting of this list of biblical reasons as to why God refuses to listen, because they object to any blame being put on the asker for the unanswered prayer. Here is an example of such an objection: "I find this list obscene. To say that God would have answered your prayers for your sick child or dying friend if only you had more fully sought to please God, or if you had confessed your sins, is misguided and cruel." [13] The fact is that we are saying nothing of the sort.

Disavowals: Inappropriate Asking

Just as it is allowable to study possible reasons for unanswered asking, it is also advisable to give a little more forethought to what we are actually asking about, to ensure that what we are asking for is not going to be subject to a divine disavowal, according to the revealed will and word of God. This should not quench intense and passionate asking. It would be ironic if we ended up overthinking an act (asking) that was essentially an expression of our ignorance. Sometimes, there are more questions we should ask before asking, that ascertain what to ask for, how to ask, and why we ask. Spurgeon thought that: "Some prayers would never be offered if men did but think ... See whether it is an assuredly fitting thing to ask." [14] In response to something asked of Him Jesus said: "You don't know what you are asking" (Matthew 20:22). Even Jesus did some 'pre-asking' asking. As we have already noted, we hear Him rehearsing for Gethsemane, talking out loud about what cannot be asked for, even though He would like to ask it: "What shall I say" (John 12:27)? This suggests that there may be much of our asking that would never make it to the official request stage if we had considered more carefully and thoughtfully the ways and the will of the Lord for our lives. We would be able to discern like Jesus those things that would be desirable to ask for, for our sake, but not appropriate to ask for, given our understanding of what makes for obedience or righteousness. We cannot possibly ask God for His blessing on something He cannot possibly bless according to His Word.

God can take no responsibility or give any support to something asked which is non-sense or which contravenes God-given laws of nature, or which contradicts His own nature and character, His will and His word. Asking for fire from heaven was inappropriate and unanswered (Matthew 17:1-8). There were things that Jesus Himself could not ask for: "to sit at My right or left is not for Me to grant" (Matthew 20:23). There were things He told His disciples that could not be asked for: "It is not for you to know the times or the dates the Father has set by His own authority" (Acts 1:7). There is no point in asking about these.

We have already noted that scripture is clear about kinds of asking that are inappropriate because wrong. It is possible to ask amiss, "with wrong motives" for the purpose of our "pleasures" (James 4:3). The answer that we want will be refused not received. Such disavowals can yet lead to a revelation of the heart and to thanksgiving, as expressed in this anonymous Puritan Prayer: "I thank Thee that many of my prayers have been refused. I have asked amiss and do not have, I have prayed from lusts and been rejected, I have longed for Egypt and been given a wilderness. Go on with Thy patient work, answering 'no' to my wrongful prayers, and fitting me to accept it."

Delays: the Waiting Game

William Gurnall, a seventeenth century pastor, described the problem well: "It proves a long voyage sometimes before the praying saint hath the return of his adventure. There comes oft a long winter between the sowing time of prayer and the reaping." [15] Scripture records something that is often asked of God by psalmists and by prophets: "Lord, how long?" (Psalm 6:3, 35:17; Isaiah 6:11; Habakkuk 1:2; Zechariah 1:12) It should be pointed out that when it comes to delayed response, the very same question "How long?" was what Jehovah and Jesus equally asked of incommunicative people. It is a two-way street. While Daniel was still asking, Gabriel came to him "in swift flight". There is perhaps something frustrating in a "swift" response that tells us that the answer will be slow in coming! What he was asking for was going to happen but not immediately. However, he was told: "As soon as you began to pray, an answer was given" (Daniel 9:23). There are delays of fulfillment that appear to us as unanswered asking, but the fact is they have been heard, and more than that "decreed" (9:25, 26, 27). Although we are not as assured as Daniel of the 'decree' being a done deal, we can be equally assured that we are heard, and equally sustained to wait. That being said, it is precisely our assurance and confidence that delay erodes.

The argument goes that the reason Jesus mentioned the need to ask so many times was because of the need to persist in asking despite delayed answers. "He knew that there would be delay in many an answer which would call for importunate pressing and that if our faith did not have the strongest assurance of God's willingness to answer, delay would break it down. And that our spiritual sloth would come in under the guise of submission and say it is not God's will to give what we ask, and so cease praying and lose our case." [16] E.M. Bounds was assuming that there will be delayed answers given the scriptural emphasis on importunity and ceaseless asking. Similarly, Spurgeon wrote: "No delay or apparent denial, however grievous, should tempt us to forbear from importunate pleading." [17] Perhaps we should be surprised at how surprised we are by delay. "Instant relief would not establish the habit of prayer." [18] Forsyth has a point. If we got what we asked for so easily then we would make an idol of faith (as in the 'faith movement') and the primary value would be what faith achieved on our terms, not what asking was as a value to God. Vindicated faith is never the ultimate goal of asking. That goal is relational union with the Lord. This is what makes our asking a holy end in itself, irrespective of answers. 'No answer' does not mean we are dealing with something that is neither 'unanswered' nor 'unanswerable.' It simply means that despite the challenge, our asking is not done, because relationship is never done.

Delay means stay: "It is hard to wait and press and pray and hear no voice, but *stay* till God answers." [19] Bounds is but one of the army of asking saints who down through the centuries have always argued for the rewards of 'staying'. William Gurnall was another: "Some prayers, indeed, have a longer voyage than others, but then they return with richer lading at last; the praying soul is a gainer by waiting for an answer." [20] Spurgeon, a great student of the Puritans, must have been influenced by this image when he encouraged his congregants to expect their delayed answers to be like ships that return more slowly because they have a bigger cargo. He went on to describe these delayed answers as coming "not only with capital but with compound interest." [21]

Having affirmed that delay calls us to be importunate, it is also important to know the red light from the green. In most circumstances, we will need to be ceaseless in our green-light asking, but there may be occasions when we need to cease and heed God's red lights. A point came for Jeremiah in his asking of God for the people when God said to him: "Do not ask for this people" (Jeremiah 7:16). God told a grieving, asking Samuel that his unresolved desires for Saul's reinstatement needed to be relinquished (1 Samuel 16:1). Asking about this was no longer of any use. It is interesting to note that it was the cessation of this asking that brought about the release of God's answer in David. Some times God gives a conviction that the asking assignment is done, and we can now wait for the answer without further importunity. "The Lord has heard my supplication; the Lord accepts my prayer" (Psalm 6:8). After the intensity of Hannah's asking, a point came when there was breakthrough: "Go in peace and the God of Israel grant what you have asked for" (1 Samuel 1:17). Despite the lack of an immediate answer, the burden may be intensified, but it may be lifted altogether.

It is a time of delayed answers that reinforces the need for a spiritual understanding that is rooted in a personal knowledge of God's ways, works, will and word. If we are like that rooted tree in Psalm 1 then the stored Word in our spirits will give sustenance, and delay will not starve us out of God's coming provision. In prison, John Bunyan went through deep turmoil as he dealt with his unanswered asking. "I have been strongly persuaded to leave off, and to seek the Lord no longer; but being made to understand what great sinners the Lord has had mercy upon, and how large His promises; and that it was not the whole but the sick, not the righteous but the sinner, not the full but the empty, that He extended his grace and mercy unto – this made me, through the assistance of His Holy Spirit, to cleave to Him, to hang upon Him, and yet to cry, though for the present He made no answer." [22] Note that it was Bunyan's knowledge of both the nature of God and the need of people that God was committed to meet, that kept him to the sticking-post. Delay weakens us to the point that, like Bunyan, we want "to leave off and seek the Lord no longer" but it is the work of the Holy Spirit in such times of weakness to empower us to keep asking and to wait, with groans if needed, until the answer comes.

It is natural to want our answers now, but delay has a way of drawing us into intimacy if we choose to trust the Lord. Intimacy is preferable to immediacy. It is also natural to assume that there is always something wrong with us. Not so, as Bunyan knew: "Seeming delays in God are no tokens of His displeasure." [23] It is possible that we are not as ready for the answer as we assumed. Delay can expose weaknesses. Faith gets tested and perhaps was not as tried and true as we thought. So many have testified to the deepening of trust and the strengthening of faith during such delay.

There are some things that we just do not learn or perceive but for such divine delays. Many have commented on the way that the revelation of God as shepherd or fortress, as shield or light, was precisely at times when the asking of the psalmist for safety or protection, for removal of wickedness and darkness, appeared to go unanswered at first. "Our needs and necessities reveal His nature." [24] They also do a very good job revealing the true spiritual topography of our nature, warts and all, so in these times of delay when our hearts are sifted and our characters are tested, we learn a lot about ourselves through them. When shaken, things have a way of spilling out. Unwelcome delay can be a welcome time of heart-searching.

The reason that delayed answers are labeled so quickly as 'unanswered' ones has to do with the difficulty of waiting. It is amazing what waiting flushes out of our overheated spiritual-radiator system. Have we ever been amazed at our lack of grace in waiting for others? There is not one of us that does not know the pains and pressures of waiting: for employment, for health, for marriage, for a child, for justice, for restoration of a relationship, for fulfillment of a dream, for a particular achievement or goal, especially for an answer to prayer for all of these. Is anything happening when nothing is happening? We can relate to the voices of scripture: "How long must your servant wait?" (Psalm 119:84) "How long O Lord?" (Revelation 6:10) They were told to "wait a little longer"! "How long till you restore the kingdom?" (Acts 1:6) It is interesting that the last recorded communication the disciples ever spoke to Jesus was this unanswered question.

It would appear then that the disciples' last moments with Jesus established the relationship between asking and waiting, asking and hope. This is hard for us because in the natural, we tend to see waiting in time as wasting of time. We readily talk of losing hope as time winds on or down. Waiting is a hold up. It is nothing happening and nothing moving; it is delay, stalling, marking time, treading water. These times tend to be accompanied by discouragement and debilitation. What affects the spirit affects the body, and the faint heart becomes the fatigued body.

You cannot read about our hope for God's will and purposes in the New Testament without tripping over the same word again and again. Listen for it: "Imitate those who through *patience* inherit the promises" (Hebrews 6:12); "For you need *patience* after you have done the will of God, that you might receive the promise" (Hebrews 10:36); "Let us run with *patience* the race that is set before us" (Hebrews 12:1); "Be *patient* until the Lord's coming ... be *patient* because the Lord's coming is near" (James 5:7-8); "I John ... in tribulation and in the kingdom and *patience* of Jesus Christ" (Revelation 1:9); "The beast was given power to make war against the saints ... this calls for *patient* endurance on the part of the saints" (Revelation 13:10; 14:12); "If we hope for that we see not, then do we with *patience* wait for it" (Romans 8:25); "*patience* of hope in our Lord Jesus Christ" (1 Thessalonians 1:3); "So after waiting *patiently* Abraham received what was promised" (Hebrews 6:15); "Since you have kept my command to endure *patiently* I will also keep you from the hour of trial" (Revelation 3:10). And the virtue is?

Life in the Spirit requires the spiritual capacity to wait. Now you understand why patience is a fruit of the Holy Spirit, of Christ's character. There is nothing natural about it, but without it there will be dysfunction in our asking. And lest we think this patience is a dour and dogged affair, it is not. How can it be unless we are reluctant to let go the grip of our will and grab the joy of His. Again, let scripture do the talking: "We *wait eagerly* for our adoption as sons, our redemption of our bodies" (Romans 8:23); "you *eagerly await* for our Lord Jesus Christ to be revealed" (1 Corinthians 1:7); "We *eagerly await* through the spirit the righteousness for which we wait" (Galatians 5:5); "Our citizenship is in heaven and we *eagerly await* a savior from there" (Philippians 3:20). You have heard of 'eager beavers' – this is about eager believers. John Stott puts it perfectly: "We are to wait neither so eagerly that we lose our patience, nor so patiently that we lose our expectations, but eagerly and patiently together." [25] Do not forget that the New Testament opens with the end of a 400-year delay in answered asking. Are we surprised that the two oldest characters on the scene who had been bearing the delay the longest, Simeon and Anna, were respectively "*waiting* for the consolation of Israel" but "*looking forward* to the redemption of Israel." (Luke 2:25, 38) The delay of answered asking invites us to similarly be 'eagerly patient', waiting indeed, but also looking forward to the answer whatever that may be. The very act of our asking is doing the will of God so we should not be surprised at the need for patience: "when you have done the will of God you have need of patience" (Hebrews 10:36). Dr. Davison writes: "To wait is not merely to remain impassive. It is to expect to look for with patience, and also with submission. It is to long for, but not impatiently; to look for but not to fret as the delay; to watch for but not restlessly; to feel that if he does not come we will acquiesce, and yet refuse to let the mind acquiesce in the feeling that He will not come." [26]

There is no question that delays can be dangerous to spiritual health. Spurgeon warned his congregants that they had an enemy who opposed their relationship with the Lord and would sponsor any wedge between them: "But we must be careful not to take delays in prayer for denials ... We must not suffer Satan to shake our confidence in the God of truth by pointing to our unanswered prayers. Unanswered petitions are not unheard." [27] Yes, he acknowledged that delays were great "trials of faith" but he was as eager to point out, as we must, that delayed answers also "give us support to honor God through our steadfast confidence in Him."

Denials: Taking No For an Answer

Unlike 'disavowals', asking which may be denied will likely be an appropriate desire, a legitimate request given present perceptions, a reasonable inquiry given current understanding. It is precisely the apparent acceptability of what is asked for that makes the acceptance of a denial so difficult. Although it is true that delays are not denials, it is easy to understand why an interminable delay will be assumed to be a denial. Having said that, there do seem to be denials and Scripture presents us with some examples. Denials were experienced by stellar saints, and one of them was the saintliest of all, Jesus. If denials were the membership qualification for this alumni group we would perhaps be less concerned about them. Moses' "pleaded with the Lord ... Let me go over" (Deuteronomy 3:23-25). The answer? Moses said, "The Lord would not listen to me. 'That is enough' the Lord said. 'Do not speak to me any more about this matter.'" David "pleaded with God for the child. He fasted and went into his house and spent the nights lying on the ground." The answer? "On the seventh day the child died" (2 Samuel 12:16). We have already discussed the denial of Paul's asking for the removal of the 'thorn in the flesh" from his life (2 Corinthians 12:7-9), as we have also meditated on the denial experienced by Jesus in Gethsemane (Matthew 26:36-46).

But let us linger with Jesus. "During the days of Jesus's life on earth, He offered up prayers and petitions with loud cries and tears to the one who could save Him from death, and He was heard because of His reverent submission. Although He was a son, He learned obedience from what He suffered and, once made perfect, He became the source of eternal salvation for all who obey Him" (Hebrews 5:7-9). Of all the things that the author could have chosen as a highlight of Jesus's life on earth, he chose Jesus's "prayers and petitions", His asking. Specifically, he alludes to the Garden of Gethsemane, to the "loud cries and tears to the one who could save Him from death." Because the asking of Jesus in the Garden was denied, we might think that God refused to listen to such a request. But the text says Jesus "was heard because of His reverent submission." It is through such asking, with such apparent lack of answering, that Jesus "learned obedience from what He suffered" and was "made perfect." The denial was a benefit.

This is not suggesting that Jesus was disobedient or imperfect. The idea here is that His response to the will of the Father was both tested and attested in this asking and in His acceptance of the denied answer. The idea of *"perfect"* here is about completion, about finishing. What we might think or hope is the answer we need to our asking, to make things perfect for us, to complete our need, to fulfill what we think our life, or our desire, or our will is all about, may not be the answers that will in fact perfect, or complete or finish what God is intending to both work into us, and work through us, for His sake, for the purpose not primarily of our present well-being, but for His eternal glory. It is this perfection of Christ that is presented as "the source of our salvation." Jesus, though his asking was denied, became the source of salvation for all who would become obedient to the Father's will. Our asking is inseparable from our obeying. God's denials are sometimes protectors of our obedience. Our response to God's denials is our ongoing obedience to the will of the Father, as supremely modeled by Jesus in Holy week, from Upper Room to Gethsemane, to Golgotha. No denial is a walk in the park – it is an agony in a garden.

But is 'grace is sufficient' a sufficient answer? Though clearly denials, we can learn from these experiences of Moses, David, Paul and Jesus that such refusals are not random or arbitrary. For Moses it was about discipline; for David it was about reparation; for Paul it was about protection; for Jesus it was about a continuing obedience to fulfill the will of God, which would be answered another way. As time passes, we may be wise in hindsight, and have a modicum of understanding. But most often, we do not know an explanation. What we do know is that God is good, that His will is perfect, and in the big eternal scheme of things, His goodness can be trusted, and does not need to justify itself because it will one day be validated, whether in this life or the next. Given that we have to wait for that, the denial is but a delay that is frozen in time until the day it will be thawed when we no longer "see through a glass darkly" (1 Corinthians 13:12). What will we see? Forsyth was clear on this one: "We shall come one day to a heaven where we shall gratefully know that God's great refusals were sometimes the true answers to our truest prayer. Our soul is fulfilled if our petition is not." [28]

In every case of denial, although the specific request was unanswered, God went to the limit to love and care for them. The denial, or what at first might have been felt as the implacable unresponsiveness of God, was wrapped in grace. As for Moses, although he was denied entrance into the land, God arranged for him to die on Mount Nebo, and there "the Lord showed him the whole land" (Deuteronomy 34:1). His feet were denied, but God let his eyes roam freely. As for David, the baby died, but the Lord gave him Solomon of whom it was said, "The Lord loved him" (2 Samuel 12:24). As for Paul, 'perfect' would have been the removal of the thorn but this was denied.

Instead, he got another 'perfect', God's grace, God's power made "perfect" in his weakness (2 Corinthians 12:5-7). What had been a messenger of Satan was transformed into an identification with the sufferings of a thorn-wearing Christ. As for Jesus, the removal of the cup was denied, but heaven was not closed for "an angel from heaven appeared to Him and strengthened Him" (Luke 22:43) thus confirming that God's will would yet make everything well. The denial meant that He could not save Himself but as a result, He saved the entire world.

So, let us ask again: is "grace is sufficient" sufficient an answer? Their responses to denial serve to tutor us. Following his denial, Moses did ask again, but in a spirit of admission of his wrong and of submission to God's will. He never questioned God's denial. David "got up from the ground", in acceptance of the denial, and "went into the house of the Lord and worshiped." Likewise, Paul submitted to the wisdom of God that purposed the humbling denial, and he accepted the grace that would make him gracious and not grieved by the denial. Jesus put the words in our mouth: "Not my will but yours be done" (Luke 22:42). Despite the pain of denial, what acceptance and worship, what submission and obedience returned to God as their final answer on that which was unanswered. As hard as a denial is, because God is good and gracious, there are rounded corners as it were to the denial. Again, Forsyth tried to capture the enigma: "Faith is sure that God refuses with a smile; that He says 'no' in the spirit of 'yes'. And He gives or refuses always in Christ, our great Amen." [29]

Deferrals: Assented but not Answered

Some unanswered prayers are divinely willed deferrals. The difference between a delay and a deferral is that the latter carries the idea that there is an agreement and acceptance between both parties. As we have discussed, our experience of delay is usually not quite so agreeable. Our asking is necessary and timely as it is being ceaselessly expressed, but it is being 'stored' to be answered another day, or another time that is even beyond our sojourn on earth. Stephen's last breath was asking for something that was answered after his death. Life running out will in no way lessen our asking – it will increase it. Answers are about timing (the moment) as well as substance (the matter): "in an acceptable time have I heard you" (Isaiah 49:8). In Scripture we observe that what is often perceived as unanswered asking is in fact a matter of God's timing: "in the fullness of time ... at the right time ... when his time has come" (Galatians 4:4; Romans 5:6; 2 Thessalonians 2:6). Personal timing was not the same as prophetic timeliness. "The moment of the response is the best possible even if we seem to have waited interminably between the prayer and its answer." [30] When we are grappling with what to us is the 'worst', it is not always easy to agree with Ellul's description of the 'best.'

Few of us have not experienced what at first seemed to us like divine dilatoriness, only to discern that it was a divinely intentional deferral. The answer was not according to my scheduled need, but when it arrived, passing time had changed our need by changing us. The answer is given to us when we have given up. It was not the answer that was too late. Rather, too late we realized that we were demanding by right what God wanted us to receive as a gift. Being gratified because my particulars have been served, gives way to God being glorified and my answer being of service to Him. There is method in His deferrals.

Then there are those deferrals that will await their activation in future ages. This has been such a provocation to the asking church through the centuries, as it asked for God's kingdom to come, as it pleaded for generations yet unborn, as it cried, "Even so come, Lord Jesus." Pastors ancient and modern have gloried in this. "God has old prayers of yours long maturing by Him. What wine you will drink with Him in His kingdom!" [31] So much of our asking awaits a time. We ask because we must, because scripture exhorts us to, but though contending we are not contentious, though imploring we are not impatient. We choose to be content and agreeable in our asking despite "the accomplishment of them not falling out in your time." [32] All of us have reaped where we have not sown, mostly through answers to another's asking. We could argue, as Pastor Goodwin did three hundred years ago, that the denouement of history is going to be the fulfillment of millions of unanswered-because-deferred prayers. "That may be one reason why God will do such great things towards the end of the world even because there has been so great a stock of prayers going, for so many ages, which is now to be returned." [33] Who would have thought that the return of our Lord was related to the returns of our deferred asking? Again, "Even so come, Lord Jesus."

Discretions, Diversions, Deprivations: Creative 'Un-answers'

It is never the heart of God to give us less than His goodness determines for us. However, as we have already seen in the Lamentations account of Israel's unanswered prayers, the delayed or deferred answers give time for some good things to be worked is us, even though they do not feel good at the time. These *deprivations* may feel like the with-holding of an answer but they are not the withdrawal of God's presence. On the contrary, when we feel there is no response, it is the responsiveness of love that seeks desired relationship not just desired request. Peter Grieg affirms this: "Sometimes He may deprive us of something in order to draw us to Someone." [34]

There is a saying that suggests that sometimes the answer to our asking is not rejected but redirected. Divine *discretions* do not deny the requests but apply their intentions and desires to different applications and outcomes. After our asking has pitched the way that things need to be, it is as if God says, "You are on the right track, but how about we do it like this not that?" Some times these redirections feel like radical *diversions*. Abraham's prayer for Ishmael was answered in Isaac. What Moses asked for himself was to be fulfilled in Joshua. David's prayers for the child who died revert to Solomon. David asked to build the Temple, but again, the answers were reserved for Solomon. Though the specific thing asked for was not delivered in the terms in which it was asked, nonetheless, this asking was not 'unanswered' but applied in a way that advanced God's glory, fulfilling his renown more than just the request.

A Tear-Bottle or a Trash-Can?

You could argue that as great as the problem of his physical and emotional suffering was for Job, it was the matter of unanswered asking that gave rise to so much tortured argumentation. The fact that this is the concern of possibly the earliest written text in scripture, suggests how foundational this matter is to the human soul. The second of two things that Job asks God to grant him is: "Summon me and I will answer, or let me speak and you reply" (Job 13:2). More than once Job seems to throw down the gauntlet, saying that at least he will answer God when He speaks: "You will call and I will answer you" (14:15). He finds a way to rationalize God's silence: "If He remains silent who can condemn?" (34:29) But at the end of the day there is the nagging thought that his asking is ineffectual. "What would we gain by praying to Him? ... It profits a man nothing when he tries to please the Lord" (21:15; 34:9). What is the point? What is the profit?

It is God himself who gives Satan an allowance to test Job, and surely his unanswered asking tested his faith. Peter argues that the suffering of our trials "have come so that your faith - of greater worth than gold ... may be proved genuine and may result in praise, glory and honor when Jesus Christ is revealed" (1 Peter 1:7). The good news is that the glory of God remains the outcome of the testing of faith. The bad news is that we may have to wait till the parousia for this to be validated and vindicated. Calvin conceded that circumstances might convince us that God has forsaken us, and that unanswered prayer sorely tests faith. His observation does not sound very comforting, that God may have us "to lie a long time in the mire before He gives us a taste of His sweetness." [35] The continuance of asking at such times, with patience, is the outworking of faith.

Talking of faith, Forsyth wrote: "The prayer of faith does not mean a prayer is absolutely sure that it will receive what it asks ... Faith is that attitude of soul and self to God, which is the root and reservoir of prayer apart from all answer ... It is what makes you sure your prayer is heard and stored whether granted or not. 'He putteth all my tears in His bottle.'" [36] The reference is to Psalm 56:8: "You have collected all my tears in your bottle. You have recorded each one in your book." Yet, like Job, we know how easy it is to give up and question the viability and veracity of asking. Why not just crumple the script of our asking and throw it in the ever-filling trash-can of unanswered prayer? The prelude to the Bible's great chapter on heroes and heroines of faith is addressing those who stood their ground "in the face of suffering" (Hebrews 10:32). "So do not throw away your confidence ... have need of endurance ... receive what is promised .... He who is coming will come and not delay" (10:37). Of course, this sounds a bit rich given the fact that delay, denial, deprivation, diversion (whatever you want to call it) is characterizing the present problem. At least it affirms us, and we know that God Himself is not unmindful that it really is a challenge for us. So we have a choice. Though there is pain in what is experienced by us as unanswered, will we throw away our request into the trash can, or will we trust our tears to the bottle?

Resting the Case

Job was feeling distant from God: "If only I knew where to find Him" (23:3). If he did find Him he "would find out what He would answer me." What he then says he will do is helpful advice. It is a two-point plan. "I would state my case before Him and fill my mouth with arguments." Spurgeon used this text to encourage Christians to "order your cause ... prepare your arguments." [37] In preceding chapters we have looked at so many things that are spiritual aids to effective asking and play their part in *presenting the case* when we ask of the Lord. The Holy Spirit does His advocating through us. We plead the case; we plead God's character and covenant; we plead His will and His Word; we plead the precedents both biblical and historical; we plead Christ. We do so with all the cognitive and affective means available, with godly knowledge and godly emotions. But when all that is done there is one thing more that is needed for our asking to be effective, especially if we have concluded our asking with an 'Amen' thus declaring 'Let it be.' We need to *rest the case* and know how to submit to the divine deliberations and decisions of the Judge who will always do what is right, by all parties: the asker, the asked of and the asked for. The fact that the jury may sometimes seem to be out for a long while may just be one evidence of how effective the asking really was. As Goodwin concluded: "When a man hath put up prayers to God he is to rest assured that God will in mercy answer his prayers; and to listen diligently and observe how his prayers are answered." [38]

The Mueller Method

There is not one of us who has not received succor from the stories of the asking saints who came before us. Mind you, their testimonies can be either encouraging (God can do the same for me!) or discouraging (Why them and not me?) depending on our present perspective. I hardly know of a book on prayer written in the last 100 years that does not refer to George Mueller, particularly when it comes to dealing with asking that goes unanswered. We might as well join the club. For twelve years (1850-1862) Mueller asked for the expansion of his work for the orphans.

> "Observe then, first, esteemed reader, how long it may be, before a full answer to our prayers, even to thousands and ten thousands of prayers, is granted; yea though these prayers may be believing prayers, earnest prayers and offered up in the name of the Lord Jesus, and though we may only for the sake of the honor of our Lord desire the answer: for I did by the grace of God without the least doubt and wavering look for more than eleven years for the full answer ... and I sought only in this matter the glory of God." [39]

Out of these 'unanswered' years, Mueller concluded that there were at least five things that he would hold as spiritually dear and non-negotiable, regardless of an answer. I leave you with his list:

1. Entire dependence upon the merits and mediation of our Lord Jesus Christ as the only ground for any claim for blessings (John 14:13-14);
2. Separation from all known sin (Psalm 66:18);
3. Faith in God's word of promise (Hebrews 11:6);
4. Asking in accordance with His will (I John 5:14).
5. Importunity in supplication. There must be a waiting on God and for God (James 5:7).

With Mueller, we will rest our case and despite being presently unanswered, rest assured.

"The God who answers by orphanages – let Him be God!" - Spurgeon on George Mueller's asking

"The reason you pray so much and give thanks so little is that you observe not God's answers … we are to take notice of His payment and give Him an acknowledgement of the receipt of it; He loseth of His glory else." - Thomas Goodwin

"Remarkable answers to prayer very much quicken the prayerfulness of other godly persons." - Spurgeon

21

When Asking is Answered

A Shocking Concern

Newsweek magazine conducted a poll to ascertain the state of prayer in America and found that a majority of adults (54%) reported praying on a daily basis, and of that number, 87% said that they believed God answered prayer.[1] Another study by the Pew Research Center similarly reported that the USA was a praying country (daily prayer by 48% of those aged 18-29, 61% for ages 50-59 and 70% post-70). Of people 50 and older, 25% reported receiving a specific answer to prayer in the past week with another 35% saying they had received several answers within the past year. [2] I hope that all the respondents were thoughtfully and thankfully amazed by the responsiveness of God to what was asked of Him.

No one is surprised when the problems of unanswered asking are raised, but given that answered asking far exceeds what is unanswered, perhaps we should be surprised at the weakness of response to these answers, as measured by little gratitude and limited worship, by a lack of appreciation for what was effected, or by a modicum of consideration about what further responses these answers require of us. The pain of what is unanswered usually shouts louder than the praise for what has been answered. This lack of response to asking when it is answered should be as significant a concern to us as our unanswered asking. We need to stop and take stock once in a while. The first thing that should move us and uncork our gratitude is how gracious God is in answering us at all, given the inconsistency and infrequency of our asking, or what Spurgeon described as "the intermittent spasms of our importunity." [3] Just to realize that our weak asking got such a strong response because of the strength of the one asked, not the one asking, should be sufficient to unstop the wells of worship for the character of God, particularly His kindness and grace.

We should be chastened by the minimal returns from so much answered asking. Should there not be more thanksgiving? As we have seen, if our asking is accompanied by thanksgiving anyway (Philippians 4:6) then this lack suggests two things: that there is a lot less asking going on than we assume, and that there is indeed a limited return of thanksgiving for all the answers received to asking. We are familiar with Jesus's healing of the ten lepers, and the sad fact that only one of them "came back ... praising God in a loud voice" (Luke 17:11-19). Given the responsiveness of our Father to what we ask of Him, He should be hearing a lot more noise.

The 'Return' of Asking – Bad and Good

This book is arguing for a 'return of asking' but the idea here is that there should be a 'return' from our answers, as with the return on a good investment. The words of Jesus have a disturbing echo: "Was no one found to return and give praise to God?" (Luke 17:18) If this incident was a rough guide to our responsiveness to God's answers to our asking, then we are looking at a 10% return. The thought that only one in ten answers may provoke a volley of God-worthy thanksgiving is unacceptable. The non-return of the other nine lepers was a bad return on the answer.

As much attention should be given to our answered asking as to our unanswered asking. God's answers should serve as a great motivation and incentive to avoid bad returns. These would include the failure: to respond with thanksgiving, to be humbled, to commit to steward the answer. Does Jesus still express surprised sadness at the ingratitude and forgetfulness that follows so many answers? The story of the Israelites, after God answered their requests for deliverance, is a salutary reminder of how soon we can forget the mercies of the Lord, and how quickly complaint and unbelief can displace the returns of gratitude and contentment.

There is another kind of return that we definitely need to avoid having once received the grace of God's answers. Having asked for the answer of forgiveness and received it, let there not be a return of unforgiveness in our hearts towards others, or a return to the confessed sin. Having asked for the answer of deliverance and received it, let us not return to a "yoke of bondage". Having asked for the answer of guidance and received it, let us not return to a pattern of self-direction. Having asked for the answer of provision and received it, let us not return to any indiscipline that accounted for unnecessary lack. Having asked for the answer of wisdom, let us not return like a fool to his folly. Having asked for a way of escape from ungodly cultural influences and received it, let us not look back like Lot's wife. These are clearly bad 'returns' on good answers.

The return of thanksgiving that one of the lepers experienced and expressed is the obvious response to answered asking, but the other nine lepers are not looking very 'obvious' right now. We are not grateful by our nature. We are characterized by Dostoevsky as "the ungrateful biped". [4] Paul makes clear that lack of thanksgiving is a sign of unredeemed life (Romans 1:21). He goes on to describe how the redeemed should respond: "Always giving thanks to God the Father for everything" (Ephesians 1:20). "God created everything to be received with thanksgiving" (1 Timothy 4:2). "Giving thanks in all circumstances" (1 Thessalonians 5:18). "I urge that thanksgiving be made for everyone" (1 Timothy 2:1). "Whatever ... in word or deed ... giving thanks to God" (Colossians 3:17). This is somewhat comprehensive. Thanksgiving is: for everything, for everyone, in every circumstance, in every word and deed, at every moment. That should cover every answer to prayer. Unfettered and unfiltered thanksgiving is the non-negotiable return of answered asking. Thomas Goodwin affirmed that "prayers answered will enlarge the heart with thankfulness." [5] Our asking is the filling between two thick slices of thanksgiving. "By prayer and petition with thanksgiving ... I will give you thanks for you answered me" (Philippians 4:6; Psalm 118:21).

Our praise is the reminder of what asking has always been about – not the answer per se but the glorifying of God. "Call upon me ... and I will deliver you and you shall glorify me" (Psalm 50:15). The psalmist's 'return' of praise is the fact that God "has not turned away my prayer or withheld His love from me" (Psalm 66:20). Commenting on this psalm, Spurgeon wrote: "What a God is He thus to hear the prayers of those who come to Him when they have pressing wants, but neglect Him when they have received a mercy; who approach Him when they are forced to come, but who almost forget to address Him when mercies are plentiful and sorrows are few." [6] How is it then that we can be so blessed yet so 'blah'? How is it that we take for granted what God has granted in answering our asking?

We Got Our Answer But Did God Get His?

How can we not be overwhelmed by the restraint of God, the humility, kindness, graciousness, patience and forbearance of our Father, who would still give us the bread and fish we need, only to watch us wolf it down, be satisfied on our terms, and miss the glory and the ultimate outcome of it all? Nine of the ten lepers who got all their prayers for healing answered, forgot that their answer actually triggered and begged another question: was the answer they got the answer that God wanted? Will the receipt of our answer provoke our praise and answer His request for our worship? Will our answer fuel our obedience and answer His request for the evidence of our professed love? Will our answer release our giving and answer His needs as presented in the needs of others? Will our answer energize our service and answer His request for workers in the harvest field? Will our answer persuade our sacrifice and answer His longing to know that we love Him more than all of these and this and that and the other? Will our answer inspire our commitment and answer His asking for our faithfulness in an intimate relationship that will be unthreatened by spiritual adultery or the back-sliding of spiritual one-night stands? Will our answer bring Him the returns He asks of us?

Observe the Answers

One reason for a lack of sustained expressive affection in response to answers is that our asking is often not imbued with expectation that trustingly lives in anticipation of what God is going to do when we ask. In his philosophical enquiry about asking, Vincent Brummer posited that "petitioning God entails that the petitioner expects an answer." [7] Sometimes the 'blah' begins with our 'might as well', 'you never know', 'can't do any harm', and 'sure hope it gets through' attitudes that precede our asking. How different this is when compared to Solomon's conviction that his requests would be "near to the Lord our God day and night that He may uphold the cause of His servant" (1Kings 8:59). Thomas Goodwin was emphatic about the need, once having asked of God, to look earnestly for the answer, and to discern what was going on while the asking continued or while waiting ensued. "It is not enough to pray, but after you have prayed you have need to listen for an answer that you may receive your prayers. The sermon was not done when yet the preacher is done, because it is not done till practiced." [8] Even so, our asking is not done until we have considered the answers that we have received.

Did You Hear a Dog Barking?

In the same way that we have seen that unanswered asking is cause for us to evaluate some things, even so answered asking equally invites some further consideration. The fact that we received an answer speaks volumes to us of the loving, purposeful provision of God, but it will also whisper a lot of affirmations and confirmations that perhaps need to be heeded for future spiritual growth and future asking. So what's up with the dog?

The asking for deliverance by the enslaved Israelites was raw and raucous: "the Israelites groaned in their slavery and cried out, and their cry for help ... went up to God" (Exodus 2:23). They were asking to get out of there, and they did not care how, but there were so many exquisite details in God's answer that served to 'quietly' underline His loving power. On the night of the Exodus, who could forget "the loud wailing in Egypt" (Exodus 11:30)? But imagine a conversation a few years later in the wilderness between Zak and Zeke.

> "Hey, Zeke, do you remember that night?"
> "Are you kidding me, Zak? My ears are still ringing with the shrieking noise of those wailing parents."
> "You know what's weird, Zeke? It's not the noise I remember but the silence. Do you remember Nimrod, that antsy dog

of mine? He never made a single whining, whimpering sound all night. What do you make of that?"

The text tells us what they were meant to make of that, if they observed the full answer. "This is what the Lord says ... among the Israelites not a dog will bark at any man or animal." But why? "Then you will know that the Lord makes a distinction between Israel and Egypt." Through the dog's silence, God speaks loudly about Himself and them. The answer to their asking that was their massive national deliverance included these details, that if considered, conveyed awesome revelations about the power of God in this world, but also about how He feels about what opposes His purposes. Do you not think that Zak and Zeke, having considered how God answered their asking on that Exodus night, would want to be sure that they always stayed on the right side of God's affections?

The point is that God's answers, when "observed", yield so many instructional encouragements, and sometimes, whimsical clues about who He is and how He feels about things, and about what is yet possible if these answers are stewarded well. It is understandable that given the relief of the answer, we are now ready to move ahead where we were once stymied, take care of what was on hold, renew our engagement with what was in limbo. Like the nine lepers, it is the most natural thing to get right on with our lives, once the brake of our unanswered needs has been released, and made way for the accelerator of answered provision. But the truth of Goodwin's observation remains that "you lose much of your comfort in blessings when you do not observe answers to your prayers." [9]

Read My Lips

"Get rid of your wine!" (1 Samuel 1:14) There was not a fluid-ounce of right discernment in Eli's pastoral counsel to the woman at the altar rail. He had confused the effects of pouring out a glass with those of pouring out the soul. "Her lips were moving but her voice was not heard." However, once Hannah had explained that she was asking at a place of "great anguish and grief" he recovered with a prophetic word: "May the God of Israel grant you what you have asked for." You know the story: He did. "She named him Samuel, saying, Because I asked the Lord for him." His very name meant "Answer"! So what did Hannah do with the answer? There was a return.

Her physical return to Shiloh sets in motion the spiritual returns of her answer, that help us to learn how to respond when our asking is answered.

"She named him Samuel" (v20). Call the answer by its name. So often we are clearer in declaring the need than discerning the answer, quicker to ask than to testify about the answer. Samuel would always bear this name. It would not change. Likewise, God's answers cannot be renamed, and we need to ensure that their identities are not redefined by doubt or negligence, ingratitude or forgetfulness. As long as he was Samuel, the remembrance of the answer was alive. Did not Hannah ask for "grace" (v18)? Was not her answer, Samuel, the grace she received? Goodwin is helpful again: "Where grace is ... there will be a continued particular thankful remembrance of it a long while after." [10] Our grace-answers should be identified with the same clarity with which we identified the needs we were asking about. Name your 'Samuel's'. Give public testimony to your answers.

"The Lord has granted me what I asked of Him" (v27). Let the first 'return' be an acknowledgement of the Lord. "The Lord has done this and it is marvelous in our eyes" (Psalm 118:23). Our answers are the Lord's "righteous acts" that solicit the worship of heaven no less: "Great and marvelous are your deeds, Lord God Almighty" (Revelation 15:3). The answer was not chance or happenstance, not coincidental or circumstantial – it was the Lord. "May the Lord grant all your requests" (Psalm 20:5). There are so many other feelings that accompany this acknowledgement, particularly the conviction of being loved. The acceptance by God of the request affirms our own sense of acceptance. Spurgeon understood this: "Answered prayers are hopeful arguments of acceptance." [11]

"So now I give Him to the Lord" (v28). God's response to Hannah became her return to the Lord. To receive an answer that we have greatly desired, and maybe waited for, makes 'grabbers' of us all. Hannah shows us that our answers are less about what we have been given, than about how they have supplied us to give back to the Lord. When David poured out the water from the Bethlehem well (2 Samuel 23:16) and when Abraham offered Isaac on the altar (Genesis 22:9), both were exemplifying this response to be willing to give back what was most longed for and asked for. The need that gets us asking, once supplied, is graciously sanctified thereby and the answer becomes the free-will sacrificial gift back to God. There is much loss when we fail to steward our answers. Even though an answer may be gained, yet there may still be a loss of possible spiritual equity.

"He worshiped the Lord there" (v28). No sooner had Hannah given her answer back to the Lord than Samuel's immediate response was to worship. I think it is a wonderful picture of the way that the instinctive and immediate spiritual response to any answer should be what we have been emphasizing all along, the worship of God. After all, this was what Jesus said would be the return on all answered asking: "I will do whatever you ask in my name, so that the Son may *bring glory* to the Father" (John 14:13). Thus we know the non-negotiable return – not our answer for our gratification, but His answer for His glorification.

The Many Happy Returns of Asking

The returns of Hannah's answered asking did not end there, and nor should ours. The text records: "Then Hannah prayed" (1 Samuel 2:1). The most obvious fruit of answered asking is simply the desire to go on asking. One of the great returns of answered asking is the encouragement to ask again. Having received the answer we need, now is the time to keep asking in the manner that God needs. But it is not only that Hannah prayed again – it is what she prayed. The observers who thought that she was just a mumbling, broken, faithless, clueless woman who was desperate for a baby, are about as misguided in their conclusion as those who think the sexually broken Samaritan woman was an air-head bimbo. It just happens that Jesus had one of his most intellectually and theologically demanding conversations with her (including about the subject of asking). What Hannah prayed could be described as the Old Testament equivalent of the Magnificat: an extraordinary manifesto for the power of God and His kingdom, that lays a foundation of truth upon which all other asking can be grounded.

The answers of God should provoke more asking for more answers. Why? Hannah's prayer reveals some of the returns of her answer:

- **"My heart rejoices in the Lord"** (v1). Jesus said that the return of asking would be that our joy would be complete. We rejoice *in* God more than *for* the answer that has been obtained. The failure to rejoice in the Lord may indicate that our asking was more self-gratifying than God-glorifying. It has been suggested that asking without thanksgiving is more likely to be about self-love. **Rejoicing is the return of answered asking.**
- **"My mouth boasts over my enemies"** (v1). Hannah knew all about enmity, "year after year" (v7) and the way that the provocation of her "rival" (v6) dominated her and bound her life. But when the righteous cry out "the Lord hears them and delivers them from all their troubles. The Lord is close to the broken-hearted" (Psalm 34:17-18). Through her answer she recovered her confidence in the face of the enemy, and her "misery" (v6) in bondage is transformed into her "delight in your deliverance." Her prayer is full of spiritual-warfare imagery. Her brokenness was not the last word. That was reserved for the brokenness of the "bows of the warriors" that were against her. "There is no Rock like our God!" (v2) **The recovery of confidence and assurance is the return of answered asking.**
- **"There is no one Holy like the Lord"** (v2). Sadly, much asking becomes so personally focused and familially functional that we lose a sense of Who is being asked and the fact that it is impossible to ask without a sense of the holiness of it all. That we can ask means something has been done about our disqualifying unholiness in order for us to approach God's holiness. The place of asking was "the holy place" (Hebrews 10:19); the Lord answers from "His holy hill ... His holy heaven" (Psalm 3:4; 20:6); when we ask we do so in and through His "holy name" (Psalm 33:21); we ask lifting up "holy hands" and ask in order that the outcome will be lives of "godliness and holiness" (1 Timothy 2:2,8). Furthermore, the return of our answer as a gift to God, in the way we have already discussed, makes the answer holy (Leviticus 27:9). Our answer will encourage our

continuance in personal holiness. **A revelation of the holiness of God and a recovery of personal holiness are returns of asking.**

- **"There is no one besides you"** (v2). Our answer reminds us that there is no other like Him, no other to whom we can go, no other love, no other will, no other hope, and that there is salvation in no other. This is the constant conclusion drawn by the psalmist-askers: "In God alone ... He alone is ..." (Psalm 62:1,6). Later Hannah says, "It is not by strength that one prevails" (v9). **A return of asking is a reinforced, reinvigorated, reassured faith, trust and hope in God alone.**

This one scriptural example is a sufficient curriculum in the returns of answered asking: joy, trust, faith, comfort, hope, holiness, obedience, sacrifice. What stewardship this invites us to, if like Hannah, we take time to consider the meanings of what was given and spoken to us by God in our answers. Observe the answers to your asking. Think a little more about your Samuel.

When the Answer Asks Things of Us

Thus far, we have assumed that the answers were good ones for us, because they accorded with what we asked for. But we have to admit that sometimes we receive answers that are not quite what we either wanted or anticipated; that are not quite understood. The classic example of this is the repeated asking of Paul for the removal of his *"thorn in the flesh"* (2 Corinthians 12:7-10). It was not taken from him, but that did not mean his "three times" pleading was unanswered. It was answered: "My grace is sufficient for you, for My power is made perfect in weakness." What a massive answer this was; the promise of a sufficient grace and a perfecting power in his life. Was there a 'return' on this answer apart from disappointment and discouragement, and the determination to just tough it out? Even this undesired and unprepared-for answer produces the return of thanksgiving and worship: "Therefore I will boast all the more gladly about my weakness." Why? So that God's answer, "that Christ's power may rest on me", would be fully accepted and appropriated. Why? "That is why, for Christ's sake, I delight in weaknesses, in insults, in hardships, in persecutions, in difficulties. For when I am weak, then I am strong." The answer God gave him was clearly "observed" by Paul and discerned, and then stewarded in a way that was not a one-time only, temporary solution. It was an answer that saved him a lot of other asking. It affected the whole of his life, the whole of his perspective, the whole of his capacity to relate to the suffering that was an integral part of his daily obedience. The huge return on this 'unanswered' answer was a life-time of perseverance and endurance, joy and obedience. So even though the answer did not seem good at first, and asked more of him, because it was God's answer, it produced good returns of praise and thanksgiving.

The Return of Returns

Let us continue to ask of the Lord, as all ten lepers did in their need. They were all motivated to be obedient and fulfill the conditions that Jesus required of them, that they satisfy the requirement to show themselves to the priest. Of course, grace outran the obedience to the law and they were cleansed on the way. But was this going to be a compliance that obtained for them the answer they wanted, namely their health, or would it be a spiritual obedience that would secure for the Father what Jesus hoped the answer would – His glory? Goodwin sums it up: "A thing obtained by prayer, as it came from God, so a man will return it to God, and use it for His glory." [12]

Let us observe and consider the meaning of His answers. Let us savor and steward the grace of His answers, with the expectation that this grace will abound in us more and more, so that our asking and God's answering will be ceaseless, and all the 'returns' will be returned to His glory, with thanksgiving. Let Goodwin have the last word: "If you observe not His answers, how shall you bless God and return thanks to Him for hearing your prayers? ... The reason you pray so much and give thanks so little is that you observe not God's answers." [13] To put it another way, the answer is never the end of the story. The answer that may have ended our need is but the means to re-introduce us to what God needs of us. Let us ask for both the return of asking, and the returns of asking. In Jesus' Name. Amen.

Postscript: Asking and You

"Asking God to do what only He can do ... doing whatever He asks of us." - From the vision statement of ASK Network

"Be not afraid to pray – to pray is right
Pray if thou can'st with hope but ever pray,
Though hope be weak or sick with long delay,
Pray in the darkness if there be no light...
But if for any wish thou darest not pray
Then pray to God to cast that wish away."
- Hartley Coleridge

"Christian prayer is marked decisively by petition because this form of prayer discloses the true state of affairs. It reminds the believer that God is the source of all good, and that human beings are utterly dependent." - Stanley Grenz

"Pray for prayer—pray till you can pray; pray to be helped to pray, and give not up praying because thou canst not pray, for it is when thou thinkest thou canst not pray that thou art most praying."
- C.H.Spurgeon

"His best answer is to raise us to the power of answering Him."
- P.T.Forsyth

22

Answering what is being Asked of Us

To Ask or Not to Ask ... That Is the Question

It would seem appropriate to end a book about asking by asking something. What is our answer to what is being asked of us? Just asking!

Thank you for getting this far and sharing this 'asking about asking'. We have different capacities and appetites, different needs and desires. Like the children of Israel gathering the manna in the wilderness, regardless of how much we get, we should expect it to be *"enough"* (Genesis 16:4-17). As we conclude this conversation, may the 'manna principle' be our shared experience. In any book, not everything is for everyone but we can trust for sufficiency for every reader. It is one thing for a dumpster truck to tip its load of soil, and quite another thing to landscape that soil. Let us ask that the Holy Spirit will do the landscaping of whatever has been deposited and received. The shapes and contours of our lives are very different. The hollows and declivities of our hearts vary. We need to be leveled and filled in different ways. Jesus used the image of 'soil' as a picture of our heart and its receptivity to His word. My prayer is that this book will have been both a deposit of some fertile soil for your spiritual growth, and also a seed-packet for you, and that the Word sown will take root and produce fruit. Jesus's word for outcome was *"crop."* We ask for such a harvest.

An Important Disclaimer

Although I have argued the need for a 'theology of asking', for a biblical validation of it beyond the circumstances of our need, it should be clear by this point that a theological presentation, descriptive as it may be of what asking is, cannot in itself guarantee that a non-asker will ask. Hopefully by now, we have seen that asking is not a subject we master, or a practice we perfect. Jacques Ellul argued that we cannot talk about prayer as if it is a topic, or we might add, even a spiritual discipline, as if it was just another spiritual skill to be attained. He wrote: "In the presence of a man who does not pray, theology loses its powers." [1] We have seen that asking is the expression and the experience of someone who is engaged in a personal relationship with Father, Son and Holy Spirit. Despite all that we have covered that relates to our asking, this book will only be effectual if it leads you to God the Father, through Jesus the Son, by the power of the Holy Spirit. The conversation we have had together about asking is not the thing itself. It is for you now, possibly encouraged and motivated by what we have discussed, to ask directly and intimately in the name of Jesus. It is not the content of this book that will fuel your asking so much as the communion of your heart with the Answerer, and you will be directing God's words to you through His Word, back to Him. Yes there are reasons for asking, but it is relationship that initiates and instructs it.

Asking Is Opposed

Of course, there will always be reasons not to ask. Asking is opposed by the enemy of our souls. To silence our asking is to cut the supply line on the battlefield. We have identified so many of the hurdles and hindrances, but we have spoken more of the help we have from the Father, Son and Holy Spirit when it comes to all things 'asking'. Please do not walk away from this book without knowing the help of His healing, if you have been bearing discouragement and despondency related to past unanswered asking that has silenced your present asking. Talking of healing, asking is God's great antidote to anxiety, the source of so much emotional, mental and physical pain. "Be anxious for nothing, but in everything ... ask with thanksgiving" (Philippians 4:6). Asking is good for your health. Ask to be freed from any diffidence about asking, whether it is rooted in fear or doubt, or a diminished sense of worth, or a lack of faith. Do not accept any rationalization that keeps you from an intimate asking relationship. If you are feeling spiritually dry, do not entertain the two bad presuppositions behind this: that asking God is determined by how we feel, as if our assessment of our feelings or energy is the determining factor in approaching the throne of grace; or that because our obligation to ask is diminished by our feelings we have a right to decide whether we ask or not. How subtly do these dissuasions become disobedience.

There are three things that commonly, but wrongly, oppose our asking if we allow them to and I urge you to begin your asking by asking the Holy Spirit to remove these three barriers that often present themselves when it comes to the need to ask:

1. **Circumstance's resistance**: It is so easy to believe that things are too far gone, we are in too deep, we have waited too long; things seem impossible, entrenched, unchangeable. We learn to adapt and say we will live with it, put up with it, accommodate it, endure it, work around it, ignore it, not expect too much from it. So we do not ask.
2. **Our reticence**: We end up characterized by our own uncertainty, faithlessness, doubt, double-mindedness, distrust, disinterest, fear, condemnation, procrastination, lack of desire, disappointment, loss of hope. So we do not ask.
3. **God's reluctance**: This is such a lie of the devil, that God is somehow asleep on the job, uninvolved, passive, mercurial, hard to please, capricious, open towards everyone but me, reluctant to respond, unengaged. So we do not ask.

These three barriers oppose our freedom to know God as our "friend at midnight" and as our "how much more ... Father". He is our 'Abba' and we are His son or daughter, so we will not accept the silence of a slave or orphan. These barriers oppose us asking boldly and unashamedly of a God who will not be shamed by any delinquency on His part towards us, of whom we can expect a trustworthy response. As Martin Luther put it, it is not about us "overcoming God's reluctance but laying hold on His willingness."

Just Ask

So what is your answer? The place to start is to 'just ask'. Have we not agreed that our asking is answering the One who first spoke to us? Begin by asking Him to help you to be a listening asker. Let me adapt the Spurgeon quotation in the preface to this chapter: "Ask for asking—ask till you can ask; ask to be helped to ask, and give not up asking because thou canst not ask, for it is when thou thinkest thou canst not ask that thou art most asking." Remember that acting comes out of asking. Ask someone to ask with you. Ask your pastors if you can start an ask-group, maybe just focusing on asking for them. Begin an 'ask group' in your congregation or in your community. In some African nations, pastors are designating one of their churches in the community as an 'asking center' open to all to come and ask of God together. Churches take turns in being that center. What spiritual unity asking encourages. Trust the burdens and instincts, impressions and tugs, the hunches and intimations that you experience in the course of a day and turn them into immediate asking. As Oswald Chambers used to say: "Never say you will pray about a thing: pray about it!" Check out sites like the ASK NETWORK site, and use their 'asking' resources, including for nations (www.asknetwork.net). Gather people to ask for your community, your city, your nation. Amazing things begin to happen when we ask.

At ASK NETWORK, our call is to *"gather all generations"* to ask God for *"all nations."* We need the interrelationship of the generations when it comes to asking: the zeal and action of a young generation and the time and attention of an older one, but both sharing a common intention and affection, as the giftings and passions are married in just asking and asking justly. We need this baton of asking to be passed from one generation to another. Moses is presented by God as an effective asker (Jeremiah 15:1) but the day came when God said to Joshua: "My servant Moses is dead" (Joshua 1:2). A new generation of askers was needed. Will you be "gathered" for this asking venture?

Take the Next Step

Our stories and journeys are so different in their co-ordinates and routes but somehow, regardless of how we get there, we all get to a place where our asking of God gets very personal. When you read the early days of David's sojourn, his asking is always of someone else. He asked of Samuel; he asked of Jonathan; he asked of Ahimelech, the priest. That proved to be the death of Ahimelech because Doeg reported to Saul that "Ahimelech inquired of the Lord for him" (1 Samuel 22:10). Asking killed him. (Hardly an encouraging thought at the end of a book that is trying to encourage asking!) But something about that asking was transferred to David because in the very next chapter we read for the first time in the narrative of his life that David "inquired of the Lord" for himself (1 Samuel 23:2). What is so heartening is that we then read, "The Lord answered him." This was a maturing experience for him. This was no longer about depending on other people to ask for him. It seems that he is so encouraged by this that only two verses later, after he shares the Lord's answer with his fearful and doubting men, we read: "Once again David inquired of the Lord." Asking was taking its place in his life as the spiritually natural response to everything. The floodgates to asking are opened here, that will result in the yet-to-be written psalms that will tutor all generations about asking, until the end of the age. Once again God answers him. All comes to pass as the Lord had answered, but before the next engagement, guess what David does? You are right! He asks of the Lord. And guess what happens then? You are right! The Lord answers him. And guess what happens next? You are right! *"AGAIN DAVID ASKED"* (1 Samuel 23:12). What follows is a wonderful question-and-answer session between David and God. Asking was becoming a life-style. To set this in spiritual cement, God sends Abigail into his life in a context in which she is an intercessor, asking David not to act foolishly in response to the folly of Nabal. Her humility, her pleading, her obeisance, her truth, her recall of God's purposes and promises are a study for David in how to ask (1 Samuel 25).

If you chose to get this far in your reading of this book, then there is no question about your heart to ask, or about the fact that you are already on a journey of personal asking, just like David. Perhaps this book has come across your path, as Abigail came across David's, as the final nudge that you are on the right track ... to stay. The asking that has begun is just going to keep on asking, just as it did for David. But a greater than David is here.

Asking to Be Well

"There is in Jerusalem near the Sheep gate, a pool, which in Aramaic is called Bethesda" (John 5:1-15). When I first visited Jerusalem, one of my favorite places to linger was beside that pool, and now, whenever I am in the Holy City, I make my way to that site. I found such sanctity there and experienced such an intimate communion and communication with the Lord, and I understand why. It was all about asking. It was Jesus's question there that initiated the conversation with the invalid that provoked his need to ask for his own healing and deliverance. God's asking of us precedes what we need to ask of Him. He sets us up for the answer we need, but have not yet asked for. Jesus asked: "Do you want to get well?" What asking should that provoke in us? Do we want to get well? Do we want it to be well with our soul? What asking for the wellness of salvation and sanctification; for the wellness of forgiveness and reconciliation; for the wellness of healing and deliverance; for the wellness of the oppressed and abused; for the wellness of comfort and the return of joy; for the wellness of the abandoned and the rejected; for the wellness of peace and sleep; for the wellness of companionship and intimacy; for the wellness of the poor and afflicted; for the wellness of the Holy Spirit and guidance; for the wellness of contentment and marital unity; for the wellness of realized promises and fulfilled hopes; for the wellness of neighborhoods and nations.

How much 'just asking' is there to do, that prepares us for much more 'just acting'? Whatever the need, do we want to get well? It is such a relief that He asks the obvious, as uncomfortable as that is at first. His asking sifts our desire and truthfulness, our motivation and values, our belief and faith. His love wants our asking, because He sees where we are at; because He is the rewarder of those who desperately and diligently ask Him, and because He wants us to be well. Within a little while, the man who Jesus addressed was telling his story. The text says that he had no idea who had asked him that question. So he called Jesus, "the man who made me well." Maybe we all need to know Jesus afresh as "the man who asked me if I wanted to be well" so that we can also call him "the man who answered my asking ... and made me well." Jesus said, "Apart from Me you can do nothing" (John 15:5). That means we are all in for a lot of asking, especially for those who have been unjustly disabled and await our intercession and intervention by whatever pools of debilitating sorrow they sit, by whatever name their Bethesda's are designated in their language of need and experience.

If you forget everything else in this book, remember the title, 'Just Asking' and remember what Dietrich Bonhoeffer said: "Our being Christians today will be limited to two things: prayer and doing justice among men."[2] *Just asking and acting justly.* By limiting ourselves to these two things our opportunities and capacities are unlimited to willingly ask according to God's will and His Word, and to act accordingly. Asking specifically is indeed the soul of prayer, so let us ask for its restoration in our lives. In the name of the asking Father, the asking Son and the asking Holy Spirit, who together are our Answerers. Amen.

Your Personal Asking...

Before you close the book, why not write down what you are asking for at this season of your life and what you are asking about, perhaps in response to what you have read and what the Holy Spirit has stirred in your heart.

Dear Father, In Jesus's Name, with the help of the Holy Spirit, I am asking you ...

Endnotes

Introduction: Asking about Asking

1. Jacques Ellul, *Prayer and the Modern Man* (Wipf and Stock, 2007)
2. Herbert Farmer, *The World and God* (Nisbet, 1935)
3. Alison Gopnik, *The Philosophical Baby* (Farrar, Straus, Giroux, 2009)
4. Paul Harris, *Trusting what you're told* (Cambridge: Belknap Press, 2012)
5. The ASK Network: www.asknetwork.net
6. George Mueller, *Answers to Prayer* (Start Publishing, 2013)
7. Klaus Issler, *Wasting Time with God* (IVP, 2001)
8. Andrew Murray, *With Christ in the School of Prayer* (Whitaker House, 1981)
9. J.I.Packer and C.Nystrom, *Praying* (IVP, 2006)
10. P.T.Forsyth, *The Soul of Prayer* (Charles Kelly, 1916)
11. C.H.Spurgeon, *The Last Word of Christ on the Cross.* (Sermon June 25th 1882) The full quote about Bunyan is: *"Prick him anywhere; **his blood is Bibline**, the very essence of the Bible flows from him. He cannot speak without quoting a text, for his very soul is full of the Word of God."*
12. George Herbert, *Prayer I* (*The Temple*, 1633)
13. C.S.Lewis, *Letters to Malcolm* (Bles, 1943)
14. Origen from his introduction to *On Prayer* (See *Origen: An exhortation to Martyrdom* translated Rowan Green Paulist Press, 1979)

Chapter 1: Asking Is For Beginners ... Or Is It?

1. Richard Foster, *Prayer: Finding the Heart's Home* (Hodder and Stoughton, 1993)
2. Karl Barth, *Church Dogmatics III* (TandT Clark, 1977)
3. B.B.Warfield, *Life of Faith* (Banner of Truth, 1974)
4. H.H.Farmer, *The World and God* (Nisbet, 1935)
5. Matthew 19: 13–15; Mark 10:13–16; Luke 18: 15–17
6. Augustine, cited in *Prayer and Modern Man* Jacques Ellul (Wipf and Stock, 2007)
7. Alison Gopnik, *The Philosophical Baby* (Farrar, Straus, Giroux, 2009)
8. *'The Creativity Crisis'* (Newsweek, July 10, 2010)
9. A.B.Simpson, *The Life of Prayer* (Christian Publications, 1967)
10. Wesley Duewel, *Mighty Prevailing Prayer* (Zondervan, 1990)
11. Story recounted by Tony Campolo and cited in Claiborne Wilson-Hartgrove *Becoming the Answer to Your Prayers* (IVP, 2008)
12. J.I.Packer and C.Nystrom, *Praying* (IVP, 2006)

13. Archibold Hodge, *The Life of Charles Hodge* (Ayer, 1979)
14. Walter Wangerin, *Whole Prayer* (Zondervan, 1998)
15. Richard Foster, *Prayer: Finding the Heart's Home* (Hodder and Stoughton, 1993)
16. B.B.Warfield, *Faith and Life* (Banner of Truth, 1974)
17. Bruce Wilkinson, *The Prayer of Jabez* (Multnomah, 2000)
18. Andrew Murray, *The Ministry of Intercession* (Oliphants, 1966)
19. Jonathan Graf, *The Power of Personal Prayer* (Navpress, 2002)
20. Thomas Fuller, *Meditations on all kinds of Prayers* (EEBO edition reprint of 1669)
21. John Owen, *A Discourse on the Work of the Holy Spirit in Prayer* (London, 1682)
22. John Bunyan, *Prayer* (Banner of Truth,1965)
23. C.S.Lewis, *Letters to Malcolm* (Bles, 1964)
24. Donald Bloesch, *The Struggle of Prayer* (Helmers and Howard, 1988)
25. E.M.Bounds, *Purpose in Prayer* (Whitaker House, 1997)
26. Bishop J.C.Ryle, *Home Truths* (William Hunt, 1887)
27. C.S.Lewis, *Letters to Malcolm* (Bles, 1964)
28. C.S.Lewis, *Petitionary Prayer* in *Christian Reflections* (Bles,1943)
29. C.S.Lewis, ibid

Chapter 2: Asking As Answering

1. Eugene Petersen, *Answering God* (Harper Collins, 1991)
2. P.T.Forsyth, *The Soul of Prayer* (Charles Kelly, 1916)
3. Ibid
4. C.H.Spurgeon, *Prayer-the Forerunner of Mercy* (Sermon, June 28, 1857)
5. P.T.Forsyth, *The Soul of Prayer* (Charles Kelly, 1916)
6. George Herbert, *The Temple – Prayer (I)* (1633)

Chapter 3: Ask, Ask, Thanking At Heaven's Door

1. John Calvin, *Commentary on 1 Timothy* (CCEL)
2. Thomas Goodwin, *The Return of Prayers* (Baker Book House, 1979)
3. P.T.Forsyth, *The Soul of Prayer* (Charles Kelly, 1916)
4. Richard Sibbes, *The Soul's Conflict and Victory over itself by Faith* (1635)
5. P.T.Forsyth, *The Soul of Prayer* (Charles Kelly, 1916)
6. John Wesley, *Commentary on the Whole Bible (vol.3): 1 Thessalonians 5:16*

Chapter 4: Towards A Theology Of Asking

1. Karl Barth, *Evangelical Theology* (Eerdmans, 1979)
2. Ibid
3. John Piper, *Solid Joys Devotional* (May, 2003)
4. D.A.Carson, *Praying with Paul* (Baker Academic 2nd ed. 2014)
5. B.B.Warfield, *Faith and Life* (Banner of Truth, 1974)
6. Friedrich Heiler, *Prayer* (Oxford University Press, 1958)
7. B.B.Warfield, *Faith and Life* (Banner of Truth, 1974)

8. Peter Baelz, *Prayer and Providence* (SCM, 1968)
9. Francis Schaeffer, *The God Who Is There* (Hodder and Stoughton, 1968)
10. Ibid
11. *Letter of Charlotte Bronte* (February 11, 1851. Her comments were upon reading 'Letters on the Nature and Development of Man' by Martineau and Atkinson
12. John Calvin, *Institutes III*
13. P.T.Forsyth, *The Soul of Prayer* (Charles Kelly, 1916)
14. J.I.Packer, Introduction to *The Death of Death in the Death of Christ* by John Owen (Banner of Truth, 1959)
15. Wayne Spear, *The Theology of Prayer* (Baker Book House, 1979)
16. John Calvin, *Institutes III*
17. John Piper, *Sermon on Jude*
18. B.B.Warfield, *Faith and Life* (New York: Longmans, Green and Co.,1916)
19. Andrew Murray, *The Ministry of Intercession* (Oliphants, 1966)
20. John Newton, *Olney Hymns* (1779)
21. Ibid
22. C.S.Lewis, *Petitionary Prayer: a problem without an answer* in *Christian Reflections* (Bles, 1943)
23. Blaise Pascal, *Les Pensées* (Penguin Classics, 1995)
24. Augustine, *Letters* Nicene and Post-Nicene Fathers Vol. 1 (Hendriksen, 1996)
25. H.H.Farmer, *The World of God* (Nisbet, 1935)
26. C.S.Lewis, *Letters to Malcolm* (Bles, 1943)
27. C.S.Lewis, *The Efficacy of Prayer* in *Fern-Seed and Elephants* (Fount, 1975)
28. C.S.Lewis, *Letters to Malcolm* (Bles, 1943)
29. Ibid
30. P.T.Forsyth, *The Soul of Prayer* (Charles Kelly, 1916)
31. C.S.Lewis, *Letters to Malcolm* (Bles, 1943)
32. Veenland and Karre, *Why ask questions?* (Topaz Issue 11, 2004)
33. C.S.Lewis, *Mere Christianity* (Bles, 1952)
34. Andrew Murray, *With Christ in the School of Prayer* (Whitaker, 1981)
35. Ibid
36. See John D. Witvliet's essay in *Trinitarian Theology for the Church* ed. Treier and Lauber (IVP Academic, 2009)
37. Treier and Lauber (Editors), *Trinitarian Theology for the Church* (IVP, 2009)
38. John Newton, *Olney Hymns* (1779)

Chapter 5: Asking and God – He Hears

1. Samuel Rutherford, *The Trial and Triumph of Faith* (Sermon, 1652)
2. Thomas Goodwin, *The Return of Prayers* (Baker Book House, 1979)
3. Karl Barth, *Evangelical Theology* (Eerdmans, 1979)
4. C.S.Lewis, *Letters to Malcolm* (Bles, 1943)
5. John Wesley, *Upon the Lord's Sermon on the Mount: Discourse Ten:* June 02 1742*)* Sermons of John Wesley ed. Thomas Jackson, 1872)
6. Karl Barth, *Church Dogmatics III/3* (TandT Clark, 1961)

Chapter 6: Asking and God – He Responds

1. Vincent Brummer, *What are We Doing When We Pray? A Philosophical Inquiry* (SCM, 1984)
2. Kenneth Woodward, *Is God Listening?* (Newsweek, March, 1997)
3. Terrance Tiessen, *Providence and Prayer* (IVP, 2000)
4. Thomas Aquinas, *Summa Theologica*
5. Origen, *Treatise On Prayer* (Origen: An exhortation to Martyrdom, Prayer translated by Rowan Green, Paulist Press, 1979)
6. Jonathan Edwards, *The Most High: a prayer hearing God* (Banner of Truth, 1974)
7. Term used by Oliver Crisp to distinguish those with views that take up the concerns of Calvin from those (Calvinists) who relate to a theological tradition with Calvin "as its fountainhead." *Retrieving Doctrine: Essays in Reformed Theology* (IVP, 2010) See Chapter 7.
8. Karl Barth, *Church Dogmatics III/3* (TandT Clark, 1961)
9. Leigh Buchanan, *It's all in how you ask* (Inc. Magazine, June 2014)
10. John Calvin, *Institutes III 20.3*
11. Oliver Crisp, *Retrieving Doctrine: Essays in Reformed Theology* (IVP, 2010)
12. John Calvin, *Institutes III 20.3*
13. Thomas Aquinas quoted by Tiessen ps.102–103
14. Thomas Aquinas, *Summa Theologica*
15. J.I.Packer, *Knowing God* (IVP, 1973)
16. Oswald Chambers, *My Utmost for His Highest* (Dodd, Mead and Co.,1935)
17. P.T.Forsyth, *The Soul of Prayer* (Charles Kelly, 1916)

Chapter 7: Asking and God – He Fathers

1. P.T.Forsyth, *The Soul of Prayer* (Charles Kelly, 1916)
2. Dietrich Bonhoeffer, *Psalms – the prayer book of the Bible* (Augsburg, 1984)
3. John Piper, *What Jesus Demands From the World* (Crossway Books, 2006)
4. A.B.Simpson, *The Life of Prayer* (Christian Publications, 1967)
5. C.S.Lewis, *A Grief Observed* (Faber and Faber, 1961)
6. Michael Reeves, *'The Trinity: the secret to a joyful Christianity.'* (Scottish Bulletin of Evangelical Theology, Spring 2014)
7. Robert C. Frost, *Aglow with the Spirit* (Bridge-Logos, 1981); *Our Heavenly Father* (Bridge-Logos, 1978)
8. Jack Frost, *Experiencing the Father's Embrace* (Charisma House, 2002); *Spiritual Slavery to Spiritual Sonship* (Destiny Image Publishers, 2006)

Chapter 8: Asking and Jesus

1. Examples would be N.T Wright, *The Lord and His Prayer* (Eerdmans, 1996); Martyn Lloyd-Jones, *Life in the Spirit-Classic Studies in John 17* (Kingsway Publications, 1996)

Chapter 9: Asking and Jesus – A Story

1. Kenneth Bailey, *Poet and Peasant* (Eerdmans, 1983)
2. D.A.Carson, *Praying with Paul* (Baker Academic, 2014)
3. Ibid

Chapter 10: Asking and Jesus – A Miracle

1. Tim Chester, *The Message of Prayer* (IVP, 2003)
2. C.S.Lewis, *A Grief Observed* (Faber and Faber, 1961)
3. Peter Grieg, *God on Mute* (Regal, 2007)
4. Augustine, commenting on John 11 in *Tractates on John #49*
5. Monty Python's Flying Circus, *Dead Parrot Sketch* (December 7th, 1969)

Chapter 11: Asking In Jesus' Name

1. Donald Bloesch, *The Struggle of Prayer* (Helmers and Howard, 1988)
2. Andrew Murray, *The Ministry of Intercession* (Oliphants, 1966)
3. Ibid
4. D.A.Carson, *The Gospel According to John* (Eerdmans, 1991)
5. R.A.Torrey, *The Power of Prayer and the Prayer of Power* (Zondervan, 1987)
6. Ibid
7. Donald Bloesch, *The Struggle of Prayer* (Harper and Row, 1980)
8. B.B.Warfield, *Faith and Life* (Banner of Truth, 1974)
9. Thomas Boston, *The Beauties of Boston* (Christian Focus Publications, 1979)
10. Craig Keener, *The Gospel of John Volume 2* (Hendrikson Publishers, 2003)
11. A.B.Simpson, *The Life of Prayer* (Moody Publishers, 1967)
12. Oswald Chambers, *My Utmost for His Highest* (Dodd, Mead and Co., 1935)
13. James Houston, *Prayer the Transforming Friendship* (Lion, 1989)
14. John Calvin, *Genevan Catechism* Q.252 (Barth words this as praying "with the mouth of Jesus.")
15. James Houston, *Prayer the Transforming Friendship* (Lion, 1989)
16. Richard Foster, *Prayer* (Hodder and Stoughton, 1992)
17. Samuel Chadwick, *The Path of Prayer* (Hodder and Stoughton, 1936)
18. Ibid
19. D.M.M'Intyre, *The Prayer Life of Our Lord* (Morgan and Scott, 1927)
20. J.I.Packer and C. Nystrom, *Praying* (IVP, 2006)
21. Thomas Brooks, *Heaven on Earth* 1654 reprinted (Banner of Truth, 1982)
22. D.M.M'Intyre, *The Prayer Life of Our Lord* (Morgan and Scott, 1927)
23. J.N.Sanders (completed by B.Mastin), *The Gospel of John* (Harper and Row, 1968)
24. John Calvin, *Gospel of John* (Bibliolife, 2009)
25. James Houston, *Prayer the Transforming Friendship* (Lion, 1989)
26. D.M.M'Intyre, *The Prayer Life of Our Lord* (Morgan and Scott, 1927)
27. Bruce Milne, *The Message of John* (IVP Academic, 1993)

Chapter 12: Never One Without The Other

1. Sinclair Ferguson, *The Holy Spirit-Contours of Christian Theology p188* (IVP 1996)
2. John Stott, *Men Made New* (IVP, 1966)
3. Donald Bloesch, *The Struggle of Prayer* (Helmers and Howard, 1988)
4. E.M.Bounds, *The Reality of Prayer* (Whitaker House, 2000)
5. C.H.Spurgeon, *Restraining Prayer* (Sermon, 1863)
6. B.B.Warfield, *Faith and Life* (Banner of Truth, 1974)
7. A.B.Simpson, *The Life of Prayer* (Christian Publications, 1967)
8. C.H.Spurgeon, *Praying in the Holy Spirit* (Sermon, 1866)
9. Alistair McGrath, *Christian Spirituality* (Oxford: Blackwell, 1999)
10. J.I. Packer, *Keep in Step with the Spirit* (Baker Books, 2005)
11. Origen from his introduction to *On Prayer* Origen: An exhortation to Martyrdom, Prayer translated by Rowan Green (Paulist Press, 1979)
12. Arthur Bennett (Editor), *The Valley of Vision: a collection of Puritan Prayers and Devotions* (Banner of Truth, 1975)

Chapter 13: Asking and The Holy Spirit – According to Jesus

1. Andrew Murray, *The Ministry of Intercession* (Oliphants, 1966)
2. E.M.Bounds, *The Reality of Prayer* (Whitaker House, 2000)
3. Andrew Murray, *The Ministry of Intercession* (Oliphants, 1966)
4. John Bunyan, *Prayer* (Banner of Truth, 1965)
5. Ibid
6. C.H.Spurgeon, *The Holy Spirit's Intercession* (Sermon, April 11, 1880)
7. C.H Spurgeon, *The Holy Spirit – the Great Teacher* (Sermon, November 18, 1855)
8. J.I.Packer in *My Path of Prayer* ed. David Hanes, (Walter, 1981)
9. Thomas Goodwin, *The Return of Prayers* (Baker Book House,1979)
10. Andrew Murray, commenting on Romans 8:26–27
11. C.H.Spurgeon, *The Holy Spirit's Intercession* (Sermon, April 11, 1880)
12. John Calvin, *Harmony of Gospels* Vol. 3 (Eerdmans, 1972)
13. Cyprian of Carthage, *On the Lord's Prayer* (Treatise 4, para.11)
14. John Calvin, *Harmony of Gospels* vol3 (Eerdmans, 1972)
15. Peter Masters, one of Spurgeon's successors at The Metropolitan Tabernacle, London.
16. John Calvin, *Institutes III*

Chapter 14: Asking and The Holy Spirit – According to Paul

1. Gordon Fee, *Paul, the Spirit and the People of God* (Baker Academic, 1996) An exception to this is a fine study of Paul's petitions by Don Carson recently reprinted as 'A call to Spiritual Reformation: Praying with Paul' and already quoted in this book.
2. H. Schonweiss and Colin Brown, *Dictionary of New Testament Theology* (Zondervan, 1982)
3. Jacques Ellul, *Prayer and the Modern Man* (Wipf and Stock, 2007)
4. John Bunyan, *Prayer* (Banner of Truth, 1965)
5. Thomas Goodwin, *The Return of Prayers* (Baker Book House, 1979)

6. Arthur Wallis, *Pray in the Spirit* (Kingsway Publications, 1970)
7. Thomas Goodwin, *The Return of Prayers* (Baker Book House, 1979)
8. Paul Gephardt, Hymn *Commit Thy Griefs* (1656) translated J.Wesley
9. James Montgomery, Hymn *Prayer is the Soul's Sincere Desire* (1818)
10. C.H.Spurgeon, *The Holy Spirit's Intercession* (Sermon, April 11, 1880)
11. Stuart Briscoe, *Communicator's Commentary on Romans* (Word Inc., 1982)
12. John Bunyan, *Prayer* (Banner of Truth, 1965)

Chapter 15: Asking According To His Will and His Word

1. *Westminster Shorter Catechism*
2. Karl Barth, *Church Dogmatics III/3* (TandT Clark, 1961)
3. P.T.Forsyth, *The Soul of prayer* (Charles Kelly, 1916)
4. D.A.Carson, *Praying with Paul* (Baker Academic, 2014)
5. Terrance Tiessen, *Providence and Prayer* (IVP, 2000)
6. P.T.Forsyth, *The Soul of Prayer* (Charles Kelly, 1916)
7. Andrew Murray, *With Christ in the School of Prayer* (Whitaker House, 1981)
8. ibid
9. Donald Bloesch, *The Struggle of Prayer* (Helmers and Howard, 1988)
10. John Calvin, *Institutes III*
11. George Mueller, in Roger Steer, *The Spiritual Secrets of George Müller* (OMF,1987)
12. Harry Blamires, *The Will and the Way* (SPCK, 1957)
13. Quoted in *The Christian Pioneer* ed. J.F.Wilks
14. P.T.Forsyth, *The Soul of Prayer* (Charles Kelly, 1916)
15. George Mueller, *The Life of Trust* (Sheldon Company, 1878)
16. John Bunyan, *A Discourse Treating Prayer* 1662
17. Eugene Petersen, *Answering God* (Harper Collins, 1991)
18. George Knight, *Christian Theology of the Old Testament* (Paternoster,1998)

Chapter 16: Asking and Acting

1. P.T.Forsyth, *The Soul of Prayer* (Charles Kelly, 1916)
2. Karl Barth, *Church Dogmatics III* (TandT Clark, 1961)
3. E.M.Bounds, *Purpose in Prayer* (Fleming H. Revell, 1920)
4. Karl Barth, *Church Dogmatics III* (TandT Clark, 1961)
5. Shane Claiborne and Jonathan Wilson-Hartgrove, *Becoming the Answer to Your Prayers* (IVP, 2008)
6. Jacques Ellul, *Prayer and Modern Man* (Wipf and Stock, 2007)
7. Donald Bloesch, *The Struggle of Prayer* (Helmers and Howard, 1988)
8. Ambrose: commentary on Psalm 1
9. Martin Luther, *Lectures on Romans* (John Knox Press, 1961)
10. Jacques Ellul, *Prayer and Modern Man* (Wipf and Stock, 2007)
11. Ibid
12. Andrew Murray, *The Ministry of Intercession* (Oliphants, 1966)
13. Ibid

14. Richard Lovelace, *The Dynamics of Spiritual Renewal* (IVP, 1979)
15. Andrew Murray, *The Ministry of Intercession* (Oliphants, 1966)
16. Ibid
17. For a discussion of this marriage of prayer and action read 'Becoming the Answer to Our Prayers' by Shane Claiborne and Jonathan Wilson-Hartgrove, already referenced in this chapter.
18. Jacques Ellul, *Prayer and Modern Man* (Wipf and Stock,2007)
19. Alan Redpath, *Victorious Christian Service* (Fleming H. Revell, 1958)
20. Joseph Conrad, *Heart of Darkness* (Dover Publications, 1990)
21. Shane Claiborne and Jonathan Wilson-Hartgrove, *Becoming the Answer to Your Prayers* (IVP, 2008)
22. P.T.Forsyth, *The Soul of Prayer* (Charles Kelly, 1916)
23. Oswald Chambers, *My Utmost for His Highest* (Dodd, Mead and Co., 1935)

Chapter 17: Just Asking Justly

1. Karl Barth, The Christian Life *Church Dogmatics* IV.4 (TandT Clark, 1961)
2. Richard Lovelace, *The Dynamics of Spiritual Renewal* (IVP, 1979)
3. C.S.Lewis, *The Screwtape Letters* (Bles,1942)
4. Gary Haughen, *Good News about Injustice* (IVP, 1999)
5. Dietrich Bonhoeffer, *Letters and Papers from Prison* (Macmillan, 1960)
6. William Wilberforce, Read *Amazing Grace* Eric Metaxas (Harper Collins, 2007)
7. Richard Lovelace, *The Dynamics of Spiritual Renewal* (IVP, 1979)
8. Christian Wiman, *My Bright Abyss* (Farrar, Strauss and Giroux, 2013)

Chapter 18: What Makes For Effective Asking

1. John Wesley, *The Sermon on the Mount Discourse* #10 June 1742 (Sermons of John Wesley ed. T.Jackson, 1872)
2. P.T.Forsyth, *The Soul of Prayer* (Charles Kelly, 1916)
3. J.Oswald Sanders, *Prayer Power Unlimited* (Moody Press, 1977)
4. Attributed to G.Campbell Morgan
5. Attributed to William Carey
6. Attributed to Martin Luther
7. P.T.Forsyth, *The Soul of Prayer* (Charles Kelly, 1916)
8. James O.Fraser, from *Behind the Ranges* Mrs. Howard Taylor (Biography of J.O.Fraser of Lisuland)
9. Kierkegaard, *Journals* (Oxford University Press, 1951)
10. Catherine of Siena, *The Dialogue 1377–78.*
11. Quoted in Christopher Hall *Worshiping with the Church Fathers* (IVP, 2009)
12. John Piper, *When I Don't Desire God* (Crossway, 2004)
13. Andrew Murray, *The Ministry of Intercession* (Oliphants, 1966)
14. John Newton, *Olney Hymns*
15. Observed by one of Melanchthon's correspondents. Quoted in E.M.Bounds *Purpose in Prayer* (Fleming H. Revell, 1920)

16. E.M.Bounds, *Purpose in Prayer* (Fleming H. Revell, 1920)
17. E.M.Bounds, *The Reality of Prayer* (Whitaker House, 2000)
18. Ibid
19. Ibid
20. E.M.Bounds, *The Necessity of Prayer* (Whitaker, 1984)
21. Steven Furtick, *Sun Stand Still* (Multnomah Books, 2010)
22. P.T.Forsyth, *The Soul of Prayer* (Charles Kelly, 1916)
23. John Piper, *When I don't desire God* (Crossway, 2004)
24. Poem by Alan Redpath author of *Victorious Praying* (Fleming H. Revell, 1957)
25. E.M.Bounds, *Purpose in Prayer* (Fleming H. Revell, 1920)
26. John Wesley, *The Sermons of John Wesley* 1872 ed. T. Jackson (Sermon Discourse #10 1742)
27. A Spiritual Maxim attributed to Pere la Combe, the Spiritual Director of Mme Guyon
28. C.H.Spurgeon, *Order and Argument in Prayer* (Sermon, July 15, 1866)
29. C.H.Spurgeon, *According to Promise* (Christian Heritage, 2001)
30. John Rice, *Asking and Receiving* (Sword of the Lord, 1942)
31. C.H.Spurgeon, *Pleading Prayer* (Sermon, February 21, 1886)
32. Andrew Murray, *With Christ in the School of Prayer* (Whitaker House, 1981)

Chapter 19: When Asking Is Unanswered

1. A.W.Tozer, *The Next Chapter Before The Last* (Christian Publications, 1987)
2. Oswald Chambers, *My Utmost for His Highest* (Dodd, Mead and Co., 1935)
3. C.H.Spurgeon, *Treasury of David Psalm 86*(Hendrikson, 1988); Sermon *Token for Good* on Psalm 86:17
4. C.S.Lewis, *Grief Observed* (Faber and Faber, 1961)
5. John Bunyan, *Prayer* (Banner of Truth, 1965)
6. P.T.Forsyth, *The Soul of Prayer* (Charles Kelly, 1916)
7. Quoted in Spurgeon's comments on Psalm 109:4 *Morning and Evening*: evening of January 15 (Hendrikson, 1997)
8. Peter Grieg: *God on Mute* (Regal, 2007) Grieg gives his check list of reasons for unanswered prayer: not common sense; contradiction of other prayers; ignoring creational complexity; life is tough and some things are unchangeably part of a creation subject to frustration and bondage; doctrinal positions that present wrong views and expectations of God; God's will is best so His refusals are the best answers; selfish motives; relationship with God is the answer, not what we are asking for; free will means others cannot be co-erced as we might wish; need for God's on-going influence; Satanic opposition bringing resistance to answers; insufficient faith; lack of perseverance; sin; justice; none of the above.

Chapter 20: When Asking Is Still Unanswered

1. C.S.Lewis, *Petitionary Prayer: a problem without an answer* in *Christian Reflections* (Bles, 1943)
2. C.S.Lewis, *Letters to Malcolm* (Bles 1943)
3. Ibid

4. C.S.Lewis, *Petitionary Prayer: a problem without an answer* in *Christian Reflections* (Bles, 1943)
5. C.S.Lewis, *The Efficacy of Prayer* in *Fern-Seed and Elephants* (Fount, 1975)
6. ibid
7. C.S.Lewis, *Petitionary Prayer: a problem without an answer* in *Christian Reflections* (Bles, 1943)
8. C.S.Lewis, *Letters to Malcolm* (Bles, 1943)
9. Andrew Murray: *The Ministry of Intercession* (Oliphants, 1966)
10. C.S.Lewis, *The Efficacy of Prayer* in *Fern-Seed and Elephants* (Fount, 1975)
11. Thomas Goodwin, *The Return of Prayers* (Baker Book House, 1979)
12. J.Oswald Sanders, *Prayer: power unlimited* (Discovery House, 1997)
13. Adam Hamilton, *Why? Making sense of God's will* (Abingdon Books, 2011)
14. C.H.Spurgeon, *Metropolitan Tabernacle Pulpit Vol. 12 #70*
15. William Gurnall, *The Christian in Complete Armour* (Banner of Truth, 1986)
16. E.M.Bounds, *Purpose in Prayer* (Whitaker House, 1997)
17. C.H.Spurgeon, *Treasury of David Psalm 22* (Hendrikson, 1988)
18. P.T.Forsyth, *The Soul of Prayer* (Regent College Publishing, 1995)
19. E.M.Bounds, *Purpose in Prayer* Whitaker House 1997
20. William Gurnall: *The Christian in Complete Armour* (Banner of Truth, 1986)
21. C.H.Spurgeon, *Daniel – a pattern for pleaders* (Sermon September 25, 1870)
22. John Bunyan: *Prayer* (Banner of Truth, 1965)
23. Ibid
24. F.B.Meyer, attributed
25. John Stott, *The Message of Romans* (IVP, 1994)
26. Dr. A.B.Davison, *Waiting upon God* (Forgotten Books, 2012 - reprint 1904 edition)
27. C.H.Spurgeon, *Morning and Evening: March 29th* (Hendrikson, 1997)
28. P.T.Forsyth, *The Soul of Prayer* (Charles Kelly, 1916)
29. Ibid
30. Jacques Ellul, *Prayer and Modern Man* (Wipf and Stock, 2007)
31. P.T.Forsyth, *The Soul of Prayer* (Charles Kelly, 1916)
32. Thomas Goodwin, *The Return of Prayers* (Baker Book House, 1979)
33. Ibid
34. Peter Grieg, *God on Mute* (Regal, 2007)
35. John Calvin, *Institutes III*
36. P.T.Forsyth, *The Soul of Prayer* (Charles Kelly, 1916)
37. C.H.Spurgeon, *Order and Argument in Prayer* (Sermon July 15, 1866)
38. Thomas Goodwin, *The Return of Prayers* (Baker Book House, 1979)
39. George Mueller, *Answers to Prayer* (Compiled from his narratives by A.E.C. Brooks, Moody Press,1903)

Chapter 21: When Asking Is Answered

1. Kenneth Woodward, *Is God Listening?* (Newsweek, March 1997)
2. Pew Research Center
3. C.H.Spurgeon, *Prayer Answered: Love Nourished* (Sermon February 27, 1859)
4. Fyodor Dostoevsky, *Notes from the Underground* (Signet Classics, 2004)
5. Thomas Goodwin, *The Return of Prayers* (Baker Book House, 1979)

6. C.H.Spurgeon, *Morning and Evening:* May 24 (Hendriksen, 1997)
7. Vincent Brummer, *What are we doing when we pray? A philosophical enquiry* (London: SCM, 1984)
8. Thomas Goodwin, *The Return of Prayers* (Baker Book House, 1979)
9. Ibid
10. Ibid
11. Spurgeon, *Tokens for Good* (Sermon on Psalm 86:17, August 22, 1875)
12. Thomas Goodwin, *The Return of Prayers* (Baker Books, 1979)
13. Ibid

Postscript: Answering What Is Asked Of You

1. Jacques Ellul, *Prayer and Modern Man* (Wipf and Stock, 2007)
2. Dietrich Bonhoeffer, *Letters and Papers from Prison* (Macmillan, 1960)

Index

Scripture Index (chapter given)

John

Acts

Romans

1 Corinthians

2 Corinthians

Galatians

About the Author

A graduate in Literature and Theology at Cambridge University, Stuart taught Literature before being called into pastoral ministry. He planted Christ Our Shepherd Church on Capitol Hill, Washington D.C. in 1987, where he continues to serve. Together with his wife, Celia, he serves as the International Director of ASK NETWORK (www.asknetwork.net) and also as a Senior Teaching Fellow for the C.S.Lewis Institute (www.cslewisinstitute.org)

Other publications by Stuart include:

A Road Best Traveled (Thomas Nelson) Out of print but available used on Amazon.com

The Advent Overture (Westbow Press) Available at Westbow Press, Amazon.com or www.mcalpine partners.com

Asking for Pastors (Ask Network) Available at www.mcalpinepartners.com

Asking in Jesus's Name (Ask Network) Available at www.mcalpinepartners.com

Printed in the United States
By Bookmasters